MORE DASHING

ALSO BY PATRICK LEIGH FERMOR

The Traveller's Tree (1950)
The Violins of Saint-Jacques (1953)
A Time to Keep Silence (1957)
Mani (1958)
Roumeli (1966)
A Time of Gifts (1977)
Between the Woods and the Water (1986)
Three Letters from the Andes (1991)
Words of Mercury (2003), edited by Artemis Cooper
In Tearing Haste (2008), edited by Charlotte Mosley
The Broken Road (2013), edited by Artemis Cooper and Colin Thubron
Abducting a General (2014)

(translated and edited)
The Cretan Runner (1955), by George Psychoundakis

ALSO BY ADAM SISMAN

A. J. P. Taylor (1994)
Boswell's Presumptuous Task (2000)
The Friendship (2006)
Hugh Trevor-Roper (2010)
John le Carré (2015)

(edited)
One Hundred Letters from Hugh Trevor-Roper (2013),
with Richard Davenport-Hines
Dashing for the Post (2016)

MORE DASHING

Further Letters of
Patrick Leigh Fermor

Selected and edited by
ADAM SISMAN

BLOOMSBURY PUBLISHING
LONDON · OXFORD · NEW YORK · NEW DELHI · SYDNEY

BLOOMSBURY PUBLISHING
Bloomsbury Publishing Plc
50 Bedford Square, London, WC1B 3DP, UK

BLOOMSBURY, BLOOMSBURY PUBLISHING and the Diana logo are trademarks of
Bloomsbury Publishing Plc

First published in Great Britain 2018

A catalogue record for this book is available from the British Library

Library of Congress Cataloguing-in-Publication data has been applied for

ISBN: HB: 978-1-4088-9366-1; eBook: 978-1-4088-9367-8

2 4 6 8 10 9 7 5 3 1

Typeset by Newgen KnowledgeWorks Pvt. Ltd., Chennai, India
Printed and bound in Great Britain by CPI Group (UK) Ltd, Croydon CR0 4YY

To find out more about our authors and books visit www.bloomsbury.com
and sign up for our newsletters.

In memory of John Julius Norwich
1929–2018

Contents

Introduction   1

Editorial Note   17

THE LETTERS   19

Dramatis Personae   427
Acknowledgements   437
Illustration Credits   441
Index   443

Introduction

This is a second selection from the letters of Patrick Leigh Fermor, a successor to *Dashing for the Post*, published in 2016. The title, like that of its predecessor, alludes to an expression often used by Paddy (as he called himself, and as almost everyone called him), 'dashing for the post'. His letters suggest that he is always writing in a rush. 'No more now, darling Diana, as I must pelt down the hill to the post,' ends one typical letter to Lady Diana Cooper. Many of his letters are headed 'In Tearing Haste' – so many, in fact, that he felt able to use the phrase as the title for a volume of his correspondence with his intimate friend 'Debo', Duchess of Devonshire. This hurry appears to have been motivated by a sense of duty, or even guilt; his letters are peppered with requests for forgiveness for not having written earlier. After heading one letter 'In Sackcloth and Ashes', he continued: 'The above should be the title of a published volume of my letters – if published one day in a hundred years' time – as <u>all</u> my letters start with abject apologies for lateness in answering ...' In another he wrote that sackcloth and ashes were 'my letter-writing uniform'. (The publishers of this volume felt that 'In Sackcloth and Ashes' would be a misleading title for a collection of such exuberant letters.)

Yet if some of his letters were written at speed, most were written with care. They are full of wit and sparkle. Some of them are long, and must have taken hours to write – indeed, some of the letters themselves show that he wrote them over a period of several days.

Letters mattered to Paddy for a number of reasons, both practical and personal. One was that he moved around a lot. He travelled widely throughout his long life, so letters were a means of informing his friends where he was and where to find him. When he did settle, it was in what was then a remote corner of the Peloponnese, where friends from England were unlikely to call unless invited to stay. Letters provided a lifeline from this isolated spot.

Paddy was a very sociable person who was often alone. Friends were important to him, and he kept his friendships in good repair by correspondence. Yet it went further than this. For him, letters were a means of reaching out to those whose company he enjoyed, of making convivial connections across the void. Paddy seems to relish the contact with those to whom he is writing, even if it is only on paper. He is psychologically and often emotionally engaged with his correspondent. He writes to give pleasure to the recipient. His prose is lively, sometimes effervescent. The warmth of his personality rises from the page. At times one senses that Paddy is writing to raise his own spirits, as if he knows that his imaginative construction of those of whom he is fond will bring him comfort and cheer.

Another reason why Paddy took so much trouble with his letters is his awareness that they might one day find their way into print. The letters themselves occasionally hint at this possibility – I have already mentioned one such hint, his suggestion that any volume of his letters, if published 'in a hundred years' time', should be entitled 'In Sackcloth and Ashes'.

Dashing for the Post received enthusiastic, even ecstatic, reviews. 'It goes without saying that nobody writes letters like this any-more, and it's a loss,' wrote Charles McGrath, reviewing the book in the *New York Times*. 'Here are descriptions and anecdotes equal to anything in his writing,' wrote Colin Thubron, himself one of the finest travel writers alive. John Julius Norwich likened Paddy to the great letter-writers of the past, among them Byron, Horace Walpole and Henry James.

When first asked to make a selection of Paddy's letters, I had little notion of what I would find. I did of course know that he and Debo Devonshire had maintained a delightful correspondence over more than half a century, which had been collected and published in 2008, skilfully edited by Charlotte Mosley. But I did not know then that those letters were matched by others – for example, his correspondence with Diana Cooper, from 1952 until her death in 1986. One could make an equally enjoyable book from their exchanges: arguably even more so, because Diana was a better writer than Debo. Paddy's letters to her were just as entertaining, and there were so many first-rate ones that I found it necessary to ration them in *Dashing for the Post*.

One reviewer of *Dashing for the Post* likened reading the letters to 'gobbling down a tray of exotically filled chocolates, with no horrible orange creams to put you off'. I crammed them in, resulting in a book significantly longer than my tolerant publisher had wanted, and even so I was obliged to leave out many tempting ones. As I wrote in the introduction, the 174 letters to thirty-seven correspondents included in *Dashing for the Post* were only the first gleanings from a hoard (scattered across six countries) containing at least ten times their number. In working on that book, I found an abundance of letters that seemed to me worthy of publication. Plenty of these I decided not to include – not because they were not good enough, but because it might have unbalanced the book to include too many letters to any one particular correspondent (such as Diana Cooper), or to have included too many written at one particular time or from one particular place. I decided too to adopt a policy (which I have continued here) of eliminating letters that to any significant extent duplicated the contents of those published elsewhere. As I was finalising my selection for *Dashing for the Post* I was already planning a second volume, so I was able to set aside a hundred or so of Paddy's best letters without too much of a pang. These form the core of this further selection. But it is refreshed by a significant quantity of letters that have come to light only since the first volume was published. This new book contains 155 letters to almost sixty correspondents, more than half of whom went unrepresented in *Dashing for the Post*.

The letters in this volume span more than three score years and ten, from October 1938 to February 2010. The first, a flirtatious letter to a teenage girl, was written when Paddy himself was only twenty-three. The last was written when he was ninety-five, a widower, very deaf, his voice already hoarse from the throat cancer that would soon kill him. As the letter describes, he had recently fallen down a flight of stairs. Despite tunnel vision, which made it hard for him to read even his own hand, he continued to pen letters that are enjoyable to read – though hard to decipher. From first to last, his letters exude a zest that was characteristic. Often they are decorated with witty illustrations and enhanced by comic verse. Sometimes they contain riddles and cringe-causing puns. Paddy's delight in language is everywhere in these letters, expressed both in a serious concern to use words correctly, and in a playfulness, showing off what he can do.

By the time Paddy had reached adulthood, one of the two achievements for which he is best known was already behind him. At the age of eighteen he had set out to walk to Constantinople (as he called it), after a premature exit from his boarding school (which would honour him later in life as 'a free spirit'). The very last letter in this book recalls 'Nellie Lemar, the wonderful looking cause of my scholastic downfall'.

Paddy left England early in December 1933, and arrived at his destination just over twelve months later, on New Year's Eve 1934. In the course of this 'Great Trudge' across Europe, he slept under the stars and in schlosses, dossed down in hostels, awoke more than once with a hangover in the houses of strangers, sat round a campfire singing songs with shepherds, frolicked with peasant girls and played bicycle polo with his host. He observed customs and practices that dated back to the Middle Ages, many of which were about to vanish forever – swept away, first by the catastrophe of war and then by communism. As Paddy puts it in one of his letters, 'a sudden Dark Age descended that nobody was ready for'. He would give an account of his experiences in what became a trilogy of much admired books, which remained incomplete at his death: *A Time of Gifts* (1977), *Between the Woods and the Water* (1986), and the posthumously published *The Broken Road* (2013).

He would spend the late 1930s oscillating between Greece, Romania, France and England. In the late summer of 1938, before departing for Romania, he left with a friend in London two trunks, which were subsequently lost with their contents, among them notebooks he had kept on his walk and letters home to his mother. The loss helps to explain why very few of his pre-war letters have survived; though two have recently been discovered and are included here. Nor do more than a handful survive from the war itself. Rather than going into the Guards, which had rated his capabilities as 'below average', Paddy had been snapped up by the Intelligence Corps, on the basis of the fact that he spoke German, Romanian and Greek; and after being evacuated first from mainland Greece and then from Crete as the Germans invaded, he had been infiltrated back onto Crete to operate under cover, liaising with the local resistance. It was during this period that Paddy planned and executed the abduction of General Kreipe, commander of the German occupying forces, a bold exploit that won him the DSO, and the other achievement for which he is best known. One letter in this book is written during this very operation, from a bitterly cold mountain hideaway in German-occupied Crete. It had started badly: Paddy had landed by parachute, but poor weather had prevented the rest of the team from making the jump, and after further unsuccessful attempts they eventually had to be infiltrated onto the island from the sea, more than a month later.

After the war Paddy worked for the British Council in Athens for just over a year – his only period of peacetime employment, as it would turn out, which ended in his dismissal. It became quickly apparent that he was 'unfit for office work'. The rest of his long life was spent as a freelance writer. Before the war he was already pursuing literary projects, and had translated a novel from French into English; though he was unsuccessful in his attempts to persuade successive generations of the Murray family to publish it. (One letter in this volume, to the American bibliophile Heyward Cutting, discusses the particular difficulties of translation from French into English.) After leaving the British Council, he accepted an invitation to write the captions for a book of photographs of the

Caribbean, a task that grew into a full-length book, *The Traveller's Tree*, published in 1950. (Paddy would invariably exceed any word limit he was given, just as he could never keep to a deadline.) From then on, though his letters betray a gnawing anxiety about lack of money, he seems never to have considered any other form of work. His experiences in the Caribbean inspired him to write a novel (his only work of fiction), *The Violins of Saint-Jacques* (1953). He was already working on a book drawing on his travels in Greece, part autobiographical, part ethnographical, which grew into two volumes: *Mani* (1958) and *Roumeli* (1966).

One of the surprises of his letters is to find how much he was preoccupied with his writing. His habitual procrastination, and his apparent readiness to allow himself to be distracted by the smallest thing, suggest a dilettante. But the letters tell a different story, of a writer always trying to steal time to write, anxious at his lack of progress, guilty at his failure to fulfil his commitments, and perpetually trying to do better. This is the refrain of Paddy's letters to his publisher, 'Jock' Murray, over a period of more than forty years. At Christmas 1984, for example, Paddy tells two friends that he has deferred a visit to London because he cannot face Jock while his book remains unfinished. Even after Jock's death, when Paddy was in his eighties, he felt it necessary to apologise to Jock's son for his presence in England by marking his letter 'NO SKULKING'.

One reason for his slow progress was that he was easily distracted. His friend George Seferis deplored his propensity for 'Penelopising', so that at night he seemed to undo what he had done in the day. (Seferis was qualified to make such a criticism, since he managed to combine a career as a diplomat with work of such a high standard that he would be awarded the Nobel Prize for Literature.) Paddy exhaustively rewrote and corrected what he had written, almost desperate to avoid errors. His torment at a mistake in *Between the Woods and the Water* is exhibited here in an agonised letter to his friend 'Dadie' Rylands.

At the beginning of his career Paddy had been encouraged to aim high, and he strove to produce the masterpiece that his admirers believed him capable of. Some thought that he achieved this in

A Time of Gifts. Yet even the acclaim this book and its successor attracted was double-edged, because it called attention to the fact that the story was incomplete. There was public as well as private pressure on him to finish the trilogy; an article in *Le Monde* mocked him as 'L'Escargot des Carpates' ('The Snail of the Carpathians'), a soubriquet that he ruefully accepted. The unfinished work hung around his neck to the end, weighing him down. Even in one of his last letters, written long since everyone else had given up hope of the third volume, Paddy reports that he was still 'toiling away'.

Paddy's domestic arrangements were unusually chaotic, even by the standards of a freelance writer. For one thing, he found it hard to resist the lure of society, and was capable of travelling across a continent for a party. (One of the earliest letters in this book mentions attending a party in Paris that had begun at one o'clock in the morning.) He seemed unable to concentrate on work in London, and sought out retreats in order to write free of distraction. He became adept at cadging houses from friends: Lady Diana Cooper's house in Bognor, Niko Ghika's mansion on Hydra, Barbara Warner's cottage in Pembrokeshire, Sir Walter and Lady Smart's manor house in the Eure. 'Mr Sponge has fallen on his feet again!' he writes in one of these letters. Being usually alone in such places, he wrote to his friends, often inviting them to stay (which somewhat defeated the object). After the war he formed a permanent bond with Joan Rayner, who became his lifelong partner, and, eventually, his wife; but they spent much of the time apart, even after they settled at Kardamyli, on the Mani peninsula. Paddy formed the habit of spending Christmas at Chatsworth, for example, while Joan, who did not share his appetite for company, preferred to remain alone, or with her beloved brother Graham. This of course meant that they often had reason to write to each other. Paddy called himself 'Mole' and Joan 'Mite' or 'Muskin'. His letters to Joan reveal an aspect of his character that he normally kept hidden: his slides into gloom and depression. He depended on her, not only for encouragement and emotional support, but for practical and indeed financial assistance. Joan was unquestionably the most important woman in his life. After her death in 2003, he was bereft. 'I constantly find myself saying "I must write – or tell – that to Joan", then suddenly remember that one can't, and nothing seems to have any point,' he wrote in reply to a letter of condolence.

But before Joan, there was 'Balasha', whom he had met in Athens in the spring of 1935. Though sixteen years older than him, she was still in her prime, and they fell in love – or, as Paddy might have put it, became 'terrific pals'. They were together almost five years, until separated by the coming of war: after 1939, they would not see each other again for more than a quarter of a century. By the time they were able to renew contact, Paddy was in love with Joan. Yet Balasha Cantacuzène had been his first love, and seems to have retained a special place in his heart. Balasha's life after the war was hard. As 'elements of putrid background', she and her family were vulnerable to persecution by the new communist regime. She tried to escape from Romania with her cousin Alexander Mourouzi, but was detained and sent back, and soon afterwards she and her sister were brutally evicted from their ancestral home. None of Paddy's letters to her at this time have survived, but a letter written to Mourouzi in 1948 expresses sympathy for the hardships they are enduring and his hopes that they may be allowed to come to the West. In 1965 Paddy was able to travel to Romania, and visited Balasha and her sister after dark, because it was dangerous for Romanians to be seen to consort with anyone from the West. Paddy, himself still youthful and vigorous at fifty, was shocked by Balasha's appearance: she was now an old woman, losing her teeth and her hair, the wreck of her former self. His subsequent letters to her are written with gallantry and tenderness: one has the sense that he is trying to include her in his life, even at long distance.

Joan recognised the sentimental importance of Balasha to Paddy, and wrote to her affectionately, as if to a member of the family. She also tolerated Paddy's lovers ('terrific pals'), and even his casual encounters with prostitutes, confident that he would never leave her. His love letters to his younger girlfriends are quite frisky – particularly his letters to Ricki Huston, the much younger Italian-American (fourth) wife of the film director John Huston.

As well as such love affairs, Paddy maintained several close and long-term friendships with women, conducted largely by letter. Though platonic, there was an element of courtly love in them; it is significant that his lady pen pals were all well born – among them Lady Diana Cooper (twenty-three years his senior) and Ann Fleming (twenty-nine years), both of whom he always addressed as 'darling'. In 1980 Paddy dug out his letters from Diana Cooper and re-read them, a correspondence that by that time had lasted almost three decades. He was very moved, he told her, 'by this record of shared delights and trust, confidence, warmth and loving friendship, and can't believe my luck, unfaltering for all these years, and still prospering in such a marvellous, happy and treasured bond, light as garlands, as lasting as those hoops of Polonius'. Another long-term correspondence was with Debo Devonshire, youngest of the lively Mitford sisters, five years his junior. Some believed that Paddy and Debo had once had an affair, but those who knew them best doubted this. To give a flavour of their epistolary relationship I have included in this volume a couple of his early letters to Debo from *In Tearing Haste*, as well as two late letters, previously unpublished.

In the late 1940s, when writing *The Traveller's Tree*, Paddy sought sanctuary in a succession of monasteries in northern France, an experience which itself would provide a subject for a short book, *A Time to Keep Silence* (1957). From these he wrote a series of letters that give a vivid picture of monastic life. Writing the letters, and observing how the monks lived, prompted him into reflections on spiritual questions, unusual subjects for him, at least in correspondence. He would return to his favourite monastery, Saint-Wandrille, several times over the next decade. Another, more temporary refuge was the 'stupendous' castle of Passerano, inland from Rome (from its battlements the dome of Saint Peter's was just discernible on the horizon), which he took for the summer of 1959. Paddy had sewn 'a vast heraldic banner, several yards square', to adorn one wall at the end of a large banqueting hall. He was tempted to fly it from the highest tower, as he admitted in a letter to Jock Murray: 'Then, when the Black Castellan of Passerano displays his gonfalon from the battlements, the peasants of the valley can hide their cattle and douse their lights and bolt up their dear ones!' To balance this attack of *folie de grandeur*, he explained that the living conditions were primitive, since the castle had not been inhabited for over five hundred years. 'There is no sanitation at all. It's all fieldwork under the trees, and the only lighting is by oil-lamp.'

Yet another refuge was Easton Court at Chagford, a hotel on the edge of Dartmoor run by an unconventional American woman and her English beau. Easton Court had been discovered by Evelyn Waugh, who wrote several of his books there; other writers had followed, including Paddy's friends John Betjeman and Patrick Kinross. From the late 1940s until the early 1960s Paddy stayed often at 'Chaggers', from which he wrote several of the letters included here. He went there to write; though another attraction of the hotel was that it offered the possibility of riding to hounds over the moor with the local hunt three times a week. Here and elsewhere, are lyrical descriptions of nature – striding out in the fields, picking his way along mountain paths, driving into the sunset.

As all this suggests, Paddy rarely stayed in one place long. In fact, he did not have a permanent home until he was almost fifty, in 1964, when he and Joan bought a piece of land overlooking the sea in the Mani, beneath the towering Taygetus mountains near the village of Kardamyli, and began building a house. Letters included here describe the search for a site, negotiations to purchase the land, and plans for the house itself and the surrounding garden. For the first few summers at Kardamyli, Paddy and Joan bivouacked in tents as the land was cleared and the house was built. Paddy took a keen interest in every detail of the design and construction, a further distraction from his writing, as he complains in a long letter to Joan. Work on the house would not be complete until the end of the decade.

Some of their friends came to visit, bringing with them a whiff of the wider world to this remote region. But much of the time Paddy and Joan were alone at Kardamyli, with just each other and their cats for company, enjoying simple pleasures such as swimming and reading. One letter tells of walking in the mountains and being followed by goats, trying one device after another to shake them off.

These letters provide accounts of Paddy's travels in Turkey and Tibet; Jordan and Syria; India and Sri Lanka; France, Italy, Spain and Portugal; Scotland and Ireland; Hungary and Romania; Central and South America, and the eastern seaboard of the United States. The incongruity of a film crew, headed by the maverick director John Huston, and a starry cast that included Trevor Howard, Juliette Gréco and Errol Flynn, on location in 'darkest Africa' is explored in two letters from a former French colonial territory, now Cameroon. Paddy was there in his temporary capacity as screenwriter, since he had adapted the novel for the screen. Another letter relates the shooting of *Ill Met by Moonlight*, the film based on the story of General Kreipe's abduction. On location in the French Alps, Paddy met a screen version of himself. 'Dirk Bogarde turned out to be absolutely charming … everything that the most confirmed snob could pray for,' he wrote to Joan.

It would be foolish to deny that Paddy had a romantic interest in aristocracy, and all its paraphernalia: genealogy, heraldry and the rest. Yet if this was snobbery, it was of a comparatively innocuous kind. There was nothing oleaginous in Paddy's relations with his betters (except perhaps, in his attitude to Her Majesty the Queen). Nor was there any superciliousness towards the 'lower classes'. Paddy was at ease in any company; he could walk into a simple taverna and soon have everyone singing. His letters contain glimpses of the great and the good: a chance conversation with the Foreign Secretary, Anthony Eden, when Paddy opens the wrong door, or a glass of ouzo under the pine trees with Harold Macmillan. They describe encounters with such varied figures as Jackie Onassis, Camilla Parker Bowles, Oswald Mosley and Peter Mandelson. But Paddy also relates his adventures with the humble: a 'picknick' with the stonemasons at Kardamyli, or a drunken feast in the Cretan mountains with his old comrades from the resistance, most of them simple shepherds and goatherds.

'He was the most English person I ever met,' recalled Agnes 'Magouche' Fielding, second wife of Paddy's close comrade,

Xan: 'Everything was *ripping*, and there was more talk of P. G. Wodehouse than of Horace or Gibbon.' Indeed, Paddy himself was something of a Wodehouse hero, in his boyish manner, his innocence, his gentleness, his sense of fun, and his tendency to get into scrapes. (One letter included in this volume tells of a high-spirited brawl, alcohol-fuelled, in County Kildare, which Paddy had provoked.) His letters are dotted with amusing and usually affectionate anecdotes about the eccentrics he has known.

There is an absence of malice in his writing, and a related unwillingness to offend. Several of his letters express anxiety that casual comments made in private correspondence may wound if broadcast. Towards the end of his life he began to edit those of his own letters in his possession, censoring passages that might cause upset, and adding the occasional explanatory note for his biographer, Artemis Cooper. Both he and Joan were distressed to read two vicious poems about Paddy written by Maurice Bowra, who had been their guest on several occasions, and whom they considered a good friend. 'I like[d] Maurice very much, which makes the whole thing even gloomier,' Paddy wrote in a letter included here. He asked for the poems about himself to be suppressed, as well as his own disobliging anagram for Bowra, 'Eroica Rawbum'.

Paddy was a philhellene, an Englishman who went to live in Greece, as Byron had done. Indeed, there was more than a little of Byron about him. Like Byron, he chose to swim the Hellespont, the treacherous strait between Europe and Asia. Byron claimed this swim as 'my greatest achievement', though he had been twenty-two when he undertook it; Paddy was sixty-nine.

In Athens after the war Paddy formed close and enduring friendships with Greek artists and intellectuals, especially the poet George Seferis, the painter Niko Ghika and the 'Colossus' of letters, George Katsimbalis; but in the mid-1950s some of these became strained by the Cyprus Emergency. This was 'an argument among friends': two nations, Britain and Greece, which had enjoyed a long history as allies. It was understandable that Greeks should feel a claim on British sympathies, since only a decade earlier, in 1940–1, they had been the only other people fighting Axis troops on the continent of Europe. Paddy felt a conflict of loyalties, between the country of his birth and the country he would make his home. The enmity was such that he felt obliged to quit Greece for a while.

In general, Paddy was not a political person. An instinctive, old-fashioned conservative, he took little interest in politics except when it touched him in some way. In a letter to Jessica Mitford (the communist sister) in 1983, he tells her that he has enjoyed her piece on Mrs Thatcher's England 'not so much for the sentiments – I rather fear that in terms of hands and bell I wring when you ring, and vice versa: too late for this old ocelot to do anything about his spots, I fear – but for the splendid jokes'. As a young man travelling through Germany in the mid-1930s he had disliked the Nazis he encountered because of their crudeness and their anti-Semitism, but he was indifferent to their rhetoric. In 1967 he reacted cautiously to the military takeover in Greece, the so-called 'Colonels' coup'. In a letter to Joan, who was in England at the time, he suggests that she may know more about what is happening than he does. 'All my spontaneous sympathies (in spite of my official views generally) are against the coup,' he wrote, 'largely because those in the provinces who welcome it are … the people one likes least in Greece.' In another letter to Jock Murray, cautiously worded to evade the scrutiny of the censor, he appeals for help to free the Greek publisher of *Mani*, who 'has been roped into durance for some unstated reason, where she still vilely is'. During the regime of the 'Colonels' he became friendly with Tzannis Tzannetakis, then in political exile, and a prominent politician (briefly prime minister) once democracy had been restored.

Paddy's magpie mind is evident in his letters. Before setting out on his 'Great Trudge' he had packed *The Oxford Book of English Verse* in his rucksack, and on the walk had committed much to memory, so that he could recite great chunks of poetry, more or less accurately, at will. He would continue to read widely throughout his life, and was able to retain much: repeatedly topping up a cornucopia of knowledge that overflowed into his correspondence. In a letter to Diana Cooper, Paddy points to 'the enormous amount of buried quotation' in Raymond Asquith's letters to his wife, 'which must mean a vast quantity of shared poetry which was in daily use, and pointless if the other correspondent couldn't spot it'. There is an enormous amount of buried quotation in Paddy's letters too, and one suspects that a significant proportion of this went unrecognised by their recipients. I daresay that some of it has gone unrecognised by the editor.

The letters themselves tell us something of the circumstances in which they were written. 'I'm scribbling this in a glassed in loggia overlooking a dilapidated Tuscan farmyard and trellis,' one letter explains; another that he is sitting in the garden of the British Embassy in Athens, with the head of an enormous Labrador on his lap. 'The sun set some time ago, I'm writing outside the studio, and it's getting darker and darker, bats wheel about among the cypresses, the sea is a fading zinc and lilac hue, and I bet this is getting less and less legible,' he writes to Jock Murray. In a letter to Harold Acton, he apologises for the smudged ink. 'I had put a glass of whisky and soda on my desk (during a thunderstorm), then all the lights went out, as they are prone to here. Fumbling for matches, I knocked the glass over, hence the frightful mess.'

Once Paddy was settled at Kardamyli, he seems to have developed a routine of rising early to work (with a half-hour swim at seven, so that he could lie on his back in the water and watch the sun come up over the Taygetus mountains), writing letters in the afternoon; often they refer to the need to curtail before the post departs. On several occasions he opens a sealed letter to add a postscript. Then he might begin work again. 'I have several times – the first time in ages – got into that wonderful, oblivious and timeless trance where meals flash by like brief irrelevances – eleven o'clock last night before I thought of dinner (just in time) and then far on into the night,' he writes in a letter to Joan.

Almost all of Paddy's letters were written by hand, though a handful were then corrected and typed. Some of them – particularly those he wrote towards the end of his long life – are difficult to decipher. 'Please tell me truthfully: could you read this letter or was it impossible work?' he asked, as a postscript to one of his last letters to Debo Devonshire. In editing his letters, I have occasionally found it impossible, and have been obliged to resort to guesswork, deciding on the balance of probabilities which word is meant.

As I have already mentioned, some of Paddy's letters are very long, ten tightly written pages or more. A rough estimate suggests that he wrote between 5,000 and 10,000 letters in his adult lifetime. That is an average of several letters a week – and of course, there would have been many weeks when he could not have written any, so the rest of the time he must have been writing more. When one reflects on this, what is most striking is the sheer amount of time and effort Paddy devoted to writing letters. Since many of them record his unhappiness at failing to fulfil his promises to his publisher (not to mention his bank manager), one is forced to conclude that writing letters took up time he could have spent writing books. But was this such a bad thing? Of course, it was regrettable that he never completed his trilogy, and perhaps sadder still that the evening of his life was darkened by anxiety about the unfinished work.

Yet we may take a different view. The letters may sometimes be penned in haste (or even 'in tearing haste'), but they are written in a spontaneous, free-flowing prose that is easier and more entertaining to read than the baroque style of his books, which at times can seem overworked. I would argue that Paddy's correspondence is part of his oeuvre, worthy to take its place alongside the work that he published in his lifetime. Now that we can read his letters at length, we can judge their worth. At their best, they are as good as any in the English language. They are utterly distinctive: Paddy's sunny nature shines through them. His letters are exhilarating; to borrow an expression he liked to use, they are absolutely 'tip-top'.

Editorial Note

Readers should be aware that Paddy's letters are not necessarily reproduced in full here: I have chosen to omit the more mundane passages which often refer to practical arrangements, or points of obscure detail of little general interest. Excisions are indicated by ellipses. I have taken it upon myself to omit repeated words and phrases and to correct the occasional spelling error, particularly in the use of foreign words and names (though I decided to retain Paddy's delightful spelling of 'picknick'). I was tempted to retain Paddy's spelling of 'Teusday', which makes aural sense, but looks so odd that I decided against. I have also standardised Paddy's somewhat erratic punctuation. As he himself would frequently lament, his handwriting is notoriously difficult to decipher, so I have sometimes been obliged to resort to guesswork, and no doubt my guesses have been wrong on occasion. In the handful of instances where I have been completely stumped, I have written 'illegible' in square brackets. I have used the same device for simple translations or other brief expository material, to avoid unnecessary annotation. Words and phrases such as book titles that Paddy underlined are usually presented in italics, to conform to standard publishers' practice. Short profiles of the people mentioned most often in the letters, including most of the addressees, are provided in an alphabetical dramatis personae at the end of the book.

In 1935, soon after completing his great walk across Europe, Paddy met 'Balasha' (Marie-Blanche) Cantacuzène at a party in Athens. She was a Romanian princess, from one of the great families of Eastern Europe; her ancestors had governed Moldavia and Wallachia for centuries. Though he was only twenty years old when they met and she was six-teen years his senior, they fell in love, and would remain together until the outbreak of war in September 1939. Much of this time was spent at Balasha's family home, Băleni, in Romanian Moldavia.

This letter and the one that follows were written from Băleni to Bridget ('Biddy') Branch, the younger sister of their friend Guy Branch; Paddy and Balasha had stayed with the Branch family at their house in Pembroke Square when they arrived in London in January 1937. In August the following year, Biddy, then still in her teens, had gone out to Romania for a six-week stay at Băleni; this letter was written after her return to England.

To 'Biddy' Branch   Băleni
October 1938   Romania

Dear Bids,

I'm disconsolate about your vicissitudes and reverses in love. Tom's[1] symbolical departure for the wide open spaces, Pat's absence in Switzerland, and Toivo's silence, altogether, are overwhelming. I think it is the right moment for me, your only faithful cavalier, to break silence and tell you that all is not lost. In fact, Biddy, it must be fun to be fancy-free, to be able to let your mind wander without any inner voice to forbid it: ready to start something. Anyway, the hecatomb of bleeding hearts that you left behind in Bucharest ought to have glutted you for a year. There are at least a dozen fancy men there who need no encouragement, and this flickering and wide-spread forest-fire abroad must surely console you for the winter's chill at home! It is like a fiery belt of beacons embracing

---

[1] She married Thomas Edward Hubbard on 23 September 1939. The other two admirers are unidentified.

all Europe from Finland – almost the North Pole – skirting the Black Sea all the way to south of Greece, in the warm bosom of the Mediterranean; and I don't know how many bonfires are smoking beside your homeward path. So what the hell.

This letter has begun a bit too 'man-of-letters'-ish, but that last phrase puts it right. It's all true, though. Nicky Chrissoveloni,[1] Paul Zanesco Alcover,[2] Ivan Ghyka[3] and all the others are yours forever. So don't you stand any nonsense at home.

Everyone misses you terribly here, and your letters are devoured from beginning to end by each of us in turn. No detail is missed – not even the Yiddish paper for Leich Ferman.[4] None of us have quite got used to your absence yet, looking on you as a fixture that is temporarily and irritatingly detained elsewhere. Tea-time is just over, and your letter and packet was brought by Mustapha [one of the staff at Băleni] just as Balasha was saying 'I do hope Biddy's reply hasn't got lost. She <u>must</u> have written,' and we were nodding our heads in silence. You would love the wintry nursery-teas that have started now, with golden piles of *cozonac*,[5] honey, toast, and salt to put on one's butter, and hot tea just right out of a huge brass samovar that steams and gurgles on a table by itself, and distorts the reflected lamplight in its huge brazen surface. The stove is piled full of logs, and everything is so kind and warm and *cardouble* [comfortable?]. Constantine[6] had just come in from shooting, with four hares already stiff under their soft fur. Balasha and Pomme[7] had been talking and playing with old papers and drawings, and their disorder swamped one lamplit corner. Ina[8] had appeared from her

---

[1] A friend of PLF's in Bucharest, scion of a famous banking family, who had been educated in England.

[2] Another Bucharest friend, 'a brilliant, funny and very gifted and unconventional young diplomat'; PLF in Cooper and Thubron (eds), *The Broken Road* (London, 2013), p. 189.

[3] Cousin of Prince Matila Ghyka (see footnote on p. 95).

[4] PLF imagines how his own surname would be pronounced in Yiddish.

[5] Traditional Romanian sweet leavened bread, stuffed with cocoa or nuts, raisins and Turkish delight.

[6] Constantine Donici, Balasha's brother-in-law, husband to Balasha's sister, Princess Hélène.

[7] Princess Hélène, known as 'Pomme'.

[8] Ina, Balasha's niece, daughter of Constantine and 'Pomme' Donici.

room and her writing, and I'd just come in from a ride that ended long after dark. Tea, and your letter, are finished now, and I have retreated to the library. A terrific wind has sprung up, knocking the branches together outside, and slamming and rattling all the doors and windows in the house.

Last week Pomme, Boule[1] and I went to Galatz[2] for the day, buying curtains for Balasha's room. They are lovely and blue ones in soft colours with a pattern of Persian flowers, like something out of Jane Austen. And, very exciting, we've put the old baldaquin on top of Balasha's blue bed, turning it into a huge blue four-poster with canopy, valences, and richly folded curtains all round. We all of us got silk for sumptuous dressing-gowns – mine is a bit too sumptuous I think; a trifle womanly, but gorgeous. We had a long luncheon [of] crayfish and other crustaceans, and Dimitri was sad to know that the pretty English *coniţa* [young lady] really had left.

Everybody has left now – Gladys[3] a week ago, and the platoons of officers and generals (but no king, it's all right Bids) who swarmed in the Maison d'Amis for the [manoeuvres]. Prue[4] doesn't seem to be coming, alas, and there are no Dereks or Anne-Maries[5] on the horizon, mercifully. Winter is closing in, and the fiercer it grows outside, the more the house comes to life, like a long strong-timbered ship on a cold sea, with all its port-holes alight, with warmth and comfort inside. We have got ourselves made warm flannel Russian shirts for the winter, wine-red, canary red, and dark blue, worn belted about the middle. A cunning man in the village is busy on our sheepskin coats.

Doina[6] is now quite mended and has forgotten all about our mournful little trio in the drizzling twilight beyond the vineyard.

---

[1] Perhaps a corruption of Balasha?

[2] A city near Băleni.

[3] Unidentified.

[4] Bridget's future sister-in-law. Guy Branch would marry Lady Prudence Pelham, daughter of the 6th Earl of Chichester, on 25 March 1939.

[5] Derek Patmore, author of *Invitation to Roumania* (1939); Balasha's cousin, Princess Anne-Marie Callimachi, who exasperated her by nonstop chatter.

[6] Doina, Cimpoi and Drâmbā are all horses' names.

Pani[1] is delighted at the approach of winter, it reminds him of Poland, and he has never been able to understand the summer. I found him putting hay into Cimpoi's manger the other evening, puffing in the dark stable, and we went into the old coach house and looked at the carriages – the pretty open one with the hood and the lamps that took us to Gara Maria [a railway station], and a magnificent shiny black one, closed in, and upholstered in buttoned leather inside. We climbed in and sat on the soft seat, and smoked a cigarette. Pani told me how he used to drive Balasha's grandfather into Galatz in it 'in the time of the Knéaz'.[2] The Knéaz used to sit inside covered in furs, with a brazier on the floor to keep his feet warm, Pani, equally fur-covered on the box, with six magnificently matched horses in front. 'Motor cars? Peuh! The only thing one notices is their stink. When we bowled down the Strada Domnească [Lord's Street] in Galatz, all six horses lifting their feet together, and me up top cracking my long whip, the policemen held up all the traffic to let us by, and everybody looked round and admired us. *Das war etwas!'* [That was something!] Pani doubled up then his hands on his knees, wheezing with sudden laughter, '*Das war etwas! … Aber jetzt …!'* [That was really something! … But now it's not the same!]

I went for a long ride this afternoon (I write to you booted and Russian-shirted, smelling of saddle polish and horse sweat. This is to put you in the mood.) I had an exciting gallop on Drâmbā in the big field where we always galloped, beside the avenue. Drâmbā jumped and writhed like a dolphin at first and then pelted along at a terrific rate, showering clods of earth and mud behind him and on me, like a dark comet. I wish you had been there on Doina or Cimpoi, and we'd have gone along, neck and neck, with stirrups almost touching, like the wind. I miss you very much on my lonely rides. You'd love the colder weather and the soft sad feeling of the fields, and the bloody and ragged sunset over those rolling hills where we went with Pomme the day it rained. Today it was magnificent,

[1] Băleni's Polish coachman.
[2] From the Russian, meaning prince or duke, as Balasha's grandfather was.

the sky torn and bleeding on the skyline with a soft grey mackerel-sky up above, like cloudy sand-dunes, or flocks of sheep, or angel-wings crossed in a regular design. The trunks of the avenue leading to the vine looked quite black, and the trees were shedding their golden and russet leaves on the damp earth all along. I saw Iou[1] and the children at the vine coming out to the lighted house like little troglodytes. Then out onto the plateau beyond the fatal ditch, down in to the valley on the left, and up into the forest beyond – now all red and gold – where we went that time I was on Moş, [Uncle] Mihai's horse, then back by that deep valley where the well is, up the other side through the dead maize stalks, and home along the little path where we heard the crickets singing in the hollow. There are no crickets now, but I met a little shepherd whistling to himself surrounded by his moving flocks bleating (baa! baa!) and tinkling their little bells in the dark. By the time I got home, [there] was a misty crescent sailing through the watery mackerel-shoals up above, and a creeping wind. Constantine's bright headlights came peering down the village street, back from shooting, making Drâmbă shine all over. We came in from the stables together, Constantine laying his gun lovingly on the billiard table.

I got a big parcel of books from Hatchards the other day, containing Gibbon's *Decline & Fall*, & the *Oxford Book of English Verse*. It made me think of the lights of Piccadilly through the rain on an autumn evening, with a wind roaring across the park, and me peering at the books in the bow-window of Hatchards. Please write long, <u>long</u> letters, like this one, just as juicy and full of description and heartburnings! I'm sure all will turn out for the best with your fancy-men, and can't feel at all anxious on that score! Please give all my love to Mayme[2] – I think of her so often, and of our happy family in Pembroke Square, and I am going to WRITE: and to Guy.

[1] Unidentified.
[2] Biddy's widowed mother, Mary Madeline, known as 'Mayme'.

God bless, Bids, and good hunting for the winter; you being the quarry and everyone else in full cry being understood.

Lots of love
Paddy

P.S. 'He that keepeth his mouth, keepeth his life; but he that openeth wide his lips shall have destruction,' *Proverbs* XIII, 3.

P.P.S. (<u>Shove</u> over, Biddy ...)[1]

To 'Biddy' Branch   6 Shepherd Market
undated [September/October 1939]   W1

Darling Bids,

Just heard 2 days ago from Guy and Prue [Branch], and then Mayme, of your engagement to Tom, and write as quick as I can to wish you every kind of happiness in your Married Life for you and the very lucky Tom. To be quite truthful, I can't help feeling a faint pang of jealousy, not in a direct way, but because it is one of the Sex's Fairest Ornaments being whipped away and put out of circulation. You know how we bachelors feel. It's always happening, but we know how to take it; we wipe a couple of salt tears out of our moustaches and pretend we are blowing our noses, then whistle a few notes of a gay little tune in a halting breath and shout angrily for another double whisky.

I'm simply longing to see you, Biddy, and hear all your news, and, of course, just exactly how everything came about. I may be able to give you lots of useful advice; I always do, don't I? I tremble to think of all the bonfires over Europe that hence forward must burn with concealed and thwarted ardour. Romania, Greece, France, England ...

I'm living in a dingy little room with jug, basin and gas-bracket in horrid Shepherd's Market,[2] at the beck and call of Old Generals who are trying to find me a job as a liaison officer. It's all very sad and depressing.

---

[1] A family joke.
[2] A square in Mayfair, associated with prostitutes since the eighteenth century.

Balasa, Pomme, Ina and naturally Constantine all send you their love, and long to see you. I do too. Please write to them Bids, and tell them all. Balasa is wretched, as you can imagine, and so am I. Hitler has a terrible lot to answer for all over the place, hasn't he?

I feel too fed up and empty to write anymore at the moment, so will shut up now, sending you and Mayme all my love. Please write!

Love Paddy
X X

P.S. Most important. Please Bids, could you send me immediately the ring you got from the bank if it is with you. Thanks, it's most urgent!

Had a terribly funny journey home with Henry Nevile,[1] one night in Venice, another in Paris. Why do we all rush to Venice as soon as War breaks out?

Shove over …

---

[1] The nephew of Eileen Ghyka (see footnote on p. 95), Henry Nevile had just left Ampleforth; before going up to Cambridge, he had come to stay the summer in Romania, first at Băleni and then as the guest of Sir Reginald Hoare, British plenipotentiary minister in Bucharest 1935–41. Sir Reginald's wife, Lucy Cavendish-Bentinck (known by her second name of 'Joan'), imagining Nevile to be much younger than his real age of eighteen, had given him bread and milk at 6 p.m. each evening, and a child's cot to sleep in; he had slipped out afterwards to join the company at dinner. At the outbreak of war, she escorted him to the station in Bucharest and tied a label in his buttonhole, inscribed with his name, address and destination. A few months later he was serving with the Scots Guards.

The next letter, addressed to a secretary at SOE HQ Cairo, was written four days after Paddy had dropped by parachute into Axis-occupied Crete, at the start of a daring operation to kidnap General Heinrich Kreipe, commander of the German occupying forces. Its light-hearted tone belies the difficulties already encountered, and the harshness of conditions on the ground. As the letter reveals, Paddy was the only member of the team able to make the jump, and was obliged to wait weeks until the others arrived. No doubt the letter was written to pass the time, and it seems unlikely that it was posted until the party returned in triumph with the captured general to Egypt three months later.

To Annette Crean   Crete (a cross marks my window)
9 February 1944

Dear Annette,

Well, here we are in the old home, at least here I am at the moment, as the second I left the car, a horrid cloud appeared that stopped Billy [Moss], Manoli [Paterakis] and George [Tyrakis] from jumping. We are expecting them tonight.[1] Then Up and AWAY!

It's great fun being back, and, of course, life is just one big whisker, as usual. It's very cold and snowy, and rather beautiful. Wish you were here. Must stop now as the runner is champing in the snow by the box-hedge in the front drive.[2] So God bless you, and my love to Nina, and all the girls, and hugs.

Love, Paddy

---

[1] In fact, bad weather would prevent the rest of the team from landing by parachute, and they were eventually infiltrated onto Crete by boat.
[2] A joke: he had parachuted onto the Omalos plateau, a bowl surrounded by jagged, snow-covered peaks, and would spend the next seven weeks living in a cave.

9th Feb, 1944.

Dear Annette, (a crow marks my
window)

Well, here we are
in the old home, at least here I am
at the moment, as the second I left
the ~~cabin~~ a horrid cloud appeared
that stopped Billy, ~~and~~ Blanche and
George from jumping. We are expecting
them tonight. Then up and AWAY!!

Its great fun being back,
and, of course, life is just one big
whisker, as usual. Its very cold
and snowy, and rather beautiful.
Wish you were here. Must stop now
as the runner is champing in the
snow by the box hedge in the front
drive. So God bless you, and
my love to Nina and all the girls
and boys. Love P......

Saucy is rather wonderful [illegible]
and the longer the more true.

HIMMEL! I AM UNDONE!

DON'T YOU DARE MOVE!

RATHER NOT!

Life in the Island

Paddy met Joan Rayner in Cairo in the final few months of the war. He was not the first to be struck by her beauty, and impressed by her calm, her good sense and her intelligence. 'Like all adorable people Joan Leigh Fermor had something enigmatic about her nature which, together with her wonderful good looks, made her a very seductive presence,' wrote the artist John Craxton, in an obituary published in the Independent in 2003. 'She was also naturally self-effacing. Even in a crowd she maintained a deep and private inner self. Paradoxically, she loved good company and long and lasting friendships. It was her elegance, luminous intelligence, curiosity, understanding and unerring high standards that made her such a perfect muse to her lifelong companion and husband Patrick Leigh Fermor, as well as friend and inspiration to a host of distinguished writers, philosophers, painters, sculptors and musicians.'[1]

Like many of those who had distinguished themselves in the war, Paddy found it hard to settle afterwards. For a brief period he worked for the British Council in Athens, but he was not a natural employee. Afterwards he tried to make a living as a writer. Easily distracted, Paddy sought out a succession of retreats where he could work in isolation – including the monastery of Saint-Wandrille in Normandy, from which this next letter was written. He had gone there to concentrate on his first book, based on his travels in Central America and the Caribbean, and eventually published in December 1950 under the title The Traveller's Tree.

To Joan Rayner   St Wandrille
Monday [early September 1948]

My darling Pet,

What a sweet funny letter. Oxford sounds as if it had been heavenly. I'm a bit more resigned to this place at the moment, and now that I've established my rights as a defaulter at Mass every day, it's not too bad. The weather has been perfect, and I have been writing away out of doors under a chestnut tree. But all the same, if I get the slightest excuse to come to London in Peggie Mathieson's[2] letter, I'm going to do so. Probably even if there isn't. There are tons of things I want to look up for the last three chapters, and I can't

---

[1] 'Muse who enlivened a distinguished generation', John Craxton, *Independent*, 10 June 2003.
[2] Unidentified.

(2 pages)

St Wandrille,

Kingdom.

My darling Pet,

View from my window

What a sweet funny letter. It Pafand sounds as if it had been heavenly. I'm a bit more resigned to this place at the moment, and now that I've established any rights as a defaulter at Mass every day, it's not too bad. The weather has been perfect, and I have been writing away out of doors under a chestnut tree. But all the same, if I get the slightest excuse to come to London in Peggie Makrigani's (probably something out letter, I'm going to do so. There are tons of things I want to look up for the last three chapters, and I can't bear the idea of your (a) enjoying London like mad without me or (b) the reverse. I really do miss you like anything. At this distance you even seem almost as nearly perfect as a human being can be, my darling little wretch — and so it's about time I was brought to my senses. So don't get too deeply sen- -imentally embroiled, for Heaven's sake-

How kind these monks are! I'm not feeling an atom more disposed to religion at the moment, but the discretion

bear the idea of your (a) enjoying London like mad without me or (b) the reverse. I really do miss you like anything. At this distance you seem about as nearly perfect as a human being can be, my darling little wretch, so it's about time I was brought to my senses. So don't get too deeply sentimentally embroiled,[1] for Heaven's sake.

How kind these monks are! I'm not feeling an atom more disposed to religion at the moment, but the discretion and good manners and general aura of kindness and sweetness of nature of these people is something extremely rare. I wander about under the trees for half an hour after luncheon with the Abbé or the Père Hôtelier every day, talking about religion, philosophy, history, Greek and Roman poetry etc. Very pleasant and satisfactory. The Père Hôtelier confided to me today that his conversion from atheism and monastic vocation was entirely under the influence of Huysmans,[2] especially later books like *L'Oblat* and *La Cathédrale*. V. interesting.

I feel <u>such a relief</u> having finished with the Windward, Leeward and Virgin Islands. The Leeward Islands were becoming a positive incubus, exorcised now, at last. Once I tackle a chapter, I find, I'm alright. After a page. But what a tormenting assidious [slothful] period of hesitation beforehand. I'm feeling much happier about this book now, and terribly excited. I'm longing for you to read and criticise the latest stuff. Must be going on scribbling now so goodnight, my darling little mite! Please go on writing, I adore your letters and they stop me from feeling like Ariadne.[3]

All my love
P
X X X X

P.S. Compline [the Night Prayer] takes place in broad daylight – 8.30 – and it's not dark for nearly an hour afterwards, which makes the evening hours seem lovely and long. But it's rather like one's

---

[1] With Cyril Connolly – see next letter.

[2] Joris-Karl Huysmans (1848–1907), French novelist associated with the Decadent movement, who became interested in monasticism. See Artemis Cooper's *Patrick Leigh Fermor: An Adventure* (London, 2012), pp. 231–2, for Huysmans's influence on PLF.

[3] Ariadne, daughter of King Minos of Crete, associated with mazes and labyrinths; maybe PLF feels lost in the labyrinth of his work. Ariadne was abandoned by her lover, Theseus, on an island, so perhaps PLF feels that he is similarly isolated at the abbey.

childhood, when grown-ups would still be playing tennis when one was supposed to be asleep. The trout rise in the Fontenelle and make little circles, and an old farmer has just ridden past on a huge cart horse to the thatched farmyard down the road. For some reason I hadn't noticed the first and last lines of Compline till tonight. They are very fine, I think – (both out of Psalms translated by St Jerome). Or is it an Epistle of St Paul? I think it is.[1]

Fratres, sobrii estote et vigilate: quia adversarius vester diabolus, tamquam leo rugiens, circuit quærens quem devoret: cui resistite fortes in fide. (Brothers, be sober, and watch, For your adversary the devil, like a roaring lion ranges abroad, seeking whom he may devour; whom resist strong in the faith.)

and

Sub umbra alarum tuarum protege nos! (Under the shadow of thy wings defend us!)

P.P.S. Important. Darling, I've suddenly remembered that I haven't [sent] Mondi Howard's brother[2] the £17 for the electric light. I'm, alas, £1 overdrawn. Do you think you could possibly send £18 to the Manager, Messrs Glyn Mills (Holt's Branch), Whitehall, SW1, and post the enclosed letter a day later. Darling, I know it's the sort of thing you loathe doing more than anything in the world (not the pennies, I mean, but writing to banks) but I do think it would be a good idea to give it back now. It might make all the difference between being allowed to live at Sant' Antonio another winter, and not. There's still more trouble though. I've lost his address. But it is Dean Farm, I know, something-something, Glos. So could you look up Ld Howard of Penrith in *Who's Who* in the London Library, and fill it in? Please, please don't be savage with boredom at all this! It won't take long.

Love P

---

[1] From the Vulgate Bible: 1 Peter 5:8–9.

[2] Edmund Bernard Carlo 'Mondi' Howard (1909–2005), writer, soldier and consular official, then serving in Rome and married to Cécile, née Cécile Geoffroy-Dechaume. His elder brother was Lord Howard of Penrith, who lived at Coln St Aldwyn, Gloucestershire. The Howards, both Roman Catholic, had recently suggested the old Franciscan monastery of Sant' Antonio, near Tivoli, as a place to work.

Paddy found his prolonged separation from Joan difficult. He was jealous of the attention she received from other men: in particular, from the writer and critic Cyril Connolly, who had already made a pass at her back in the summer, when she had been with him in south-west France, taking photographs for a travel book which he never found time to write. In his letters to Joan, Paddy referred to Connolly as 'the Humanist', or 'the H' for short.

To Joan Rayner   St Wandrille
Tuesday [October 1948]

My darling Mopsa,

Just got your lovely two letters. Hooray! Darling, you have been efficient and brisk. The pullover is the smartest thing that has ever been seen in Saint Wandrille.

So the H has been very attentive, eh? Hm. 'I can-no-longer-live-without-you,' I suppose. Well, bugger it, neither can I. Oh dear, what fun London sounds! Late at night is a dangerous time. I wake at night at 1.00 a.m. when you are letting yourself into the flat for a last drink with whoever you have been dining with, and pray to Saint Wandrille to put the words 'thus far and no further' into your mouth … Grrr! …

Longer letter tomorrow.

All my love, my darling pet from Paddy

From Saint-Wandrille, Paddy moved on to the monastery of Saint-Jean de Solesmes in Sarthe, near Le Mans.

To Joan Rayner   Abbaye de St Jean de Solesmes
Tuesday [December 1948]   Sablé
                                                                Sarthe

Darling sweet little mite,

Thank you so much for your letter, and please forgive me for being so slow in writing. This is going to be in a terrific hurry, as the post is leaving the village in a few minutes. I'll write you a better one after Compline this evening.

Alas I didn't get here till Sunday, as there was no through train on the day you left … Felt frightfully ill. It must have been Groddeck[1] as I recovered at once on meeting François de La Rochefoucauld,[2] who asked me to a St Germain-Balthus-type existentialist party in his bedroom in the Montana,[3] beginning at 1 a.m., if you please. Club St Germain first, then a wonderful party. He lives in a minute room with a beautiful Mlle Schwob.[4] 50 people came (please don't hate me). He is our stern hostess's son, a great beauty and funny, and a capable musician. You will like him. (I repeat, rather timidly, no hatred, darling, please!)

Then here. A much dourer, more Victorian, forbidding place than St W[andrille]. The Plainsong is amazing, but, from every other point of view, it's a dungeon compared to my old home. A lovely comfy room, however, shaded lights, open fire etc. But I don't want to stay long. Please wire at once, my darling pet, and tell me any plans you have made, and if I have time to stay two days at the Trappe.[5] I can't bear to stay away from you much longer. What about the Betjemans?[6]

My minute rodent, I love you and miss you more than I can say. Do let's get married and live happily forever. I simply can't be without you. (What a funny 3 months! You and your H[umanist], me and my abbeys, thank Heavens everything is alright now.) I wish this letter were not so hurried. Did you get my short letter to Isobel's?[7] I do hope it went to the right number. Write or wire at once, my dear little muskin.

All, all my love to darling muskin & mopsy, Your JEMY[8]

---

[1] The physician Georg Groddeck (1866–1934) is regarded as a pioneer of psychosomatic medicine.

[2] François de La Rochefoucauld (1920–2011), duc de La Rochefoucauld, duc de Liancourt, duc d'Anville. His mother, Edmée, was a women of many parts: poet, writer, painter, philosopher and mathematician.

[3] Le Montana, a hotel and nightclub in St Germain-des-Prés.

[4] Annabel Schwob de Lur (1928–2005), singer and writer who modelled for Schiaparelli. She married the painter Bernard Buffet in 1958.

[5] La Grande Trappe, a Trappist monastery in Normandy, where PLF would spend ten days in late December 1948.

[6] John Betjeman and his wife Penelope had invited Joan and PLF for the weekend.

[7] The artist Isabel Rawsthorne (1912–92), second wife of the composer Constant Lambert.

[8] PLF signed himself as 'JEM' or 'JEMY' in letters to Joan – probably an acronym, but of what I have not been able to discover.

While living with Balasha at Băleni in the late 1930s, Paddy had befriended her cousin Alexander Mourouzi, and together they had explored the Danube delta.

During the war years Paddy had been unable to communicate with Balasha or anyone else in Romania, then an enemy country. After the war ended the victorious Soviet Union imposed a harsh communist regime upon the defeated Romanians. Aristocrats like the Cantacuzènes were regarded as enemies of the people; their property was confiscated and their activities monitored. In the summer of 1948 Balasha and Mourouzi tried to escape to Greece in a small boat, but they were caught and briefly imprisoned.

No letters from Paddy to Balasha during this period have survived, but the following letter to Mourouzi – though written in guarded terms because of the danger that it might be intercepted and read by the authorities in Romania – gives some indication of his sympathies. Paddy tries to comfort his friend by reminding him of the life he had known in pre-war Paris. The letter is translated from the original French.

To Alexander Mourouzi   Abbaye de Solesmes
6–9 December 1948   Sablé sur Sarthe
                                     Sarthe

My dear old friend,

Did you ever receive an immensely long letter that I sent you from Guatemala in January, describing my trip there, etc., and in reply to your long and beautiful letter concerning the dreadful *pumpute* [upheaval]? Please forgive me for not having written since. As I explained to Francesca,[1] it's not through lack of friendship or indifference, but from a horrible kind of vanity or perhaps humility, I don't know which, that led me to put off, day after day, writing a letter that would be less than I would have hoped, or disappointing, or imbued with a background of hairshirtedness. Every day my responsibility to write something substantial grew, widened, deformed, until little by little it assumed the proportions of needing to write the entire *Divina Comedia* in order to fill the silence that through my stupidity and vanity I'd allowed to develop,

---

[1] Unidentified.

the result of childishness as well as odious egotism and [not] lack of friendship. I'm making such a meal of this because you understand this kind of state of mind, so I hope that you will try to excuse it. Now the news I hear from Lucienne[1] is so awful, that it completely demolishes this absurd edifice, so I am diving in feet first.

All my plans and suggestions I have put in a letter to Francesca – sadly nothing very much, but all I can come up with at the moment. I don't know the current conditions alas but I imagine them to be extremely difficult – I mean travelling conditions, getting around, getting out. But it's wretched, all Lucienne's friends, mine too, are, one and all, unsettlingly and utterly broke. However, I'm sure that, collectively, we can scrape together something, but nothing compared to what is needed. If by some miracle you manage to get past the last accursed frontier, it will give you the means to steady yourself for a month or two, until something can be arranged. I'm ashamed to be writing so ineffectually, which is why I am castigating myself for being so helpless. I beg you not to think that, just because I am comfortably situated on this side, I lack the imagination to grasp what it must be like: the privations, the humiliations, the troubles that surround you. I can imagine them all too well and I wish I could be there to share them with you rather than giving you useless and naïve advice. I tried as hard as I could to come to Romania after the war but, given the nature of the work I had been involved in during the war, it was completely out of the question.

As you know, Lucienne, who is terrific, received your letters and convened a meeting of your friends at her house: Bernard [—],[2] and Bernard brought Babette. She is now firmly on the Left, which I grasped both between the lines and from hearing her speak, but I feel sure she'll do no harm. Apart from that, she seems kind, good-natured and well-disposed, but alas incapable of doing anything to help. [—] was full of ideas, none of which sadly were feasible. And

[1] Lucienne Gourgaud du Taillis, born Lucienne Haas (1898–1982), artist, a friend of Balasha Cantacuzène's in Paris.
[2] PLF left the surname blank, perhaps to protect the identity of 'Bernard', or perhaps because he had forgotten it.

while I really liked Bernard, it was the same story. Reggie S[1] wasn't there, so I went to see him at his studio in a little street off the Rue des Grands-Augustins. We talked at length about you and your life in Paris, a huge delight for me. He showed me a painting he'd done of his apartment – that you know – in the Rue de la Harpe: two shutters open out onto a dizzying view of tumbledown red-tiled roofs and smoking chimney stacks, the vague contours of the Rue de la Huchette and the Rue du Chat-qui-Pêche, while in the background the tower of Notre Dame stands out against a spring sky. All the joy, the air, the light, within it. He paints terrifically well and in a few weeks' time is having an exhibition, posters are already going up across Paris. He and I went through the various options, starting with contacting friends on the Left, that is if we could find them. I found myself saying that I felt it would be a complete waste of time, things being as they are. I now wonder if it was the right thing to say. What do you think?

He had another idea, about a Romanian who comes and goes, not left wing, the contact being a local restaurant owner. I went to meet him five times but he never showed up, then making it known, via an intermediary, that he wanted nothing to do with it. I don't have to tell you that no names were exchanged.

Reggie told me that he thinks it better he doesn't write, as too many letters would only draw attention to you. However, like the others for that matter, he sends you his best wishes, fondest memories and looks forward enormously to seeing you (!). The day after our meeting, I set out to follow the little plan he had drawn, starting at the Rue Soufflot, then down to the Place Adrien Herr.[2] The plaque by the door still bore the name of 'Grandmaison'.[3] I passed under two arches, and found myself in a little garden where the flowers had all passed their best. Then up into a funereal hall (noticing a pile of folded napkins stacked up against one of the dining room windows). Eventually

[1] Unidentified.
[2] PLF probably means the Place Lucien Herr, close to the Rue Mouffetard.
[3] Perhaps a reference to a member of the de Grandmaison family, which had connections with the Russian nobility.

an old servant appeared who told me that Grandmaison had died during the war and that the staff had all changed. How sad it was! I asked if I could go upstairs 'to take a look'. She refused, in an extremely ungracious way. Once she'd left, I tiptoed up the staircase (worn down by the feet of Popo, Martine and Montet!), until I reached the mezzanine at which point the old Gorgon reappeared and chased me out, yelling like a banshee, as if I'd been planning to rob or rape someone. I spent half an hour on the terrace of the little bistro that you get to by a kind of ladder, where I had a beer and watched the goings on in the boarding house of the girls' school opposite, but above all remembering those wonderful stories of yours, laughing out loud, to the astonishment of the only other customer, an old plumber complete with tool bag. Then, down at street level again, I cut through the Rue l'Arbalète to the Rue Mouffetard and the Rue Monge where I visited the mosque. Walking up the astonishing Rue Mouffetard I reached the Pantheon and thence to the Jardin du Luxembourg, down to the Boul[evard] St Michel. Two more beers at Chez Dupont and then, by way of Place St-André des Arts, found my way back to the minuscule hotel where I used to live, at the corner of the Rue de Seine and the Rue Buci, above a horse butcher's. Looking out of my window I used to see the whole of the Rue de Seine market, fish, vegetables, practically blocking the lanes. My bedroom was on the corner where I would look down on three horses' heads apparently nailed to the floor below mine, which always gave me a pleasing sensation of driving a troika.

The life of this *quartier* revolves around the Place St-Germain-des-Prés, and the Cafés Flore and Deux Magots, Royal St Germain and La Reine Blanche serve as a kind of fortress to the doctrines of the existentialism of Jean-Paul Sartre, a philosophy which consists of a special kind of walk, accent, clothes, hair-style etc. and which leads to regular punch-ups with the anti-existentialists. The atmosphere, the life, are delightful. I know that you are familiar with all of this and I am sure that, in spite of all your difficulties, though it seems impossible now, you'll be back here.

Are you writing now, A[lexander]? I so enjoyed what you wrote back then. I fear that the current situation – the anxiety and loss you're having to endure – is hardly conducive to work. As for me, I'm trying to turn myself into a writer. I find it terribly hard but since it's the only thing I like, I have to persevere. I've had a few articles published recently and I'm busy writing a book about the journey from which I've recently returned. The least distraction – even the most boring thing – is excuse enough to prevent me from actually working and this is the reason I hide myself away in monasteries. I spent five weeks in the Abbaye de St Wandrille in Normandy, two weeks here, and tomorrow I leave for La Grande Trappe for ten days. It's the only means I have of writing anything alas. I believe that we both suffer, literarily speaking, from the same evil – an inability to start and a lack of faith in what we do because of our high standards – a thing brilliantly described in *Oblomov* by Goncharov.[1] Write to me soon, tell me what you are thinking, reading, writing. I have absolutely no idea how, but I feel sure these vicissitudes will be overcome and that Byzantium will be saved.[2]

With fraternal greetings, affectionately, Patrick

---

[1] Ivan Goncharov, *Oblomov* (1859). See footnote on p. 398.
[2] PLF uses this expression metaphorically to mean 'all will be well'.

Encouraged by Harold Nicolson, who had taken an interest in his writing, Paddy sent a copy of his poem 'Greek Archipelagoes' to John Lehmann, editor of the 'Penguin New Writing' series. This may have been awkward for Paddy, because ten years earlier he and Lehmann had clashed at a cocktail party over the issue of support for the Spanish Republic. They had 'locked horns in a furious debate', and 'unforgivable things' had been said, or so he told his biographer Artemis Cooper half a century later: indeed he claimed that they never spoke to one another again. This letter suggests otherwise. The poem appeared in Penguin New Writing, No. 37, *published in 1949.*

To John Lehmann   Hôtel de la Louisiane
undated [December 1948]   Rue de Seine
                                                          Paris 6ème

Dear Mr Lehmann,

Thank you for your letter, which I have just received at the end of a chain of re-directions. I am delighted that you enjoyed the poem about the Greek archipelagos, and very excited at the thought of seeing it in Penguin New Writing.[1]

I left the Abbaye de Saint Wandrille a week ago and find Paris bewilderingly noisy; and before returning to England, am going to see what the Monastery of La Grande Trappe, on the Norman–Breton border, is like. A week of absolute silence should be a valuable and curious experience in the present century.

I will certainly telephone you when I return to London, and look forward very much to meeting you.

Yours sincerely
Patrick Leigh-Fermor

[1] John Lehmann had launched the 'New Writing' series in 1936, as a bi-annual anthology published in hardback format by the Bodley Head. In his launching 'manifesto', Lehmann announced that 'New Writing … does not intend to open its pages to writers of reactionary or Fascist sentiments'. In November 1940 the series transferred into the Penguin format, and 'Penguin New Writing' ran for forty issues, until September 1950.

Cyril Connolly's infatuation with Joan was a complicating factor for Paddy, but the two men were able to maintain cordial relations nonetheless.

To Cyril Connolly   Pienza
undated [February/March 1949]   Prov. di Siena
                                                                      Italy

Dear Cyril,

I got a rather gloomy Ovid-in-exile[1] letter from Xan [Fielding] today, which made me think of *Horizon*.[2] I remember paying for a year's subscription, but forget whether I gave you his address, which is P & E a, 100 HQ C.C.G, BAOR[3] 15. If I did, please forgive me for bothering you with it again. I know it will cheer the old boy up.

Joan and Hamish[4] disappeared down the Road to Rome[5] four days ago, and I settled in this small town – a village really – built on a cone, and heavily walled. The Tuscan hills are 2 inches deep in snow, as far as I can see, to the mountains of Latium, the Marches, and Umbria. A permanent cyclone blows through the piazza, nearly blowing one away, like the last picture in *Struwwelpeter*.[6] There is a vast Piccolomini Palace,[7] and an amazing Renaissance cathedral, both built by Pius II. An old priest, and urchin, and two old dames assemble once a fortnight in the latter for the *mysterium tremendum et fascinans*.[8] The remaining houses of Pienza grovel round these two

[1] Ovid was banished from Rome to Tomis (now Constanta, Romania) by decree of the Emperor Augustus. PLF's comrade, Xan Fielding, served with MI6 in Germany after the end of the war, and perhaps felt himself similarly exiled.
[2] An influential literary magazine edited by CC. It ceased publication in 1949.
[3] [Political and Economic Administration?], Control Commission for Germany, British Army of the Rhine, a catch-all term for British troops stationed in Germany.
[4] James Alexander Wedderburn 'Hamish' St Clair-Erskine (1909–73), second son of the 5th Earl of Rosslyn.
[5] Perhaps a nod to Hilaire Belloc's *The Path to Rome* (1902).
[6] The last picture in Heinrich Hoffmann's *Der Struwwelpeter* (1845) depicts 'flying Robert' being borne up into the sky when the wind catches his umbrella.
[7] An Italian noble family prominent in Siena. Two Piccolomini became popes: Pius II and Pius III.
[8] A phrase coined by the theologian Otho, meaning the experience of God.

buildings. Graf Piccolomini, the palace-dweller,[1] is in Rome, so no chance of oiling into a four-poster ... The cold is appalling, and there is no heating except those Balkan charcoal braziers. Macaroni at every meal, cheese made out of granite, and wine that is sometimes what one might call *de saveur gamine mais de lampée franche*,[2] at others, like slipping a bit and snaffle into one's mouth. Too much even for me.

I did enjoy our last evening. Please give my love to Lys,[3] and I hope to see you both in a month.

Yours ever, Paddy

P.S. The Tuscans pronounce 'c' as 'h' – *'un pollo deharne'* etc. Very ugly and difficult.

The innkeeper in Tarascon described how a maquis friend carried secret documents *'caché dans le cul'*,[4] and added *'Je n'aurais pas pu faire ça. Il faut avoir le temperameng...'*[5]

Paddy returned to the monastery of Saint Wandrille in the late spring of 1949.

To Joan Rayner   St Wandrille
Wednesday [May 1949]

Darling,

What a lovely, funny letter, & what good news.[6] Hip-hooray. I'm longing to be there, and will, if I may, the very moment

---

[1] Count Alberto Piccolomini d'Aragona, a direct descendant of Pius II.

[2] 'Cheeky but to be gulped down chilled', a quote from J. K. Huysmans's novel, *Là-Bas* (1891).

[3] Lys Lubbock, CC's common-law wife: they were not married, though she had changed her name to Connolly by deed poll. 'Lys is very pretty and prattled of housewifely things like linoleum and dry rot,' Frances Partridge noted in her diary, 'while Cyril kept the conversation relentlessly on literary subjects, particularly his own writings ...'

[4] 'Up his bottom'.

[5] 'I couldn't have done that. You have to be that way inclined.'

[6] Joan had written: 'I can have Barbara [Warner]'s flat for as long as I like for £8 a week. Isn't it heaven & it will be perfect for you to write in.'

the chapters are up to date, which will be soon. I've decided to leave Cuba, Jamaica and Haiti II (+ Santo Domingo) – the last 3 chapters – till I get back, and rush through everything up till then, as the publishers and printers will have plenty to go on with.

So that's the *jam redit et virgo!*[1] Darling, I can't remember for the moment who Ann Dunn is.[2] Is she the one that was supposed to be in Ireland, and wasn't, something to do with P. de Bendern?[3] How lively London sounds, every body's changed places. It's like 'Sir Roger de Coverley', the bit when people gallop from opposite ends, link arms and swing round while everybody watches and claps, and then whoops! away again and all change. I wouldn't mind a day or two of it now, as long as we neither of us performed leading roles. I don't think I could bear any change now.

It's lovely and quiet here, but it is quite failing to cast the same sort of spell on me that it did last year. Everyone is just as kind and the place as peaceful, but I must have undergone a *dégonflement* [change of heart], rather like Sarah[4] in Rome; which is rather childish at my age. I grudge the time I have to spend in church, which I have cut down to just over an hour a day; but both at awkward times. Perhaps having written and talked about St Wandrille so much has dissipated some of the charm. It's rather sad if writing about something burns up one's interest in it, and it has to be discarded after that.

---

[1] A phrase from Virgil's 'Eclogue IV': *Iam redit et Virgo, redeunt Saturnia Regna* ('Astraea returns, returns old Saturn's reign'). Astraea was the Greek goddess of innocence and purity, associated with justice: one day she will return to Earth, inaugurating a new Golden Age. PLF means here: 'So that's the good news!'

[2] Anne Dunn (b. 1929), artist; daughter of the Canadian steel magnate Sir James Dunn (1874–1956) and his second wife, former musical-comedy actress Irene Clarice Richards (1898–1977).

[3] Patricia de Bendern (née Lady Patricia Douglas), (1918–?) who was married to Duff Cooper's secretary, Count John Gerard de Forest (alias Count de Bendern) though they would be divorced in 1950. Nancy Mitford described her as 'the greatest home breaker in Paris … She is simply lovely & perfectly wicked, a very bad combination', Charlotte Mosley (ed.), *Love from Nancy: the Letters of Nancy Mitford* (London, 1993), p. 196.

[4] Unidentified.

Amy and Smartie[1] came here yesterday and we had a lovely long and talkative luncheon at Villequier, then drove to see the ruins of Jumièges,[2] and back here for Vespers, which seemed to impress them both. They send lots of love to you.

Darling, I must stop now, and carry on my journey through the Leeward Isles. It's rather like eating prunes for supper that you refused at luncheon. 'Go on, eat them up, you're not going to have anything else until you've got them down.' Ugh. I'm feeling rather gloomy and *dégoûté* [sick of everything] at the moment and wish I was with you, my darling pet. Don't fall desperately in love with anyone till I get back!

Write as often as you can.

100000 hugs and kisses from
Jem

I wonder what to do about Haiti for *Horizon*. Would you ask Cyril if he would still like it?

To Joan Rayner   Lisbon
undated [March/April 1950]   Portugal

My darling pet,

I wish, I <u>wish</u> you were here. I arrived an hour ago by bus, don't know anybody, can't understand a word anybody says, and the division between me and depression was, for about ¼ of an hour, tissue-paper thin; but I took measures to thicken it, and am safe now. I'm in a wine shop off one of the minor squares of Lisbon, a towering, bottle-lined place, with a hand-knitted marble inlay floor and spittoons and three or four ragged men in velour hats at the end of an echoing vista. As an atmosphere, *sympa* (as they say),[3] and promising.

[1] Sir Walter and Lady Smart (see dramatis personae).
[2] A Benedictine abbey, abandoned in the French revolution and now ruined.
[3] Meaning 'friendly' in French.

Now, quick recapitulation. I went to Annie Rothermere's[1] after you left, it was very nice – Robin, Mary,[2] Peter Q[uennell], etc. Then I did what I imagine to be 'tying up all the loose ends' (*penses-tu!*)[3] all through the afternoon; had dinner with Anne Millard[4] at that Greek restaurant with the *kapheneion*[5] – [illegible], and then went to the Gargoyle,[6] (where Anne soon left) and spent the evening, first upstairs, then drinking brandy in David [Tennant]'s flat, with Phillip [Toynbee], David, Derek Jackson[7] & [the artist] Francis Bacon. David was entirely unboring and informative about Spain. We were all rather drunk. Derek and Francis exchanged pecks between drinks like two bullfinches in a cage. It was rather sweet, and utterly un-rebarbative.

Well, I caught the ship at Liverpool next day (the fellow-tourist passengers were quite fun: two priests of St Vincent de Paul, heading for Indian parishes 1,000 miles up the Amazon – beyond Manaos, the ship's Brazilian terminus – two terrible Scotch nurses, an elderly, mincing Ambassador's niece with bony wrists a-clink with seals and amulets, and a nice old Portuguese historian). The ship stopped (to my surprise, I don't know why) at Oporto, so I got off there, stopped at a 5/-[8] pension, and had three weeks' dirty

[1] Ann Rothermere (1913–81), née Charteris, granddaughter of the 11th Earl of Wemys, was a close friend of PLF's. In 1951 she would divorce her husband, the newspaper proprietor viscount, and marry the writer Ian Fleming.

[2] Robin Francis Campbell (1912–85), soldier and painter, and his second wife Lady Mary Sybil, née St Clair Erskine (1912–93), daughter of the 5th Earl of Rosslyn (and sister of Hamish).

[3] 'Don't bet on it!'

[4] Married to the diplomat Guy Millard.

[5] The White Tower in Percy Street, Fitzrovia.

[6] A private members' club on the upper floors of 69 Dean Street, Soho. Founded by the Hon. David Tennant (1902–68) in the 1920s, it closed in 1978.

[7] Professor Derek Ainslie Jackson (1906–82), nuclear physicist and a jockey who rode in the Grand National three times. Among his six wives were Pamela Mitford, Janetta Woolley and Barbara Skelton. He left Janetta for her half-sister, Angela Culme-Seymour. A bisexual, he is said to have enjoyed a threesome with Francis Bacon and Anne Dunn.

[8] 25p in decimal coinage; about £8 in today's value.

shirts laundered by the old peasant woman there for 3/-[1] in three hours. I went to see San Francisco, a lovely Manueline[2] church, and then the late 18th Century Association building of the English Port Growers. An entrancing building like a beautiful English country house on the banks of the Douro, all out of granite, with a fine English 18th century façade, a wonderful flight of granite stairs, and delicious rooms full of Queen Anne and Chippendale furniture, the most delicately festooned plaster ceiling in libraries and ballrooms and saloon after saloon; full, too, of the portraits of old port-growers in full-bottomed and tie-back wigs, then regency stocks; all of them, one of their descendants told me, as, glass in hand, we walked from room to empty room all bright with polish and beeswax, squires, scholars (see *They Went to Portugal* by Rose Macaulay) like Whitehead,[3] and Warre the Eton headmaster,[4] with an occasional duellist and blackguard, and a galaxy of Peninsular War heroes. He asked me to dinner at his house at the mouth of the Douro, where I met a Madrid colleague of yours[5] called Cobb, who seemed rather nice, and very instructed about Portugal. They gave me two tremendous bottles of port which I carried away with me, when I left by bus this morning. He is called Ron[ald] Symington, a charming, shy friendly person with an equally nice wife.[6]

I left Oporto by bus at dawn – so beautiful, across an iron rainbow of a bridge poised above the windings of the Douro; and, as we rattled on, a lovely sylvan upland world emerged – forests of Mediterranean pine and the clean pale blue air I've been longing

[1] 15p in decimal coinage; about £5 in today's value.
[2] Portuguese late Gothic: a sumptuous, composite Portuguese style of architectural ornamentation from the first decades of the sixteenth century.
[3] John Whitehead, British consul in Oporto, 1756–1802.
[4] PLF may be confusing the Peninsular War commander Lieutenant General Sir William Warre, who was born in Porto, with his nephew, the headmaster of Eton, Rev. Edmond Warre, who edited his uncle's *Letters from the Peninsula, 1808–1812*, published in 1909.
[5] Joan, who trained as a cypher clerk, had been deployed to the British embassy in Madrid in 1943.
[6] The Symington family, owners and proprietors of Graham's, have been associated with port production since the seventeenth century.

to breathe, sinking to valleys full of young yellow-gold corn and olive groves with the peasants scything hay and leaving it in silver green swathes under the trees; solid-wheeled ox-carts, and women in bright, scallop edged woollen scarves filling tapering kegs with the slats and hoops painted different and jarring colours, at monumental fountains. Vines are putting pale green shoots out everywhere, and anemones and poppies are scattered over everything. Once we sank into a marshy valley, where the fen was coated with lilies, and an old bridge crossed it, span after span under osiers, like the shallow trajectories of a bouncing ball. The bus stopped at Coimbra for an hour at midday, so I managed to clamber up to the university and see those three staggering library rooms with their galleries poised on slender gilded and upturned obelisks[1] and, just before the bus left, the Manueline church of Santa Cruz, with an organ sprouting trumpets like the Last Judgement, and *azulejos* [tiled walls] depicting the exploits of Vasco da Gama. We stopped for a tantalising ten minutes at Batalha, the abbey erected in the 14th century (very English or French looking) to celebrate the victory of Portugal over Castille. There are the tallest late Gothic pillars in the nave I've ever seen, and a lovely tomb of the victorious king, Don João, and his English wife, Phillipa of Lancaster (John of Gaunt's daughter, mother of Henry the Navigator – the Infante Henrique, as they call him here). The King's and the Queen's hands are joined; pretty and grave and moving. Then south again, to the other great abbey of Alcobaça, which celebrates his victory over the Moors; and went to the coast, where the sailors wear Portuguese tartan shirts (like Dick's) and tasseled jellybag hats and go to sea in queer, brightly painted, spike-prowed boats. They are descended from the Phoenicians, and look it.

South again then, between castled hills, to Torres Vedras (the centre of Wellington's line against Soult and Junot[2]) and finally,

---

[1] The baroque library at the University of Coimbra was built in the early eighteenth century.
[2] Between 1809 and 1810, during the Peninsular War, Wellington had three lines of forts constructed to defend Lisbon against any offensive by Napoleon's marshals; and *in extremis*, to cover the evacuation of his forces.

after a violet and amber sunset, into Lisbon after dark, where I've found a room for the night up seven flights of stairs in a back street off one of the squares. Incredibly sordid, but run by a blue-grey-chinned ex-village schoolmaster and his peasant wife – v. kind, like all the Portuguese I've met; they really are nice, soft, sweet people, but with none of the bite and toughness of the Spaniards. I long for that. We drank half of one of my bottles of port together, and they directed me here.

Dinner (which I've eaten while writing this) was half execrable, half delicious: the bad part was the cod, the *bacalhau*, with potatoes and spinach; the good part, *vinho verde do minho*, green i.e. new, young red wine, *pétillant*; it has a head on it like Guinness when poured out, which quickly subsides; excellent; and the soup *à la Alentejana*, with a poached egg in the middle, and green on the surface with some saw-edged leaf. I asked what it was, and the waiter wrote down: *coentros, erva da margem dos rios*; a sort of cress, I think, a herb from the river's margin.[1]

My darling, I think I'll catch the bus for Evora (E. of Lisbon) tomorrow night; cross the Spanish frontier at Badajoz, and then go south through Estremadura to Seville, and so to Andalusia, and Julian's:[2] fitting in, if I can, late Maundy Thursday and Good Friday of Semana Santa [Holy Week] in Seville. All rooms will be taken, I think, so I'll put my luggage somewhere, and sleep on a bench. I'm longing to be at Grazalema, these long bus journeys are fairly tiring, but they give me a lovely, half forgotten feeling of every inch of my long body aching, my eyelashes caked with dust, and an accumulation of such a quantity of dazzling beauty in my head – falling one on top of each other like a pack of cards, which I won't be able to shuffle and deal till I've been quiet for a day or two – at Grazalema, I hope – and there is so much to come between then & now.

[1] Coriander.
[2] The anthropologist and ethnographer Julian Alfred Lane Fox Pitt-Rivers (1919–2001), lived in the Andalusian village of Grazalema.

I've missed you much, my darling angel, and I <u>do hope</u> you'll come to Spain. Please, please do. Above all, don't worry and fret and drown yourself in some awful English balloon-glass, which I'm sure, is the un-truest crystal to guide anyone.[1] I'm off on one of those searches, (which I bet will end in a *bec de gaz*[2]) for a *fados*[3] singer on the other bank of the Tagus that the Portuguese historian told me about. All, all my love, my darling, darling, little Joan, and very many ex-rodentish hugs.

Love love love
Paddy

A guitarist, followed by a tame claque of soaks, has just entered; a nice drunkard's whispering guitarist, with his familiars quietly singing and humming the refrain.

Please give my love to Graham, if he's at Tumbledown.[4]

<u>Come to Spain</u>. There is some intrinsic health and sense in these deluges of wine and pale clear blue sky. It strikes me that I've been not very clear (too diffident out of not wanting to interfere with your right of choice) to let you know how much I miss you and love you. Also, Spain and Andalusia are unfair trappings. I love <u>you</u>, but come for <u>them</u>. It'll be alright, my poor darling, sweet, sweet Joan. You as a friend and a lover are almost (not quite) equally precious things. This language (Portuguese) is incomprehensible – no vowels, it might be Polish, with all these consonants – an endless succession of the syllable 'Shoinsh'.

P.

---

[1] i.e. don't drown your sorrows in brandy.

[2] Gas lamp.

[3] A form of song following a traditional structure, characterised by mournful tunes and lyrics, often about the sea or the life of the poor, and infused with a sentiment of resignation, fatefulness and melancholia.

[4] PLF refers to Joan's brother, Graham Eyres-Monsell. 'Tumbledown' was PLF's nickname for Dumbleton Hall, the family seat on the border of Gloucestershire and Worcestershire.

To Joan Rayner   Jerez de la Frontera
8/9 April 1950

My darling pet,

I've had rather a full, but uncoordinated time since I last wrote to you. I was woken up early by the couple in my pension (both of whom came from the Azores), and all the people Robin Fedden had given me letters for were out of Lisbon, so I was befriended all day by a fat, kind Nico Baltazzi-Nicky Melas[1] figure called the Count of Mafra[2] and went with him to see the Manueline churches and the most splendid collection of state coaches in the world. We had luncheon in a Taverna-ish restaurant called the Leão d'Ouro (Châteaubriands the size of Baedekers smothered with béarnaise, but first great plates of clams cooked with onions, garlic, saffron and sliced pimento, with a soup sauce better than any bouilla-baisse). He's a godfather of about 18 people, but a bachelor-type of person of the Athenian variety,[3] warm, kind, convivial, very Micky-ish. I dined at his house, then we visited several friends, ending up with a very nice Portugee called John Marques, who is married to Mrs Belloc Lowndes's daughter; charming, intelligent, freakishly lettered and erudite.[4] Here we drank too much, and, on the way out in the moonlight, I'm sorry to say, Mafra fell down the stairs (he is an enormous man) and broke his collar-bone. I saw him home to bed.

Eastwards across Portugal next day, lovely rolling hills, covered with olive and forests of cork oak and castles on islands in the Tagus

---

[1] Fedden (see dramatis personae) and Melas were two old friends from Athens who had served with PLF in Albania in 1940, while he was attached to the HQ of Greek III Army Corps. 'We roared around in the car I'd been given like the three Musketeers,' recalled Paddy (Cooper, *Patrick Leigh Fermor*, p. 128).

[2] Francisco de Mello Breyner, 5th Count of Mafra (1894–1963).

[3] PLF means to indicate that he was gay.

[4] The Portuguese journalist Luiz Marques had been educated in England. In 1938 he married Susan, younger daughter of the novelist Marie Lowndes (1868–1947), née Belloc (elder sister of the writer and historian Hilaire Belloc).

and across the Spanish border at Badajoz; across Estremadura, through the Sierra Morena, and into the suburbs of Seville at 10 o'clock on Maundy Thursday night. The town was chocked with the Semana Santa crowd, and one moved about a furlong an hour. The first people I met, of course, were Bill & Annie Davis[1] with Eldred (?) Curwen,[2] Mrs [Peggy] Bainbridge,[3] a loathsome munitions millionaire called Sir Douglas Orr-Lewis[4] with his diamond-smothered Russian girlfriend. All awful except for Bill (whom I like, I must say) and Annie (who I would like more if she was a fraction more intelligent). I nearly lost them in the mob outside the church of the Mararena, where there must have been about 10,000 people who burst into a furore of clapping and cheers as the enormous Mararena virgin came out (every one murmuring *Mira la! ¡Mira la! ¡Qué bonita, la guapa! Qué fotografía!*[5] etc.), preceded by a hundred Roman soldiers in full armour and huge ostrich feather plumes, soldiers playing slow-marches on muffled drums etc. (You've probably seen it.) I managed to crawl into the sacristy while they were all, cigars in mouth, dressing up, and hundreds of boys putting on velvet and gold dalmatics and ruffs, all in candle-light under white baroque vaults – the closest one could get to the Funeral of Count Orgáz.[6] The procession went through the narrow streets of the poorest quarters, and the Mararena's balda-quin got caught again and again in the clothes and tramlines, and had to stop even more often for *saetas* – improvised sung tunes in a minor key from windows – some of them wonderful, slow

[1] Both Americans, living in Malaga: Annie Davis, née Bakewell, from a wealthy Pittsburgh family, sister of Cyril Connolly's first wife, Jean; Bill Davis, a New Yorker, who carried a silver-topped cane and referred to his wife as his 'squaw'.
[2] Unidentified: probably from the Curwen family of Workington Hall, Cumberland.
[3] Daughter of an Indian Army colonel and the estranged wife of Emerson Bainbridge, a rich Guards officer and ardent Mosleyite; her first love had been Ian Fleming and in 1936–7 she had been involved with Cyril Connolly.
[4] Probably Sir (John) Duncan Orr-Lewis, 2nd Baronet, whose Canadian father made a fortune from shipbuilding and armaments manufacture.
[5] 'Look at her! Look at her! The beautiful, the pretty one! What a photograph!'
[6] A Goya painting usually referred to as *The Burial of the Count of Orgaz*.

and heartbreaking howling ones of enormous complexity. I'm sure the only criterion of these is whether or not they make the hair on your nape prickle. I wandered about till 8 a.m., the town still full of processions, but all the soldiers smoking, and the cafés full of *cagoulards*[1] jovially drinking with their hoods rolled up, next to whores whose brothels had just shut – the claustrophobia was as dense as Les Saintes Maries [de la Mer],[2] but it had a mood of Goya, Greco and Doré that was extraordinary. A lovely turquoise dawn over Seville, and the streets fuller than ever. I was put up on the sofa of a student I met in a café, which was as well, as the few hotels I had tried at were full.

The same thing all next day (lunch & dinner with the Davis's, who were avid for London gossip), and to bed in the most beautiful and cheap pension in the Santa Cruz quarter – a lovely *Mudéjar*[3] patio, and a monkish, whitewashed room like the one we had in Antigua (Guatemala). I'd long ago reached saturation point, and won't be able to see read or hear about anything to do with religion for quite a long time. I could never see the Semana Santa again, and think the Spaniards – the Andalusians anyway – must have a good strong streak of insanity.

Yesterday Bill, Orr-Lewis, Curwen and I drove out to see the six bulls for Sunday's (today's) fight, and sat drinking white wine & eating langoustines on a terrace above their pen, and then I caught a train for Cadiz (where I had telegraphed Julian [Pitt-Rivers] to telephone me – a general breakdown had kept us out of touch and I was beginning to despair. Trains and buses – how right you are darling! – are <u>hellishly irregular</u>.) I fell asleep in the train, woke up with a start at a station I thought was Cadiz, and only realised as it steamed away that it was Jerez, so took a broken-down taxi

---

[1] Members of a French fascist organisation in the 1930s, named after the French word *cagoule*, a hood with openings for the eyes, worn by members of the organisation at secret meetings.

[2] Les Saintes-Maries-de-la-Mer is the gypsy capital of the Camargue, where an annual festival attracts up to half a million people.

[3] A style of medieval Iberian architecture and decoration, particularly of Aragon and Castile, strongly influenced by Moorish taste and workmanship.

all the way to Cadiz, a lovely drive along the Guadalete across the Cadiz salt-flats. A French-speaking workman in Cadiz spoke with hatred of the boss here,[1] and of the poverty (which, as you know, knocks you flat the moment you get here), of the general suspicion and nark-ridden and haunted atmosphere; of villagers bumped off and their bodies put on mules and led round the countryside as an example against feeding maquisards, etc. etc. I had to come back here today (after looking at the Murillos and Zurbaráns[2] in Cadiz), and am meeting our host in his local town at the end of a bus journey tomorrow. It sounds so lovely, and I do long to be there. I'm tired of travelling, and still shagged out from Seville. The country is so beautiful – all a brilliant green, with smears of some lilac herb, and dazzling white villages, and Jerez (which I reached at sunset) full, even now at 1.00 a.m., of perambulating citizens and the smell of orange blossom and cyclamen. This café is still crowded, half the women are in combs and mantillas from the morning's ceremonies, the balconies are hung with armorial carpets, and the tauromachic[3] clubs full of old men arguing behind their plate-glass club windows. J[ulian]'s house, apparently, is on the eyebrow of a steep gorge – I long to lie there in the sun, & work and talk and not move. Do, do come![4] I expect I'll get a letter from you tomorrow. My bus leaves at 6 a.m.! More news later.

All my love, my own darling, and many hugs and kisses from
M[ole]

I'm staying at a minute pub here full of peasants, bull-herdsmen etc., and mules and saddlery piled in the hall. How nice they all are.

[1] Possibly a reference to the Spanish dictator, General Franco. Four lines preceding this one in the original letter have been heavily scored out.
[2] The artists Bartolomé Esteban Murillo (1617–82) and Francisco de Zurbarán (1598–1664).
[3] Related to bullfighting.
[4] She did.

In the summer of 1947 Paddy had met the publisher Jock Murray (sometimes referred to as 'John Murray VI', signifying that he was sixth in line to bear the name of the famous old firm). Jock Murray was not only an exceptionally tactful and patient editor, but a firm friend to his authors: one who was also willing, if necessary, to act as financier, counsellor and representative, and even, on occasion, to undertake chores or run errands on their behalf.

To Jock Murray   Astros
12 April 1951   Tsakonia
E. Coast of Peloponnese frontier of
Argolis and Laconia

My dear Jock,

Thank you for your last letter. I've forgotten where I wrote to you from – Yannina or Souli or Preveza.[1] Anyway, from Preveza I went S. to Missolonghi of holy memory, thence E along the north coast of the Gulf of Corinth, and N. into the Ætolian mountains from Naupaktos (Lepanto) to an extraordinarily remote valley where all the villagers have been professional beggars from time immemorial. They are taught to twist their arms, walk with a limp, even to sham dead, from their tenderest years. The companions of the bogus corpses collect cash from mugs in foreign parts to pay for the funerals of their comrades who have died suddenly – they exhibit the corpse – and then, in the middle of the night, they and the corpse do a bunk with the collection. In the good old days they wandered all over the Balkans, Hungary, Romania, Asia Minor and Russia, as far as Kamchatka and Nizhni Novgorod, returning with vast fortunes. Their little villages bristle with churches endowed by them, the size of cathedrals. I filled a notebook about them, also with their curious secret language. I hastened thence by bus to meet Joan, learning lots of exciting London news.

I got a letter from Ian Fleming[2] (Kemsley Press) suggesting that the Dropmore Press published a limited edition of a book with the

[1] He wrote from Zitza, near Yannina, on 18 March.
[2] Ian Fleming (1908–64), wartime intelligence officer, publisher and writer, creator of the James Bond novels. After the war he began working for the Kemsley newspaper group. In 1952 he would marry his long-term mistress Ann Rothermere.

two monastery articles. I got his agent to cable him, asking him to consult you about this, saying that you had a plan of publishing them in a long book containing many such articles, later on. As the Dropmore Press only publish limited, deluxe editions (never, according to their brochure, exceeding 700 signed copies), I don't think this should interfere with our plan, as we will aim at a far wider audience, and with a much fatter book. What do you think about this? It would produce a welcome £150 or guineas for Greek travels. I am in favour of it, but leave the decision entirely in your hands. Do let me know about this.

A lovely surprise came from the Royal Society of Literature, saying they had awarded a Heinemann prize (also to Mervyn Peake[1]) to *The Traveller's Tree* of £100, tax-free! Hip-hooray!

Joan and I set off from Athens a few days ago, to Nafplio via Mycenae and Epidaurus, and set sail at dawn this morning for the Tsakonian coast of the Peloponnese (Leonidion or Astros will probably be the only coast towns marked on your map). We arrived here an hour ago, and sit drinking ouzo while mules are arranged for our departure into the interior. It's a fascinatingly wild and remote mountain region, notable as the only place in Greece where a sort of ancient Greek is spoken, owing to the isolation of the district – it's a kind of Doric-Laconian, quite incomprehensible to the rest of Greece. We strike over the hills to Leonidion, then south to Monemvasia (ancient Malmsey of the crusades and the Duke of Clarence's death-butt[2]), right down to Cape Malea at the tip of the eastern prong of the Peloponnese, then north to Sparta and Mystras, and clean across the Taygetus range into the Mani (central prong), home of the vendetta. And so on. The weather is beginning to be perfect – cloudless skies, brilliant blue sea, dotted with islands, pale blue mountains of the [illegible] stretching inland. I'm finishing a long Meteora[3] article for *Cornhill*, which will follow

[1] For Peake's novel *Gormenghast* (1950).
[2] In Shakespeare's *Richard III*, Act I, Scene 4, the Duke of Clarence is drowned in a butt (or keg) of Malmsey wine.
[3] The pillars of tall rocks with monasteries on the top, near the town of Kalambaka in central Greece.

this hot foot. No more for the moment – Joan sends love – she is knitting something out of rust-coloured wool the other side of this tin-table – All the best!

Yours ever, Paddy

Can we use the R. Soc of Literature's award on the cover anywhere? Perhaps it's not a grand enough award.

P.S. Delighted with 2nd Edition and Voodoo picture.

Richard Howland, an architectural and art historian, who had been associated with the American School of Classical Studies at Athens since the 1930s, had carried out excavations in Athens and in Corinth. He was remembered by friends and colleagues as 'a debonair socialite', 'a consummate gentleman of the old school', and 'a wonderful raconteur'.

Paddy was staying at Gadencourt, the Normandy farmhouse lent to him by Sir Walter and Lady Smart, friends from wartime Cairo days. They wintered in Egypt, allowing Paddy to stay at Gadencourt and write while they were not there.

To Richard Howland   c/o Lady Smart
undated [postmarked 3 January 1952]   Gadencourt
                                       Pacy-Sur-Eure
                                             France

My dear Dick,

How funny! I was just thinking about you, and determining to write belated New Year's Greetings when rat! tat! tat! on the knocker, and in comes the *facteur* with yr astonishing Miró Christmas card. You cld have knocked me over with a (wait for it) feather. Dick, how are you? It's lovely to have even a brief hint of your doings. Are you going back to the Agora next/this summer? I don't know if I shall manage to get to Greece. I'd love to, but it rather depends on dough. That book has now come out in the States, and is about to in France, so perhaps something will roll in. Not much seems to have so far, or I've spent it all years ago, or something! I've settled down here for the winter solid to get through my book on Greece – it's fearfully hard work, and rather difficult, but I'm enjoying it immensely. I've been lent this little farmhouse by my absent hostess (she's charming, and a Syrian, which makes me think of the area as Eure of the Chaldees[1]). My house-scrounging technique is becoming suspiciously slick; I must watch it. Joan has just left after spending Christmas here with her nice brother, and expressly told me to send her love if I wrote. She will [come here] off and on, and I sneak off to Paris for a day now and then. If you come to [the] Eure before May, come and stay a bit. It's rather nice – cold outside, but huge fires indoors and lots of books. At the moment there is a wind straight from Novaya Zemlya, mist like a leak from the *Nibelungenlied*,[2] and, when that lets up, a downpour that gives you the sensation of being in a diving-bell. But when you can see it, it's charming, rolling country, with a big river, the Eure, winding through willows and cypresses and bare poplars, cloudy with mistletoe receding in Holbein-ish vistas. The inhabitants are moustachioed, calvados-logged Merovingians – stunted, clogged and monosyllabic, which is a mercy, and there's no temptation to royster with them. Don't you think my hostess has a splendidly Sheridan-esque name?

Scene: Bath. Enter Lady Smart, Sir Volatile Quicksilver severally, and unobserved, Mr Sneak.

Lady S: Zounds, Sir Volatile, are you not well?

Sir V.Q.: Madam, I swear your ladyship's eyes wreak more carnage than powder and shot! Two salvoes have battered down the demilune and the barbican, the citadel (touches his breast) is taken, and the garrison shows the flag of truce (mops eyes with handkerchief).

[1] The city of Ur of the Chaldees is mentioned in the Book of Genesis as the birthplace of Abraham.
[2] The *Nibelungenlied* ('Song of the Nibelungs'), an epic poem in Middle High German, and source for Wagner's Ring Cycle.

Lady S: La, dear toad, we must console the toad for his surrender. (<u>They embrace.</u>)

Mr S: Tut! I must straight to my Lady Viper, and inform her of the issue. (<u>exit furtively, etc., etc.</u>).

No more room left, but Dick, do write and tell me your news, and probably see you later in the year. Happy New Year, and all the rest!

As ever, Paddy

In the early 1950s Paddy came to know Lady Diana Cooper, a glamorous figure then in her sixties; in her prime she had often been described as the most beautiful young woman in England. An actress on stage and screen, married to a prominent Conservative politician, she was a celebrity, the subject of countless portraits, profiles and articles in newspapers and magazines.

She and Paddy would maintain a correspondence until her death, almost four decades later. His letters were written to amuse and entertain; they were affectionate and not a little flirtatious, despite the twenty-three-year difference in age. Paddy usually addressed her as 'darling'; she addressed him as 'Paddles'. 'Being alone with you is what I like best, a delight of which I can never tire,' he would write to her in March 1953.

The following letter was written after he and Joan had spent a weekend with Diana and her husband Duff at the exquisite eighteenth-century house, the Château de Saint-Firmin, that they rented in the grounds of the Château de Chantilly after he had retired from his last post as British Ambassador to France.

To Diana Cooper Gadencourt
3 May 1952 Pacy-sur-Eure
Eure

Dearest Diana,

How wretched it was, all separating after that lovely luncheon at the Coq Chantant, end of the happiest stay anybody has had for years and years. It really was perfection from start to finish, <u>and thank you both 1,000s of times</u>. Heavens, what a lot we laughed. I think the funniest actual <u>incident</u> was Lady Rootes's[1] visit – I wonder what she would have been like if Joan hadn't taken the edge off her, as it were. I wake up in the night even now, on the brink of screaming at the memory of that terrible alligator face. I wonder if she has the Evil Eye? It really is so seldom that one has absolutely perfect times, when one is unbetterably happy the whole time, that I think one ought to wallow like anything in retrospect as well as at the time – I'm still trailing clouds of glory from Chantilly, and remembering conversations and jokes and Duff reading Swinburne and Browning so beautifully, while you listened in a quiet transport of blubbing:

(Two liquid baths, two weeping motions
Portable and compendious oceans),[2]

and our lovely out-of-doors luncheons by the *glycine* [wisteria]-covered stables and in the front of the house; also our strange walk after the hunting tea, following a paper chase of iguanas and toucans and jaguars and all one's favourite animals; and the Grand Meaulnes Priory[3] with the beautiful children and that black Satanic bandog. Lots of heavenly things to think about for ages.

The drive to Paris wasn't nearly as bad as Joan feared – she whizzed along, charioted by Bacchus and his (wait for it) pards,[4] and it was mugget mugget all the way. We dined out of doors opposite the

[1] Probably Ruby, Lady Rootes (née Duff), second wife of the motor manufacturer, Sir William ('Billy') Rootes.
[2] From 'St Mary Magdalene, or the Weeper', by Richard Crashaw (*c.*1613–49).
[3] PLF often referred to Alain-Fournier's novel *Le Grand Meaulnes* ('The Lost Domain') (1913) when describing somewhere ancient, remote and dilapidated.
[4] 'Away! away! for I will fly to thee,/ Not charioted by Bacchus and his pards' – these lines, from Keats's 'Ode to a Nightingale' always made PLF laugh – no doubt thinking 'pards' ['leopards' abbreviated] sounded like the vulgar abbreviation for 'partners'.

Odéon with Isobel Lambert, poor Constant L's widow,[1] and after Joan and she had gone to bed, I had a bout of noctambulism, ending up in the small hours in a faintly louche place called the Café de l'Echaudé, just off the Place de Furstenberg, where Delacroix's studio is. At the next table in this extraordinary grotto sat five immense negroes – jet black, with beautifully shaped heads, talking quietly together in some African dialect. One was eating a plate of bright orange spaghetti, the others were throwing huge ivory dice in a tray lined with green baize, with lovely long [illegible] and ebony hands. I scraped acquaintance, of course, and learnt that four were Wolloffs from Dakar in Senegal, the other a member of the warlike Fong tribe of Dahomey, where most of Voodoo comes from. After a few *fines à l'eau* [brandies and water] they were all singing, very quietly, a southern Saharan war song, and tapping the tom-tom measure with those long fingers. The Fong told me he came from a grand family that once ruled from Abomey, in Upper Dahomey, to the Haute Volta river, and that on the ruler's birthday 100 years ago, sometimes as many as a thousand tribesmen were beheaded – one after the other, with huge scimitars. Towards the end of the ceremony, the Prince would sometimes get bored, and move off to dinner while the holocaust went on, skipping the last hundred or so. I like to think of this immense black potentate in a green and scarlet brocade toga, stifling a yawn, waving democratic-ally to the cheering populace under the skull-decked battlements, and sauntering indoors with his glittering retinue while the rest of his chopping was rushed through … (something hallucinatory about decapitations – poor Lady Jane Grey's head falling off, all Ascham's teaching, the Latin & Greek & arithmetic & philosophy & geometry suddenly expiring on the straw like a puff of smoke[2]). I got to bed in the end shortly before dawn. We had luncheon at the Cretan place, where of course I couldn't resist another lump of camel,[3] so arrived back here burning with a hard, gem-like

[1] The Composer Constant Lambert had died the previous summer.

[2] The scholar Roger Ascham (*c*.1515–68), tutor to the future Queen Elizabeth, visited Lady Jane Grey at Bradgate House, Leicestershire, and was impressed to find her reading Plato while everyone else was out hunting. This encounter was the subject of several romantic nineteenth-century prints.

[3] PLF's term for *pastourma* – highly seasoned, air-dried, cured beef.

flame,[1] and, owing to the previous night's wanderings, feeling older than the rocks on which I sat …

We're off tomorrow, stopping for a last valedictory guzzle at the Cygne at Totes, outside Dieppe[2] (✗✗ ❦❦ *quenelles de brochet à l'épicurienne, langouste à la Newburg, poulet maison* etc.). I hate leaving here [Gadencourt].[3] It's looking lovely in the moment, in the big wildish garden behind the house that you never saw, where I am writing this under an apple tree. Blue and white irises everywhere and a tremendous smell of wisteria, very lyrical now just as evening comes on – a sad and elegiac feeling: big soft shadows on the newly mown grass under the trees, the sound of a pair of clogs clumping home on the other side of the hedge, navy blue swallows darting and wheeling, and a nightingale from the trees over by the Eure, ¼ mile away. It's just about time Pierino[4] would [be] shutting the shutters at Chantilly, and the idea of that lovely first drink of the evening (that unconscious, magnetic, almost sleepwalking convergence on the frescoed chamber of mysteries that only an expert on animal and bird migration could explain) begins to blossom in all our minds. The saddest thing of all is that this breaks up Chantilly & Gadencourt being (almost) neighbours. No more pricking across Normandy & the Ile de France to meet for gastronomic Fields of the Cloth of Gold halfway! Must stop now, as it's getting too dark to see. Many many thanks and love to you both again, dearest Diana, and see you in a few days in London.

Love from Paddy

[1] PLF is quoting Walter Pater on Leonardo da Vinci: 'To burn always with this hard, gem-like flame, to maintain this ecstasy, is success in life,' *The Renaissance: Studies in Art and Poetry* (1873). Here he probably refers to heartburn.

[2] L'Auberge de Cygne, formerly a famous old hotel on the road between Rouen and Dieppe. Over the centuries its guests have ranged from D'Artagnan to General Eisenhower. Maupassant set his short story *Boule de suif* at L'Auberge de Cygne, and Flaubert wrote part of *Madame Bovary* there.

[3] PLF seems to have thought that he was leaving Gadencourt for good, though in fact he would return there for another long stay in 1956.

[4] Pierino Chitto, manservant at Chantilly.

If you are free for <u>a second</u> in London, do please telephone Joan on MUS 8566. My permanent address is (please put it in your book!) Travellers, Pall Mall, S.W.1, WHI 8688 (U.K.)

P.S. Dreamy Joan, wandering in the Palais Royal yesterday afternoon to take some photographs, sat down on a bench, where she was soon joined by a young man who gazed at her with great sloe eyes, and said, '*Madame, on dirait que le soleil joue à cache-cache aujourd'hui.*'[1] Isn't that a charming overture?

To Diana Cooper   Cimbrone
17 July 1952   Ravello
                                            Golfo di Salerno

Darling Diana,

I loved your breakdown letter, waiting for Pierino to come and tug the Simca back to Chantilly with the station-waggon, like *The Fighting Temeraire* in reverse;[2] and pray for some other small mishap and another letter. Alas, I only got it after it had travelled all over the place, on the brink of leaving England, and have been on the move ever since, which is the reason for this rather rude delay in answering. The awful thing is that I expect you are both on the high seas at the moment, and this letter has as little chance of reaching you quickly as if I put it inside a bottle and threw it out of the window into the Gulf of Salerno. I do wish we were all together here, bathing and talking all day and lying about and reading out loud, like that heavenly last stay at Chantilly shifted south. As it is, things here are alright, but far from ideal. I'll tell you all about it later on.

---

[1] 'Madam, one might say that the sun is playing hide and seek today.'
[2] PLF refers to J. M. W. Turner's famous painting, which shows the hulk of the warship being towed by steam-launch to its last berth before being broken up.

Like everyone else I met, I was tremendously excited and cheered up by the birthday honours,[1] mixed with the feeling that it was about time too: why hadn't the brutes done something about it years ago? You're probably both bored by the general enthusiasm about it by now, but that, and Ld Alexander's peerage at the end of the War,[2] seem to me to be the best of such events since heaven knows how many years. I heard Sir Duff had chosen Norwich, which has a splendid ring of the eighteenth century and Grand Whiggery: it's also a v. nice second title for future earldoms, when we'll all have to start thinking again. I know such themes rather bore you, but you must forgive plebeian jubilation and there's nothing bucks one up more than nice things happening to one's friends.

It seems a century since seeing you. I wish I'd gone to that ball in the Kentish Rotunda.[3] Anne Tree swore she'd work it, but forgot. I went to stay with Daphne & Henry[4] 2 weeks ago for a vast ball at Longleat, which was great fun and unbelievably rowdy. Xan and Daphne had just arrived back separately from Crete, looking like a couple of Mohicans, and seemed more gone on each other than ever – all very harmonious and congruent at the moment, as Henry is happily involved in Virginia.[5] I do hope to God they've all got the sense to keep it so, as they are all so nice except perhaps, Virginia, who is lovely but slightly a conceited ass, I think, and with nothing of Viola's dotty and impulsive charm. Also went to stay with Sachie & Georgia [Sitwell] (who I believe imagines you are

[1] Duff Cooper had been made Viscount Norwich in the Queen's birthday honours list, announced in mid-June.

[2] Field Marshal Alexander (1891–1969), reckoned by some to have been the 'foremost British commander of the war', had been made viscount in 1946. In 1952 he was elevated to an earldom.

[3] Mereworth Castle in Kent is a copy of Palladio's Villa Rotunda, just outside Vicenza. It was then owned by the artist Michael Lambert Tree (1921–99) and his wife, Lady Anne Evelyn Beatrice Tree, née Cavendish (1927–2010), later a prison reformer.

[4] Henry Thynne, Marquess of Bath (1905–92), and his wife Daphne, née Vivian (1904–97).

[5] Daphne Bath was having an affair with PLF's close friend and wartime comrade Xan Fielding, while her husband had become involved with Virginia Tennant, née Parsons (Iris Tree's niece), the estranged wife of the Hon. David Tennant. Both would divorce and marry their partners. Virginia was painfully shy, in contrast to her mother Viola.

slightly cross with her about something) at Weston. Mme Massigli[1] and Winnie were also there, she rattling away nonstop and he occasionally vouchsafing a few guttural and staccato reptile noises but, as far as any sense went, totally incommunicado. It is like somebody who has Passed On attempting to communicate through an inexpert medium. Other stays were with Alan Hare, who was in the same racket that I was during the War,[2] in Suffolk (where Ran Antrim[3] came over for the day and, after an evening of fast and furious swigging, surged out into the dark, tripped on the scraper, and lyrically stumbling, hid his face amid a cloud of privets[4]) and in Joan's mother's house (where old Meadows is agent). The day before leaving we went on a lovely Rape-of-the-Lock expedition[5] in a barge with Annie Fleming and several other people along the canals behind Paddington in the dark – past all sorts of derelict warehouses and the back of the zoo where disgruntled Mowgli-esque noises from behind bars indicated that all the dumb chums were being put to bed. Rustic couples, entwined on the banks among dockweed and cow-parsley, leapt guiltily apart at our silent approach.

We finally set out with painter friend J. Craxton[6] 1½ weeks ago in a long dangerous looking jet-black 1932 Bentley that Joan has got hold of, of which she pretends to be ashamed (saying it's bounderish etc.) but which I think she secretly loves: rather like someone disclaiming all association with a negro lover … It goes like the wind. We stopped a night at Gadencourt with Lady Smart, and spurred on south next day, gazing hungrily over our shoulders at the road leading to Nantes and Chantilly; through that rather flat country of the Upper Loire. Not very exciting, except for an occasional Romanesque basilica

---

[1] Madame Odette Massigli, wife of the French ambassador René, who spoke with a lisp.
[2] The Hon. Alan Victor Hare (1919–95), son of the 4th Earl of Listowel, diplomat and businessman, served with SOE during the war, and with the Foreign Office after; managing director, Financial Times Ltd 1971–78, chief executive 1975–83.
[3] Randal McDonnell (1911–77), 8th Earl of Antrim.
[4] 'And hid his face amid a crowd of stars', from W. B. Yeats's poem 'When You Are Old' (1893).
[5] PLF refers to Belinda's journey on the Thames up to Hampton Court in Pope's poem 'The Rape of the Lock' (1712).
[6] The artist John Craxton (1922–2009), who illustrated the covers and prepared maps for PLF's books.

(Fleury, la Charité, Paray-le-Monial etc.) and some lovely Puss-in-Boots castles; but we ate lots of delicious fish out of the Loire, notably a lovely pike at la Charité, with some freezing Pouilly from a few miles downstream; over the Alps at Mt Cenis, and along the beastly Ligurian coast, and inland to Lucca and Pisa. What lovely towns they are! We stopped at Tarquinia for the night to see those extraordinary Etruscan tombs again, and on through the Maremma ('Verbenna down to Ostia, Hath wasted all the plain ...'[1]) to Rome, and on and up into these rocks through Caserta and Pompeii.

Is it my imagination, or did you spend your honeymoon here?[2] It certainly is the most staggering place. Again, I do wish it was a sort of transplanted Chantilly at the moment! Our host here is an immensely kind American balletomane with an ex-ballerina wife[3] but with a terrifying gift (now for a lump of disloyalty and ingratitude!) for endless platitudinous disquisitions on all the most boring themes under the sun, which kills the conversation ... STONE DEAD. All this turns the dinner bell into a knell tolling, instead of the Tocsin of the Soul.[4] None of us, in the movement and change on the yacht in Greece last year, seem to have noticed this dreadful latent power; but here, static in the villa, we're up against the ropes and dizzy with punishment. But I'm the luckiest of the lot as I can escape all day to a secluded library under the pretence of writing, well out of range. But otherwise, it's great fun. Freddie is in tremendous form, Margot Fonteyn as pretty as ever, and it's rather absurd to complain. I think Joan and I will be here till the end of the month. In the flurry of departure, I forgot your letter with your summer's programme, in London. Where will you be during the next 2 months, in case our roads crossed? Do please let me know.

[1] From Thomas Babington Macaulay's *Lays of Ancient Rome*.
[2] They did spend part of their honeymoon at the Villa Cimbrone.
[3] PLF and Joan, together with Craxton, the ballerina Margot Fonteyn (1919–91) and the choreographer Frederick Ashton (1904–88), had been guests of a rich American attorney, Thomas Hart Fisher, and his wife Ruth Page, also a choreographer and a former dancer, who had rented the famous Villa Cimbrone, in Ravello on the Amalfi coast. The previous summer the same group had cruised in the Cyclades aboard a chartered caïque, *Elikki*.
[4] '... that all-softening, overpowering knell,/ The tocsin of the soul – the dinner bell', Lord Byron, *Don Juan*, v, 49.

Must stop now, and trudge into Ravello. Very much love to you both dearest Diana, and also from Joan; & Freddie instructs me to send 'love & devotion'. Do please write!

Paddy

To Diana Cooper   Travellers Club
13 December 1952   Pall Mall
                                                    London

Darling Diana,

Thank you for your lovely long letter & postcard and many apologies for delaying so long in answering. It was really because I wanted to find out the date of the Monastery book's appearance.[1] I have only just been able to discover that – alas – it won't be out in time for Christmas, only sometime early in January. Isn't it sickening? I was longing to give it away as Christmas presents and I loved the idea of your doing so. Poor Diana, what a beastly homecoming that sounded, and what hell it must be without fickle Jacqueline – hasn't she got a younger sister? I do hope Louise de Vilmorin's[2] operation went off alright. How horrible it sounds. Two publishers here have told me *Madame De* is selling like hot-cross-buns.[3]

I got the typescript of *The Violins of Saint-Jacques* the other day, my Caribbean island story. It's about 160 pages long and needs a great deal of polishing and pruning apart from maddening typing mistakes. I would have sent you a copy if I weren't afraid of it arriving after you had left France; so it would be better to hand it over when you appear here if you can face the sweat of reading it, a) because

[1] *A Time to Keep Silence* (1957).
[2] Louise de Vilmorin (1902–69), novelist, poet and journalist, and heiress to a great family fortune. She had a slight limp that became her trademark. As a young woman she had been engaged to Antoine de Saint-Exupéry, but the engagement had been called off. She was a notorious femme fatale, with many lovers, and was for some years one of Duff Cooper's mistresses.
[3] Vilmorin's novel *Madame de...* (1951), translated into English by Duff Cooper, which was adapted into the film *The Earrings of Madame de...* (1953), directed by Max Ophüls and considered a masterpiece of French cinema.

there's plenty to criticise in it and b) if you liked it at all, I'd love to dedicate it to you as a sort of present.[1] I think they are going to publish it fairly soon, probably with some illustrations & vignettes etc.

The weekend with Rowly and Laurian Winn[2] was rather fun. Rowly and I motored up together, the others (Laurian, Ld Euston and his boring, rather smug and pretty fair wife,[3] Jim Lees-Milne,[4] and Priscilla Bibesco[5]) going by train. The car broke down near Peterborough, and we had to be towed into that depressing town, where we kicked our heels in miserable back streets for five hours while new bits of the motor were being welded and hammered; then pricked northwards through Doncaster and mist and a slight snowfall with slagheaps looming out of the dark like great pyramids – either old and derelict and covered with bryony and bugloss – I insisted on inspecting one – or crowned with red burning crests like Hecla or Stromboli[6] – then, stretches of moor and dale where we lost our way again and again, finally arriving at Nostell Priory[7] at 11.30. It was a great, pillared, dark and splendid thing floating in mist, and inside, of an enchanting, rather delicate, magnificence – room after room designed by Paine and Adam[8] with almost every stick of furniture by Chippendale, each room like a lovely casket with pretty garlanded mouldings over the ceilings and eccentric and elaborate looking-glasses and quantities of rather fine pictures – a splendid huge one of St Thos.

[1] He did.
[2] Earlier in the year PLF had acted as best man when Rowland Winn, 4th Baron St Oswald (1916–84), married Laurian, daughter of Sir Roderick Jones and the novelist Enid Bagnold. The marriage was in difficulty from the start, and they were divorced in 1955.
[3] Hugh Denis Charles FitzRoy (1919–2011), Earl of Euston and heir to the Duke of Grafton, was married to Fortune Smith, for many years Mistress of the Robes to the Queen.
[4] The architectural historian and diarist James Lees-Milne (1908–97) was instrumental in the transfer of country houses from private ownership to the National Trust.
[5] Priscilla Helen Alexandra Bibesco (1920–2004), the daughter of the Romanian Prince Antoine Bibesco and his wife Elizabeth (herself daughter of the British prime minister, H. H. Asquith).
[6] Both volcanoes.
[7] A Palladian house in West Yorkshire. In 1953 the house and its contents were given to the National Trust.
[8] Nostell Priory was built by the architect James Paine (1717–89), with a wing by Robert Adam (1728–92).

More & family by Holbein.[1] I don't remember a single ugly thing there. But no disorder or patina of contemporary life! – sewing things, books, papers, etc. It has apparently only been used as a sort of shooting box or assembly place for race meetings by Rowly's uncles, for decades and decades; and he and Laurian had some of the bewilderment that a couple of Red Army corporals might feel suddenly billeted in Tsarskoë Selo;[2] & they were rather touching and sweet. No confidences in the car, nor later, alas; but both of them seemed much less nervy and on edge than in France. Perhaps it's alright after all? ... It was jolly cold, in spite of innumerable huge coal fires from the neighbouring mines. By daylight all was snow and mist, with the bare, black soot-covered trees leaning over frozen artificial lakes. These were spanned by colonnaded bridges that sailed away and disappeared in this faint white mist – all so dim and pale and like a Chinese painting that it was impossible to tell whether there was ice on the water till one threw pebbles that went skidding over the surface with a twittering noise. Two village boys came whizzing out of the white cotton wool on skates and then vanished again like ghosts. We all longed to join them, but there were no skates. We scattered a troop of phantom deer on the way back.

Last weekend I went to stay with Prof. Dawkins,[3] a don at Exeter Coll., Oxford, who is 82, and a tremendous authority on Byzantium and Greece and such a tireless talker that one has to sit up till 4 a.m. every night after tremendous, port-laden dinners at Exeter or All Souls, while Dawkins gasses away (fascinatingly) in a high falsetto, often getting so carried away with enthusiasm that he flourishes his two rubber-tipped walking sticks (he is lame) over his head, to the peril of half-a-century's growth of bric-a-brac that chokes his room. He starts up again at nine in the morning, like a giant refreshed by his 5 hours' sleep. I sat next to the Master of

[1] An early copy of a lost original.
[2] A former residence of the Russian imperial family.
[3] Richard MacGillivray Dawkins (1871–1955), Fellow of Exeter College, Oxford; director of the British School at Athens, 1906–14; Bywater and Sotheby Professor of Byzantine and Modern Greek Language and Literature, 1920–39.

Exeter[1] on Sunday night (a rather charming pince-nez-ed old stick, the world's authority on Catullus and Propertius). The other dons were talking about the war in Korea. He didn't participate in this, but in a moment of silence, vouchsafed in a sepulchral voice: 'They say the next one is going to be a Class War,' then, gazing up into the rafters, and speaking in tones of faint and meditative soliloquy, he went on: 'I think it's the only sort of War I should enjoy …'

Darling Diana, it is gloomy your being so long in France, and only staying in London such a short time. I do hope I'll be there – Barbara Warner is coming back to Charlotte Street,[2] and I'll have to clear out somewhere. If you stayed in London on the 20th, would you be free at all – for a meal or anything? If you were, I'd do <u>anything</u> to be there, in London I mean. Do <u>please</u> write a word almost at once, to say if you'll be free at all, and (please) don't punish my delay in writing by silence! I so long to see you again, and send

lots & lots of love
Paddy

P.S. <u>Night thoughts written in moments of insomnia</u>:

Harbourmaster: What's your name ?

Whale: Whale.

Harbourmaster: What's your cargo?

Whale: Whalebone and blubber.

Harbourmaster: Crew?

Whale: One.

Harbourmaster: Name?

Whale: Jonah.

Harbourmaster (shouting below): Any complaints?

Jonah (off): Yes. Claustrophobia and seasickness etc.

[1] The classicist Eric Arthur Barber (1888–1965) was then Rector of Exeter College, Oxford.
[2] The flat in Charlotte Street that she had rented to Joan for the past two years.

To Diana Cooper   Tivoli
26 March 1953   Italy

<u>After dinner</u>

Darling Diana,

Here we are at last – but not quite! Miss Edwardes[1] was away from her villa – in Rome I think – when I turned up in Tivoli this evening so I'm staying for the night in the hotel near the Temple of the Albunean Sybil (I just see her circle of pillars outside in the dark, by the light of the window of the dining room of which I am the sole incumbent). I believe you and Duff were here on your honeymoon, which, as at the Villa Cimbrone in Ravello, I always seem to be sleuthing unconsciously. (*Freud en dirait long*,[2] I dare say!)

What a lovely afternoon at the zoo; I always have such fun with you (almost scans). There was something immensely nostalgic about that vast red balloon of a sun, with a thin bar of cloud across it, seen through lovely London's bare trees, reminding one of happiest childhood afternoons, with back to tea and blazing coals through nursery wire firescreens ahead when one got home, a heavenly fuggy smell of the carpet always within six inches of one's nose, looking through picture-books, as one breathed in the fluff.

I had to pick Annie Fleming up that evening, after she'd had dinner with the Edens[3] (or was it the night before, and did I tell you all this? Apologies if so). Well, half a dozen cops – part of Tito's bodyguard, still hanging about, no doubt[4] – were lurking in the hall of 1 Carlton Gardens.[5] I said I wanted to pick someone up who'd been dining

---

[1] PLF was renting rooms in the Casa Sabina in Tivoli from Miss Edwardes, an Englishwoman.

[2] 'Freud would have a lot to say about that.'

[3] Sir Anthony Eden (1897–1977), Foreign Secretary 1951–5, and his wife Clarissa (b. 1920), née Spencer-Churchill.

[4] Josip Broz Tito, known as Marshal Tito (1892–1980), President and Prime Minister of Yugoslavia, had arrived in Britain, the first communist head of state to visit the country.

[5] Official ministerial residence of the Foreign Secretary.

with Mrs E; was put in a lift and sent up to the third floor; marched along a rather homely looking passage, opened what I thought was a drawing-room door and there was the foreign secretary in bed, with open despatch boxes all over the place, looking very silvery and smooth. 'Do come in,' he said (we'd never met) – and then with a *dégagé* [relaxed] wave at the litter all over his bed – 'I'm just trying to catch up with some arrears of bumf.' Wonderful ease, three minutes of the lightest possible amity and banter. The ease was tremendous – after all, I might have been one of the trigger-men of Catholic Action, that well known Balkan Underground Committee ...[1] I finally found Annie and Clarissa (in a sweeping tea-gown), one floor down, and went off with Annie to a night-club I'd never been to before called the Eldorado. There were only two other couples there and I think we drank far too much, as I remember our taking shoes and socks off and padding around through delicious tangoes barefoot, which caused a slight row with the manager, somehow smoothed out in the end. Dinner next night, and sitting up drinking a whole bottle of Armagnac, with Annie and Peter Q[uennell] till nearly four and then off, over the waves of the Channel next morning, cradling the happiest kind of hangover. At Vallorbe the French *douaniers* discovered my passport was four months expired but I managed to talk my way across the Swiss frontier, to Montreux, to get it renewed at the Consulate there. My word, what a gloomy town. Silly Swiss mountains that you think it common to abhor reflected in a soppy lake and an empty Nineveh of palace hotels everywhere, [and] that accent that makes you want to cut your throat.

Lovely waking up in Italy next day; ragged black clouds over the strange Maremma, and Etruscan towns whizzing past in the half-light ('Verbenna down to Ostia, Hath wasted all the plain; Astur hath stormed Janiculum, And the stout guards are slain'[2]); then out into a lonely unbreathed Rome. I parked my luggage in the Bocca di Leone, walked up the steps of the Capitol to the Piazza Aracoeli,

[1] PLF's positive view of Eden would soon change, because of what he saw as Eden's obstinacy in the Cyprus Emergency.
[2] See footnote on p. 64.

gazed over the empty city – Coliseum, Forum, arches, and the pimply circumambient hills – and gave myself over to Gibbonian musings:

Nouveau venu, qui cherches Rome en Rome
Et rien de Rome en Rome n'aperçois
Ces vieux murs, les vieux arcs que tu vois
Les vieux palais, c'est ce que Rome on nomme
Vois, quel orgueil, quelle décadence, etc.[1]

(If, which I strongly doubt, you can't place that, answer on first page, above the vignette of the Castello Meleto in Chianti.)

I came by bus here this evening. Darling Miss Edwardes [is] away in Rome (to pick me up?), so I walked back three miles to Tivoli, and am just beginning my fourth grappa after a solitary dinner in this empty building. I adore this sitting alone and pretending to be an 18th century Traveller of Mark,[2] having dismissed doctor, valet and postilions before setting down to an evening with Horace and Propertius, and suitable reveries. Tremendous weeks of work ahead, which makes me feel very excited.

So good night, dearest Diana. I do adore you, and wish you were here, and that we were about to spend hours talking away. I wonder if you'll come to Central Italy at all. <u>IMPORTANT</u>. Please tell me if any of those bulb-patterns have exploded legibly.[3] I was sorry to have missed them. And please write as often as possible!

Lots of love & hugs from Paddy X X X

P.S. Had dinner with Ivan Moffat[4] last night in Rome.

---

[1] 'Newcomer, who seeks Rome in Rome/ And nothing of Rome in Rome can find/ These old walls, these old arches that you see/ These old palaces are what Rome is called/ See, what pride, what decadence ...', from Joachim du Bellay, *Les Antiquités de Rome* (1558).

[2] i.e. of distinction.

[3] PLF had planted bulbs in patterns of words at the Château de Saint-Firmin.

[4] Ivan Moffat (1918–2002), screenwriter and film producer, 'a tremendous crony of mine'. His mother, Iris Tree, was also a friend of PLF's.

To Joan Rayner   Casa Sabina
10 April 1953   Quintiliolo
                                                        Tivoli
                                             Provincia di Roma

Darling Joan,

A great day! George is over and done with at last![1] I finished it this morning, after having translated 20 to 30 pages of the typescript a day, which was a tremendous amount. I have done 350 closely written pages of manuscript since arriving here, and altogether it is 450 pages: which just shows what can be done! It's a great weight off my mind, and now all is clear for [the book on] Greece at last, and I'm about to plunge into it.

The excitement of finishing this and getting rid of it has been spoiled by the bloody news that the *Sunday Times* did <u>not</u> pay that hundred quid into my bank as they faithfully promised several times over: the result has been a disaster – cheques not being paid etc. – shaming beyond words. I first learnt of it by a furious letter from Randal McDonnell. I hate to think of the havoc and the mess it has caused. I have sent a violent S.O.S. telegram to Lambert,[2] but no answer yet. I suppose they just forgot, but it's callous and inexcusable after I'd explained at great length just how vital it was. Bugger bugger bugger! Miserable shits. I can't sit still – or do anything! – till I know what's happened. Don't you think it's the limit?

It is fantastically quiet here, perfect for writing. I get up at 8, have breakfast with Miss Edwardes, and then vanish from 8.30 till 12.30 in a room opening onto the garden downstairs, return there after luncheon 12.30–1.30, and stay there till suppertime at 7.30 at night, sitting up talking to Miss Edwardes till 9.30 or ten, then downstairs again till 12 or 1. I sometimes go for a walk before dinner, down

[1] PLF had been working on an English translation of George Psychoundakis's memoir, eventually published as *The Cretan Runner* (1955).
[2] J. W. Lambert, then assistant literary editor of the *Sunday Times*.

among the ruins and olive trees. If I didn't have so much work to do, it might be a bit depressing. As it is, it's perfect. I have arranged to contribute 10/- a day for food – she won't let me pay anything for the two rooms I use. She's awfully sweet. I have been reading Percy Lubbock's *Roman Pictures*[1] out loud after dinner. She said the other night that she read Pickwick [Papers] all through, and only laughed once, and read it through years later carefully to find what it was that had made her laugh, but couldn't find it…

I've not even been inside Sant'Antonio[2] yet. The lessee, Tony Scarisbrick, came to luncheon three days ago – very curious, not very sympathetic, I thought. But the talk was all in Italian, as a very amusing schoolmaster, speaking no English, came too. I don't think I'll learn any Italian this time. I've got a 'method' that I read in bed, but always fall asleep on the same page.

On Easter Monday, John Russell[3] (to whom I'd sent a card with my whereabouts) motored out and took me to Palombara, where Maurice Bowra was, with another couple called the Spinks. They were in a little rustic bar, and Maurice was streaming with sweat, roaring with laughter, talking at the top of his voice, rather tipsy – at his best. It was tremendous fun. John had brought some vodka & caviar (Aliki was in Belgium) after which, lots of red wine, and a walk to a ravishing 6th century Basilican church in a valley full of cherry blossom called S. Giovanni in Argentella – remote, lost, unknown place and unspeakably charming.

No more now, darling – please forgive me being such an age writing, but I wanted to get this damn George book done. Any

---

[1] Percy Lubbock (1879–1965), who lived most of his life in Italy, was an essayist, critic and biographer. His *Roman Pictures* (1923) was reviewed in the *Sunday Times* as 'a book of whimsical originality and exquisite workmanship, and worthy of one of the best prose writers of our time'.

[2] A former monastery near Tivoli built over a Roman villa, believed to have belonged to the poet Horace, where PLF had stayed in 1949 while writing *The Traveller's Tree* (1950); now owned by the Landmark Trust.

[3] John Wriothesley Russell (1914–84), diplomat, was married to Aliki Diplarakou, the first Greek Miss Europe.

reviews of [*A Time to Keep*] *Silence*? Do send any. How lovely your party sounded!

Lots and lots of love & hugs
from Old Mole

To Diana Cooper   Castello della Rocca di Porto Ercole
undated [June 1953]   Orbetello
                                                                 Toscana

Dearest Diana,

I've just bought this measly little nib in the village underneath this castle, and writing with it is like trying to tame a crippled tarantula! I was frightfully sorry to learn Duff (in an Italian newspaper) has been ill, and do hope he is better now. Did it wash out the Coronation?[1] If it didn't, do please send a tremendous account of it. I feel a bit of an exile on this rock, engaged on a protracted and Laocoön-like struggle with the last part of my book about Greece.[2] It seems endless.

Now – are you coming to Italy at all? To Tuscany or Rome? If so, <u>do please</u>, on your way to the capital, rescue me for a day from this Zenda[3] I've incarcerated myself in. It's at the end of a peninsula sticking out of the coast of the Tuscan Maremma, a colossal ruined Aragonese bastille built in the 16th century against the Barbary pirates – a labyrinth of barbicans, glacis, inner wards, demilunes, redoubts etc., and at vast extent. Great lumps of it have fallen away, and there are corn- and hayfields and lots of poppies and a couple of ricks, even inside the battlements. I live in two rooms – rather dark hell-holes – and eat as well, for 1,000 lire a day, which isn't bad. About 30 peasants live a troglodytic life in various dungeons and

---

[1] The coronation of Queen Elizabeth II had taken place on 2 June at Westminster Abbey.
[2] Laocoön was the Trojan priest who warned his fellow citizens against trusting the 'gift' of the Wooden Horse. The gods sent two sea serpents to silence him. Here PLF probably refers to the ancient Greek marble *Laocoön and His Sons*, now in the Vatican, which depicts Laocoön's agony as he struggles to free himself and his two sons from the serpents' embrace.
[3] A reference to Anthony Hope's *The Prisoner of Zenda* (1894).

holes dotted about the castle, and the whole thing is owned by a small hunchback spinster – a schoolmistress from the Abruzzi – who acquired it twelve years ago in settlement of a debt. The rockface falls perpendicular to the sea beyond the *enceinte* [surrounding wall], except on one side, where it is connected with the little port, which, in its turn, is linked by an isthmus to the mainland, running between dismal salt-flats and lagoons. It's very windy – there have been apocalyptic thunderstorms these last few days, like illustrations for Mrs Radcliffe or Sheridan le Fanu;[1] these have now been replaced by a cheerful, unflagging scirocco. Otherwise, it's perfect. I don't think Joan will like it much, when she finally appears.

I wandered about Tuscany and Umbria for ten days last month with Peter Quennell (I can't remember whether you share the Waugh–Sykes antipathy?).[2] He was an absolutely charming companion, never grumbling and great fun, which dispelled my misgivings, as one did a lot of it on foot, like palmers,[3] with knapsacks. We met in Siena, spent a day in S. Gimignano, then went to Montepulciano, Chiusi, and round Lake Trasimene to Perugia, thence to Assisi, along the Apennine foothills to Spello and Spoleto, across a small range to Todi, and then slowly along the winding upper reaches of the Tiber – dreamy, oil-green loops reflecting poplars and oak trees between sad and beautiful hills, all with castled villages on top, and tiered in that queer Umbrian-Tuscan way, on frameworks stretching from olive to olive, a Courbet melancholy hanging over everything, & so back to Perugia, where, after a journey to Gallio, we separated.

When he'd gone, I went by bus via Terni and Aquila to Salmona, in the Abruzzi, where I met an old drunken friend of mine, called

[1] Both Gothic novelists.
[2] 'Have you ever noticed how everything beastly begins with Q?' Evelyn Waugh wrote to Ann Fleming. 'Like Quennell and queers and the queen, quibbles, quod, quagmire, quantum theory, queues, quiffs, most Quentins, questionnaires, quarrels – well, everything.' In another letter, to his friend and future biographer Christopher Sykes, Waugh expressed his antipathy for Quennell, whom he nicknamed 'Fuddy Duddy Fish Face'.
[3] PLF refers to the pilgrims to the Holy Land, who returned bearing a palm branch to signify where they had been.

Archie Lyall,[1] drinking his tenth solitary grappa on the Piazza del Duomo. We set off next day to a village called Cocullo, at the end of a remote blind-alley of the mountains, to attend the feast of a local saint called St Dominic the Abbot (or 'of Sora'), not to be confused with the great St D., founder of the Order. He is a tenth-century local saint, who rid that part of the Abbruzzi of wolves, bears and snakes – but only for a while, as thousands of peasants flock there on the first Thursday in May to be made proof against snake bite and rabies for the next year. The village was full of wonderfully coloured clothes and crabapple faces (one old shepherd, in rawhide moccasins and cross-gartered like an Anglo-Saxon messenger, was playing some bagpipes made out of the patched inner-tube of a motor). Thousands had slept in the church, which reeked like a stable. There were some very queer goings-on: queues of peasants on their knees advancing in turn and pulling the chain of a bell with their teeth (it had once hung outside St D's hermitage). Then they brought bits of rubble from the same place to scatter over their fields to ensure a good flock, and a young priest rubbed them all over with a cylindrical reliquary in which hung one of St D's teeth on a chain, now a vast discoloured fang. Crusts of bread, to be fed to their livestock, were also blessed with the same relic. The next move was up to the image of the Saint, which was kissed and stroked in transports – bits of coloured wool were rubbed against him, and tucked away in pockets & bodies – all this to ward off rabies and snakebite and toothache till next Saint's Day. But the climax of everything was when the life-size image was carried out into the village square. Dozens of boys and young men were waiting, holding live snakes between each of their fingers – four per hand, a tremendous tangle, some of them whoppers over two inches thick and a couple of yards long. These were lassoo'd and festooned all over the Saint, about a hundred of them, till he was a great writhing & hissing figure, with serpents twisted round his crozier, and in and out of his wire halo. The procession lasted two hours

[1] Archie Lyall (1904–64), traveller, linguist, author and intelligence officer, with a reputation as a raconteur and bon viveur. An SIS colleague remembered that he 'carried a revolver in case of accidents and a monocle in case of serious trouble'.

to the tune of Verdi's triumphant march from Aida and various Sousa[1] pieces. Snakes everywhere, girls even waving them from housetops. After fireworks, we processed back to the church where the image was de-snaked, and put back in his niche.

The snake-catchers – *i serpari* – catch them weeks ahead, in a semi-swoon among the rocks, when they are coming round from hibernation, and get their teeth out (and their poison) by making them bite bits of cloth, which they then jerk sharply away. There were lots of people buying them afterwards, mostly peddlers, who use them to collect a crowd, then open a suitcase of combs or watches or celluloid thumbs-ups ... There was even a quack doctor from Bologna who bought a kicking sackful to melt down into rheumatism ointment. I got one for 400 lire, a beauty speckled grey and green, 1½ yards long, with clever little black eyes, and motored back to Rome, with it crawling all over Archie's car.[2]

After having luncheon at his flat on the outskirts, I took a tram to the Via Giulia, where I was going to stay the night with the Rodds.[3] But when I put my hand into my coat pocket to pull it out, it wasn't there – it must have crawled free in the tram, and probably caused pandemonium later. Or perhaps it crept out, and is now asleep on a sunny ledge of the Colosseum or the baths of Diocletian or, best of all, the Temple of Asclepius. I reported its loss at the police station in the Campo Marzio. It cheered all the carabiniers up a lot; but there was never any sign of it.

Ivan Moffat & 2 other friends stayed here last weekend, which was great fun. He's as bright as a button and very funny indeed, and we sat up all the last night cooking steaks and emptying nearly a demijohn of wine, among the rocks by the sea, under the *schloss*,

---

[1] John Philip Sousa (1854–1932), American composer and conductor, known primarily for marches.

[2] PLF wrote an account of the snake-catchers for *The Spectator*, published under the title 'Serpents of the Abruzzi', on 5 June 1953, and reprinted in an anthology of PLF's occasional writings edited by Artemis Cooper, *Words of Mercury* (London, 2003), pp. 68–72.

[3] The Hon. Gustaf 'Taffy' Rodd (1905–74), named after his godfather, King Gustavus of Sweden, and his wife, Rosemary Rodd Baldwin (1917–92). His brother Peter was the estranged husband of Nancy Mitford.

until daybreak. Lots of lovely singing. It reminds me of that funny 'Doll-to-Doll' letter you read me out loud at Chantilly last autumn. Graham, Joan's brother, turned up two days ago, and we had a slap-up meal in Orbetello, which was nice after the dreary mileage of macaroni I get here every day.

The 'Violins of St J' came out in the last *Cornhill* and appears as a book in two months – also, in America (hooray!) and there's an 'option' from a film company so I may be under a miniature v. necessary shower of gold later on. I wish these things didn't take such aeons. I'd love to get it printed in France, which I don't think would be very difficult. Louise de Vilmorin might be able to advise? I wonder if I could write to them – or could you ask advice when you saw them? – if it's not a nuisance? My dream would be, when a publisher is found, for Louise to translate it – she'd do it so beautifully and it would only take a few days. I wonder if you, Diana, could fly a very tentative kite here, or is that difficult or a bore? She's probably far too busy with her own stuff anyway. I'll get a copy of the book sent to you the second it appears, naturally.

Very many commiserations again about Duff's wretched illness, and please give him *touts mes souhaits* [greetings] and wishes for getting better. And please write and illuminate this gloomy keep. Lots of gossip would be the very thing; to here, if you write quickly (which, <u>my word</u>, I think I deserve after your more than Cistercian silence!), but to Rome if later; and lots of love, Diana darling,

from Paddy

P.S. Two weeks ago I was trudging down the hill, when I saw a magnificent yacht in the bay flying the white ensign, and when I reached the quay, there were two Englishmen in a launch struggling with Italian to a fisherman on shore. It was the work of a second to wander up as interpreter, and (you've guessed) it was Loel Guinness,[1] whom I've never met, and man with a horse-like

---

[1] In 1951 Group Captain Thomas Loel Guinness, MP (1906–88), married Gloria Rubio Alatorre (1913–80), socialite and fashion icon, becoming her fourth husband. One of her lovers was Duff Cooper, who wrote of her: 'I have never loved anybody physically so much or been so supremely satisfied.'

face called Du Cane.[1] I managed to get asked on board for some
delicious whisky (no meal, alas!). I was a bit disappointed in
Gloria, who I had somehow imagined to be a raging beauty; but
thought Guinness charming. I think they must have imagined
I was a rather affable tramp. A nice interlude, but how heavenly
if, which you might so easily have been, you'd both have been
opening a bottle of champagne in that smart white drawing room
in the stern!

P.S.S. Can't help thinking what a ghastly [illegible] bore it must
have been about robes, crowns etc. if they couldn't be used[2] in
the end!

*The Reverend Canon Frederick Shirley (1890–1967) had become head-
master of the King's School, Canterbury, in 1935, three years after Paddy
had been expelled, ostensibly for holding hands with the daughter of a
local greengrocer.*

To Canon Shirley   Tuscany
22 June 1953   Italy

Dear Canon Shirley,
    Thank you very much indeed for your kind letter, which reached
me here yesterday after many halts on the way. It was very good to
have news of the school – it certainly has changed since my day,
in numbers and academic glories! It's an immensely impressive list.
I wondered who the Fellow of All Souls was.[3] I go and dine with
them from time to time, staying with old Professor Dawkins (82

[1] Commander Peter Du Cane (1901–84), designer of fast boats and managing director of
the shipbuilders Vospers. He had served in RAF 601 Squadron with Loel Guinness.
[2] i.e. at the Coronation. Duff Cooper was too ill to go, but Diana went.
[3] David Edwards (b. 1929), who had been a pupil at the school, was elected a fellow of
All Souls, Oxford, in 1952. He would later write a biography of his former headmaster,
F. J. Shirley: An Extraordinary Headmaster (1969).

this year) at Exeter, as he is a great authority on Byzantine and Modern Greece, and especially on the life in the mountains & islands, which I am writing a longish book about. Alas, it looks as if I'm going to be abroad some time, but I would love to talk informally about Greece and Crete sometime when I get back, if you don't think it would bore people.

I had rather a topsy-turvy career at Canterbury, which came to grief in mid term, I'm sorry to say! Since then I wandered about Europe a long time, and rather lost touch with the school. I used to meet and dine with my housemaster, Mr Macdonald, fairly often in London, until his sad death. The only other master I have re-met was Mr Reynolds (whom we used to call 'Piggy'). I wonder if any of the others are still there – Mr Egerton-Jones, Mr Stanier, Mr Harris? If they are, please remember me to them.

I leave for Greece via Brindisi at the end of the week, and will spend about two months wandering about Epirus, Ætolia and Acarnania, thence to Athens, and then possibly to French Equatorial Africa, to visit Albert Schweitzer,[1] as the *Sunday Times* want somebody to write about him before he dies. I believe he's immensely old.

Thank you again for your letter. I have occasionally wandered through the buildings in a rather Scholar Gipsy-ish fashion[2] when staying with friends in Kent; next time I'll certainly look in, if I may.

Yours sincerely
Patrick Leigh Fermor

[1] Albert Schweitzer (1875–1965) was a French-German theologian, organist, writer, humanitarian, philosopher and physician, best known for founding and sustaining a hospital in Lambaréné, French Equatorial Africa (now Gabon). He had been awarded the Nobel Peace Prize in 1952. The journalist James Cameron visited Lambaréné in 1953 on behalf of the *News Chronicle*. Though he found significant flaws in the practices and attitudes of Schweitzer and his staff, Cameron resisted pressure from his employers to publish an exposé.

[2] Matthew Arnold's poem 'The Scholar Gipsy' (1853) is prefaced by a story from two centuries ago, of an impoverished student who abandoned his studies to join a band of gypsies, and learned their arcane secrets. Even two centuries later, his shadowy figure can still be glimpsed in the Berkshire and Oxfordshire countryside, 'waiting for the spark from Heaven to fall'.

To Diana Cooper   Dumbleton,
30 January 1954   England

Darling Diana,

Only just got your letter, owing to silly re-directions by the Travellers [Club]; so many apologies for delay. I wonder whether you will be in Rome at the end of Feb, beginning of March? Some publishers (Verschoyle) want me to do an essay on the Torlonia ball,[1] and I hope to fly out. It would be heavenly if you were there – I'll stay several days and we might go on some lovely jaunts near Rome, meals at Tivoli, etc. – It would be tragic to hear you had just left. Do please try and fit Rome into your wanderings then;[2] we might all try and go to this wonder-ball together, if you were in the mood for such a thing. (I'll be able to wear my miniatures [medals], which I've always longed to do, in vain so far. I hope there will be thousands of archdukes and Infantas in the Golden Fleece ...)

I thought of writing to Jenny[3] (but I don't know her address in the Forum) to see if she or somebody in the Embassy could wangle an invitation to this thing. I'm sure there would be no difficulty in getting one, as the purpose is to record the occasion in deathless prose. I thought of Jenny especially, as the essay is for a book of *Memorable Balls* (of all magnificent titles)[4] to which she has contributed a glowing account of the Beistegui one.[5] <u>Could</u> you sound her, if it is not too much of a bore for her (or you)? Also,

---

[1] Balls had been held at the magnificent Villa Torlonia in Rome for a century or more. As many as 2,000 guests would be in attendance.

[2] She joined PLF in Rome towards the end of February.

[3] Jenny Nicholson (1919–64), journalist and daughter of the poet Robert Graves; married to Reuter's bureau chief in Rome, Patrick Crosse.

[4] James Laver (ed.), *Memorable Balls* (1954). There is no account of the Beistegui ball in the book: indeed, no account of any ball later than 1910.

[5] At the Palazzo Labia on the Grand Canal in Venice, where the double-height ballroom is decorated with frescoes by Tiepolo. The 1951 ball hosted by Don Carlos de Beistegui ('Charlie') has been described as 'one of the most lavish social events of the twentieth century'.

could you ask Jenny what the exact date of it is, as the *Sunday Times* might want me to do something about it. Many thanks in advance for all this.

I wonder how you are, Diana darling. I'm sure that the only remedies at times like these[1] are a retreat into a Trappe [monastery] of some kind, or travel, movement & change. You may well have chosen the best one; if it doesn't work, why not try the other for a fortnight, unless it would depress you beyond bearing. I long to see you to know how you really are, and your plans and so on, though you probably haven't any beyond the immediate future. San Vigilio would obviously be no good, because of too many memories – what about Como or Maggiore, with a gladstone bag full of books? No good? What we all need at difficult times is a sort of giant nanny, a she-Grenadier[2] ten feet high to boss one about and no nonsense, off to bed with bread & milk, console one or tell one not to sit there moping, scrub one firmly, tuck one up and read one to sleep. If I could breed some of them by careful crossing of strains, my fortune would be made ...

After leaving Michael, Annie & Bridget at Birr,[3] I went back to my old haunt at Luggala,[4] and, at a nearby hunt ball of the Kildare Hunt – 'The Killing Kildares'! – met my doom by getting into a murderous brawl with several enormous pink-coated thugs. It was about 3.00 in the morning, and everybody was reeling. Nobody knows how it started, though I believe it was my fault for not gauging (with my misty perceptions) the depths of unraggability of the hunting Anglo-Irish.[5] Anyway, there we all were, slamming

[1] Duff Cooper had died suddenly on 1 January 1954, aged sixty-three.
[2] Grenadiers were originally chosen from the strongest and largest soldiers.
[3] Lawrence Michael Harvey Parsons (1906–79), 6th Earl of Rosse, Irish peer whose family seat was Birr Castle, brother of Lady Bridget Parsons; and his wife Anne, née Messel, mother from her first marriage of Anthony Armstrong-Jones (Lord Snowdon), who in 1960 married Princess Margaret.
[4] The Co. Wicklow house of Oonagh, Lady Oranmore and Browne, née Guinness (1910–1995), who was then romantically involved with the historian and broadcaster Robert Kee (1919–2013).
[5] PLF provoked the brawl by asking whether it was true that the 'Killing Kildares' were in the habit of buggering their foxes.

away at each other like navvies – Whizz! bang!! Slosh!!! – I was being dealt with by ½ a dozen great incarnadined Nimrods; Robert Kee dashed to my rescue, only to be brought down by Roderic More O'Ferrall,[1] and the scarlet maelstrom surfed over them and me. The Macgillicuddy of the Reeks's sister-in-law plunged into the middle and fetched me one on the top of the head with her ringed fist … result of all this for me, a split chin, two enormous black eyes & three stitches in Dublin.[2] Phew! They are fading away now, and only a faint nostalgic mauve afterglow still lingers. A sharp lesson.

I'm writing this at Joan's mother's house (at Dumbleton), in spite of the deceptive paper. There was a heavy snowfall last night, and the white fields stretch away under a pale grey sky, into which the bare elm trees ascend like maps of deltas: a Brueghel winter landscape dotted with enormous rooks.

Do please write again almost at once, dearest Diana. I wish I were in Rome. Must stop now, darling Diana, and please write again as soon as possible. Are you coming here soon?

Love from Paddy

P.S. Here is a 16th Century anon. post byzantine Greek peasant poem[3] I discovered in an old collection the other day, which I translate word for word. Very eerie and sad, I think.

Black swallows out of the wilderness
And white pigeons by the edge of the sea,

---

[1] Roderic More O'Ferrall (1903–90), passionate foxhunter and owner of the Kildangan stud farm, now owned by Sheik Maktoum.
[2] PLF was rescued from the melee by Ricki Huston, Italian-American fourth wife of film director John Huston. She drove him to Dublin, where a surgeon was got out of bed to administer stitches.
[3] Unidentified.

Flying so high, when you come to my homeland
Fly to my courtyard and give them a message:
Tell my poor wife she must watch no longer.
Let her turn nun if she wishes, or marry
Or dye her dresses and live in mourning.
But wait and sigh no more. I am never returning.
For they have married me here, in distant Armenia,
To an Armenian girl, the child of a witch,
A witch who casts a spell on the stars and the sky.
A spell on the birds and they fly no longer,
A spell on the rivers that stops them flowing,
A spell on the ships that keeps them from sailing,
A spell on the sea and the waves fall silent.
She has cast a spell on me. I shall never come home.
When I set out, there is rain and snow,
When I turn back, sunlight or starshine.
If I saddle my horse to come, the horse is unsaddled;
If I gird on my sword for the journey, the sword is ungirded;
If I write down words with my pen, they are all unwritten,
And I shall never come home.

While she was holidaying in Greece, Diana Cooper allowed Paddy to stay in her house by the sea at Aldwick, near Bognor Regis.

To Diana Cooper   c/o You!
8 March 1954   Bognor

Darling Diana,

Well, I must say, this is absolutely marvellous. After telephoning two days ago, and sending a wire this morning, I reached Bognor by train after dark, got into a car that brought me here like a homing swallow, rapped at that pretty little pavilion, and there was Miss Wade,[1] as severely tweeded as a marchioness, soon leading me through the dark garden to the welcoming lamplit windows, into the hall, along a brief labyrinth of passages into this charming room, where all the lamps were on and a coal fire blazing merrily. I can't sleep in Miss W.'s house, as minute Artemis (my hostess in your absence)[2] is there with her nanny; so a heavenly room has been made ready immediately over this one. The little restaurant along the road is shut in the evenings, so for tonight Miss W. gave me some delicious brawn in her pleasure-dome, and here we are. The plan is to eat down the road for luncheon, and lay in cold goodies from the grocer for the evening, which is perfect, as, working alone, I sometimes don't want to eat till about midnight. Also she suggests my getting Mrs ____, the gardener's wife, for an hour each morning for a suitable pittance to tidy up etc. Miss W. insists on doing breakfast herself, though I'm quite capable of boiling a pot of tea. She seems very kind and austerely friendly and eager to make one feel welcome and at home. I do hope all this is alright. I have forewarned [her] about lighting, fuel, telephone bills etc., and will go to great lengths not to be a nuisance. She doesn't seem nearly as displeased to have her hibernation broken as one might expect.

It's very dark and misty outside and I can hear the sea crashing away somewhere near; also an odd noise like far away gunfire, a sort of muted report growing faintly louder, then all the windowpanes rattling. Must be artillery practice. Slightly eerie and like the war. I love this room. I made a dash for that alcove up two steps where there is a woollen portrait of the Iron Duke in sampler stitching, and what should be the first book to meet my eye? *The Prisoner of Zenda*! I'll take it up to bed with me ...

[1] Lady Diana's maid.
[2] Diana Cooper's granddaughter, Artemis, then an infant, who would eventually write PLF's biography.

All went off well at Auberon [Herbert]'s[1] ducal soirée last Thursday. The Dss of Kent appeared with both her sisters, all three looking very decorative and Winterhalteresque, I must say.[2] With them was Sir Malcolm Sargent,[3] who is ghastly, rather like a dressy hôtelier or road-house proprietor who will call one 'old man'; and also Dick Howland, the very nice American archaeologist I put down on your list for Athens. He'll be there in a week or so; I told him to find you, as I'm sure you'll like him. Auberon very capable and unrattled, having risen annealed after sleeping off his three-day hangover. At various points in the evening I could hear his urgent voice muttering into each sister's ear in turn, 'Ma'am, I've got you down on my Ukrainian committee ...' following up this opening with the intentness of somebody selling patent medicines or a vacuum-cleaner, coiling both arms round his neck till he comprised a Laocoön-group. All this had an agreeable follow-through for me by being asked to spend all Sunday at the Dss's house in leafy Bucks: playing a rather simplified kind of word making & word taking called 'Scrabble' after luncheon, a drive to Windsor after

[1] Auberon Mark Yvo Henry Herbert (1922–74), who lived at Pixton Park on Exmoor. A militant Catholic, he opposed his sister Laura's marriage to Evelyn Waugh, who never forgave him for this. PLF met him in Wilton's in 1940, ordering a vodka with tomato juice, Worcester sauce, lemon juice, pepper and salt – which he refused to call a Bloody Mary, since this 'traduces the name of a noble and deeply wronged Queen'. Like PLF, he had a gift for languages, and he campaigned on behalf of the peoples of Eastern Europe over-run by communism. According to his entry in the *Oxford Dictionary of National Biography*, Herbert's great disappointment was that the Conservative Party never gave him a safe seat in the West Country. 'The mastery of tongues, which was his special gift, and his awkward sympathies for the oppressed, appeared to respectable Conservatives disqualifications for public office and proof of some incurable eccentricity – an impression heightened by his unreliability in mundane matters.'

[2] Princess Marina of Greece and Denmark (1906–68), known after her marriage to the Duke of Kent as the Duchess of Kent; with her two sisters, Princess Olga, who married Prince Paul of Yugoslavia; and Princess Elisabeth, who married Count Carl Theodor of Törring-Jettenbach.

[3] Sir Harold Malcolm Watts Sargent (1895–1967), conductor, organist and composer, nicknamed 'Flash Harry'.

tea where I wandered plebeianly under Harrison Ainsworth[1] oaks while the three royal ladies saw the Queen Mother; back, dinner, with the same trio & the Duke of Kent (who seemed extraordinarily polite, bright, interested in literature, languages, painting etc., not a bit what I had expected from photographs in which he always looks ill-kempt and surly);[2] then arrival of neighbours, paper and 'the game'[3] in various forms. By far the best read, most intelligent and fly at all this was Pss Olga; Ctss Törring a tremendous duffer. Altogether, great fun.

Had luncheon with Freddie Ashton & Margot Fonteyn & Joan next day, both hotfoot from American triumphs, and dinner with Julian and Michael Pitt-Rivers, poor Mike being due to appear in the dock for buggery next Monday.[4] Did you ever meet him? He's absolutely delightful: quiet, charming, learned, witty, heart of gold etc. It's a real calamity. He carries it off splendidly. Both brothers seem to think he'll get off because of the scarceness of evidence and (chiefly) because the police have behaved like such swine. I wonder if they have just incantated themselves into this mood ... If they are wrong, I suppose it means 2 years in quod.

11th March

This is all working out wonderfully, and I'm slugging away like a pneumatic drill. I've laid in lots of stores – sausages, tomatoes etc.,

[1] William Harrison Ainsworth (1805–82), historical novelist, author of *Windsor Castle* (1842).
[2] Prince Edward, Duke of Kent (b. 1935), son of Princess Marina, inherited the title at an early age following the death of his father in an aeroplane crash in 1942.
[3] An after-dinner game, with similar conventions to charades.
[4] In the summer of 1953, Lord Montagu of Beaulieu offered his friend Peter Wildeblood the use of a beach hut near his country estate. Wildeblood brought with him two young RAF servicemen, and the four were joined by Montagu's cousin, Michael Pitt-Rivers. At the subsequent trial, Pitt-Rivers, Montagu and Wildeblood were brought before the courts, charged with 'conspiracy to incite certain male persons to commit serious offences with male persons'. After an eight-day trial they were found guilty; Pitt-Rivers and Wildeblood were sentenced to eighteen months and Lord Montagu to twelve months in prison as a result of these and other charges. Their case led eventually to the Wolfenden Report, which in 1957 recommended the decriminalisation of homosexuality in the UK.

bracing Bovril for the small hours ('Lady Diana's very fond of that,' Miss Wade says: 'she likes it with milk in …'), and bottles and a syphon gleam encouragingly on the corner table – also a jug full of daffodils. The weather has been almost cloudless, though coldish, except for last night, when there was a sea-mist, and I took myself into Bognor after dark, ate a solitary dinner over the *Prisoner of Zenda* in the Norfolk Hotel, then to see *The Heart of the Matter* in the cinema behind the Arcade. (What a rotten end it has.[1])

It's looking very pretty and there are any number of crocuses & primroses out on the lawn.

Your letter has just turned up, after the Patras-Olympia trip. I do hope you are enjoying it; it's a bit hard to make out. I love your descriptions, and recognise every single step. Do go to Mycenae and Epidaurus – the latter is the most peaceful and calming place in the world. I wish I'd been there at Olympia. Three years ago, in mid-summer, Joan and I found some horses and rode from there clean across the mountains of Arcadia to Tripoli, via Bassae, taking five days, sleeping out on hay on village threshing floors, and moving off again by starlight to avoid the heat of the day; watching the stars flicker out one by one by one, the sky paling to turquoise till the sun came bounding up beyond the mountains, stretching our long shadows the wrong way across rocks & asphodel & thistles as we ambled along.

No more now, dearest Diana, but please write as often as you can, and tell me all! I'm gnawed with terrible envy. Fondest love from Paddy.

XXXX

P.S. Yes, of course I'll tell everyone, on spec, about the letters' loss, my indelible shame.[2] There were only a few, thank heavens. Two shirts and a pair of trousers are also missing, so they must have been pinched along with them – presumably sometime during the hour-long wait before we took off from Rome.

---

[1] Though a Catholic, the protagonist, Henry Scobie, commits suicide.
[2] PLF had lost an envelope filled with letters of thanks from Lady Diana to those who had written her letters of condolence on the loss of her husband. (See *Dashing for the Post*, pp. 83–4.)

P.P.S. Important.

Do get in touch with a very old friend of mine called Tanty Rodokanaki;[1] he's written several excellent books, fought in a number of wars, had [mules] killed under him like horses, and is one of the most brilliant and most amusing and cleverest talkers in Greece. He'd adore you, and I know you'd be amused by him. I can't think how I forgot to tell you. I've sent a cable, unless this misses you for several days, as I do want you to see him. He'll make you laugh a lot. He was very mixed up in my early Romanian love life when I was about twenty.

The editor, critic and bibliophile John Davy Hayward (1905–65) was a close friend of T. S. Eliot. His scholarly works included editions of Rochester, Donne and Swift, and the anthology The Penguin Book of English Verse *(1956).*

To John Davy Hayward   c/o Ghika
23 June 1954   Hydra

Dear John

It's no good, I can't get any decent anagrams out of your name – nothing to touch Bowra's 'Eroica Rawbum'[2] ... I struggled with it all one day last week in a tortoise-like train across Yugoslavia. Ljubljana, Zagreb, Belgrade, Nish and Skopje crawled past while I fought with that intractable assembly of letters. I realised I was beaten by the time the train crept into the Macedonian gorges, and put the meagre results into play form[3] next morning, as we puffed along between the Aegean and Mt Olympus, close under

---

[1] Constantine Pandia 'Tanty' Rodocanachi (1877–1956). Before the war PLF translated his novel *Ulysse, fils d'Ulysse* into English. His wife, to whom he had been introduced by Balasha Cantacuzène, was Romanian.

[2] PLF's anagram for Maurice Bowra.

[3] A few lines from a play incorporating anagrams of Hayward's name were appended to this letter.

the haunt of the Pierian Muses themselves – Polyhymnia, Calliope, Euterpe[1] must have drifted in through the window of the wagon-lits, an invisible *Notre Dame des Sleepings*.[2] So little to show for so much toil!

It is splendid here. The island is about 3 miles from the Argolic coast of the Peloponnese, and the house (borrowed from the painter Niko Ghika) is a huge rambling white empty thing on top of a rock above the Aegean. One leads an amphibious life, and there is a vast white studio to scribble away in. A pretty good billet, and the most accomplished bit of house sponging I've done for ages. Joan got here last week too, after an hilarious stay with Eddie Gathorne Hardy[3] in Beirut. We both fondly hope Annie [Fleming] will come here in about a month, with Eroica. Joan sends her love too. I'm sorry the anagrams are so feeble!

Yours ever, Paddy

P.S. Couplet on the Ruins of Shepheard's Hotel:[4]
'Neguib and Nasser now the courtyards keep
Where "lions" and lounge-lizards once drank deep.'[5]

[1] Three of the muses with their attributes: Calliope (epic poetry), Euterpe (flutes and lyric poetry) and Polyhymnia (sacred poetry).
[2] A reference to Maurice Dekobra's bestseller *La Madone des Sleepings* (1925), then being filmed for the second time, with Erich von Stroheim playing the sexologist Dr Siegfried Traurig.
[3] The Hon. (Ralph) Edward Gathorne-Hardy (1901–78), one of the original 'Bright Young People', the model for Miles Malpractice in Evelyn Waugh's *Vile Bodies* (1930).
[4] Shepheard's Hotel, once the most famous hotel in Cairo, was burned down in January 1952, in the anti-British riots that led to the Egyptian revolution.
[5] A pastiche of *The Rubaiyat of Omar Khayyam* (first published in English 1859).

As one of the first Europeans to travel through the southern Arabian deserts, Freya Stark was already well known as an explorer and travel writer when she met Paddy in Egypt during the war. She was one of the stars of John Murray's list; in all, she wrote more than two dozen books on her travels in the Middle East and Afghanistan, as well as several autobiographical works and essays. Towards the end of August 1950 she spent a day with Paddy and Joan as guests of the British ambassador, Clifford Norton, and his wife Noel Evelyn (known to friends as 'Peter'), at their cottage near Piraeus. 'Yesterday we had a cheerful party down here with Paddy Leigh Fermor and Joan,' she wrote afterwards to her husband, Stewart Perowne: 'Paddy looking in this wine-dark sea <u>so like</u> a Hellenistic lesser sea-god of a rather low period, and I do like him. He is the genuine buccaneer.'

To Freya Stark	Poste Restante
29 June 1954	Hydra
	Greece

IN TERRIFIC HASTE TO CATCH BOAT.

Darling Freya,

I'm writing this to Asolo,[1] although I know you're in darkest Anatolia – or most luminous Lycia? – because I don't know any nearer forwarding address. The thing is that Joan and I have borrowed Niko Ghika the painter's house in Hydra till the end of September, I hope, and it would be lovely if you made it on the caesura, for a few days, on your return journey westwards. Derek[2] too, either with you, or if you came by separate routes.

---

[1] Stark owned a villa in Asolo, in the northern Veneto.

[2] Stark, then sixty-one, was travelling with an unlikely companion, the portrait painter Derek Hill, almost twenty-five years her junior. When he remarked, on their first evening together, that he was thinking of keeping a diary, and perhaps writing about their journey, 'a glacial expression descended over her face'. 'No, Derek,' she said. 'I think that would be very rude to me. I am the writer. You are the painter.' In a letter to Jock Murray she confessed that she felt like 'strangling him at frequent intervals'. She parted from him, she said, 'with that wonderful feeling of exhilaration which seems to visit me when I drop a man'; Caroline Moorehead, *Freya Stark* (Harmondsworth, 1985), pp. 120–1.

I do hope you are having an exciting and rewarding *hadj*; I envy you immensely and long to hear all your sagas. Perhaps you will unfold them over ouzo and retsina, hotfoot from Rûm [Anatolia], on this very hillside.

It is not a bit luxurious – a big, white empty thing on top of a rock built by one of the prosperous old Hydriot captains – Nico's g-g-grandfather – on the cash made running the British blockade for Boney during the Napoleonic wars – but it has many compensating charms – you would certainly be one. Joan is in Athens, but I know would send love. Do scribble a line from the heart of Karamania[1] or the shores of Van.[2]

Love Paddy

I hope Diana [Cooper] is coming here in Sept.

Now that he had finished translating George Psychoundakis's memoir, Paddy was able to resume work on his own, much-postponed book about Greece, which he had first discussed with Jock Murray in 1947.

To Jock Murray   Poros
19 July 1954   Greece

Dear Jock,

I've got Miss Boulanger's letter[3] yesterday with the first instalment of Ghyka's translation, which seems to me absolutely tiptop.[4] I tremble to think <u>what a hash</u> anyone else might have made of it (judging by 'The Tree'), and am glad we stuck to our guns. I have suggested one or two very small emendations, and airmailed it back to him this morning, with counsels of urgency, so he will probably send it to you within an hour of receipt. It might be as well to telephone him when you get this.

[1] The southern coast of Asia Minor.
[2] The largest lake of Turkey, in the far east of the country.
[3] Jane Boulanger was rights manager at John Murray.
[4] Matila Ghyka's French translation of *The Violins of Saint-Jacques* would be published by Albin Michel in 1956.

Good news about Albin Michel[1] biting, though I have a secret snobbish hankering for Gallimard; but any port (or <u>nearly</u> any!) in a storm! <u>Can we wangle another translator's fee from them for Matila?</u> He really is so terribly broke. I'm so glad that something of his is under consideration for *Cornhill*.

I'm delighted about the 1000th *Cornhill* and long for it to arrive. Many thanks for copies of *The Tree* and *Violins*.

Any decision about *Over the Hills* yet? It's about a furlong ahead with me by now. Last week I thought it would be a photo-finish with *Running into Danger*.[2] But the latter has mysteriously dropped behind …

Now, about George's <u>map</u>, the <u>incomplete</u> tracing of which I left at Auberon Herbert's. What I suggest is this: that we get the indexer going at once, and all proper names sent out to me. I can get the necessary maps from our Military Attaché here, also tracing bumf, and send you a filled in map in no time.

Do you know if *The Phoenix Nest* has ever been used as a title? I'm beginning to toy with it as a possible for my present magnum opus.

Patrick K[inross] came here for three days, then Cyril Connolly and his bride,[3] which was not as difficult going as it might have been. The Great Eroica Rawbum comes next month. Don't be disturbed about this, as I seclude myself for <u>7 hours a day</u> in my hermitage in the bowels, and am working like anything, and allowing nothing to interfere. My diligence fills everyone with awe. I'm allowing myself a week's hol at the beginning of Sept, but till then the grindstone and my nose cohere.

All the best,
yours ever
Paddy

[1] Albin Michel and Gallimard are both French publishers.
[2] Suggested titles for PLF's English translation of the book by George Psychoundakis, eventually published as *The Cretan Runner*.
[3] PLF did not much like Connolly's second wife, Barbara Skelton.

P.S. You ask what should happen to the *Cornhill* fee for the pseudo-Betjeman.[1] Yes, could you please have it sent to Hambros, also anything accruing from *Realités*[2] and Michel. Do you think we could get the Treasury to give permission for another £200?[3] I hope to stay here till mid-October, and will need it fairly soon. There are other ways, but that is best!

P.P.S. Since Amiot-Dumont's advance before publication, we don't seem to have had a word from them – not a *centime*, and not a single cutting.[4] I saw the book boldly displayed in several Paris windows. Could we ask Mrs Bradley how things are going?

To Diana Cooper   c/o Mr Nikos Hadjikyriakos-Ghikas
1 June 1955   Hydra
                                                               Greece

Diana Darling,

A letter has been sizzling to the boil for the past 2–3 weeks, when suddenly, ages late, along comes yours; so off the fire with it and here goes.

Why I seem to be a sluggard in answering is that we went to Cyprus (where I had to give 2 lectures for the British Council) and then to Beirut to see Eddie Gathorne-Hardy and George Seferis, the Greek poet-ambassador there (the T. S. Eliot of Helios[5]), being away over three weeks, during which time the idiots in the post office, undirected by anyone, forwarded letters

[1] PLF's parody 'In Honour of Mr John Betjeman', first published in the *Cornhill Magazine* in the summer of 1954. See *Dashing for the Post*, pp. 85–6.
[2] A French-language illustrated magazine, published between 1946 and 1978.
[3] Foreign exchange controls meant that UK nationals were restricted in the amount they were allowed to take out of the country.
[4] A French edition of PLF's *The Traveller's Tree* was published by Amiot-Dumont under the title *Les Caraïbes* in 1953.
[5] PLF had formed a lasting friendship with Seferis while working for the British Council in Athens after the war.

to the Consulate in Athens, where yours must have roosted in a pigeonhole for over a week before taking wing back to Hydra and finally alighting here.

I wonder why Matila Ghyka[1] said that about our leaving here in mid-June! I hadn't written to him for ages, and don't think it is true; though the Athens Ghikas may suddenly decide to come here, as they might have any time during the last few months. But, alas, I think the end is in sight – and this month? two? perhaps a bit more ... The difficult thing is they keep encouraging us to stay on and on and assuring friends they are delighted, but obviously one must move long before the faintest hint of the reverse was perceptible. So, darling, if you are coming to Greece this summer, come soon! It's not quite as nice as last year, as Sophia and her husband are back with the Ghikas [in Athens] ... and now we have a local Albanian oaf who can't cook for toffee. He is much closer to the animal kingdom than the human, and would be happiest grazing peacefully in a field. Also the electric machine in the town has gone wonky and we only have lights two nights on, two nights off, which means a lot of play with petrol lamps and candles. These are all delible faults and it is still heavenly, in its primitive way, and you would easily rise above them.

I say, what an exciting plan about the *Eros*![2] Do you think you can pull it off? I would simply love to come, especially, if, as you think, it might be at the end of August or beginning of September, which, especially Sept., is the best time of all for these islands. Joan, alas, thinks she ought to go home & look after her mum. Do try hard! You might come here first, if we are still installed, and be picked up. Any way, if it doesn't come off, do let's go on a lovely jaunt somewhere, not too desperately expensive if possible, as I will

[1] Prince Matila Costiesco Ghyka (1881–1965), Romanian novelist, mathematician, historian, philosopher and diplomat, married Eileen O'Connor, daughter of a British diplomat. An English-language edition of his memoir *The World Mine Oyster* was published in 1961, with an introduction by PLF.
[2] Diana Cooper was hoping to borrow the shipping magnate Stavros Niarchos's second-best yacht, *Eros II*, for a cruise in September.

be able to get hold of a hundred quid, I think, but not much more; though I may strike lucky with something. I have hopes of being finished then, and ceasing to be a bore to you, Joan, and all one's friends. It has been really intolerable. I keep thinking of you at Chantilly, and wishing I were there, but it's far too magical and exciting to do a great deal of work, and I've got to shed my burden (like Christian after the Slough of Despond[1]) before being free again. I wish I wrote faster.

Cyprus was detestable, the Cypriots sullen and, in a wet way, disaffected, the English the sweepings of the Colonial Office, well-intentioned, unimaginative, blundering, stubborn and fifth-rate. What an idiotic and unnecessary mess our new prime minister has landed Greece and England in over that island! Pray God Harold Macmillan handles it better;[2] though, thanks to the idleness and bad manners of his predecessor,[3] it's become from child's play an Augean stable.[4] I wish I'd been at Chantilly when he was there, to try and pick up what he feels about it. Do tell me all about his stay. I bet he's a 1000 times better boss for J.J.:[5] more guts, less smarm. Please expand about him.

The only day I enjoyed in Cyprus was driving to the tomb of Umm Haram, Mohammed's aunt, whose uncle stumbled there, pitching her onto a rock and breaking her neck. It's a little congerie [jumble] of domes and cupolas and minarets in a great clump of

---

[1] In The Pilgrim's Progress.
[2] Sir Anthony Eden had become prime minister two months earlier, in April 1955; Harold Macmillan had succeeded him as Foreign Secretary.
[3] Relations between Britain and Greece were being poisoned by British policy towards Cyprus. Greek opinion had long regarded the island of Cyprus, a British colony, as rightfully Greek. A nationalist popular movement named EOKA agitated for unification with Greece ('Enosis'). The situation was complicated by the presence of a substantial Turkish Cypriot minority on the island. Impatient with the lack of progress, EOKA had declared an armed struggle against British rule. The British authorities responded to the insurgency by declaring a state of emergency: the new governor of the island, Sir John Harding, formerly Chief of the Imperial General Staff, took unprecedentedly harsh measures to improve the security situation.
[4] One of the labours of Hercules was to clean the stables in which Augeas, King of Elis in the Peloponnese, kept 3,000 oxen, and which had not been cleaned for thirty years.
[5] Diana Cooper's son, John Julius, had recently joined the Foreign Service.

trees with shady fountains and pigeons fluttering and cooing everywhere, a *hodja*[1] in a huge white Mohammed II turban as painted
by Bellini,[2] sitting cross legged and silent, fasting for Ramadan, in
a great expanse of carpets, lanterns and green crescented banners
hanging in faded sheaves, the muted cooing echoing in vaults, the
sunlight slanting into the penumbra cut up into thousands of dust-
moted prisms and cylinders by the intricacy of lattices. All this
standing on the edge of a wonderfully mournful salt-lake still as a
looking-glass, in which the reflected minarets hang upside down a
few miles from the church where Richard Coeur de Lion married
Berengaria.[3]

I hadn't been to Beirut since the war, when, after being in hospital for ages in Cairo after a long time in Crete, I spent about
a month staying with May Spears[4] on the hills above. All the
European glamour has gone – red-lined *spahi* cloaks,[5] kepis, spruce
dashing English regiments and so on, but traces of jaded sophisti-
cation still linger in that domed and tram-haunted city. We stayed
in an old Maronite Christian hotel – Grand Hotel Bassoul – which
must have been the house of a Turkish Pasha or Wali in the past.
Herman Melville stayed there in 1860, and Gertrude Bell, I was
surprised to hear, discovered a robust young Syrian, kept him
in her room for a fortnight in an indissoluble embrace and only
let him out again when he had become a hollow-cheeked, etiol-
ated and stumbling wraith. The place reeks of Flecker.[6] It is half

[1] Muslim schoolmaster.
[2] Gentile Bellini's portrait of Sultan Mehmet II, painted in 1480, hangs in the National
Gallery, London.
[3] Berengaria of Navarre, traditionally known as 'the only English queen never to set foot
in the country', married Richard I on 12 May 1191, in the Chapel of St George at Limassol
on Cyprus.
[4] Lady Spears (1886–1968), the American novelist and amateur painter Mary Borden.
Known as 'May', she was married to Major-General Sir Edward Spears (1886–1974),
British Ambassador to Lebanon. During his stay, PLF sat for his portrait.
[5] The French North African *spahi* (light cavalry) regiments wore red jackets.
[6] The poet James Elroy Flecker (1884–1915) worked in the consular service in the eastern
Mediterranenan. PLF is thinking of Flecker's verse-drama *Hassan* (1922).

oriental – huge seraglio-like rooms dotted with plush Pierre Loti furniture[1] and brass things under a patina of dust, half Beckford & Horace Walpole, with gothic windows divided up by slender laths into the sort of tracery there must have been across the casements of Strawberry and Fonthill.[2] It was very pleasant lying there on enormously high beds in cool dilapidated rooms, listening to the clatter of trams, the cries of vendors clanking brass objects and muezzin answering muezzin, a faint rank whiff of kebabs and spices drifting in through those mock crusading windows. Occasional fierce argument between Druzes. (A friend of mine, during the war, was staying in the Normandie hotel in the next room to a brother officer in the Scots Guards called Bernard Bruce, who was engaged in a great love affair with a princess of the Djebel Druze. One night there was a great amorous hullabaloo next door, and finally a sudden crash of furniture collapsing followed by a few seconds' silence, and Bruce's voice saying *Oh, princess, vous avez cassé le printemps de mon lit.*)

The main reason for going to Beirut was to read great lumps out of my book to George Seferis, whose opinion I value more than anyone's about literature dealing with Greece. Thank heavens, it went well & encouragingly. He & his wife, Joan & I went to Byblos together, – you probably know it – the oldest continuously inhabited city in the world – Hittites, Assyrians, Phoenicians, Egyptians, Greeks, Romans, Saracens, Crusaders, Turks, Lebanese, French, Maronites, Jesuit fathers, Armenian grocers. Next day we went with E. Gathorne-Hardy – a charming, erudite, funny, David-Herbert-vintage[3] exquisite, working at the Embassy – to Baalbek, which I had never seen. I was bowled over by those colossal columns & the apricot and tired gold colour, the acanthus-explosions,

---

[1] Pierre Loti (1850–1923), naval officer and novelist, known for his depictions of 'Eastern exoticism'.

[2] Strawberry Hill and Fonthill Abbey, the Gothic Revival houses of Horace Walpole and William Beckford.

[3] The Hon. David Alexander Reginald Herbert (1908–95), socialite and interior decorator, described by Ian Fleming as 'the Queen of Tangier'.

the Vanbrugh semicircles of pillars and scallop-roofed Kedleston alcoves[1] under broken pediments that should be ensconcing statues of Marlborough or Turenne in togas and Roman armour and full-bottomed wigs, with marshals' batons propped on their thighs. It was very peculiar, leaving these Augustan precincts, to find oneself nose to nose with over a hundred camels of a bedouin caravan, with, balanced on their humps, chestnut-coloured men scowling through kohl under joined blue eyebrows and headdresses; occasionally a matted girl tattooed all round the nose and chin like blue dribble; all of them padding off somewhere on feet like expanding boxing-gloves.

We had dinner with the Peakes[2] the night we got back, with my publisher Jock Murray & his wife & Baba Metcalfe[3] & Ld Feversham,[4] who had been to Petra together then back here, where the Murrays came for two days, leaving with a great sheaf of MSS. Osbert Lancaster[5] came for two days as well, bristling and as cratered as a planet, his eyes swivelling in their sockets as, in cavernous sub-Bowra, last year's gossip was retailed. Both he and the Murrays moved on from here to Spetsai an hour south of here, the next island stepping-stone, where the Alan Mooreheads[6] have taken a house. Do you know them? I don't, but everyone seems to like them very much. I believe we are going to meet for luncheon either here or there next week. I think these islands will be awful in

[1] PLF is referring to the façade of Kedleston Hall in Derbyshire, the south front designed by Robert Adam to resemble a Roman temple, with six tall columns supporting a portico, and a double-armed stone stairway leading to the entrance: inspired, it is said, by the Arch of Constantine in Rome.

[2] Sir Charles Peake (1897–1958), British Ambassador to Greece (1951–7), and his wife Catherine.

[3] Lady Alexandra Metcalfe (1904–95), daughter of Lord Curzon, Viceroy of India, called 'Baba Sahib' by her father's Indian servants, and the nickname stuck. She was the last surviving witness to the Duke of Windsor's wedding to Mrs Wallis Simpson in June 1937.

[4] Charles William Slingsby 'Sim' Duncombe, 3rd Earl of Feversham (1906–63).

[5] Osbert Lancaster (1908–86), cartoonist and author, who had been press attaché in the British embassy in Athens after the war, while PLF was working for the British Council. Like his friend and collaborator John Betjeman, Lancaster was a John Murray author.

[6] The Australian writer and war correspondent Alan Moorehead (1910–83) and his wife Lucy.

another two years. The remoter islands of the outer Cyclades will be the place then – Ios, Pholegandros, Amorgos, Icaria, and the more desolate islets of the Dodecanese ... Our immediate visitors are going to be Eddie Gathorne-Hardy, Patrick Kinross, perhaps Nancy Rodd [Mitford] for a day or two. What about you? At the moment, Joan's childhood neighbour Coote Lygon[1] is here, a farmer, spectacled and what Americans call homely, quiet and very nice, sister of the two more spectacular ones. We spent an enjoyable evening yesterday reading aloud from *The Voyage of the Beagle*, grave and comic descriptions of fauna in Patagonia and Tierra del Fuego. This island has been suffering from a plague of horseflies for the past few days. They are unknown here – why should they visit this horseless rock? – and I think they must have been blown here by a dreadful scirocco last week, straight from the Sahara like those armadas of pelicans hustled by hurricanes for thousands of miles across the Caribbean sea when the wind fills their pouches. These horseflies are almost as big as wrens, and their proboscises, destined to pierce the withers of a Suffolk Punch, are as sharp as bradawls; denied their legitimate quarry, they assault us as we step naked from the sea and riddle us like colanders. They have immense *cloisonné* turquoise eyes of disarming integrity, but never look one straight in the face, I'm sorry to say, as though they were weighed down with heavy secrets. There are also a number of centipedes about, and always in some muddle trying to crawl up walls and falling off, floundering in puddles, going down drains or getting trodden on. One would think that, with all their advantages, they would have gone further. They make one proud of being a biped ...

I'm very excited, as Cretan George's book is out (they are sending you a copy) and has had a splendid review in the *Sunday Times* by Dilys Powell.[2] I wish Mr H. Macmillan would read it – it

[1] Lady Dorothy 'Coote' Lygon (1912–2001), fourth daughter of the 7th Earl Beauchamp, a spinster until her unexpected late marriage to Robert Heber-Percy in 1985, two years before his death.
[2] George Psychoundakis's *The Cretan Runner*. Dilys Powell's favourable review of the book appeared in the *Sunday Times* on 22 May 1955.

might drop a scruple or pennyweight of favourable feeling towards Greece (a country he actually knows very well). Do try and persuade people to buy it if you get a chance, as it's the poor charcoal-burning author's only chance of making any dough and escaping from the beastly vendettas brewing for him in Crete. I've read two books I've loved recently: *Cards of Identity* by Nigel Dennis and *Going to the Wars* by John Verney.[1] Have you got them? If not, please let me know and I'll have them sent.

Do make Pam pursue the *Eros* play![2] Think, the whole archipelago and the Levant! I've written a long thing in my book (which Stephen Spender is printing in one of the next two month's *Encounter* – the new *Horizon*) evoking all the different parts of Greece – mountains, towns, rivers, islands etc. – by the sounds that conjure them up, pages and pages, which I'll send when I get a typed copy, as bait.[3] I had a rather frivolous piece in last month's in the form of a letter,[4] as an afterthought to the great debate that has been going on about Logical Positivism, between Freddie Ayer who has just been here and Philip Toynbee, my drunk friend. (I mean, taking me as *l'homme moyen sobre* ...[5])

I must finish this and get it off, Diana dearest. Do please write back at once so that I can catch up; and fondest love, hugs, embraces and devotion

from Paddy
X X X X X X

[1] *Cards of Identity* is a novel, a satire on psychology and class prejudice. *Going to the Wars* is a memoir of the author's service during the Second World War.
[2] PLF hoped that Stavros Niarchos might be influenced by his mistress, Pamela (ex-wife of Winston Churchill's son, Randolph) to lend Diana Cooper his yacht.
[3] The piece, 'Sounds of the Greek World', did not appear in *Encounter* until the following June. PLF used it again as the final chapter of *Roumeli* (1966).
[4] 'Sense and Nonsense: a Footnote', *Encounter*, May 1955.
[5] 'The averagely sober man.'

George Seferis deplored Paddy's failure to make progress with his book on Greece. 'Tell him that he should stop gathering material,' Seferis had written to Joan on Christmas Eve 1954: 'he should throw away all his notes and concentrate on writing ...'

'I am afraid he is too much "Penelope-ising" with that book,' Seferis continued, referring to Odysseus's wife, who each night undid the weaving she had done during the previous day. But Paddy was incorrigible, as this letter shows.

To George Seferis   c/o Mr Nikos Hadjikyriakos-Ghikas
Greece

27 May 1955

Hydra

Dear George,

Thank you so much for your card with the news that the picture of my lost youth[1] is now under your hospitable roof. I do hope it's not too much of a nuisance. Lock [it] in an attic, like Dorian Grey, and may the proxy stigmata of my vicissitudes accumulate under the cobwebs. If anybody kind and long-suffering should ever be leaving for Athens during the next two months, and could bear to bring it, would you ask him or her to drop it at the British Embassy there, % Lady Peake, or Hamish Mackenzie?[2] Rolled up, it shouldn't be too cumbersome ... Thank you very much indeed for having taken so much trouble about it and many apologies for the boredom. It isn't a very good picture, but I know my mother is very keen on having it. '*Ça dégonfle* [deflates] Paddy' as Máro [Seferis's wife] would say ...

Osbert [Sitwell][3] came here for a couple of days and has moved on to Spetsai to stay with Alan Moorehead. (One could move through the whole archipelago like telling the beads of a rosary.)

[1] See footnote on p. 97.
[2] Second secretary at the British embassy in Athens.
[3] Sir Francis Osbert Sacheverell Sitwell, 5th Baronet (1892–1969), writer, brother of Edith Sitwell and Paddy's friend, Sacheverell Sitwell.

Do you know anyone in Athens who could write a decent review of George Psychoundakis's book? I ask without shame as he (naturally) will get all the pennies from it and it is his only chance of ever getting any money and, perhaps, escaping from τὰ οἰκογενειακά του [his family problems].[1] A good review of the English version in an Athenian paper might encourage a Greek publisher to take it on. Is it the sort of thing you would care, or have the time, to do?

Joan has ordered Heywood Hill to send you a copy of *Cards of Identity* by Nigel Dennis, an author neither of us had heard of before, which gives one the same kind of pleasure, very rare in English, as *Paludes* or *Les Caves du Vatican*.[2] Let us know what you think of it.

Do you remember a letter I wrote to the *Καθημερινή* [*Kathimerini* – a Greek newspaper] last autumn, asking for certain information about μάγγες [*manges*][3] etc.?[4] (I know you read it, because you expressed your fears to Joan that I was Penelopising too much – and so I am.) None of the answers were any good until two months ago. I got an immense bundle of 20 closely (and exquisitely) written foolscap sheets, a complete treasure chest of extremely recondite, and (according to all who have seen it) absolutely reliable information, giving full etymologies, tracing the history of the χασάπικο [*hasapiko*][5] back to the Byzantine Roman 'macellaricum' & quoting a host of authorities. They were sent by a Mr Kosta Papadopolos of 11 Michael Mitzaki St, Athens. Since then, we are in constant correspondence, and the last letter is 50 pages long, answering questions about Lazi, Pomaks, Kizilbashi in Thrace, the Paulicians, the Cumans & Pechenegs (Πατσινάκοι), the possible

[1] A Cretan vendetta in which Psychoundakis's sister was killed.
[2] *Paludes* (1895) and *Les Caves du Vatican* (1914), by André Gide, both favourites of PLF's.
[3] A *mangas* (pl. *manges*) is 'a working-class man who displays excessive self-confidence or arrogance as well as unusual appearance or behaviour (e.g. dress, movements, vocabulary, tone of voice)'. Paddy refers to the *manges* in *Roumeli*.
[4] PLF's letter was published on 8 December 1954. His chief concern was with the etymology and meaning of the Greek words and terms.
[5] The *hasapiko* (literally, 'butchers' dance') is a Greek urban folk dance in 4/4 time originating from Istanbul and Asia Minor and performed in a highly disciplined way by two or more people in a row.

Jewish origin of the Lacedaemonians![1] (see chap 12, Second Book of the Apocrypha – but don't worry – I'm keeping it dark!), the Trapezuntine crypto-christians of Of,[2] all the Μουσουλμανοφανεῖς [ostensibly Muslim] of Asia Minor, the Pelasgo-Phrygian descent of the Tsebékides[3] etc. etc. He obviously knows good ancient Greek, as well as Turkish, Persian and Arabic. George K[atsimbalis] is absolutely enthralled, as he's a complete mystery man. He has asked everywhere, and discovered that he is a 'well known scholar' (according to someone in the National Library) married to a 'well known actress' that no one's ever heard of. I think he must be about 60, a refugee from Asia Minor. He writes terrific *Katharevousa*.[4] Whenever George goes to the N. Library, he has always just left five minutes before … He ends his last letter with the words 'I must apologise for my delay in writing, but I suffer from a serious heart disease which has held me up. But I have done nothing else but prepare this letter for the last fifteen days.' I simply must find him when I go to Athens next, and, if possible, organise a meal with him, George, Niko [Ghika], and Joan. I wish you were going to be there. The extraordinary thing is that all this volume of information is documented and cross-checked, and bears no similarity at all to the splendid mythopoetic exegeses of Thanos.[5] It reminds one of Auden's lines:

[1] See *Mani: Travels in the Southern Peloponnese* (London, 1958), pp. 8–11.

[2] Of is the name of a river valley east of Trebizond (Trabzon) in northeast Turkey (the area often known as Pontus).

[3] PLF must mean the *zeibekides* (*zeybeks*), irregular Turkish troops living in western Asia Minor. They gave their name to the *zeibekiko* dance, which is the other chief traditional Greek urban dance from Asia Minor, along with the *hasapiko*. It is in the thrilling 9/8 rhythm and is performed by a single dancer, showing off his or her agility and individuality.

[4] A form of modern Greek conceived in the early nineteenth century as a compromise between Ancient Greek and the demotic Greek used at the time. By the twentieth century it was seldom used except for official purposes.

[5] Thanos Veloudios, a friend of PLF's in Athens. While serving in the Greek air force in Turkey during the Greco-Turkish war in 1920, he had landed his plane outside the Ottoman military academy and hoisted the Greek flag up its mast. His passionate interest in Greek folk rituals and their origins was such that he dressed in velvet *fustanellas* (skirts as worn by the *evzones*, the elite soldiers from the Greek Presidential Guard).

... Lone scholars, sniping from the walls
Of learned periodicals,
Our facts defend,
Our intellectual marines,
Landing in little magazines,
Capture a trend ...[1]

but still more of Browning's 'Grammarian's Funeral':

So, with death's grappling hands at strife,
Ground he at grammar;
Still, in the rattle, parts of speech were rife
While he could stammer.
He settled *Hoti's* business – let it be!
Properly based *Oun*,
Gave us the doctrine of the enclitic *De*,
Dead from the waist down![2]

I was shattered to learn, two weeks ago, that poor [Professor] Dawkins[3] had died. He fell down dead suddenly crossing the quad in Wadham. Maurice Bowra rushed out, and there he was in a heap. 'He looked like a child as he lay there,' Maurice writes, 'with none of that anguish which he had on his face as he hobbled along on two sticks. I shall miss him very much, as he belonged to a wonderful old cultivated world.' I got a very cheerful, lively, posthumous letter from him two days after.

It was a great delight seeing you and Máro again in Beirut, and very many thanks for kindnesses. Do try and get to Greece, and come here for a few days. The hillside under my window is dotted with women in faded pink and blue skirts cutting the corn with

---

[1] From 'Under Which Lyre: A Reactionary Tract for the Times' (1946).
[2] From Browning's 'A Grammarian's Funeral: Shortly after the Revival of Learning in Europe' (1855), slightly misquoted.
[3] See footnote on p. 67.

sickles. They have knocked off for the moment, and are sitting round among the sheaves under a tree, almost, but not quite, overflowing the shadow of an olive tree, like a flock at midday. Joan sends lots of love to you both.

Yours ever
Paddy

Of the Mitford sisters, Paddy was especially close to Deborah, Duchess of Devonshire, but he was also friendly with several of her siblings, including Nancy, who came to stay with Paddy and Joan on Hydra in June 1955. In her letters she addressed Paddy as 'Darling Whack', and Paddy & Joan as 'Mr and Mrs Whack'.

To Nancy Mitford   c/o Niko Ghika
8 August 1955   Hydra
                                                     Greece

My dear Nancy,

Thank you so much for the beautiful Corbusier[1] font. It arrived yesterday, when Niko was here for a couple of days, so I didn't fail to rub it in, to the rousing strains of our anthem. Yes, of course I'd like to be a founder member of the league.[2] Members unknown to each other meeting clandestinely should display a crumpled copy of *L'Humanité* and an empty sardine tin respectively as proof of *bona fides*.[3] The password should be '*propre*'

---

[1] Charles-Édouard Jeanneret, known as Le Corbusier (1887–1965), pioneer of modern architecture.

[2] Nancy Mitford had proposed a league against Le Corbusier, whose church at Ronchamp was completed in June 1955.

[3] Le Corbusier had visited the Soviet Union and undertaken several commissions for the Soviet government; *L'Humanité* is a French newspaper associated with the Communist Party. PLF thought that Le Corbusier's *Cité Radieuse* in Marseille (1947–52) looked like stacked sardine tins.

[clean], with counter-sign, of course, *'gai'*[1] – like 'St Hélène', 'Schönbrunn' in *L'Aiglon*.[2]

Poor Cyril [Connolly] mopes about the house,[3] but seems to cheer up at meals (those gastronomic wonders), but only like the conditioned reactions of Pavlov's dogs that dribble at the sound of dinner-bell, whether followed by a meal or not. Beef steaks are sometimes almost as effective on broken hearts as on black eyes. I wish we had some. Maurice [Bowra] arrived last week, so the house cheerfully booms and reverberates. Cyril and I sleep out of doors and are woken up each morning by the barking of the Non-U Indicator[4] which announces Christo's arrival.

Coote's house is a great success, a sort of branch office in the port.[5] The Mad Boy[6] has just been staying; Patrick [Kinross?] is there now and also Coote's coz., Ly Lettuce A. Cooper styled Duchess,[7] who I didn't know. Rather a surprising appearance, slightly Bruce Bairnsfather,[8] like a clean-shaven Old Bill; but

---

[1] *'Tout est si propre et si gai!'* Nancy Mitford would exclaim, 'whenever a particularly squalid or doleful scene came in sight'. See p. 272.

[2] 'Sainte-Hélène' and 'Schönbrunn' are the passwords used between the Maréchal Marmont and Séraphin Flambeau in Edmond Rostand's play *L'Aiglon*, first performed in 1900.

[3] Connolly's second wife, Barbara Skelton, was having an affair with the publisher George Weidenfeld.

[4] PLF was looking after a dog called Spot, who 'barked like mad' at some visitors, but not others. 'I'm afraid old Spot's an unerring Non-U indicator,' commented Nancy Mitford. Her article 'The English Aristocracy' (*Encounter*, September 1955) had suggested 'a useful formula: U (for upper class) speaker versus non-U-speaker'. See p. 272.

[5] Coote Lygon was working as social secretary at the British embassy in Athens, and living in a house near Piraeus.

[6] Robert Vernon Heber-Percy (1911–87), 'a wild and pugnacious character', who had inherited Faringdon House and its estate in Oxfordshire from his companion, the eccentric composer and novelist (Lord) Gerald Berners. Before meeting Berners he had a brief but hectic career in the cavalry, acted as an extra in Hollywood, worked in a Lyons Corner House (until spilling soup over a customer), and helped run a nightclub.

[7] Lady Lettice Mildred Mary Ashley-Cooper (1911–90), daughter of the 9th Earl of Shaftesbury, and great-granddaughter of the 1st Duke of Westminster.

[8] Cartoonist: creator of the character 'Old Bill', curmudgeonly soldier in the trenches of the First World War, with walrus moustache and balaclava.

very nice. My *oraison funèbre* [funeral oration] in the cathedral of Herakleion went splendidly. No nerves for once, so I was able to send long Demosthenian periods ringing and echoing round the central dome and its attendant cupolas ... V. gratifying.

Many thanks for the cutting.[1] It's very good but wicked indeed and has caused much amusement and anger but no harm. You might have used Roger [Hinks]'s[2] remark after being shown over the Agora: '<u>Now</u> I really understand what agoraphobia means!'

I feel very excited at the approach of the yachting trip,[3] whatever the human hazards, and although the whole archipelago will be still tainted and reeking from E. Maxwell's[4] presence.

Everybody sends lots of love and wishes you were here!
Love Paddy

---

[1] Nancy Mitford's article, 'Wicked Thoughts in Greece', *Sunday Times*, 24 July 1955; republished in Charlotte Mosley (ed.): *A Talent to Annoy: Essays, Articles and Reviews, 1929–1968* (1986). She described Athens as 'probably the ugliest capital in Europe'.

[2] Roger Hinks (1903–63), art historian with a particular interest in Caravaggio; director of the British Council in Athens, 1954–9.

[3] Aboard Niarchos's yacht.

[4] Elsa Maxwell (1883–1963), American hostess, scalp-hunter and gossip columnist, said to have introduced Maria Callas to Aristotle Onassis; she is parodied as Edythe Van Hopper in Hitchcock's film *Rebecca* (1940).

Paddy left Hydra in the autumn of 1955. The ill feeling engendered by the situation in Cyprus was poisoning relations between Britons and Greeks. An official at the Greek Aliens Office on Hydra attempted to have Paddy and several other British nationals deported; and though this attempt came to nothing, it unsettled him. There was a heated exchange between Paddy and his old friend George Katsimbalis on the subject of Cyprus. 'I'm in such despair about it all,' Joan wrote to Seferis. 'George refused to dine with Paddy & me on my last night in Athens, which upset us dreadfully,' she continued. 'What are we to do? I can't think about it any more without bursting into tears.'

Paddy was once again able to borrow Gadencourt, the Smarts' house in Normandy, where he would remain until the following summer. But his unhappiness about the unpleasantness surrounding the subject of Cyprus persisted. 'Things get worse and worse,' Joan wrote to Seferis from Gadencourt in the spring of 1956. 'It is most depressing to be classed with Anthony Eden and hated for it …. Paddy has got so depressed that he can't finish his book, or rather, the first volume, which is supposed to be published this year.'

To Joan Rayner   Gadencourt
February 1956

Hurray No Hanging![1]

Forgot: Had dinner with Costa[2] on Wednesday. He was rather nice and touching.

My darling Muskin,

First of all, a trillion billion thanks for the most lovely dressing-gown I've ever seen. It really is the most sumptuous, sombre-splendid robe imaginable, the sort of thing in which an 18th century Whig magnate would trifle his mornings away among the busts and folios of a vast library while artists display pictures

[1] Presumably a reference to the Cyprus Emergency.
[2] Greek photographer Costa Achillopoulos, PLF's collaborator on *The Traveller's Tree* (1950).

and little turbaned blackamoors bring in madeira and glasses on silver trays and fallow deer graze under the oaks outside ... The initials are beautifully done, the colours lovely, and it fits as if a team of haberdashers had spun me in the middle of a cocoon of tape measures. Thank you very much indeed, darling!

I say, what exciting news about Yeomans Row![1] It sounds absolutely perfect, just the right size and a lovely street, near everything and with a very nice unpompous tradition. Isn't it where Freddie [Ashton] lives?[2] I do think it's clever of you. It would be so wonderful, apart from all else, to have somewhere to park books and all the vague moss that rolling stones somehow contrive to gather – and as you say, a perfect thing to swap against an Hydra *quelconque* [or anywhere] abroad (though I don't think actual Hydra would be much good until this bloody mess is over). I do long to hear how it all goes, and feel rather ashamed not being there to help, though I'd probably be a hindrance.

Now, at long last, a rough diary. I didn't write immediately after telephoning, as I wanted to include later events.

Getting to Paris, I had a lovely luncheon with Nancy [Mitford] (the Colonel,[3] a writer, Cora Caetani[4] and Lilia Ralli[5]), and in the afternoon, saw Mrs Bradley the agent and Albin Michel the publishers, and was excited to learn that *Les Violons de St Jacques* is coming out at the end of this month (I have now got three copies – I won't send it, but keep it till you arrive. Not very exciting cover, too much print on it; but lovely type. 350 francs). In the evening I picked up Eileen and Matila [Ghyka] at P. L. Weiller's[6] house in the Rue de la Faisanderie and took them to a sumptuous dinner at the Roi Gourmet. They seemed very happy in Paris – P.L.W. had lent them an entire flat

[1] Joan was in the process of buying a house in London, in Knightsbridge.
[2] It was.
[3] Nancy Mitford's lover Gaston Palewski, a colonel in the Free French Army during the Second World War, whom she had met in 1942, while he was in London attached to General de Gaulle's staff.
[4] Cora Caetani (1896–1974), née Antinori, married to Michelangelo Caetani.
[5] Jean 'Lilia' Ralli (1901–78), Greek-born socialite, lifelong friend to Princess Marina, friendly with Cecil Beaton.
[6] Paul-Louis Weiller (1893–1993), French industrialist and philanthropist.

in the largest of his many houses, with servants and as many meals as they wanted: a wonderful treat for them. Eileen and I got rather drunk and we all laughed a lot. Diana picked me up there, and off we set for Chantilly, my plan being to have a luxurious 3–4 days change, half work, half hol. It was absolutely lovely, as there was nobody else there. Nearly always Diana drove off to luncheon in Paris or else-where and I spent the day scribbling and having lovely meals in front of the fire, dinner with Diana in the *trumpoil* room,[1] then talk, crosswords, reading aloud, long playing records. Chantilly at its best, in fact. I forgot to say that my back by now was quite alright except for an occasional twinge. On what turned out to be the coldest day of the year I went for a long walk along the Senlis road, and when I got back, suddenly felt the whole thing starting again. Diana (like us too) is inclined to be rather no-nonsense about physical ailments, but it became so bloody that even she was convinced I wasn't shamming, and so I was packed off to bed, where it got so bad, especially in the mornings after waking up, that it was hard to find a comfortable pos-ition to be in, or to reach for anything. However, all this was looked after by a local doctor and a cheerful nun looking like a merry wife of Windsor came in to give injections and manage my back with some red-hot anti-phlogistine stuff, and the injections, pills, arse-bombs [suppositories] at night etc. saw to it, and kept one in a delicious semi-dopey state for almost five days, in the end wobbling about on two sticks. During this time Lilia Ralli and Odette Pol-Roger[2] came out to dinner by car with one of J[ohn]J[ulius]'s colleagues in Belgrade, and the roads to Paris were so frozen, skiddy & accident ridden that they had to stay, everyone drinking mulled wine round my bed, which was rather fun. I felt wonderfully pampered & rather wallowed in it. When I had been hobbling about a day or so, getting every minute better, Diana drove into Paris to see a great specialist who did a general check up, X ray etc. Says no slipped disc, only two (as far as I could make out) rheumatic torn muscles in the lumbar

[1] A small room at Chantilly used as a bar was covered with a series of *trompe-l'oeil* panels by Martin Battersby.
[2] Grande dame of the champagne family; a friend of Winston Churchill's.

region, which though this can hurt like hell, are absolutely nothing. Of course, by the time I got there, my two corroborative walking sticks were no longer necessary.

Matila and Eileen came out to Chantilly for luncheon and spent most of the day there, which they loved (they are back in St Scholastica's now, poor dears). By now I should have been back in Gadencourt, but 3 factors: 1) Marie's brother's death at Fécamp, for which she and Charles [servants at Gadencourt] went to Brittany, where he was buried, 2) the burst pipes which had inundated the kitchen & dining room & 3) the impending week-end with Annie[1] and Peter [Quennell] & the Ball almost at once afterwards – all these, cumulatively, lured me into staying on.

The weekend was heaven, consisting of Diana, self, Peter, Annie, Ld Gage[2] & Judy Montagu;[3] starting by a rendezvous at the Ritz, where every one drank a great deal of vodka, and (D & Ld G. had to have luncheon somewhere else) then a hilarious luncheon with lots of hot wine & Calvados in a bistro on the quais, as it was a Siberian, but beautiful day. We spent the afternoon in the Musée Victor Hugo in la Place des Vosges but were too late for the Carnavalet[4] which we had also planned, so R.V. [rendezvous] with Diana and off to Chantilly. It really was fun. Ld Gage is very nice, slightly moth-eaten, untidy, looks more like a painter or writer, v. knowledgeable about literature, music, heresies etc. We all laughed until the tears flowed at dinner. Annie got rather drunk in a very nice way (so did all, I think) and danced a wonderful ballet to the gramophone, which really was rather good. Sunday next day, with a huge luncheon party expected. Annie, Peter, Ld G. & I, wrapped up like Captain Oateses, set off across the park, which was quite empty and

[1] Ann Fleming (née Charteris, later Rothermere).
[2] Henry Rainald Gage, 6th Viscount Gage (1895–1982), who had inherited the title at the age of only sixteen.
[3] Judith Venetia 'Judy' Montagu (1923–72), daughter of the Hon. Edwin Montagu and Venetia Stanley, one of PLF's 'terrific pals'.
[4] Musée Carnavalet in the Marais, the museum of the history of Paris.

glittering white with snow, all the lakes frozen, teams of ducks and swans flapping about bewilderedly, and about a dozen beautiful herons. Three fallow deer turned up the other day! The castle looked like some giant Russian or Polish palace – on the pools a few people were skating and we wished we could too, so rather commonly slid about, then made our way, frozen by now, to the stables & then to The Tipperary bar in Chantilly for Guinness and coffee with calva[dos], also some pâte & gherkins, a great deal of wild and cheerful conversation, the atmosphere being like that after ski-ing in Austria or Switzerland. So back to luncheon, ravenous once more. There were (wait for it!) the Jebbs,[1] Fd Marshal & Mme Cattroux,[2] Rory Cameron (not too bad),[3] André de Staercke[4] (also sends love), & Ld & Lady Ismay.[5] I sat next to Ld Ismay, by Diana's design, and we talked a great deal about Cyprus, about which, as far as I can make out, his views are identical with ours! He thinks the only thing is a grand sweeping generous gesture on our part, or 'the eastern Mediterranean is useless for any NATO defence purposes as it is, apart from the loss of friends'. I was delighted and very surprised. What a charming man he is, and (I'm sure!) sound as a bell. Lots of Dumbleton talk, in a discreet way. Luncheon wasn't too bad, in spite of their usual horror on Sunday, and the miracle was, they were all away soon after three, and not even the threat of a dropper in. So we had another lovely walk in the icy woods, tea and rum, and another cheerful dinner. Alas, Peter & Gage left next day, to be replaced by Ali Forbes,[6] about whom Annie feels just as you do, and I must say, me; though he was better

[1] Sir Gladwyn Jebb (1900–96), British Ambassador to France, and his wife Cynthia.
[2] General Georges Catroux (1877–1969) and his wife Marguerite.
[3] Roderick ('Rory') Cameron (1913–85), waspish American writer and influential interior decorator, who lived on the French Riviera.
[4] André de Staercke (1913–2001), former political advisor to the Belgian prince regent.
[5] General Hastings Lionel 'Pug' Ismay, 1st Baron Ismay (1887–1965), Secretary General of NATO, who had been Churchill's chief military adviser during the Second World War.
[6] Alastair Forbes 1918–2005, boorish writer, journalist and reviewer.

than I've seen him. He had just returned from Tangiers, where he had seen Cyril & Baby,[1] but was immensely discreet as though he had been sworn to silence (I shouldn't have thought he was Cyril's type much). It seems that B. is off for a kiff-smoking jaunt among the Atlas Caïds (or perhaps with someone Ali refused to mention), while Cyril returns to Malaga. What news your end?

Next day – Ball day[2] – everyone seemed to go to Paris by different ways: I with Annie & Aly, reading out loud from Claud Cockburn's autobiography[3] which seems marvellously funny. Annie, Diana, Judy & Lady Lambton[4] (who was met in Paris) had appointments with various people, connected with their costumes. I [set] off to a theatrical outfitters in Montmartre, not certain what to be, hankering a bit after Death's Head Hussar as Rupert of Hentzau,[5] but all was so tatty, that I decided on Bulwer Lytton, found lovely cravats, fobs, satin ties, flowered waistcoat etc, but rather a dreary, grey thick tight frock coat, & felt a bit distressed. Luncheon at the British Embassy, then, (very strange) everyone had to go to Mme de Noailles to get 'passports' with their fictitious names on, date of birth etc, profession. After this, all the women went to Guillaume the hairdresser to get their hair set for fantastic sums, all meeting at Pam Churchill's at 9 for a moving dinner with women's hair all in glue, each of them disappearing behind the scenes in turn for a final £10 twist of the tongs by M. Guillaume, who had been bought (to the fury of all Paris, which was the point) for the evening by Pam C. Diana went as Lady Blessington, wonderful claret coloured velvet dress,

---

[1] Cyril Connolly and his second wife Barbara Skelton, who would be divorced later that year. She would marry the publisher George Weidenfeld (1919–2016) immediately afterwards.

[2] The Countess Marie-Laure de Noailles was giving a ball to celebrate Mardi Gras, and had invited her guests to dress as writers and artists from the fifteenth or nineteenth centuries.

[3] The journalist Claud Cockburn had just published his first volume of memoirs, *In Time of Trouble* (1956).

[4] Belinda ('Bindy'), Lady Lambton, née Blew-Jones (1921–2003).

[5] The dashing, well-born villain who gives his name to the title of the 1898 novel by Anthony Hope, the follow-up to *The Prisoner of Zenda*.

with puffed sleeves painted like ermine, false *anglaises* [ringlets] that I wasn't crazy about, but a great success on the whole; Annie absolutely charming in a Josephine-Marie Louise dress, a great diamond star and a small empire tiara as Harriet Wilson, Pam as some kind of Elizabethan, Kitty Giles & Ly Lambton in 1890 dresses, with huge Boldini hats smothered in birds and osprey plumes as Mrs Patrick Campbell & Lady Windermere, Frank Giles[1] as a very convincing Bernard Shaw, P. L. Weiller as François Premier, Judy Montagu as George Eliot, Walter Goetz[2] as Cruickshank; and several others. I forgot to say that before setting off (I'd settled at the St Romain for the night, not being able to face the Louisiane) I changed my horrid coat for my wonderful new dressing gown, which looked magnificent with all the rest, and solved all! So, off we went to the ball.

There were lots of people standing to see the arrivals in spite of falling snow, and inside this enormous house, the floor and stair carpets were scattered with playing cards, which gave it an amusingly raffish look. Of course I'd lost my 'passport', so it was rather difficult to get in, and needed a long confab of butlers, and the backing of the others & everything written out anew. People went up one by one to blasts from trumpets, their bogus names and dates were announced, up the strewn stairs to Mme de Noailles dressed, I think, as a very abstruse Nerval[3] heroine with great ivy clad branches sprouting like antlers from her monstrous head. But – and this was the great point of the whole thing – the splendour of the costumes knocked one sideways. It is the sort of thing one could never see in England. Not only the splendour, but the literary research, punctilio, exactitude

---

[1] Frank Giles (b. 1919), foreign correspondent and later editor of the *Sunday Times*, married to Lady Katherine 'Kitty' Sackville.
[2] Walter Goetz (1911–95), German-born artist and cartoonist, came as the English caricaturist and illustrator George Cruikshank (1792–1878).
[3] Gérard de Nerval (1808–55), writer, poet, essayist and translator. In fact, Marie-Laure de Noailles went dressed as the heroine of 'Délie, *objet de plus haute vertu*', a poem by her ancestor, the sixteenth-century poet Maurice de Scève.

and perfection of detail. One was all at once surrounded by Ingres, Davids, Delacroix, Watteaux, Clouets, Van Loos etc. of unimpeachable verisimilitude and often of great beauty. It had been so planned that nobody was redundant. There were lots of quite funny ones – a cissy Pierre Loti in naval uniform, D'Annunzio, Petrus Borel with removable wolf's head;[1] a lovely Italian girl dressed as a Sargent picture of Ctss Annina Morosini. Numbers of monks, *abbés mondains*, a cardinal or two. Quantities of powder & patch, as you can imagine. It seems the buffet was awful. The drinks were plentiful and good. But there was scarcely anywhere to sit. Diana, Annie, Harold Acton[2] & I managed to make a huddle for an hour or so, but not at a table. It was lovely seeing Harold as Beckford, very convincing indeed, with powdered hair <u>planted</u> for the evening it looked, strand by strand on his bald pate.[3] Georges Bernier[4] was very good as some revolutionary poet – Fabre d'Eglantine? – with a powdered wig but open collar, as in portraits of Mirabeau; Peggy [Guggenheim][5] rather [illegible] 'Marquise', Henri Kell an excellent Incroyable [Scarlet Pimpernel]. I was very much on the look out for Balthus,[6] who was there but no luck. One awful American woman had actually come as Joan of Arc, can you beat it? with a breastplate and a fleurs-de-lys covered skirt. There were some very good Grandville[7] animals and fabulous, faintly

---

[1] Petrus Borel (1809–59), writer, subject of a biography by Enid Starkie, *Petrus Borel: The Lycanthrope* (1954).

[2] Harold Mario Mitchell Acton (1904–1994) writer, scholar and aesthete. As an Oxford undergraduate in the early 1920s he had declaimed passages from *The Waste Land* through a megaphone from the balcony of his rooms (an episode fictionalised in Evelyn Waugh's *Brideshead Revisited*, through the character Anthony Blanche).

[3] William Beckford (1760–1844) novelist and art collector, and eccentric recluse, was notorious for his extravagance.

[4] Georges Bernier (1911–2001), founder and editor, with his wife Rosamond, of the arts magazine *L'Oeil*.

[5] Marguerite 'Peggy' Guggenheim (1898–1979), American art collector.

[6] The artist Balthasar Klossowski de Rola (1908–2001), known as Balthus.

[7] J. J. Grandville (1803–47), caricaturist.

anthropomorphic creatures from Brueghel or Bosch. I think you would have liked it for about an hour. Almost the best was a queer actor-manager called Peter Glenville,[1] who went as Byron just after swimming the Hellespont, streaming with transparent green oilskin, crusted with winkles, mussels and limpets, a-drip with seaweed. Wonderfully good-looking. Annie fell for him, having heard he was only <u>nine</u> parts queer. But her face fell when it turned out, on first hand authority from a queer informant, to be ten.[2] I stayed very late, talking to some Breton bagpipers who, about five, suddenly filled those emptying halls with pibrochs, and then trailed unsteadily to bed. Well, I'm glad I saw it, but feel (now) a secret theory that it is not a higher level of taste and of literacy that makes the French do this sort of thing so much better, and above all more earnestly than we do. I think it's a subconscious longing to resurrect and piece together a history that events have mangled, buried, hung drawn & quartered; a few hours of exorcism of Vichy, Dreyfus, F. Faure,[3] Boulanger,[4] the Commune, Sedan, Napoleon III, Louis Philippe, and even Napoleon & the Fall of the Bastille, though many would stop here: a compensation process that is probably officially satisfied in England by crowns, coronets, robes, tabards, redcoats & bearskins, pierrots, cowboys, long noses, or drag.

Well, that was that. Back to Chantilly for an afternoon & night to collect everything and recover, then here, everyone back to England, Diana off to Rome, me back on the evening train, getting here after dark. It was terribly cold, in spite of dear Marie's fires. Awful description of turning up in the morning after the pipe burst, finding a foot and a half of water (it sounds incredible) in the kitchen, several inches in the dining room

[1] Peter Glenville (born Peter Patrick Brabazon Browne) (1913–96), actor and director.
[2] Glenville's life partner was the American impresario Hardy William Smith (1916–2001).
[3] Félix François Faure (1841–99), President of France at the time of the Dreyfus affair, who died in flagrante.
[4] Georges Ernest Jean-Marie Boulanger (1837–91), nicknamed 'Général Revanche', French general and politician who advocated aggressively nationalist policies.

(none, thank God, in the living room), bailing, sweeping, drying, plumbing, poor Marie & Charles! Sue all in black for her brother; she found some consolation in describing the funeral, the quantities of wreaths, the reverence of the Bretons – '*ils se taisaient pendant une heure – pas même un murmure, monsieur! Les gens d'ici feraient bien de les imiter; en Normandie on se croirait à une foire...!*'[1] Thank heavens, there is absolutely no visible damage. But it almost seems as if the cold has got into the house's bones. Even un-*frileux* me[2] finds one's teeth chattering, though I've been back 3 days now. Perhaps I ought to light a fire in the dining room. I felt terribly depressed at first. This is the nadir of the year, black, spiteful weather, a bitter wind, ragged inter-mittent snow, the roads either ice or slush, everything raw and hostile. Darling, for God's sake wait a week before coming here. I wouldn't dream of encouraging anyone as it is at the moment, even the austerest. I feel bloody lonely and gloomy & miss you like anything, but I at least have got the remedy of throwing myself into a wild orgy of work. You would simply loathe it as it is; but everyone says it can't possibly last more than another few days, and the house will warm up. I'll light fires upstairs for two or three days before you come. This month is in the year what 5 a.m. is in relation to the twenty-four hours. There was nothing like it last time.

Enough of all that! Darling, what lovely news about your new gramophone! Following your instructions, I have only risked playing this one a bare minimum. The Beethoven has got slightly buckled, and makes a dreadful sound! Frank Giles has got the full libretto of *Don G[iovanni]* from the Mozart Society – in Italian & English – It's pre-war but probably still obtainable. Don't forget the missing D.G. record! Could you bring a lot of Easter cards

---

[1] 'They were completely silent for an hour – not even a murmur, monsieur. The people around here would do well to copy them. In Normandy it's like being at a fair.'
[2] PLF appears to mean that he doesn't usually feel the cold.

for Greeks? Also Paul Bloomfield's book (*Remarkable People?*)[1] and *British and American Philhellenes during the Greek War of Independence* by D. Dakin. (International University Booksellers, Store Street, W.C.1. 25/-)? Also Lawson *Greek Superstitions*[2] from the London Lib? I'm sending the Arabian Nights to Chesham Place tomorrow.

Darling Musk, I'm so sorry having been such a rotten letter writer. I always promise to develop the art of brisk letters frequently, instead of widely spaced deluges like this which probably no one reads. I meant to every day, but got in a sort of dopey trough of inaction in bed, then into a whirl ... André de Staercke (I think he's got a secret passion for me) has sent me a remarkable *Personal Religion in Ancient Greece* by a Dominican called Festugière, which is my bed and meal-time reading.[3] Very odd for a monk. Has anyone heard of him? I've also got, from Diana, a most extraordinary autobiography (stopped at proof stage by request of her family) called *Candles in the Sun*, by Lady Emily Lutyens (Eliz. Lutyens' mother, Billy Wallace's grandmother), about Krishnamurti & the whole theosophist movement.[4] I think you'll like it. V. v. odd.

My darling little Mopsa, lots and lots of hugs & kisses from your old

[1] Paul Bloomfield, *Uncommon People* (1955).
[2] Douglas Dakin (ed.), *British and American Philhellenes during the War of Greek Independence* (1955); J. C. Lawson, *Modern Greek Folklore and Ancient Greek Religion: A Study in Survivals* (1910).
[3] André-Jean Festugière (1898–1982), *Personal Religion Among the Greeks* (1954).
[4] The book was published the following year.

To Diana Cooper   Gadencourt
24? March 1956

Diana darling,

I do hope Saturday's gloom has evaporated. You did sound forlorn over the telephone. I'm sorry to hear about gentlemen not
complaining, when I cast my mind back to my frequent jeremiads –
though, I must say, it's nothing to touch the elegiac note that Joan
can achieve on occasions, as doleful a sound as the booming of
a bittern at dusk across a November fen ... It would be impossible, however, for the gloomiest not to cheer up this morning.
Not a cloud anywhere, sunbeams ricocheting from every window
pane, a number of unassuming flowers appearing for the first time,
fingertips crackling with St Elmo's fire.

Maurice [Bowra] was in tearing form, and Gadencourt's
cobwebs were fluttered by many a guffaw. Coote is still here,
I think a bit downcast at the prospect of her Currer Bell existence
in Constantinople,[1] or perhaps it's the effects of a hornbook[2] that
never leaves her called *The Slim Gourmet*.

I found two jays' feathers yesterday just before dinner and gave
them to Joan and Coote, who stuck them into their hair like Tiger
Lilies. Marie came in with the drinks a moment later and I asked
her '*si elle ne les trouvait pas follement* [foolishly] *chic?*' She gave
them a look, said, '*C'est un genre ...*' and went out.

Lots of love, darling Diana, and many anaconda hugs

from Paddy
XXXX

P.S. I've just learnt from a book that all Quakers are colour-
blind. Did you know this? I suppose they see everything
chocolate-colour.[3]

---

[1] Currer Bell was the pseudonym of Charlotte Brontë.
[2] A primer.
[3] Several of Britain's leading chocolate manufacturers were founded by Quakers.

Joan Rayner, later Joan Leigh Fermor, photographed at Epidaurus in 1946.

A moustachioed Paddy takes a quiet moment in German-occupied Crete. This snap was taken only a few days before the abduction of General Kreipe.

Paddy on horseback in Guatemala, 1948.

Balasha Cantacuzène, probably in the 1930s.

Paddy on the rocks, photographed in Greece by his lover Marie-Blanche Cantacuzène, known as 'Balasha'. This picture was taken in 1936 or 1937, when he was twenty-one or twenty-two and she was in her late thirties.

Paddy could rarely resist the temptation to sing or join a dance. This photograph was probably taken in Crete, after the war.

A lunch at the Vasilenas Taverna in Piraeus, 1954. Facing the camera is Stephen Spender; opposite him, smoking a cigar, is the 'Colossus' of Greek letters, George Katsimbalis; further back, wearing spectacles, is the painter Nikos ('Niko') Hadjikyriakos-Ghika. Between Ghika and Paddy is Natasha Spender.

Paddy enjoying himself in Greece.

Paddy examines a relief at his friend Aymer Maxwell's house on Evia.

Relaxing at Niko Ghika's house on Hydra, 1955. Paddy and Joan lived there for almost two years in the early 1950s.

The Ghika house on Hydra, later destroyed by fire.

Paddy examining the manuscript of his book *Mani*, 1955.

Paddy first spotted Deborah ('Debo') Mitford – as she then was – at a regimental ball in the 1940s, though she did not notice him at the time. They came to know each other as acquaintances at London parties in the early 1950s; but their friendship took off in the mid-1950s, when they began to correspond regularly. By this time, she was married to Andrew Cavendish, the 11th Duke of Devonshire, with a family of young children. Their correspondence would continue until Paddy's death, more than half a century later. Over the years Paddy was often a guest at one of the Devonshire houses, Chatsworth in Derbyshire or Lismore Castle in Ireland. The letter below was sent after his first stay at Lismore.

Paddy sent inscribed copies of each of his books to Debo. 'Look here, honestly, it's awfully good, frightfully good,' he would say; and she would reply, 'All right, Pad, I will try one day,' but it seems that she never did.

There was speculation that Debo and Paddy had once been lovers, but those who knew them best doubted this. The editor of their letters has described their relationship as 'a deep, platonic attraction between two people who shared youthful high spirits, warmth, generosity, and an unstinting enjoyment of life'. As their correspondence has been published separately, only two introductory letters are reproduced here, with a couple of late, previously unpublished letters towards the end.

To Deborah Devonshire   Gadencourt
undated [May 1956]   Pacy-sur-Eure

Darling Debo,

Your letter was a marvel and a lovely fat one. I revelled in every single word, and laughed a lot and love your flat-out, headlong way of writing. It plunged me back in Lismore – staying there and all the fun, jokes and everything were by far the nicest thing for me this year – and also gave me a dash of the gloom of an exile wandering far away from Eden. I say, what do you mean about me not liking gardens? I love them, and that one especially, in particular with a glass in hand and the key lost, lawns in stripes, but some grass under trees so long that one gets back slightly late for dinner, festooned up to the knees in cuckoo-spit.

Alas, I ought to resist the temptation to implore you to come to Paris now, as I am bombarded by my publisher daily to have the manuscript of the book[1] in within the fortnight, or else it won't be able to come out this year – and I've only got this house till the end of June. However, if you *did* come to Paris, I need hardly say that I'd be there faster than an arrow from a bow ... I thought of trying to get you to come and stay here, but it wouldn't be sensible at the moment, as I'd have to be closeted with this blithering book in a muck sweat of creative fever, leaving you and Joan alone all day in double agony of shyness. BUT, I do hope you'll be in London for the last half of June, when I'm coming over purely on pleasure bent, and rather hoping to be practically inseparable from your side. DO PLEASE TRY! We could do innumerable glorious things. I long to do lots more dancing for one thing, and make you stay up long past bedtime, also to take that river steamer to Greenwich. Do let me know about this, and what hopes there are. I do hope you haven't got a million beastly thwarting plans! The truth is I worship & long to see you, and keep thinking of things to talk about.

The sun pours down here and I scribble a lot in the garden, planning to arrive in London brown and gimlet-eyed, ready to win friends and influence people.[2] Two swallows flew into my room this morning and circled round for twenty minutes. I suppose it's too late, but it would be nice if they built a nest against one of the beams that cross the ceiling. The windows would have to be left open even in a deluge. One of them kept banging against a window instead of flying out. I put it in my pocket, went out to the lawn where some people were. I said 'Watch me throw a stone over that enormous tree,' took it out and threw it up into the air. It fluttered up into the firmament and everyone was amazed!

[1] *A Time to Keep Silence* (1957), an account of PLF's sojourns in monasteries in France and Cappadocia.
[2] A reference to Dale Carnegie's bestseller *How to Win Friends and Influence People* (1936).

Do please write at once and tell your plans, and an autobiography of your immediate past.

With lots of love from
Paddy

P.S. A published report recalls in 1952 that fornication was responsible for over 32,000 illegitimate births. So THAT'S what it's caused by! I'm glad they've put their finger on it at last ...

In 1956 shooting began of Ill Met by Moonlight, *a film based on the book by Paddy's deputy, 'Billy' Moss, about the abduction of General Kreipe. Most of it was shot on location in the French Alps.*

To Joan Rayner   Au Grand Lierne
Summer 1956   Auribeau-sur-Siagne
                                                           Alpes Maritimes

My darling Musk,

I've been meaning to write for days, but life has been such an odd and insane whirl that it has seemed hopeless to settle down for even a minute.

Xan [Fielding], Daph[ne Bath] & Emmerich Pressburger[1] were waiting at Nice airport – which I finally reached at 1.00 o'clock in the morning, as a woman whose entire family had been killed that afternoon in a crash took my place – and off we went to Beaulieu[-sur-Mer] for the night, and next day with Micky [Powell] up several dozen hairpin bends to the crests of the Alpes Maritimes above Menton, where all the nobs of the hundred-strong film unit camped in a vast chalet, as the shooting in the Castellane gorges was over, and they had embarked on the crossing of Mt Ida.

---

[1] Emeric ('Imre') Pressburger (1902–88), Hungarian-born screenwriter, who collaborated with the director Michael Latham Powell (1905–90) on nineteen feature films between 1939 and 1957.

Dirk Bogarde[1] turned out to be absolutely charming, and not only everything that the most confirmed snob could pray for, but a wonderful quiet under-actor (if you see what I mean). It is extraordinary what a difference there is between the script and the actual performance when it is shot. Each scene is rehearsed again and again, and even the text itself is radically changed, which gave one loophole after loophole for insisting on important changes. The only one I'm not happy about is Manoli [Paterakis],[2] who seems far too indefinite a personality. Billy [Moss] is excellent, also the General (Marius Goring), George [Psychoundakis], and the Cretans are very convincing. All the scenes that I saw seemed tip-top in feeling and verisimilitude, and, in spite of my fears, I feel excited and impressed. The scenery is dizzily precipitous and like the White Mountains and Ida, and Xan and I have managed to make the corroborative detail life-like. I'm very glad I went. I am slowly convincing them, too, that the dentist and sentry-stabbing scenes are dead wrong, and adjusting Billy's role. I think it will be a magnificent film in the end. It will certainly be a very exciting one.

But, in spite of all this, life 'on location' is hell – endless waits and hanging about, and constant crowds filling one with misanthropy and agoraphobia – fleets of cars, truckloads of stage Germans and swarms of 'Cretans', megaphones, cameras and cameramen, 'props' & make-up men, 'continuity' & script girls, odd hands, producers, directors, experts etc. The atmosphere has much of the gloom of an army transit camp. I shared a table in the chalet with Daph, Xan, Dirk Bogarde & David Oxley (Billy), lots of champagne was drunk and it was great fun. Even so, I couldn't bear it for more than a week, and telephoned the Grand Lierne. Madame

---

[1] Dirk Bogarde (1921–99) was playing PLF, who described him to Debo Devonshire as 'slim, handsome, nice speaking-voice and manner, a super-gent, the ghost of oneself twelve years ago'.

[2] 'He was my guide and closest Cretan friend in the island,' PLF would write to Debo Devonshire after Paterakis's death in 1985, 'hand in glove in all sorts of risky ventures, a man in a million, two years older than me, v. funny with a hawk nose, piercing eyes, and vast knowledge of the mountains'; Mosley (ed.), *In Tearing Haste*, p. 235.

Primet answered, Yes, they had a room, so along I came. Alas! *'Mon mari est décedé il y a deux ans du'une scirrhose de foie, on ne fait plus de cuisine'*[1] – so I took a small room, and have my meals – not a patch on the old ones – in an upstairs room *en pension* chez a Mme Berthet. But still, I can write in the garden (no longer the priest's, alas, but belonging to someone in Cannes and in charge of a rather gaga old caretaker and extracting the key from him each morning is a lengthy operation). A smart, very expensive restaurant has been opened on a knoll five minutes from the village. It is abhorrent and attractive at the same time, but a pity that it is there. Otherwise, it's charming. I've bathed several times in the icy Siagne, and gazed at several games of boules trying to pick up the rules. They are all such experts, especially at cannoning each other's balls to tremendous distances, that I haven't dared to approach or ask questions. There has been a steady Mistral the last 2 days which has slightly frayed everybody's tempers, like the scirocco in Auden's poem.[2] I'm rather hoping to oil my way to S. Maugham's house for a day when Annie is there, so have sent her my address in hopes. Meanwhile the death grapple with my book continues.

What news of Diana, and yacht plans? I've just written her ℅ Chips,[3] but perhaps you have been in touch. Darling, why don't you come here? It would be wonderful if you had your car, to spin about these hills a bit, as one has slight claustrophobia in this hot weather & wind, and one could make gastronomic *fahrts* [outings], now that the home oasis has dried up. [Illegible][4] knocked up one and half centuries, but the pitch here is pretty bumpy – the bowling, however, as good as ever. Darling, the people at 32 Hans Crescent

---

[1] 'My husband died two years ago of cirrhosis of the liver, so we don't cook any more.'
[2] 'Scirocco brings the minor devils: A slamming of doors At four in the morning Announces that they are back...', from W. H. Auden's 'Cattivo Tempo' (1949).
[3] Henry 'Chips' Channon (1897–1958), Conservative MP and diarist.
[4] In censoring his own letters long afterwards, PLF has scored out a name beginning with the letter 'P' or 'D' – presumably because the coded sentence alludes to some form of disreputable behaviour.

have got some pyjamas & a shirt or two from the laundry – could you bear to collect them? Please give my love to Graham. I rather envy you those quiet woods & lawns. I look forward to the yacht like anything – don't lose heart over it!

Heaps and heaps of love, hugs & kisses, my darling muskin, from your Mistral-ruffled

Mole

Ann Fleming was a close friend of Paddy's and one of his favourite correspondents.

To Ann Fleming   Auribeau-sur-Siagne
Monday [August 1956]   Alpes Maritimes

Annie Darling,

I escaped two days ago from the top of the French Alps where the film of the capture of General Kreipe is in full swing – the crossing of Mt Ida. I must say, it is terrifically exciting. Dirk Bogarde, who is doing me, is charming, a brilliant actor, super U in gesture and manner (rather more than one, perhaps), and the whole thing is bewilderingly strange. It's very odd seeing truckloads of Germans in steel helmets bawling 'Lili Marlene', blocking those peaceful Alpine passes.

All the same, I was glad to get away. Fleets of cars, technicians, camera men, props and make-up men, 'continuity girls', megaphones, cohorts of dawdling extras – agoraphobia strikes like a mallet.

Do appear in this part of the world soon. Telephone will get me any morning, and probably afternoon. This is a minute village on top of a green cone in the hinterland between Grasse and Cannes – 10km from both, and I spend my day scribbling in M. le Curé's leafy garden overlooking the meanderings of the ice-cold Siagne, most bracing of rivers. What is M. Maugham's[1] telephone number?

[1] The novelist and playwright W. Somerset Maugham (1874–1965), who lived at the Villa Mauresque on Cap Ferrat with his companion, Alan Searle.

I might ring and ask when you are expected, and pave the way for oiling in there for a day in a rather underhand way, by leaving a message asking you to ring, if you see my wheeze.

Anyway, Annie darling, do please write at once. It will be heaven seeing you.

Love

Paddy

X X X

Ann Fleming described what happened next in a letter to Evelyn Waugh written on 27 August, 1956:

When I arrived at the Mauresque there were letters postcards telegrams awaiting me; so Willie suspected a plot to use his house as a hotel and angle an invitation for a lover. Paddy was invited for lunch and arrived with five cabin trunks, parcels of books and the manuscript of his unfinished work on Greece strapped in a bursting attaché case; despite this inauspicious start luncheon went like a marriage bell ... so when coffee was finished I was not entirely surprised to hear Willie invite Paddy to stay and the minions carried in the trunks to a magnificent suite and Willie pointed to a splendid desk and said 'you c-can w-w-w-work there'. But, alas, that evening Mr and Mrs Frere of Heinemann[1] came to dinner and Paddy who never travels without a bottle of calvados appeared more exuberant than one small martini could explain. The conversation turned to tropical diseases and Paddy shouted at length on the stuttering that typified the College of Heralds, I intervened with a swift change of topic and thought the situation saved, but Frere (nasty man) made us all angry by saying that no author wrote

[1] Alexander Stewart Frere (1892–1984), managing director, chairman and eventually president of William Heinemann Ltd, publishers.

for anything but profit; this put my voice up several octaves as
well as Paddy's; worse was to follow while I was endeavouring
to include our octogenarian host in the conversation by
praising his garden, our octogenarian host remembered
that it was the feast of the assumption – no newspapers no
gardeners – he cannot bear to see the flowers unwatered and
the gravel unraked nor can he believe in assumptions – while
he haltingly complained of religious holidays Paddy broke in –
'darling Annie, when I was with Robin Fedden at the Louvre
we saw the vast Mantegna painting of the assumption and
Robin said with that delightful stutter "that is a m-most un-
un-w-warrantable assumption"': Alan [Searle] and I exchanged
glances of despair and the evening was wrecked, the Freres
left at ten o'clock, Willie saw them to the door returned to
the unlivable living room and said 'goodbye; you will have
left before I am up in the morning'. He then vanished like a
primeval crab leaving a slime of silence; it was broken by Paddy
who cried, 'Oh what have I done, Oh Christ what a fool I am'
and slammed his whisky glass on the table, it broke to pieces
cutting his hand and showering the valuable carpet with blood
and splinters. Alan and I were reduced to mad laughter; but in
the morning Alan reported that imitations of stuttering drove
Willie to frenzy and the car was ordered to drive Paddy and the
cabin trunks to St Jean. When I went to tell Paddy the car was
at the door he was sweating with fear and hangover and trying
to strap the manuscript into the attaché case, unluckily he had
put it on the unmade bed and the last tug tore the sheet, a
noise like Smee in Peter Pan and a huge three cornered rent. It
was a sad end after so promising a beginning.[1]

[1] Extracted, by kind permission, from Mark Amory (ed.), *The Letters of Ann Fleming*
(London, 1985), pp. 184–5.

Easton Court Hotel, in Devon, had been discovered by Evelyn Waugh, who wrote several of his books there; other writers followed, including Paddy's friends John Betjeman and Patrick Kinross. Like them, Paddy would often use it as a bolthole to write in over the next ten years.

To Ann Fleming   Chagford
undated [November 1956]   Exeter

Darling Annie,

Turning idly through the pages of my favourite author yesterday – *The Violins of St Jacques*, in this case – I was suddenly electrified by a passage I had completely forgotten, in which the villain comes out very badly on the score (among other things) of imitating somebody's stammer to his face, which is a contributory cause to an exchange of challenges to fight a duel! The stutter-mimic is such a <u>swine</u> in the book, that it would be obvious to anyone that I would never willingly emulate him. Do you think I should send it to my late host? If you've got a copy, do read the section pages 72 to 82, and advise. Stuttering is obviously destined to play an important and dangerous role in my life. Perhaps it is a mercy King George VI is dead – otherwise I would have certainly found myself, at some curious party arranged by the Queen Mother for the King to meet some of these writer Johnnies, happily telling him the whole Maugham saga ...[1]

Love Paddy

[1] The late king also suffered from a stammer.

The Easton Court Hotel's location on the edge of Dartmoor enabled Paddy to ride to hounds as a break from writing. This letter was written to his sometime lover Judy Montagu, who lived in Rome; Paddy would remain friends with her after their affair was over.

To Judy Montagu   Easton Court Hotel
undated [winter 1956]   Chagford
                                                           Devon

Darling Judy,

I hunted today, the first time since 1938. After pounding along for leagues, I found myself 'checked' outside a wood beside a giant, lantern-jawed man on a huge horse, while a great deal of whip-cracking, horn-blowing and yelping was going on in the undergrowth. A delinquent hound, smothered in filth, sat virtually with legs akimbo in front of us, looking from one to the other and occasionally scratching its ear and yawning. The silence was becoming oppressive, so at last I said, in a voice that was hardly my own and pointing with my borrowed crop, 'That hound's taking it easy.' The huge, dark-eyed and bloodshot face of my putative interlocutur swivelled slowly in my direction, fixed me for several seconds, but never uttered a word ...

Love, Paddy

To Jock Murray   Chagford
27 January 1957

Dear Jock,

All goes well and I am forging ahead in an all-out attempt to finish [*Mani*] this week – though nothing more from Miss Johns [the typist] so far, in spite of desperate appeal!

I'm terribly exercised by two problems and bring them up with some misgiving. One is that I had got a far bigger bill than I thought here – nearly £180, with millions of cigarettes, etc., of which I paid £100[1] out of the lump you so kindly gave me; now I suppose it is creeping up again, on top of the remainder. I know Carolyn[2] would never dream of mentioning it, but I do feel that as Miss Hepburn[3] and I are the only source of income in these lean winter months, I would terribly like to pay in another fifty quid, to show I'm not taking it too much for granted. The other is a bit of nightmare, for your ear alone. My mama, being frightfully ill and operated on twice last summer, and thinking that everything, not only a stipulated maximum sum, was payed for by the Nuffield Trust I had fixed up, somehow contrived, poor dear, to run up a nursing home bill (Rayland's Nursing Home in Brighton) for the alarming & catastrophic sum of £247. I have promised them to settle this by degrees before the end of this year, and, if all goes well, should be able to manage this. As a matter of fact, I think I will talk to my very nice bank manager, explain the whole thing, and see what we can do. But I ought, I think, to do this viva voce, rather than by letter, with all the documents etc. The thing is, to quieten these people, I said, a couple of weeks ago, that I would start by giving them £50 within a month. So I wonder if, by any wild stretch of anticipation & prestidigitation and kindness on your part, we could contrive to let my bank have at least one hundred quid, to cover these two dollops of fifty. I'm terribly reluctant to suggest this, but I do feel that once this present work is off my hands and into yours, I will be able to turn to other things and straighten things out during an interim. It's a difficult time for all this to crop up, and I do look forward to bringing some money <u>into</u> the house of Murray, instead of constantly trying to wheedle it <u>out</u>. Neither of these problems – especially the first – are grounds for throat-cutting; but they are the most dreadful worry.

I wish I'd contrived to get a vast sum off those film people now all this has cropped up, instead of being so hoity-toity. One never

---

[1] About £6,000 in today's value (2018).

[2] Carolyn Postlethwaite Cobb, proprietor of the Easton Court Hotel in Chagford.

[3] The actress Audrey Hepburn (1929–93), then one of Hollywood's most popular box-office attractions, took refuge in Dartmoor and south Devon out of season to escape the hullabaloo.

knows, they <u>may</u> cough up some enormous *douceur* [bribe] later on. When I said I didn't want any dough for advising them last year (on the grounds that no Cretans in the film were getting any), Powell said 'Well, we'll have to give you a Rembrandt, or something.' So perhaps ... To show you my singleness of mind at the moment (!) I am resisting the temptations of Tantalus[1] and <u>not</u> coming to London to see the opening of the film[2] next week (31st). There are constant maddening telephone calls from publicity, B.B.C., television people etc., connected with all this. But I don't want to have anything to do with it all until I have made my position viz-à-viz the film clear in a *Sunday Times* article <u>after</u> it has come out and been reviewed; which (the article) will probably do in any question of Rembrandt.

Now for some cheerful news, after all this. I went hunting yesterday (<u>one</u> day a week is my plan for an anti-cobweb – not my hosts! – measure) and we had a stupendous run, finishing at Gidleigh, and from there lickety-split over hill & dale (Mr French's horse 'Flash' sailing over all obstacles like a swallow) right over the flank of Meldon Tor, then down to the common and killed under the very walls of Chagford with all the citizens craning from their windows.

After the poor wretch [the fox] was broken-up ('an old offender, a sly devil he was ...'[3]) the gory mask was crammed into my hands with a great slap on the back from the master. It is being packed off to the Army & Navy stores tomorrow for stuffing & mounting. Carolyn <u>was</u> pleased! The dreadful object is now hanging up in a bucket, and it makes those dogs Born & Bill howl for hours on end.

Yours ever
Paddy

P.S. Did you manage to read any of the typescript [of *Mani*]?

---

[1] Tantalus's name has become a proverbial term for temptation without satisfaction: he was punished by being made to stand in a pool of water beneath a fruit tree with low branches, with the fruit ever eluding his grasp, and the water always receding before he could take a drink.

[2] *Ill Met by Moonlight.*

[3] Source unidentified.

To Diana Cooper   Abbaye St Wandrille de Fontenelle
22 April 1957   Rançon

My darling Diana,

It's very strange to be here again, and oddly enough for once, the changeover from the mid-twentieth century to Carolingian or Valois times went as easily as winking. It's 8 a.m. and I'm just back in my room – a lovely big one with a huge desk and enormous windows looking out on millions of chestnut candles – after a breakfast of brown bread & coffee standing up in the refectory. Early for <u>one</u>, but the monks have been up since 5, when they sing Matins and Lauds. Dom Gabriel Goutard, the charming & scholarly old abbot, is away ill, alas, but I was greeted by the Prior, the F. Guestmaster and the Père Bibliothècaire with great kindness, like a long lost friend. One of the extraordinary things about a place like this is the amount the monks manage to get into the day. They work like blacks at their various tasks, covered in filthy old 'working habits' – hoods and cowls made of dungaree – in the woods, in the kitchen garden, in the bootblack factory etc. – you see them all over the place – and yet they go to church seven times a day. A few peals on the bell, and there they are, trooping black & spotlessly clad in flowing habits and as orderly as slow-marching guardsmen, up the aisle, bowing to each other, genuflecting, fanning out symmetrically to their unchanging stalls, stooping their tonsures over vast breviaries, while others follow glittering with splendid vestments, candles, censers, mitres, a crosier (when the abbot is here) as if their only plot were the practise of ritual and the perfection of Gregorian plainsong. But, the moment it's over, they are dispersed at once all over the green monastic landscape, in the thick once more of some backbreaking secular task. I think it is this strange conjunction of silence and *recueillement* [contemplation] with this busy exploitation of every second of the day that shames and goads one out of selfish and moody sloth. Anyway, I got off to a whizz-bang start and have already written more here than I have done for any week in London recently. 'Now doth time waste me'[1] – but not at this second, thank God! This curious regimen seems to convert one's brain from a rusty heap of kettle-choked scrap-iron into a swift and smoothly working piece of machinery.

Darling, what a lovely Easter. It was simply splendid throughout and stuffed with bumper moments. Everyone in thunderous good form. I did love it, and many many thanks (also apologies for you know what …) The most exciting part was hearing those glorious chapters out of your book.[2] Well done. All qualms over – incapability of any of one's nearest & dearest to do anything good etc. It's going to be a vast and deserved success. (Why not split into two vols? Double the pennies?)

It's a resplendent morning here – a cuckoo and lots of thrushes & blackbirds hard at it, and, when I peered into the stream that turns through the Abbey grounds – '*ruissel et fontaine de merveilleuse beauté*', in mediaeval chronicles[3] – there were about a dozen trout hovering under the bridge, noses upstream and managing to remain stationary against the current with only the most economical and imperceptible twitches of their tails. Do write. I'll be here another week or so. Many thanks again, darling Diana, and fondest love & hugs

from Paddy
X X X

Love to Annie, if still there.

If you can come here for a jaunt & outing, 8.45 to 9.45, 11.45 to 12.30, or 1.45 to 4.45 are best telephoning times – *préavis* [advance notice] best. If you are motoring to England, it might be a good detour. I can't tell you how I'd love it. But it's miles.

---

[1] 'I wasted time, and now doth time waste me', Shakespeare, *Richard II*, Act V, Scene 5.
[2] Lady Diana Cooper's autobiography would be published in three volumes, the first, *The Rainbow Comes and Goes*, in 1958.
[3] PLF had quoted this phrase in *A Time to Keep Silence* (1957).

'My life has taken a queer temporary turn,' Paddy wrote to his close friend and former wartime comrade Xan Fielding. 'John Huston got hold of me soon after we broke up at Lismore last year, to do the script of Romain Gary's Prix Goncourt book, Les Racines du Ciel *['The Roots of Heaven'], a queer, diffuse, bulky, rather brilliant book about a sort of Jean-Gabin-esque resistance fighter who leaps to the defence of elephants in French Equatorial Africa. I was put up in an hotel in Paris – St James and Albany – for most of the winter, and scribbled away like a wild cat, conferring every two days, sometimes more, with Darryl Zanuck, who is the owner & producer of the film. A very strange man with a pepper & salt moustache, bright blue eyes and a colossal cigar, which he mashes to a pulp between irregular teeth, a barrier for a loud and rasping voice. We got on very well, and eventually out I flew to F. E. Africa with him & J. Huston, arriving at Fort Archambault, on the banks of a winding crocodile-haunted river, the savannah around being full of elephants, lions, panthers, jaguars, giraffes & buffalo. We live here in a huge stockade containing scores of huts ... All pretty odd.'*

To Joan Rayner   'Roots of Heaven'
26 February 1958   Box 99
                                  Fort Archambault[1]
                          French Equatorial Africa[2]

My darling Musk,

Well, here we are at last, and very queer it is, and rather wonderful. Zanuck,[3] Huston[4] and I set off on Monday night, a tremendous press party at the airport with champagne corks a-pop; we touched down at Marseilles, then slept till we woke up in Fort

[1] The French colonial name of the city now known as Sarh.
[2] French Equatorial Africa, a federation of French colonial possessions comprising the countries now known as Cameroon, Gabon, Chad, Central African Republic and Congo-Brazzaville.
[3] Darryl Zanuck (1902–79), American film producer and studio executive.
[4] John Huston (1906–87), American film director, screenwriter and actor.

Lamy, a sprawling dusty town under blazing stars which faded while a turquoise dawn broke. We drove into the town for 1½ hours. Some of the men were nearly naked, others wore *galabias* [hooded gowns], many carried *assegais*. We saw a robed chief on a gloriously caparisoned horse, a man walking before him carrying a sabre. All jet black, tall & shambling, the women in gorgeous coloured elaborate dresses with their hair a page-boy arrangement of tiny plaits. Then by plane again, flying low to tiny Fort Archambault, over scrub and trees, where one gazed down at fleeing herds of antelope, spotting elands, kudus and buffalos, rhinoceros, patterns of elephant tracks, but no elephants so far. Ft Archambault is much smaller than F. Lamy, a tree shaded village really, with a few European houses and shops (Portuguese and Greek) and a sprawling fringe of conical African huts, each one surrounded by a compound of plaited-palm-trash walls haunted by dogs, goats and humped cattle and women pounding manioc. Zanuckville, two miles out, by the banks of the Shari river (no bathing because of crocodiles and bilharzia) is a vast matting compound full of beautifully built pretty matting bungalows, except for five thick-walled white rooms in a row for the nobs (I have one at the moment, but will have to shift when the stars turn up). All have showers & mosquito nets. It has been an endless series of conferences ever since we arrived. Two aeroplanes are in alternate compounds – life is slight hell – slightly too like the army – but could be worse. I have a huge huge Ubango tribesman slave talking Sango and a little French. He is constructed out of jet-black satin. Huston seems charming and is very funny, but there may be shoals ahead. I forgot to say that in Paris I was sent to a tropical outfitters and given a tin trunk-load of tropical kit – bush-shirts, several kinds of foot gear, a wonderful anti-solar sombrero, a camouflaged suit to deceive elephants in, and a khaki anti-social yashmak in which one swathes one's head like a Tuareg.[1] The local Greek community is all from Lesbos,

---

[1] The men of the Tuareg people of the Sahara cover their heads and faces to ward off evil spirits, and as protection against the searing sun.

Imbros and Samothrace. Thanks to General Kreipe (!) I am bidden to a great banquet given by the leading grocer tonight.

Last night, just before sunset, I wandered along the banks of the Shari. It was wonderfully quiet and remote, feeling slightly melancholy. Negroes were fishing with spears and bows and arrows, others drifted by in dug-out canoes, and, overhead, swarms of great-crested cranes, herons and ibises were wheeling and homing. The country here is utterly flat: scrub, elephant grass and low forest – thorn, occasional mango or breadfruit-looking trees and many carobs. A little way off I came across a nice French administrator with a bungalow among the reeds. Round him gambolled a black dog and a tame eighteen-month-old lion, as nimble and jolly as a kitten, climbing all over me as the Frenchman gave me a whisky and soda and told me how the Ubangi still kill and eat their elderly villagers, even digging up corpses, and occasionally sacrificing girls. The locals are a mixture of Catholic, Moslem and animist. They are very childish and backward and do not smile easily. The atmosphere is not entirely a happy one, and the thing that slightly invalidates it for our kind of travel is that one is, willy-nilly, a kind of white boss and the locals are utterly, utterly remote. I may change my ideas about this, I long to see the mountainous Foulbé country in the Cameroon.

Darling, I think I'll be here at least three weeks, so do write quick and forward letters (the first Archambault address is the right one). I've got to finish this in a hurry for the usual reasons!

Lots of fondest love & hugs
Greetings to Peggy[1]

---

[1] Their housekeeper.

To Joan Rayner   20th Century Fox
22 March 1958   Boîte Postale 83
                                                        Maroua
                                              French Cameroon

My darling Musk,

I'm so terribly sorry to have been such a monster about writing, but things have been so hectic and <u>addling</u> that it has seemed impossible, though of course I should have scribbled short almost daily notes. I'll try and do something of the kind in future.

The whole outfit assembled soon after my last letter. Errol Flynn (Forsyth), Trevor Howard – the one who had Graham's Viennese job in *The Third Man* – marvellous – Paul Lukas (Saint Denis), Juliette Gréco (Minna), some splendid negroes for the African parts, and Grégoire Aslan – the one who did the Bey in 'He who must Die!' – as Habib; he is splendid.[1] I lived in a V.I.P. group consisting of a row of little bungalows in the vast mushroom town – Zanuckville! – outside Fort Archambault, which were inhabited by Zanuck, Gréco, Huston, Howard, Flynn & self. They all bore me a bit except Huston, Gréco & Flynn. But the former is really a tremendous mountebank with very little beneath it. Flynn is a tremendous bounder, but awfully funny and rather touching in a way. He and Howard breakfast off brandy and go on all day, but he manages to act wonderfully. My real pals are J. Gréco and three friendly cronies of hers, very intelligent, properly educated and funny, like a bottle of champagne after the maundering anecdotage of the Americans. This clique within a clique rather irritates everyone else – too much laughter and too many private jokes. Zanuck is not very happy about it,

---

[1] Errol Flynn (1909–59), Australian-American actor known for his swashbuckling roles; Trevor Howard (1913–88), English actor who became a star after appearing in *Brief Encounter* (1945); Paul Lukas (1894–1971), Hungarian actor, who won the Academy Award for Best Actor for his performance in the film *Watch on the Rhine* (1943); Juliette Gréco (b. 1927), bohemian French actress and singer; Grégoire Aslan (1908–82), known as 'Coco Aslan', ethnic Armenian actor and musician.

as it separates him from Juliette G, who he watches like a hawk quite without reason, except that she seems to have taken a fierce dislike to him, and is exasperated with incarceration.[1] It's all rather sad. The odd thing is, that under the rasping voice and the cigar, he has got a heart, I think, of gold. The general level is appallingly low. I feel the kind of permanent irritation that must have irked the exiled Athenian at the Court of Artaxerxes in Cavafy, disgusted with his satrapy and longing for the austere standards of the [illegible] and the Agora.[2]

We shifted from French Equatorial Africa to the French Cameroon last week by air. Marona is a little town inhabited by heavily robed Foulbé, many of them on horseback, splendid jet-black Moslems with geometrically gashed cheeks, living in a labyrinth of rush-topped huts, rather like thatched *trulli* in Apulia. But the mountains round about are a chaos of volcanic rocks that look like a herd of petrified elephants. One is inhabited by stark naked animist savages without a stitch of clothes on, thunderstruck at the sight of a cigarette or an ice-cube, the men with enormous trunk-like tools dangling, the women with their eyes surrounded by painted spectacles of ochre. They gather round us on the rocks while the film company with all its gear and myrmidons goes through its bewildering evolutions, and gaze and gaze. All this would be fascinating if I were alone with you and a friend or two. It's hell like this, in a sort of compulsory army-cum-compulsory-Sunday-school atmosphere. I am seeing everything too darkly today. I have escaped from the Belsen camp we inhabit and have taken an empty white house which is pretty-good hell (but better nevertheless) with an idiot Foulbé for the servant. I forgot to say

[1] Zanuck was having an affair with Gréco.
[2] A reference to C. P. Cavafy's poem 'The Canon':

'...And how unblest the day when you give in/ (when you have lost yourself, and you give in), /and you depart, a wayfarer for Susa, /and come before the monarch Artaxerxes/ who welcomes you with favour at his Court, /offering you satrapies and things akin. /And you, despairing, you accept those honours, /those that are not the honours you desire./ Your soul is hungering for other things: /the praises of the Demos and the Sophists, - /the difficult, invaluable 'Well done'; /the Agora, the Theatre, the bays...'

Friedrich Ledebur[1] arrived a few days ago, he may move in too. He speaks with such nostalgia of that day at Gadencourt, and begs me to send love. I wish we were there. You would have gone mad here. I would like to leave really, but it looks as if we are here for another fortnight, before returning to France. I work like hell, re-writing things in the light of local conditions at the last moment. I have a terrible time stopping them dressing up animist aboriginals as Tunisian beys in flowing robes. I have even acted talking parts in three different scenes, when they have been short. When we move from here, we continue for another two weeks in the Camargue – with any luck I'll be out of it by then ...

Please forgive this moaning letter, my darling, and its lateness – it's [only] the second letter I've written for a month. I have read three more pages of Valery Larbaud.[2]

Heaps and heaps of love

from JEMY

Please! A maddening favour! Could you like an utter sadist send at once, airmail here, *The Tree*, *The Violins*, *T. to K. Silence*, *C. Runner*, and, if it exists in my bookcase, the French *Violins*. Thanks darling, and sorry. I say, what a bore and a torment about Πέγκι, το κοριτσάκι μας [Peggy, our little girl]![3]

[1] Friedrich von Ledebur (1900–86), Austrian-born character actor who gained international recognition after playing the role of the South Sea islander Queequeg in John Huston's film *Moby Dick* (1956).

[2] Valery Larbaud (1881–1957), French writer and translator; his best known work is *Fermin Marquez* (1911), said to have been inspired by his boyhood at boarding school.

[3] Their housekeeper, Peggy, had given in her notice.

To Nancy Mitford   London Clinic!
last day of February [1959]

Darling Nancy,

Debo tells me you're bedridden too, so this is a consoling line
from a fellow invalid. I do hope all goes well; it is wretched for you.

I'm here for pretty unglamorous reasons: quite literally, arse &
elbow, the latter caused by a riding accident in Africa last year, which
sounds alright, at least. Both points were dealt with by a surgeon called
Sir Ralph Marnham,[1] whom Debo styles the Knight of the Thousand
and One Bums.[2] This place, which is considered a hell hole, isn't bad at
all: lovely leisure for writing letters and doing crosswords and reading
Agatha Christie and Gibbon and drinking half-bottles of champagne
that friends bring. I rather wish I wasn't going out tomorrow.

Just before coming in I went to stay with mad Auberon [Herbert]
for a stag hunt (a hind, rather, just now). It turned out to be the
run of the season, a lovely cold bright day, steep hills & bare woods
and fast brown streams that we crossed and recrossed: 36 miles,
ending with an 8 mile point[3] full tilt. I got given a slot,[4] like you,
which is why I've brought it all up!

It was a horseman's farewell to his fork. All I could do now is
leap astride an air cushion as to the manner born and look part of
the chair ...[5]

I do hope all goes well & that you are out and about in no time,

With love from Paddy

---

[1] Ralph Marnham (1901–84), knighted in 1957; Serjeant Surgeon to the Queen,
1967–71. Joan was treated by Marnham for 'the all too familiar woe' later that year.
'I'm glad you've done something about it,' PLF wrote to her, '– at least we've both
complied with that vital strategic maxim (Livy, Caesar, Clauzewitz, Foch), securing
one's rear.'
[2] A play on words, alluding to the collection of Arabic tales published under the title *One
Thousand and One Nights*, also known as *Arabian Nights*.
[3] A straight line distance made good in a run.
[4] A cloven deer hoof.
[5] PLF had been suffering from haemorrhoids.

Towards the end of 1958, during a brief stay in Rome, Paddy had become involved with Lyndall Birch, daughter of the novelist Antonia White. Their romance had been interrupted when he had left for England, for the publication of his book about Greece, Mani: Travels in the Southern Peloponnese. *Paddy returned to Italy the following spring, keen to renew the love affair. Looking for somewhere to work, he found an uninhabited castle, within striking distance of Rome (described in detail in his letter to Deborah Devonshire of 27 July 1959), and asked if he could rent a couple of rooms there. The owner laughed and said: 'You must be mad! You can have the whole place free.'*

To Lyndall Birch   Castello di Passerano
Monday, mid-(late?) May 1959   Lazio

Darling Lyndall,

What a shame missing you last night. It was quite fun. I liked both the girls, but found the two surviving young men hopeless, and Borghese[1] unspeakable. With the shining exception of you (and Iris [Tree] and Judy [Montagu]), I'm getting fed up with female society, which seems to be the only kind available in Rome and its environs; and the occasional masculine society which comes one's way is so hopelessly vapid and useless as to be non-existent. Where are the Cyrils, the Maurices, the Philips, the Ivans, the Stephens, the Isaiahs, the Eddies, the Raymonds, the Roberts?[2] Where indeed? This reads like the wail of lovelorn flapper.

And, if it comes to that, where are you? I can't take much interest in life at the moment unless you are somehow involved in it, in the present or the impending future. I expect you are waiting in the wings made up trying to read, waiting to be called for the fifteenth re-take.[3] Try and escape here for a day and a night

[1] The playboy prince, 'Tinty' Borghese.
[2] Cyril Connolly, Maurice Bowra, Philip Toynbee, Ivan Moffat, Stephen Spender, Isaiah Berlin, Eddie [Gathorne Hardy?], Raymond Mortimer, Robert [Kee?].
[3] Lyndall Birch had a small part in Fred Zinnemann's *The Nun's Story*, starring Audrey Hepburn.

or so when you are finished – I know you probably can't. But I do love it so.

Paola and Francesca[1] (how funny that sounds[2]) are longing (or so they said) to come here some evening. But what paragons can we find for them? (So many princes and counts, but hardly one human being!) What about Mr Franchetti[3] for one, whom I so sadly missed? Can you think of another possible? We might try and get Rina to cook a rustic meal and eat by candlelight at that long baronial table, instead of mobbing a trattoria. Could you bear this in mind (N. Pasolinï[4] any good? too tame and formal? Our lover Renzo?[5]) Do chew on this project, bearing in mind that it is about a million times less important and pined for than your coming here on your own and turning a bastille into a palace.

I wonder how this past half year will seem to us both, wherever we are, in twenty years' time; what effect (as everything that happens to one shapes one in some degree) it will have had on us both? I dare say our helpless, unwilling and, on your side, innocent mangling of each other will seem barely comprehensible.

It started off a lovely day, billions of birds, but the cuckoo has mysteriously fled for the last few days, before he could change his tune. Then it clouded over and rained cats and dogs and I felt at my desk as though thrust up into the heart of the rain, also like a khaki fish peering out of its aquarium. I'm writing this in a deckchair on my knees among the sodden artichokes at the end of the battlements (the ivy and dockweed and cow parsley drenched all round, but no rain falling) in an attempt to find a sunset vantage

[1] Paola Rolli, Lyndall Birch's closest Italian friend, one of Fellini's casting directors; and her friend Francesca Patrizi. Francesca's mother, the Marchesa Patrizi, was a writer.
[2] In the first volume of *The Divine Comedy*, Dante and Virgil meet Francesca and her lover Paolo in the second circle of hell, reserved for the lustful.
[3] Baron Giorgio Franchetti, collector of modern art and ancient motor cars.
[4] Count Niccolò Pasolini dell'Onda, a young lawyer who would later write a history of his family.
[5] Possibly Renzo Avanzo (1911–89), film actor, scriptwriter and producer, a friend of Judy Montagu's.

point. It's not too bad. There's a turquoise blue sky and long tragic crimson bars of cloud beyond the battlements, also, at last, my black bar and three lion heads flapping from a mast on the tower, but the grey death-like moment and the sudden drifting valedictory gust ('The bright day is done and we are for the dark!'[1]) is at hand. So it's Gallicano[2] for me, I think.

Goodnight, Lyndall, dearest one, and see you in a day or two.

love Paddy

(Almost dark now.)

To Jock Murray   Castello di Passerano
25 June 1959   Gallicano nel Lazio
                               Provincia di Roma

Dear Jock,

Many apologies for this dreadful delay! It was caused, mainly, by the fact that a ghastly film company temporarily moved into the castle and made it such hell that I took flight in disorder to Rosie Rodd's house in Ansedonia. I am there now, but will be encastled again (as above) within the week, d.v. [God willing], with Joan (also turned up last week) to lighten the medieval solitude.

The owner of the castle, approached by these insidious monsters for permission to shoot in the castle, said he had lent it to me, and they must tackle me. Meanwhile, they had so excited the famers and peasants with promises that I felt it dog-in-the-mangerish [to refuse] – as they had been v. decent to me (the farmers etc.) – so I weakly said yes . . .

Now! Could you possibly manage a rather splendid advance on the vol on which I'm engaged? Earmarking for tax, motor-cars, castles, bills, family commitments, surgical benefits, nursing-homes and a swarm of minor financial gadflies have stung me to a

---

[1] Shakespeare, *Antony and Cleopatra*, Act V, Scene 2.
[2] Gallicano, the nearest town to the Castello di Passerano. PLF means that it was time to go into town and pass the evening.

standstill. The great thing would be to pay this into the bank, and make them stand up and cheer.

I think you will like the new book. It starts with me tooling away from the Theodosian walls of Constantinople, across eastern Thrace, into the heart of the Rhodope Mountains, and a whole world of unparalleled wonders. It is going well, a work to foster.

All the best, with renewed apologies,

Yours ever
Paddy

To Stephen Spender   Castello di Passerano
26 June 1959   Gallicano nel Lazio
                                                Provincia di Roma

Dear Stephen,

I wonder if the enclosed would be any use for *Encounter*.[1]

I have become the guilty and clandestine owner of the ravishing things which the verses celebrate. They were chanced upon by a peasant near this castle, who is a pal of mine, while ploughing last autumn, along with a seated, headless, lion-flanked statue of Cybele (also mine now!). This boy, Silvio, had them hidden under straw in a tufa [limestone] cellar in a barn full of Maremmana oxen,[2] and it was very exciting putting them under the pump, then looking at them by dead of night, under a lantern on the table of the farm kitchen.

The feet and tree trunk are both on a slab, and like Cybele, the tree is almost two feet high. I can't think who originally stood on the feet, leaning on the tree. Phoebus, Bacchus, Diana, Ceres? As hinted in the verses, there are no giveaway attributes.

---

[1] See end of this letter and footnote on p. 152.
[2] A breed of cattle reared in the Maremma, a former marshland region in southern Tuscany and northern Lazio.

As you see, I've taken one or two minor liberties with the alcaics; but, however akin to English, it seemed the right metre.

I'm scribbling away in this extraordinary borrowed castle, a great scowling medieval thing, uninhabited till now for four centuries. So pretty rough stuff. It stands on a spike above a ruffling Canaan of treetops.

Joan (arrived last week) says you've been in America, but I hope you're back now. Any chance of Rome? You ought to see this castellated phenomenon.

Love, Paddy (also to Natasha)

P.S. My ownership of these bits of marble is criminal and secret. How to smuggle them home? Mum's the word.

On Two Marble Feet and a Marble Tree dug up by a Ploughman in Latium

Sleeping in darkness, the tip of a chisel
Once tapped me awake, a snowfall of splinters
Dissolving the thicketed marble
And looping me about with weightless sunbeams,

Leaning me here on the stem of an oak-tree.
Was there a circle of wide leaves, a fillet,
A wreath round my forehead? A sickle,
Poppies and wheat-ears entwined, an unstrung

Bow in my hand, a wand plaited with tendrils?
A long flute or berries? None can remember.
The shade of vine leaves over water,
Sheaves, instruments, the voices of reapers,

Pigeons alighting there, the touch of children,
Fingers on drawn strings, some pillars and meadows,
Sunsets along the floor and moonlight
And tired words of decay in the senate;

Sieges recalled, theatres in Bithynia,
Parthian troubles and rumours from Egypt,
Fluteplayers and laughing and whispers,
The track of comets, the soul, and omens –

All these there were, and uncountable summers;
And, finally, talk of strange men and watch-fires
And flight; then a moulting of garlands
And cups forgotten on the mosaic.

Newcomers' voices spoke in the portico,
The steel flickered and sparks lit up the fragments
And stopped all the flutes and scattered me
For blind centuries under the harvests.

Steel found me again and here stands the oak-tree.
I lean there no more. But my shining feet are
Unfettered, a heel ready lifted
For flight into the woods or for dancing.

To Deborah Devonshire
27 July 1959

Castello di Passerano
Gallicano nel Lazio
Provincia di Roma
Abruzzi

Darling Debo,

This non-writing won't do at all; so bags I break silence, in order to seize the advantage and put you in the wrong, before this sly move occurs to you.

Don't be fooled by the splendour of the address at the top of this paper; I set it myself at a local printers. This castle is a huge empty thing of spell-binding beauty on top of a leafy hill overlooking a froth of treetops and cornfields surrounded on three sides by classical mountain ranges whose names need not concern us, and on the fourth by the Roman Campagna and the dome of St Peter's in the distance, indicating – too near! – great Rome itself. The castle hadn't been inhabited for 600 years, so it meant putting windows in and borrowing, buying or hiring furniture (all of which has ruined me). It looks rather marvellous, but there is not a drop of water running. Two beautiful girls called Loredana and Gabriella come wobbling gracefully up the castle ramp twice daily with great brass pitchers on their heads. I won't enlarge on the loo situation ...

Some nuns in Tivoli sewed me a huge heraldic banner, which I fly from a mast on a tower (Fermor's answer to Lismore). I have been building up a fictitious character for myself: the Black Bastard of Passerano, and like to think that when I unfurl my banner from the topmost battlements, all the trembling peasants of the valley look askance and cross themselves, dowse their lights and hide their cattle and bolt up their dear ones. Actually, most of my time is spent driving car-loads of white-clad little girls or Fauntleroys into nearby Gallicano nel Lazio for first communion, or the castle women – there is a farm grovelling at the foot of the ramparts – to market: the Black Sucker of Passerano, Il Succho Nero.

There used to be masses of nightingales, but they've vanished now, but there are plenty of owls which sometimes get in and flap silently round for hours among the oil lamps and candles, having rashly flown down a spiral stair inside a tower; also frogs, crickets and nightjars. The atmosphere at night is like the castle in *Hamlet* by William Shakespeare.[1]

---

[1] A teasing allusion to the duchess's apparent lack of interest in literary works.

The discomfort is almost beyond sufferance. Some of this is caused by rats, which, rather intimidated at first by my usurping their age-old suzerainty, are getting the upper hand again. I think Joan was rather taken aback by all this. The other night, hoping to foil the ants (which I forgot to mention), she put a basin of water on a table, and inside this, a jug with a plate on top containing a loaf for breakfast tightly wrapped in brown paper, and, balanced on top of this, a saucer with butter in. Next morning I was reading early by a window in the same room – the banqueting hall! – when I was roused by a rustle; there, his hind legs on tiptoe on the basin's rim, stood a tall rat carefully unfolding a hole in the bread paper with his forepaws and nibbling in felicity. I threw my book at it – *The Age of Elegance* by Arthur Bryant – but missed. The rat sloped off perfunctorily, but turned back halfway to the door and resumed his post in half a minute. I thought I'd better let it rip. So there he crunched, the butter wobbling to and fro on top, looking at me out of the corner of his eyes with a victor's glance … Next night, Joan found a large scorpion nestling on her. So I suppose it's time to draw stumps.

We are now in the cool heights of the Abruzzi, great Alpine mountains about 100 miles E. of Rome, in a village called Ovindoli. The cattle here are a wonderful body of cows. At dusk, a bell is rung from the church tower, and, quite unaccompanied, all gather from their fields at a never changing rendezvous, and head for the village by the hundred. Once in the market square, they split up and mooch off along various lanes to the houses where they live and tap on the door with their horns and out comes a girl or a grandmother and lets them into a comfortable cellar for the night.

Lots and lots of love from
Paddy

'As you see, I've removed to Ischia,' Paddy wrote to Jock Murray in August. 'The castle became unbearably hot and rats, owls, ants and scorpions had resumed their interrupted reign. We escaped to the Abruzzo which was perfect, but could only have rooms available for a week; so came here, and discovered a cool flat on the edge of Forio with a wide balcony looking out over orange-groves and the sea where I sit (as now) and scribble away under a wickerwork awning, charging down into the sea every few pages. I plan to stay on here for a bit ...'
In fact they were to remain on Ischia several more months, welcoming a succession of guests, including Lyndall Birch, who was astonished by the friendly reception she received from Joan.

To Lyndall Birch   Forio d'Ischia
1 October [1959]

Darling Lyndall,

I've been meaning to write for days to find out whether you caught that boat alright, after my miserable car succeeded in wrecking your last day. I was awfully worried all the time you were here because your precious hol was turning out so differently, so very much more restless, fragmentary and dispersed, than it should have been and what I'd meant it to be. I'd hoped for lots of work done by both, long bathes and sun-wallowing, early evenings and up again with the lark next day. I'm afraid Diana's interminable stay[1] wrecked the whole thing, and all work or peace of mind for me as well. It really was an agonising time and I wouldn't go through it again for anything. But I do hope it didn't entirely ruin your stay. There were some nice bits: Janetta [Jackson] and Ivan's visit, Ali's tragi-comic conclusion[2] and the arrival of Debo & Co. Annie left a couple of days after you – next day, I think – and I <u>do wish</u> you could have stayed on (though I know you couldn't) because everything was glorious from then

---

[1] Diana Cooper's stay had been extended because of a paralysing bout of depression, meaning that she occupied the only spare room in the house for longer than expected.
[2] Alistair Forbes, who assumed that PLF and Lyndall Birch were still having an affair.

on, ending up with a lovely visit to Capri which was fun, laughter and oddity throughout, a huge success. I hated it when that broke up.

I'm glad you liked and got the point of Debo. I adore her. One of the bright points of this last phase for me was seeing the point of Tom,[1] who I liked, and approved of, by the time he left, immensely. He seemed very taken by you indeed. Do put me abreast of later trends.

Everything has been much quieter since Capri. I've contrived to settle into a quieter and a fairly diligent rhythm, up early, work all day, frugal cold lunch and salad at home, left ready-laid by Giovanna, now and then a smart outing with Harry & Maria Carmela[2] in depraved Mimosa's boat,[3] dinner with them and Iris [Tree] – a great click – then bed. A gay evening looms ahead tonight; Iris, Hambledens & Henry & Virginia Bath, who turned up yesterday. He's a wonderfully funny and odd creature. I heard the following conversation ten years ago, at dinner, when Henry was sitting next to Julia Strachey:[4]

H. (urgently) Now! Take the sexiest thing of the lot – Sex! (anxiously) I say, you are married, I hope?

J. Yes

H. (relieved, flourishing his hands in the air) Well, you see what I mean, then!

---

[1] Lyndall Birch was being pursued by Thomas Egerton (1918–98), racehorse breeder, and a friend of Princess Margaret.

[2] William Herbert 'Harry' Smith, 4th Viscount Hambleden (1930–2012), descendant of the founders of the stationers W. H. Smith, and his wife, Countess Maria Carmela Attolico di Adelfia.

[3] Marina ('Mimosa') Parodi Delfino (1927–2009), a renowned Italian beauty, the daughter of a rich Italian industrialist family, who was first married to a Brazilian millionaire playboy, 'Baby' Pignatari, then to Prince Ferdinando Del Drago. As 'Queen of Ischia' she was given honorary citizenship of the island where she owned a magnificent villa. Anyone of any importance was entertained extravagantly there.

[4] Julia Strachey (1901–79), novelist; niece of Lytton Strachey.

The only thing that's wrong with this island (apart, of course, with it's not being Greek, but can't blame it for that) is that it's so hard to stay awake. I only keep myself from nodding off with the greatest effort, and getting a paragraph written is a hero's work.

The house looks very pretty at night. I've hung lengths of African cloth behind both those Passerano marbles, and it has been cold enough twice to have blazing fires. If you <u>can</u> get off for a long weekend, do try and come. It's all very different, and you could sleep and work in Diana's & Debo's room (which should have been yours, anyway), which I use as a study. Or you could have mine with its fire and galleon of a bed. It's beautiful, cool weather now (after sinister days of suicidal sirocco), autumn all right, and a trace of sadness at sunset, but soon abolished by lights and fires.

Write and send news, and

much fond love from Paddy

P.S. Stephen Spender wrote last week and is tremendously enthusiastic about your marble poem, which he is printing before the year's out.[1] I <u>am</u> pleased.

[1] PLF's poem 'On Two Marble Feet and a Marble Tree Dug up Last Autumn by a Ploughman in the Roman Campagna', dedicated 'For Lyndall', appeared in the January 1960 number of *Encounter*.

Almost forty years later, Paddy would still be trying to persuade Murrays to undertake publication of his translation of Paul Morand's Isabeau de Bavière *(see, for example, his letter to Jock's son, John, of 10 February 1998).*

To Jock Murray
New Year's Day 1961

12 Kallirhöe Street
Makriyannis
Athens[1]

Dear Jock,

1) I write in Sackcloth. I can't think why I have been such a long time writing, and very many apologies included.

2) You will be pleased to hear that I have been making considerable progress. After one or two false starts, I settled in a room in the old Neon Hotel in Nauplia[2] and really got going, only breaking off to come here for Christmas and the New Year. I stand Godbrother to an old Cretan pal at the marriage of his son tomorrow, and then rusticate once more, either back at Nauplia or in a room in Delphi, deciding within the next 24 hours. But here will get me, as I will arrange a good quick forwarding system by the bus people. The book has been forging forward. I wish I hadn't let it lie for so long, as it takes quite an effort to warm up the cold notes; but it's all right once this is done. (I also wish I'd known how expensive it was to 'buy the crown' at a Greek wedding!)

3) Hambros [bank] tell me that you just kindly sent them £200, for which v. many thanks. It was timely as the barrel was empty, and still is! I am very pleased you advised me to put that £500 on one side for taxation, as that is looming at last, and this sizeable sop should quiet them for a time. I am hoping against hope that the glorious American & German reviews have brought in lots of money, as it is

---

[1] Joan had bought this small house in Athens with an inheritance after the death of her mother. Though they had to endure constant noise of pumps, diggers and pneumatic drills while a road was being built only yards from their door, it helped to have a base in Greece while they were looking for somewhere permanent to settle.

[2] A port at the northern end of the Argolic Gulf of the Peloponnese, now more generally transliterated as Nafplio.

desperately needed, as my ebb in faraway Greece is very low indeed – I won't depress you by saying <u>how</u> low. So if something <u>could</u> be sent to Hambros against these future or present foreign royalties, do try and wrench it free, and let Mr Teasdale have it. (Two hundred is what I am praying it might be.) I feel very guilty badgering you when you have had so little from me for ages; but I hope and think this bread cast upon the waters will return many times over, even if it is after many days. I'm working hard to reduce the number.

4) Heinemann's professed to be thrilled and delighted with the Ghyka corrections and introduction[1] and propose, as they put it, to show their gratitude in tangible form, although none was asked for; but nothing so far.

5) Something entirely different, including a slight saga, and rather nice. Before the war in Romania, I translated, rather well, I think, a book of Paul Morand's[2] called *Isabeau de Bavière*. (Morand's wife Hélène is Romanian, and both were friends.) The 'Isabeau' in question is Isabella of Bavaria,[3] the Queen of Charles VI, the well-beloved King of France,[4] and the book, which was a

---

[1] PLF had translated Matila Ghyka's memoir *The World Mine Oyster* (1961).

[2] Paul Morand (1888–1976), diplomat and author, was a collaborator with Vichy. He was eventually elected, at the fourth attempt, to the Académie française in 1968, despite the protests of President Charles de Gaulle, who refused to receive him at the Elysée Palace.

[3] Isabeau of Bavaria (c.1370–1435), eldest daughter of Duke Stephen III of Bavaria-Ingolstadt and Taddea Visconti of Milan. She became Queen of France when she married King Charles VI in 1385, at the age of fifteen or sixteen, though she always spoke French in a heavy German accent. Later, when Charles's madness (see below) rendered him incapable, she became regent to her son, the dauphin, and was blamed for the civil war that followed, denounced as adulterous, meddlesome, scheming and spendthrift, and even accused of being a witch.

[4] Charles VI (1368–1422) was only eleven when he inherited the throne of France in the midst of the Hundred Years' War. The government was entrusted to his four uncles, who squandered the resources of the kingdom for their own benefit. In 1388 Charles dismissed his uncles, and political and economic conditions improved significantly, earning him the epithet 'the Beloved' (*le Bien-Aimé*). But four years later he suddenly went mad, slaying four knights and almost killing his brother. From then on he suffered frequent bouts of insanity, attacking servants, denying he had a wife and children, and claiming that he was made of glass: he became known as 'Charles the Mad' (*le Fou*). In 1430 he signed the infamous Treaty of Troyes, disinheriting his offspring and recognising Henry V of England as his legitimate successor to the throne of France.

pre-war best seller in France, and I think Morand's best, was done in brilliant dialogue form. It all goes on in the thick of the 100 Years' War, involving Philip the Bold and John the Fearless of Burgundy, Henry V and the English invasion, with Agincourt and the Earl of Bedford's occupation, all told from the French end. There are revolts and battles and witchcraft and palace revolutions and every kind of exciting mediæval goings on, the whole being done after considerable research and brilliantly carried off. Now! I somehow lost my typescript of it, which I believe to be the only one, with some luggage I left behind in a house later bombed when leaving for the Middle East as a soldier, France having already fallen, which held up all question of publication. When it disappeared, I forgot all about it. Now, all of a sudden, last month Hélène Morand writes to me saying she has found a complete copy of my translation, while going through a cupboard in Paris! So I have arranged for her nephew, who is now here, and just escaped from Romania after 25 years, called Nicky Chrissoveloni, to pick it up in France in a fortnight's time and deliver it to you when he comes to London a few days later. He's a charming and brilliant chap, an old friend,[1] so please make a bit of a fuss of him when he turns up with it. I would like to have had another look at it after all these years, but as it's the only surviving version, I don't want to risk it. I think you'll agree when you have a look at it that the thing is remarkable, and my idea is: why not publish it? I can't remember who we had in mind as a possible publisher before the war; but they are perfectly prepared to let me place it – so where else but 50 Albemarle St?[2] The only drawback is that Paul Morand had a bad record during the war. He was a career diplomat, and remained on under Vichy, becoming Pétain's ambassador in wartime Bucharest, which was why he wasn't elected to the Académie française last year – you may remember all the rows and the fuss. But the thing is, he didn't do anything criminal, and, if he had done, *Isabeau* was written long before. I don't know how much all this ought to weigh with us. But

[1] They had become friends in Bucharest in 1934.
[2] Address of John Murray publishers since 1812.

I'm sure you'll have no doubts about the quality of the book. For later reference, his address is: M. Paul Morand, 3, Avenue Charles-Floquet, Paris (I think VIIeme). I long to hear your views. It might turn out to be a splendid thing for all of us.

No more now, dear Jock, except renewed apologies for my slowness in every kind of writing, both books and letters, and the best wishes to one and all for 1961.

Yours ever
Paddy

I must now go out and buy candles as tall as a man, ribbons, crowns, boxes of sugared almonds and countless other gewgaws that Godbrothers have to provide against tomorrow's wedding. If only I'd realised all this when accepting!

Soon after his affair with Lyndall Birch petered out, Paddy became involved with Enrica 'Ricki' Huston, the fourth and much younger wife of film director John Huston. At forty-six, Paddy was closer to her in age, though still fourteen years her senior. It seems that he was a generous lover. 'With most men it's just take, take, take,' she told a friend, 'but with Paddy it's give, give, give.'

The Hustons lived at St Clerans, an eighteenth-century mansion in the west of Ireland. Their marriage was troubled, not least because Huston was so often absent from home making films.

To Ricki Huston   Château de Chassy
undated [postmarked 28 April 1961]   Montigny-en-Morvan
                                        Nièvre

My darling Ricki,

We always seem to be corresponding from castles, and here's another. I'll tell you how I got here in a minute, but first, thank you so much, Ricki dear, for telephoning to Joan on your way through London. She was very touched, me too. I do hope your arrival in

Paris, and Tony's & Anjelica's,[1] went off all right, that beds were soft, shops full, chefs diligent and dentists kind. It's odd to think of you through a film of Galway rain, after the Thessalian plain, the sierras of the Pindus and nomads' land, transported from Lethe to the Shannon ...[2]

Things improved a bit in Rome after my last letter. Judy [Montagu] suddenly decided she wanted to go to Paris, after a long telephone chat we had with Diana, now an exile from Chantilly in the Rue de Lille, and Balthus and his nymphet[3] were leaving on the same day, so we determined to hit the Aurelian Way in a two car-convoy, stopping for a few days at Balthus's castle – here – on the way. *Ainsi fut dit, ainsi fut fait.*[4] There were two lovely picnics between this decision and pushing off, the first in the gardens of the Villa Medici, under a clump of ilex trees with my beautiful Mycenaean wreath hung on a moss-covered stela of Janus, and another among some Etruscan tombs at Cerveteri, near Viterbo. Your and Judy's pal Hubert Faure[5] turned up in Rome with a beautiful American girl two days before we left (not a patch on mine, though, I may say) and participated in a giant evening at Natalie's,[6] full of Boucompagnis, Ruspolis, Borgheses, etc. ...[7] My word, how pleased I was to see the last of Rome and its denizens.

Well. Both cars foregathered on the island at 9.30 on Friday morning, and off we set through grey weather, over the Campagna and the Maremma, me Hustoning through the defiles of Montefiascone and Radicofani as to the manner born, with a cheerful luncheon in the Piazza in Siena, lasting far too long, then off along the amazing new *Autostrada del Sole* to Bologna. This journey, which used to take hours of coiling up and down over the Futa Pass, now

---

[1] Ricki Huston's children, Walter (known as 'Tony') and Anjelica.
[2] PLF had holidayed with Ricki in Northern Greece.
[3] Balthus lived with his niece, Frédérique Tison, thirty-two years younger than him.
[4] 'No sooner said than done.'
[5] Hubert Faure (b. 1919), French-born company executive based in America, who married a Rockefeller.
[6] Natalie Perrone (1927–2004), daughter of the Vicomte and Vicomtesse de Noailles.
[7] PLF was scathing about Roman society.

whirlsjone along one of the wonders of the world, straight through the Apennines, along the top of vast airy viaducts with deep canyons beneath, and then through long tunnels like the insides of neon-lit boa constrictors, with miles of mountains overhead. It all took place in a violent rain and thunderstorm, with deafening claps echoing along the tunnels, the ends zig-zagged with lightning, and then, the deluge, one's journey sounding like league on league of calico being ripped asunder nonstop. The car, thanks to all your instructions, shot through this apocalyptic world like a bullet, with me in a sort of trance at the wheel. A major emotional experience, exaltation laced by an Angostura-dash of misgiving: sensations long blunted for old hands like you. But what an anti-climax, to branch off limping into the bumpy local labyrinth of ordinary roads again, after soaring through the firmament like a destroying demon out of Dante, crackling sword cast aside and mackintosh wings a-draggle, a grounded Lucifer. But then, slowly, farms, castles, churches and oxen became visible, all obliterated till then by rain, speed and space.

In colonnaded Bologna, at the Papagallo [Parrot],[1] we had a great feast of turkey pumped full of cream over which thin slices of white truffle were guillotined. At the next table, a tall & suspectly distinguished man (who should have been advertising shirts with one eye covered,[2] gazing down the double barrel of a custom built Purdey or telling it blindfold among lamplit first editions) struck us all as familiar. English? American? English passing as American, or American as English, or Canadian as both? Anyway, we all bowed and waved, not to hurt his feelings (typically English & French to cut people when travelling). He acknowledged these salutes with a grave hauteur, and turned out to be Dean Acheson.[3]

A torrential Autostrada again next day, with Modena, Reggio Emilia, Parma, Pavia, Piacenza and Alessandria swishing invisibly by, then back to ordinary roads again after a hundred miles in as many

[1] A famous old restaurant, popular with celebrities, film stars, etc.
[2] PLF refers to the Hathaway shirt campaign, which made the name of the advertising guru David Ogilvy.
[3] Dean Gooderham Acheson (1893–1971), US Secretary of State 1949–53.

minutes with pounding heart ... Then, after a happy gluttonous break at the *Due Bue Rossi* [Two Red Oxen][1] in the last town, hell for leather for Turin, Lombardy and Piedmont screaming past, then corkscrewing breakneck up into the mountains of Savoy, swirling through Alp after Alp, Fermor in the lead, a tenfold Hannibal-Huston hell-bent for the frontier dusk train lift at Bardonecchia, with Balthus-Balthus and his nymphet hot wheel behind, pirouetting down precipices only to soar again ... how I blessed those gentle lessons of the Pindus passes![2] We got out just in the nick in the station yard, a strange light in our eyes, like the person in Kubla Khan who on honeydew hath fed and drunk the milk of Paradise.

How much better the first French dinner, in the station hotel at Modane (owing to the late hour) seemed than anything we'd had at The Parrot or The Two Red Oxen! Leek soup, trout, and a fillet ... Then the luxury of French roads in the dark, the soft swoops between a million headlamp-lit poplars, sailing over rushing streams and through shuttered villages, no triple Hs here [see above], just a full tank and a full heart and motion like a peaceful and never-ending sigh. We got to the Hotel Pernollet at Belley (✗✗ ❀❀) at midnight, having driven just over 400 miles since Bologna, a record for one day in my brief career on wheels. You probably know this heavenly place, about 150 years old, with rooms like caskets smelling of lavender, beeswax and *eau de javel* [bleach], with plenty of brass and lace and wallpaper patterned with nosegays of faded flowers, and vast Empire beds, stoutly carpentered for embraces, that cruelly underline a traveller's solitary estate. We stayed here two nights, to guzzle and rest from our journeys, drifting all day about the passes of Dauphiné and the Jura. They have a wonderful fish at Belley, a distant cousin of the *omble*[3] you get at Chambéry, a sort of deep still water trout called a *lavaret*, delicious and quite

---

[1] A hotel restaurant in Alessandria, founded in 1741.
[2] After their holiday together in northern Greece, PLF had driven south with Ricki to catch the ferry to Bari, and then on to Rome. During the journey she had an opportunity to improve PLF's primitive driving skills.
[3] Arctic char.

unlike anything else.[1] They only swim in the Lac du Bourget nearby, and in Lake Como hundreds of miles away, and in none of the intervening ones, two fortuitous rock pools from prehistoric times, I suppose, when all these mountains were underwater. It seems they live hundreds of feet down, the lines being lowered into the abyss on winches, often emerging after hours of winding with only one fish. No wonder they're worth their weight in radium.

Judy turned up trumps as a travelling pal. Hamstrung and gagged by various woes in Rome, her spirits shot up at the idea of the trip, and all has been happy chat and laughter. Frédérique the nymphet still remains an enigma: is she 13 or 30?[2] Apart from startling flashes of knowledge about astronomy and zoology, her conversation, in the teeth of appearances, supports the first hypothesis. She is a great one for a hop-skip and a jump with hands clapping with excitement and plaits flying; also, she has five dolls in a special basket, one of which closes its eyes and gurgles; and she stops at every newsagent to take on a new armful of Mickey Mouse comics. Of course all this may be to please Balthus-Balthus; perhaps she devours Proust and Schopenhauer on the sly …

I wish you'd had more of a chance to drink in Balthus. I like him more and more. He's a beautifully distinguished and well finished off product, intricately and reconditely cultivated and wonderfully funny. There is a sort of half complicity about the nymphet situation almost as though it were an elaborate joke; though of course it's nothing of the kind.

So here we are at last in his castle, in the Morvan, between Avallon and Vézelay, dreamlike green rolling country full of trout streams and spinneys full of bluebells and ragged robin. The château is like one out of *Puss-in-boots* or *Beauty and the Beast*, tall, that soft suet French colour I adore, with high windows and four cylindrical towers topped with red-brown tiled extinguisher cones

[1] Not in fact a trout but a whitefish, similar to the powan found in Loch Lomond or the gwyniad in Lake Bala (Llyn Tegid).
[2] Frédérique was about twenty at the time of this letter, having lived with Balthus since she was fourteen.

and surrounded by billowing chestnuts crowded with their pink and white candles. Rank grass sweeps right up to the walls, dotted with dandelion clocks. I'm writing out of doors in the corner of a walled orchard and can hear two clogged peasants scything this grassy jungle and singing in patois. Lilac and weeping willow droop, cats stalk along the roofs of barns, guinea fowl scuttle through cow parsley, a sheepdog pants in the shadow of an elder bush, huge geese descend through rushes to a carp- and pike-haunted pool, and embark. The fairy tale aura thickens as the hours accumulate. Inside, all is soft grey and faded mauve, with huge black and white squares or worn rose coloured tiles under foot, beds in curtained alcoves and tall windows looking out over the tops of chestnut trees, full of birch (and at night, of nightingales) and drifting white flotillas of clouds in full sail. Sitting up in bed in the morning, I can see the hill opposite scattered with a flock of sheep, then successive hues of forest and a belfry or two. How I wish I was doing and seeing all this with you.

We all set off to Paris in a day or two (where Joan comes), catching Diana for a day before she finally departs. I'm staying jolly luxuriously in Natalie's wing of Marie Laure de Noailles' house at (N.B!) 10, Place des États Unis,[1] a stone's throw from the Étoile, and remaining, I think, about a week. Then London; then I don't know quite what, except that it must be a frenzy of long neglected work. As you can guess, my darling Ricki, I'm busy churning round plans of seeing you again as quickly as possible. Paris doesn't seem very propitious for either of us, but dark and delicious schemes are beginning to bubble and crystalise for later. I can't really bear the idea of seeing you with other people, and grudge the idea of their presence bitterly. I've been asked to Lismore, and wonder, with racing pulse, whether the green island might offer some secret refuge for a glorious, headlong reunion? Do let's allow these dark and splendid thoughts to germinate. I really do long for you. It's no good people trying to fob one off with twelve pairs of tudor firedogs,

---

[1] The Vicomtesse de Noailles lived at 11 Place des États-Unis, Paris. See next letter.

a basket of pineapples, Britannia metal snuffboxes, tickets for the circus, an Edwardian kaleidoscope with amusing slides of the 1900 exhibition or the bound works of Sir Walter Scott; one knows what one wants, and nothing else will do. Our journey remains far more real than anything since, and I wish we'd been able to go on and on. Of course I pine for the joys of brinkmanship and, indeed, for long plunges at last into the deep end amid spreading rings; but also for all the fun and laughter, and complicity and heaven of everything else. I must stop this now, and try and post it in Vézelay, where we are heading anon for a wonder lunch. God bless you, my dearest darling Ricki, and tons and tons of

fond love from
Paddy
X X X X X

To Ricki Huston	c/o Viscount de Noailles
6 May 1961	Paris
Thursday	France

IN UTMOST HASTE

My darling Ricki,

It's too maddening. I put 10, not 11, Place des États Unis, in my letter to you; and of course, 10 is to let and empty; so, should you have written, I won't get it for months, probably posted back unknown to you. Hell and damnation!

My plans are, to return to London, Chester Row,[1] on Sunday and to set off for Lismore for about 10 days next Wednesday. Do you think you could possibly dine in Dublin on Wednesday Night? If so, I'd set off for Limerick junction next afternoon. Do try! You know how I pine for you. If you could, do, like a saint, write to London at once, advising me where to stay in Dublin etc. Then we might make

---

[1] In 1956 Joan had bought a small house in Pimlico, No. 13 Chester Row, SW1.

some heavenly plan for post-Lismore days. I feel rather a-flutter with excitement at the possibilities of all this. Of course, my darling Ricki, I do understand that it may be difficult or impossible for you; but if it is humanly feasible, try and circumvent, dodge, outwit, foil and checkmate any impediments. It would be a glorious triumph, and a joyful clanging asunder of golden gates with countless rockets soaring and exploding and a massed fanfare of long shafted trumpets.

Judy [Montagu] and I are sumptuously installed in this vast mansion (Joan is down the road chez Derek Jackson): hushed vistas of Louis XV furniture, labyrinths of gilt and brocade magnificence, looking down into a courtyard where pigeons flutter and croon about among pink candled chestnut trees, with the roar of Paris muffled somewhere in the distance. Vast doors, with doors within doors, sweep silently asunder as one comes in from the street, click after click admits one to deeper and deeper mirrored meanderings, all activated by unseen hands. Very grand, but a bit eerie, as if [illegible], spies and eunuchs were observing one's every step from inside gigantic Ming vases and through giant portraits of Noailles after Noailles: Eyes and No Eyes ...[1] No question of sneaking in in the small hours with five negresses, or any rot of that kind ...

No more for the moment, my sweet darling Ricki, except please write at once. (I'll telephone from London, if that's alright); and love and a trillion hugs

from Paddy

To Ricki Huston   Lismore Castle
undated [postmarked 13 May 1961]   County Waterford
                                                            Eire

Ricki darling,
    'The loine to Galway's very busy. Oi can't guarantee less than two hours delay,' say the beasts at the exchange. Worse than yesterday.

---

[1] A play on words.

What can they be so busy about? Giant shamrock combines merging, a million bog-oak pigs changing hands; or are the wires a-murmur with the voices of an army of lovesick Galway ladies and their swooning Waterford paramours? What are the wild wires saying?[1] Anyway, I've fled the cold billiard-room in despair, and have settled under a terrace, with the many-towered castle below, buoyed among tree tops, and Andrew's bold banner beating from the topmost turret (but no more boldly than mine at Passerano ...).

Darling, you <u>were</u> an angel to meet me in Dublin like that; and I'm so glad, in spite of all our vicissitudes and reverses, that we had that wonderful golden evening drive and fireside dinner and blissful time – even if the cup was dashed from one's lips, as one might or might not say. <u>I do hope</u> all is well there. I loved your house, and sigh for those ravishing rooms.

It's great fun here: Debo, Andrew [Devonshire], Mark [Ogilvie-Grant], Nancy [Mitford], an amusing aunt of Andrew's called Lady Maud Baillie, and tonight, Eddy Sackville-West. There's lots of lolling in the garden and sneaking off to the Lismore wine-vaults, a sawdust-scattered drinking hell in the village, with Andrew. Cuckoos are seldom out of earshot, and the Blackwater flashes below, far below, as the salmon leap there, winding away under caverns of enormous trees so thick with ferns and parasites and so looped and festooned with creepers that it might be the Zambezi or the Limpopo.

Now I must dash off with this to the post, and see how soon it gets to you express. Could you, angelically, give me a ring when you get it to see if it's any quicker that way? I do miss you. God bless you, my darling sweet Ricki, and oceans of fond love and hugs from

Paddy

X X X X

---

[1] A reference to Paul Dombey's repeated question to his sister Florence: 'What are the wild waves saying?' in Charles Dickens's *Dombey and Son* (1846–8).

To Ricki Huston   Lismore Castle
17 May 1961   County Waterford
                                                         Ireland

Darling Ricki,
    The castle's population has thinned down considerably, to
a mid-week minimum. Kitty Mersey[1] left for Derreen in Kerry,
where she lives, yesterday morning, Nancy went to stay with Eddy
Sackville-West, leaving only its chatelaine [Debo] and self, which
is lovely and peaceful: long mornings writing on a card table under
a magnolia on the crenellated upper terrace which I have made
my *querencia*,[2] and, yesterday afternoon, a tremendous walk along
the Blackwater, the vast trees leaning over it more tragically than
ever. Sometimes it runs straight for a mile or two, a diminishing
vista like a watery Champs Elysées, then winds again with islands
and weirs, with sudden flights of swans and cormorants' heads
projecting from the flood in the manner of periscopes and huge
herons drifting lazily overhead from wood to wood. We left the
banks uphill through a steep and almost impenetrable spinney,
thick with willow-herb and ragged robin and clumps of that giant
broccoli and cow parsley two yards high, it might have been the
haunt of mammoths and dinosaurs in those imaginary pictures, in
children's books, of prehistoric scenery; in reality it only harboured
some woodpigeons, a cuckoo, a number of blackbirds, and it
seems, quantities of foxes and badgers. A woman in a cottage the
other end of it said no one had been through it for fifteen years,
and, slashing one's way through the dappled wilderness, one could
believe it. She gave us some tea and Guinness and currant-buns,
then we thumbed a lift back here in a lorry. This afternoon a lovely
ride looms ahead, involving Royal Tan[3] and Another. (Bags I the
former.)

[1] Debo's 'wife', her close friend Lady Katherine Petty-Fitzmaurice, Viscountess Mersey
(1912–95).
[2] The part of a bullring where the bull takes its stand.
[3] Winner of the 1954 Grand National.

You're quite right about Roderic M.O'F.[1] (Haven't seen him since my fighting days.) I think he comes the day after tomorrow, also Andrew and several others, a popular weekend, in fact. Then Dublin! I long for it, and the other single unit of increased population at 8.30 on Tuesday.

With lots of love from Paddy X X X

To Ricki Huston   Cliff Cottage
Nine days after the Fast of St Samson the   Fforest Farm
Innkeeper [17 July] 1961   Dinas
                                                            Newport
                                                        Pembrokeshire

My darling Ricki,
    Well, I made it by the skin of my teeth, by chucking all ideas of cabs and taking the tube from Green Park Station and whirling through London entrails – a glittering gut through that inert clay carcass stuffed with flint arrow heads and the skeletons of mammoths ...
    [INNER VOICE: Get on with it.
    SELF: Very well.]... and just catching the Fishguard train, charging through mild sunset pasturelands towards the Celtic fringe. The train was full of a pretty tough horde of returning Irish awash with Guinness and all called Paddy. Alone at my table reading *The Late Lord Byron*[2] and judiciously puffing at a Romeo and Juliet [cigar], an aloof and fastidious Sassenach, I had no difficulty in quelling any primordial interior voice from the bogs responding, as you and your brood soared overhead. I blew surreptitious kisses to a plane, but it was going so high and fast they may not have made it. Anyway, it might have been the wrong one; just think of a nun starting up in outraged bewilderment

---

[1] See p. 83.
[2] Doris Langley More, *The Late Lord Byron: Posthumous Dramas* (1961).

from dozing over her beads and her breviary and glaring at the neighbouring squireens ... I got to Fishguard at four and drove to this wuthering height in the rain, the car waking a number of gulls who seem to think they own the place; to bed, and up next day to rainy and studious solitude, my only fellow lodger being a rather noisy bluebottle who has perfected the art of dodging during his years of incumbency.

I keep on finding myself smiling clean across my face at the thought of all the fun, laughter, delight, bliss, excitement & magic, all still inextinguishably aglow from last week. You <u>are</u> a lovely present to suddenly get, my darling Ricki, and I do feel grateful to life for suddenly tilting this cornucopia and setting all these treasures cascading so generously and gratuitously round one. No stint there: all laughter among wine glasses and under leaves and fierce, moon-flaunting death grapples in what seem like half-lit palaces, tents and caves; and gentle and loving recoveries with my hands full of dark silk and warm alabaster;[1] and lighter paces through nocturnal towns as empty as a room, built, one might think, with no ulterior motive beyond the re-echoing of private laughter and themes like cats amidstream.[2] I <u>must</u> find out about a Soho HQ. I see brown, embossed poppies on the wallpaper, coronation mugs and china cats and spaniels on the mantlepiece with ribbons on their pretty necks, *The Last Rose of Summer* on the wall, *The Monarch of the Glen*, and *The Last Charge at Waterloo*; perhaps a 1911 Mazawattee Tea gift calendar, with blossom and Fujiyama, and a giant brass bed in which the lucky ones who have taken sanctuary there can lie loosely coiled, listening to soft gear changes beyond the blue lace curtains and Italian colloquys about *tortelloni alla Bolognese*, *lavaggio* [washing], *ingrassaggio* [lubrication], and, of course, the procrastination so sadly prevalent among cats in Dolomite rivers, so

---

[1] In her reply, she teased him about 'the dark silk and warm alabaster', suggesting that he might have used some of these literary gallantries before.
[2] Perhaps a reference to the sounds of love-making?

unlike the decisive and masterful toms of the Arno, the Po and the Tiber;[1] these and other delightful themes, only blotted out now and then by embraces, until it's time for lunch or dinner or breakfast …

Lots of love and hugs, Ricki darling, Paddy

P.S. I'm wearing one of my lovely Greek shirts, the slatey one. I love to think of those three spectacular tailors stitching away at them for weeks, cross-legged among the cobwebs.

To Ricki Huston   Dumbleton
27 July 1961   Evesham
Gloucestershire

My darling Ricki,

What a lovely letter from Achill. If only the carpet underfoot would suddenly begin to fidget, then, making up its mind, sail out of the open window with me on it, away over the bean fields and elm trees, then a bit of open country where the jettisoned table and chairs could harm neither man, beast, nor crops over St Geo's channel and lose height over the Mayo coast, and then, rolling itself into a funnel as we approach the Diamond Hotel,[2] tilt me, as from a chute, into the right one of those whitewashed beds by peat light. I got this glorious letter ½ an hour before leaving Wales and re-read it halfway here in the churchyard in Abergavenny and drove on singing at the wheel through the East Wales and border counties, a lone rolling forested pre-Domesday Book world. The only thing that worried me was your far too modest thought that anything in my letter might have been written before like some awful trick with dog-eared card from a well-thumbed pack.

[1] See footnote 2 on previous page.
[2] Ricki Huston had been staying at the Amethyst Hotel.

The last two or three days in Wales went in preparing for exodus here, finishing a terrific chapter (or so I hope) and in going with 3 ornithologists to 3 remote islands of the Pembroke coast, all with windy Viking names, Skokholm, Skomer and Grassholm, the Welsh equivalent of your stormy habitat. The first two were full of hordes of puffins, guillemots, shearwaters, razor bills, cormorants and shag, and the third – Grassholm – which is little more than an acre of crag about twelve miles out among stormy waves, was inhabited by 50,000 gannets (pause here to refill your lovely grey pen) crowding together on every inch of rock like snow (redundantly, as they already sparkled with millions of years of droppings), croaking raucously, wheeling, edging, barging, getting their furry grey chicks to peck mackerel from their gullets, and diving from more [than] 150 yards in the air, shooting sheer into them, with wings folded like atomic missiles or screaming bombs. They are huge, bigger than geese and amazingly beautiful with great elegant raking black tipped wings and swan necks. I've never seen anything like it, one of the wonders of the world, like Angkor or the Grand Canyon. Phew! Poetic epithets in Norse, sagas for the sea are 'The Whales' Acre' and 'The Gannet's Bath': *Hronsaker* and *Ganetenbaep*. I can't get over them. Seals also crowded thick.

Well, here I am, scribbling away again like mad. I slip away on Sat[urday] for the night to Henry & Virginia Bath, to see some people walk netless and on tightropes across the Cheddar Gorge, from where I'll telephone you on Sunday morning, probably before you get this …

Lots and lots of fond love & hugs, darling Ricki,
from Paddy
X X X X X X X

In 1961 the satirical revue Beyond the Fringe, *written and performed by Peter Cook, Dudley Moore, Alan Bennett and Jonathan Miller, had a hugely successful run at the Fortune Theatre in London's West End, after previewing in Edinburgh and in the provinces. Though certain war veterans felt that the sketch titled 'The Aftermyth of the War' was insensitive, this letter suggests that Paddy was not one of them. It was addressed to the Fortune Theatre.*

A few weeks after writing this letter Paddy met Bennett, then an aspirant academic, at the opening of Peter Cook's Establishment Club in Soho. Paddy, who was accompanied by John Sparrow, the Warden of All Souls, claimed to have gained entry by climbing through a window.

To Alan Bennett and Jonathan Miller   13 Chester Row
9 September 1961   London, SW1

Dear Mr Bennett and Mr Miller,

I hope you will forgive me for writing. It is not specifically to reveal my admiration for Beyond the Fringe – though I would not let this opportunity slip without doing so, a thousand times over – but to transmit a snatch of conversation during the war. (This is *à propos* of 'The Suspense is Killing Me'.[1])

The soldier-servant* of a friend of mine had been a prison warder before the war. I asked him if he had ever participated in an execution.

S.S.: 'Dozens of them. I never liked it. I always tried to cheer them up, like, on the way to the scaffold.'

Me: 'What on earth did you say?'

S.S.: 'I always used to say, "Keep your chin up, cock, and you'll go off nicely."'

The whole thing was magnificent. I especially enjoyed the Proustian miner[2] and the Logical Positivism piece.[3] Please don't

---

[1] A sketch about a man awaiting execution, performed by all four members of the cast.

[2] 'The Miner', a sketch performed by Cook about a miner who wanted to become a judge but couldn't because 'I never had the Latin.' In an attempt to raise the intellectual level of the conversation, he asks one of his fellow miners: 'Have you heard of Marcel Proust?' and receives the reply, 'No, he must work down another mine.'

[3] 'Oxford Philosophy', performed by Bennett and Miller.

think that your self-restraint in not calling the latter 'On the Ayer'[1] went unobserved.

> Yours sincerely, Patrick Leigh Fermor

* Interesting sociologically.

To Ricki Huston   Au Fer à Cheval
Wednesday [postmarked 31 October 1961]   Locronan
                                                         Finistère

Darling Ricki,

Thank you so much for sending those glorious francs, and also for the toothpaste and the lovely spiky-based nailbrush. They arrived at the very second that I was sallying forth to buy one, and I bet it would not have been nearly such a nice one. No spikes on the back, for a start. Above all I do humbly beg your rosporden[2] for being such a slowcoach writing.

I <u>did</u> feel glum and lonely, digging in here after you had to bugger off. Not getting that pavilion was a real disaster. I do wish I'd never seen it, as my present quarters are far from ideal for my purposes. How could they be? And yet one can't waste all one's days scouring Brittany for the perfect habitat. I've done it a certain amount, but all in vain, and I'm continuing to flog myself to work in this horse-shoe, and fairly successfully. But it's uphill work.

It seems ages since you were here. It <u>was</u> marvellous, from the first moment in France at Châteaubriand at St Malo till the last outside our marvellous madhouse in Pont Aven.[3] What amazing

[1] A play on words: A. J. Ayer (pronounced 'air'), Wykeham Professor of Logic at Oxford since 1959, was the best-known proponent in English of logical positivism, a movement in philosophy developed in Berlin and Vienna in the 1920s.
[2] Perhaps based on an Irish pronunciation of 'your Honour's pardon'? There is a village called Rosporden in Finistère, close to Pont Aven, where PLF and Ricki Huston had been staying.
[3] A picturesque Breton river port made famous by Gauguin and the Pont Aven school of artists.

luck finding such a haven! I can't get over the amount of <u>time</u> there seemed for everything. God knows, we weren't up with the lark – at least, not in the usually accepted sense – and yet the days seemed infinitely elastic, with time for slow lunches, endless dalliances over shrimps and oysters and muscadet, hours of talk, hundreds of miles of travel, dozens of villages and churches and inlets, menhirs, Gregorian chant, a few moments reading, drinking and dancing with the Merry Wives of Locronan, and entire crowded lifetimes in bed; glorious extinctions and phoenix-like resurrections (I hope the last is the right word …) Whereas now, in this dark granite solitude, the enormous bell in St Ronan's seems to toll the quarters at five minute intervals, and it's sunset about an hour after getting up. We <u>were</u> lucky! Everything was radiant and well-starred throughout. You were an angel, and what a bold and dashing one, to alight so splendidly in this duchy.

I'm writing this in the empty crêperie in the square, I hear shuffling clogs and neolithic exchanges in Breton in the bar next door. I wonder what they are talking about. Last year's Great Toadfest? Shrimping prospects? How to circumvent the danger to traffic offered by fallen beetroots? *Il faut savoir* … A very nice tortoise-shell cat has just come slowly and purposefully pacing across the flagstones, thinking the room was empty, then stopping dead and looking clean through me with vast grape-green eyes. I'm afraid he can read me like an open book. The thing about cats in motion is that they are always up to something. They know what they're heading for, and are out to win. Unlike dogs. These just hang about, rather like humans, wasting the best years of their lives in purposeless lounging, pointless activity and random hobnobbing. Dead Sea Fruit. Good time Charlies.

No more now, my dearest darling Ricki, except a billion thanks for everything, and lots and lots of fond hugs, kisses & love from Paddy.

X X X X

P.S. A huge truckload of giant pigs has just driven past. I wonder if this spells marvellous <u>bacon</u> somewhere.

To Ricki Huston   Easton Court Hotel
4 February 1962   Chagford
                                           Newton Abbot
                                            Devon

Darling Ricki,

Riddle: What is the difference between outdoors and indoors, in the country, in England, in winter? Answer: Outdoors it rains cats and dogs while indoors dogs and cats reign.[1] This is a rough outline of the situation here, but I don't mind, as for the last ten days I've been striking oil, from a literary point of view, such a gusher that it's hard to keep pace with it: all day long, from immediately after breakfast till late at night, wheels turning, pumps thundering, shift replacing shift, no labour disputes, wildcat strikes, occupational diseases or disruptive propaganda. Deadline Camp is a happy camp. The deadline seems to be about the first of March (for Mexico);[2] whether it's this time limit that has initiated this sudden blockbusting or whether, more classically, country austerity and solitude has straightened the path for the descent of the Muses, I simply don't know. Spells like this have something of the insane buoyancy of a hot love affair. Are they a substitute for it, or is it the other way about? And what about the two running high at the same time? It can happen, and the buoyancy becomes explosive. One of them has to steady up, as a rule, and cede precedence to the other. Nevertheless:–

[write on one side of the paper only]
Examiner Muse or mistress?
Candidate Both!

To hell with all that . . .

---

[1] One of PLF's favourite riddles, which appears in several of his letters.
[2] PLF was planning to go to Mexico with Joan, to gather material for a book; but though he had obtained a promise of funding from the new *Sunday Times Colour Supplement*, Jock Murray was not keen, and the trip never happened.

How are you, my darling Ricki? I do miss the looming ahead of some dead-secret joint plan, which has played such a part in the last ten months. We'll dissect all this sometime, and I fear I won't come out of it too well. You do, impeccably.

I broke away from this writing table yesterday for a most wonderful moorland hunt. It was a lovely clear cold day with infinitesimal rain hanging in the air so that one was always pounding towards a rainbow; and so high on the moor that one got a peculiar aerial feeling of the actual curve of the earth sloping away from one dizzily on all sides and it was such miles away that hacking home over bridges and through unknown villages and down endless unfamiliar mazes of lanes all took place in the dark, so that when I got back here, I almost felt as if I were from China or Peru. Do you know the feeling?

Fond love & hugs to you, dear darling Ricki – it's 3 a.m.!

from Paddy

This letter, written from Tuscany and never completed, is included to show Paddy in one of his periodic troughs of depression. He was trying to make progress with another book about Greece, the follow-up to Mani.

To Joan Rayner   Montepulciano
4 June 1962

My darling Joan,

… I've been in rather a rotten state, I'm sorry to say, but am getting out of it. <u>And about time too</u> – I don't mean about getting out of it, though I'm glad I am – but being in a rotten state; some good may come of it.

NEXT DAY. I was going to launch into a huge wallow of gloom and self-flagellation last night. I'm glad I knocked off, because today I feel fine, and would have had to tear it up and start all over again, as it would no longer have been true. The main cause of all this gloom is my slowness at writing. I <u>wish</u> I could get a move on, and don't know what's the matter with me. I've got about half of that wretched chapter done, with the utmost fuss and bother, smoking, pacing up and down, putting on the gramophone, and mouldering in my chair. I hope that I haven't done my brain in with smoking, or something – i.e. that it's not an organic thing like busting a wrist. My scorn of psychiatry in the past is rapidly on the wane. My plight at the moment is a sort of anti-mescalin jag, where everything is not enhanced, but lessened: chairs, walls, floors, far from being touched with magic, are not even chairs, walls and floors, but sub-c's, sub-w's, sub-f's ... not even neutrals, but actually on the wrong side. The rain, wind and cold here have been, in spite of all Origo[1] said, far worse than for many years. Sunset's the bad time, when all this side of the town is grey and cold far too early, with St Louis Blues looming, while the other side of the town is bathed in lovely lingering sunsets and it's all but impossible not to make a dash for the battlements at S. Biagio.[2] I've thought several times of Bagni di Lucca, or taking a room on the west side of the town, and then thought of 'Ithaca' and 'η Πόλις' ['The City'],[3] and decided to stick it out. Anyway, I'm going to Rome the day after tomorrow, and then to Athens, I hope in under a week, so hooray! Of course, it's not all been like this and I've been for some lovely walks, also to a few neighbouring towns and villages for late lunch – all of them better than here, as far as food goes. The day before yesterday I went – in a downpour – to a charming little town called Monte S. Savino – full of buildings by San Gallo[4] and Sansovino (his home town)[5] and had some delicious minestrone and eggs in a downstairs den full of peasants...

---

[1] Antonio Origo, husband of the English writer Iris Origo, who lived nearby.
[2] San Biagio is a Romanesque church outside Montepulciano. It does not have battlements.
[3] Both titles of poems by C. P. Cavafy. PLF reflects that there is no point in moving to another place, as in the second stanza of 'The City':

You won't find a new country, won't find another shore. /This city will always pursue you. You will walk/ the same streets, grow old in the same neighborhoods, /will turn gray in these same houses. /You will always end up in this city. Don't hope for things elsewhere:/ there is no ship for you, there is no road. /As you've wasted your life here, in this small corner, /you've destroyed it everywhere else in the world.

[4] Giuliano da Sangallo (c.1445–1516), sculptor, architect and engineer.
[5] Both the church and the cloister at Monte San Savino were renovated by Andrea Sansovino (c.1467–1529) in the early sixteenth century.

Joan's inheritance from her mother made it possible for her and Paddy to realise a long-nursed ambition to settle in Greece. Soon after abandoning the last letter he headed for Athens to resume his search for a house. At first he and Joan planned to convert one of the towers that dot the western coastline of the Peloponnese. His attention was focused on the coastal village of Kardamyli, which he and Joan had visited while he was working on Mani.

To Joan Rayner   12 Kallirhoë Street
26 June 1962   Athens

Darling Joan,

I'm so dreadfully sorry about the lateness of this. I was in the middle of a long letter begun in Montepulciano and continued in Rome, pages and pages, and it was idiotically still unfinished when I came here – and now, in my multiple changes of address here, it seems to have evaporated, which is absolutely maddening and frustrating. But in a way, perhaps it's all to the good, as I got fearfully gloomy and depressed in Montepulciano, and simply loathed Rome, and the letter was really a long jeremiad about the awfulness of Italy (and me) and pretty melancholy reading. Anyway, darling, to hell with all that!

Coote was away,[1] on a yacht with the Hares[2] and Mark [Ogilvie-Grant] for a week when Ian [Whigham][3] and I got here, and there was no chance of getting the key from the number you thoughtfully sent that night, so I burgled it in the usual way with Ian's help, and luckily found a key in the ashtray. Coote was due back in two

[1] Coote Lygon was staying in their house in Kallirhoë Street.
[2] Alan Hare (see footnote on p. 63) and his wife Jill.
[3] 'A delightful man, rather formal-looking, piercing blue eyes, a cheerful face. Extremely gifted for languages, drawing, painting and talking,' PLF wrote in a footnote to *In Tearing Haste*. 'Much in our life as he was a great friend of Joan's brother, Graham.'

days, so I camped there, then set off with Ian (Tony[1] couldn't come at the last moment) for Kardamyli …

Ian was a glorious companion all the time, and an invaluable adviser. I think he's one of the funniest people I've ever met, so there were lots of laughs throughout.

I rented a Fiat 1100 for £30 (four days) and off we set. Lunch at Ay. Theodori,[2] bathes, night in Kalamata, to Kardamyli next day, chez Socrates Phalireás, who sends love and was a great ally throughout.

1) It turned out that the <u>tower</u> belongs to the state, the adjoining ruined house to a gymnasiarch [supervisor of an athletic college] in Kalamata, and the pretty house across the square beside the church to two half-mad megalomaniac spinster hags, indirect descendants of the Mourtzinos boys, both of whom, by rights, ought to be in an asylum. They have a frantic devotion to their ancestral acres, and burst into screams at the idea of selling. Socrates reasoned with them, they wavered, changing their minds every five minutes, quarrelling with each other and with us, then embracing us, then hurling curses and prophecies out of the Apocalypse, finally stickling about a field which we would have had to have had, for the bare minimum of privacy, finally, thank God, turning into immovable mules. I say thank God because, even if we <u>had</u> been able to buy it, they would have made the neighbourhood intolerable to us, as they insisted on an open right of way clean through the middle for them and their all-devouring goats, and would have been on top of us, screaming, all day long. They have voices that carry 5 miles, and verbal diarrhoea. One of them spoke, without a single comma, for 1 hour 20 minutes, with shrill mad terrifying scream, embracing in her discourse the atom bomb, the wickedness of the Turks, the end of the world, the vice of foreigners, the beast of Babylon with the harlot on its back, with a cupfull of abominations, fire, swords and brimstone. I felt dead at the end of it, grateful to slink away, abandoning the whole thing. I would willingly have throttled her. Ian listened with considerable astonishment. I must say, the place looked marvellous, but we're well out of it. Also, (sour grapes!) it's

[1] Tony Massourides, a lawyer friend who had offered to act for PLF and Joan in purchasing any property in Greece.
[2] Agioi Theodori, a coastal village near the Corinth Canal.

6.

and orange rock, ribbed and cliffed like the
mountains near Leonidion, and, like them,
flaring crimson at sunset. ~~In~~ Through high
clefts of these one glimmers goey glimpses of
the highest Taygetus. But ~~nothing~~ overpowers
or impends. There is not a house in sight. Nothing
but rocks, trees, mountains and sea. It's called
Kalamitsi.

MOUNTAINS.   TAYGETUS.

Kardamyli, about 2 miles.

water road.

Stoupa.

Wooded
Slope
Olives

Ravine

walled path

Ravine

A
Zhut.
Kalamitsi

B

marble
beach

olive terraces

pebble
beach

rocks

rocks.

rocks.

little ravine

S E A .

⅛ mile?

Castle rock

far too much in the village, and, as Ian pointed out, would have cost thousands to render habitable. We looked at several other sites, but all were no good, for one reason or another.

2) In despair, we drove down the coast to the village of Stoupa for a bathe and a quick look at a rather jolly *panagyri* [festival] for Holy Ghost Day. (We saw a mule being ridden into the sea to be washed, which gave rise to Ian's joke: '*Mule Marinière!*') On the way there, about two miles south of Kardamyli, we saw a peninsula jutting between two valleys, ending in crescent-shaped beaches, covered with olives and cypresses, and determined to bathe there on the way back, dazzled by the beauty of the place. This we accordingly did, walking down into a gently sloping world of the utmost magical beauty, descending shelves of grass going gently down to the sea, thick with magnificent olive trees and cypresses and lots of other trees: one or two stone pines, a *celtis australis* (hackleberry: Ian's expertise), almonds, oranges, lemons, pomegranates, pistachio, carobs, an ibex, lentisk, mulberry, cistus, capers, every kind of plant and shrub. The ledges are almost lawn-like, not small buttresses, but 15 yards across and 20 yards long. The last one juts in a growth of shrubs and cypresses over some rocks and caves almost ten yards below, then deep into blue-green sea. This peninsula is in the middle of a wide open bay, with rocky headlands at either end, the tip facing southwest, and can never be in shadow of the mountains, except, perhaps, at dawn. The view is an enormous sweep of sea, bounded by the headlands, off the right hand one of which, due west, is the island with the castle on it, about half a mile away, and beautifully and dramatically placed. The sun is visible until its last gasp. Behind, the peninsula mounts, forested, and melts into a great conch of grey and orange rock, ribbed and cliffed like the mountains near Leonidion,[1] and, like them, flaring crimson at sunset. Through high clefts of these are glimmering grey glimpses of the highest Taygetus. But nothing overpowers or impedes. There is not a house in sight. Nothing but rocks, trees, mountains and sea. It's called Kalamitsi.

[1] On the eastern coast of the Peloponnese.

Kardamyli

Friday.
Date?

IN HASTE.

Darling,

Here are the snaps, jolly bad ones, giving an idea of the splendour of the place, but better than nothing.

1) View of the peninsula from the Kardamyli road, looking South. The ink line vaguely indicates the boundary of the property

2, 3) ditto.

4). This is on one of the ledges, where possibly the house might stand, roughly indicated by X on snap 3. Castle rock island in mid distance.

5) Bad snaps from the slope hillside South of Kalamitsi. Boundary interest in. The Taygetus have vanished & in the picture!

(7) The valley that marks the South border of plot B.

Letter to Joan Rayner, sent from Kardamyli in June 1962

Paddy began negotiating to buy the land near Kardamyli. The negotiations proved complex, and it would be a year and a half before the purchase was complete.

To Joan Rayner   Spetsai
undated [summer 1962]

Darling Joan,

Thanks so much for your lovely long letter – all you say fits in almost exactly with what I feel we should attempt ... If we get the land, I think the house should overflow from one terrace to another, giving it two levels. We might incorporate a cypress or so into the building ... I see a dovecote at a suitable distance. Petro, the nice peasant, was swathed in muslin when Tony [Massourides], Rania & I left last Sunday, back from the hives, of which there are a number, and gave us some lovely honey, tasting of all the herbs that abound there. I forgot to tell you that when we swam round the rocks under 'the house', we came into a great stalactitic sea cave, full of odd [snowbrite?] limestone formations like petrified mushrooms bulging from the cave walls, and a little freshwater spring.... Lovely and cold out of the sunlight. I wish I'd had goggles. It's said to be stiff with fish there, so perhaps we ought to learn how to catch them – lines? traps? guns? – to throw them straight into the pan or on the *skara*.[1] We might have one of the white domed ovens, as in the village, & bake our own bread. There were ladders leaning against the olive trees, pruning and grafting in progress. I think the size and atmosphere of this main room should remind one of Arkí.[2] The appearance and mood of the

[1] Barbecue.
[2] A small almost uninhabited Greek island in the southern Dodecanese.

place is half Calypso's cave, half the orchard where Odysseus found his old father Laertes at work. That's what's so lovely, this inter-penetration of sea and rocks with olives, cypresses, sweet-smelling shrubs; marine and georgic with that hectic sunset amphitheatre of precipices behind, and the phantom Taygetus [mountains] looming; and oh! No yachts, no nightclubs, no beachwear, no dropping in, no smartness, no competition, no development. Nothing except leisure for reading, writing, bathing, prancing, shade for eating & drinking and sleeping, glades for wandering, vantage points for talking. I must stop all this, and seize the wooden edge of this table. No more now, my darling. I'll send the snaps tomorrow, and any further bulletins.

tons & tons of love/hugs
Paddy

To Ricki Huston   Mill House
19 August 1962   Dumbleton
                                                   Evesham
                                                   Worcester

My darling Ricki,

Rome seemed like a plague city after Athens, quite empty, dissolving in heat and dust and the Tiber reeking like the Limpopo or the Zambezi; you expected hippos and alligators, but only got Romans. I only stayed two nights, and made a solitary get-away to Tivoli, ate an outcast's trout at the Temple of the Sybil,[1] then mooched about among the olives above the ruins of the villa of Quintilius Varus, where we spent that heavenly after-noon, with the whole of the dusty campagna below, till the sun began to set behind the just visible dome of St Peter's. Then off next day in our old friend the Sunbeam Rapier, through Viterbo, Montefiascone, Aquapendente to the Radicofani Pass, a lovely

[1] PLF means the hotel nearby (see p. 69).

landscape of Upper Latium, all tufa mountains tufted with ilex woods, lakes Bracciano and Bolsena gleaming far below through oak branches, Poussin's and Claude's Italy. In Siena, I discovered, in a lane, a really magnificent restaurant; seafood from Leghorn, guineafowl, turkey, wild boar, all kinds of unItalian wonders. Not a foreigner there, only serious guzzlers, viz., a napkinned bishop & two canons, three local journalists, a critic from Florence, a bank manager, an assize judge on circuit and a mystery Tuscan with a pretty French mistress – lucky dog! It's called Le Campane. Do write it down, and I hope I never find you munching in one of those tourist *trattorie* on the piazza. Florence was full of the latter, i.e. tourists (one always hopes to be exempt from the epithet) – and there was also some monkish congress, so the place was brown with friars. The *Autostrada del Sole*, next day, was not quite the explosive experience it was last year – no rain, thunder or lightning – but amazing nevertheless. Bologna & Milan sailed past unseen, then I crawled, with a thousand others, along the side of Lake Maggiore, which I hadn't seen since I was eight with my pa, and spotted a melancholy pebble beach below Baveno where I remembered playing ducks and drakes with him till sunset. This sunset, however, came as I was climbing up that twisty road into the Simplon pass, untravelled by me heretofore, huston on huston [on and on] into the dark Gothic north, a vast distance down into pitch darkness, and then flat, to tame Ouchy under Lausanne, where I stayed at a grand dull hotel, and was glad to leave. I can't help finding the Swiss the scum of the earth. Ah, the delight of France next day! Those endless, sunny poplar avenues flicking the shadows of their trunks across one's path as one swish-swishes through beech forests and hills, under castles and belfries with the prospect of one's first French meal for months goldenly looming! This materialised gloriously, at (N.B.) *Chez Guy* at Salins: *écrevisses à la nage*, two wonder-trouts, a pigeonneau, wood-strawberries, Jura cheese, with ½ bottle of Sancerre, 1 bott. of Burgundy (Nuits St George). I wish you'd been there, as I wished often on the way. So, fortified and singing, on to Dôle, Dijon, Avallon, Auxerre and Sens, to Fontainebleau, arriving chez Charles de Noailles[1] in time for a splendid dinner, in Mme de Pompadour's old love-nest, finding the place full of familiar faces i.e. Peter Quennell & wife, Natalie Perrone, David McEwen[2] & Betty Robilant, the pretty American married to a Venetian you met at that dinner where you sang so captivatingly; also, slightly irritatingly, her nice husband Alvise[3] ... All rather fun after a few months of ungracious living; including a long ride through the forest, first since breaking my wrist, startling great troops of stags, lonely huge antlered creatures with their hornless better halves, which went bounding away into the wilderness. On to Normandy next day, peering at the stained glass through binoculars at Chartres on the way, reaching my old friend Lady Smart on the Eure by nightfall. England next day, this filthy rain, the first for months, greeting me before I'd been one hour in the kingdom, and not stopping ever since. Since then, I've been scribbling here, and return to London on Tuesday. Well, those are my movements. What about yours?

S.O.S. The Post's about to leave, so: –
No more now, dearest Ricki, except write at once, and tell me your news and plans, and do let's meet.

Tons of love & hugs
from Paddy
X X X

No time to reread, so forgive illiteracies.

---

[1] Vicomte Charles de Noailles (1891–1981), gardener and patron of the arts. His wife Maire-Laure was once asked: 'Charles, he likes men, or does he like women?' She always replied: 'Charles? He likes flowers.' In fact he preferred men, as she discovered early in their married life, when she happened to come to his bedroom one afternoon and found him in bed with his gym instructor. But the incident was not discussed. They lived lives in part separate, in part together, and in many ways as a devoted couple, telephoning and writing to each other every day when they were apart. And even when in the same house, she would write him a letter and push it under his door, and he would promptly reply.
[2] David Fraser McEwen (1938–76), soldier, younger brother of Rory McEwen (see p. 293).
[3] Conte Alvise di Robilant (1925–97), managing director of Sotheby's Italy, and his American wife Elizabeth Stokes, from whom he was later divorced. He was found murdered in his apartment in Florence in 1997.

To Joan Rayner   Lismore Castle
25 April 1963   County Waterford
              Ireland

Darling Joan,

It _is_ strange and exciting to think of you in Crete and I wish I could be padding slowly behind under a _saríki_[1] of darkness, or better still, as a total newcomer. I wonder if you went to Koustogérako and saw Manoli.[2] I rather hope Johnny [Craxton] took you to the mountains between Ay. Roumeli and Sphakia – Anopolis etc. – which sound wonderful; and what about the south coast, west of Souyia, all unknown to us; or for that matter, Siteia on the East – Toplou monastery and so on? I can't wait to hear about it all.

The Welsh adventure with Robin [Fedden] over Easter was an unqualified success. We motored north, through the rainy midlands and Shropshire on Thursday and had dinner, just over the Salop–Montgomery border, within a few yards of the northern end of Offa's Dyke, with Tony and Dunstan Curtis,[3] who have settled in a little manor-house there; then motored onto to a town called Machynlleth on the Dovey river, which separates Montgomery from Cardiganshire, setting off [on foot] next morning, in bright cold sunlight, straight up the northern slopes of Mt Plynlimon, a wonderful verdigrissy, sulphuric brackeny mountain, third highest in Wales. The top is an endless wilderness and we ate bacon sandwiches by the source of the Severn, which gushes out of a meadow and then cascades down a cliff of black slate. So on all day over endless undulations, through hollows and plateaux and over watersheds, very wild, druidical and desolate, not meeting a soul all day except an old shepherd who could scarcely speak English, reaching a little town called Llanidloes towards nightfall, dog-tired and aching but unbowed, having walked 30 miles almost nonstop. Next day, in drizzle and

[1] A turban of thin silk, fringed with black, worn by Cretan men.
[2] Manoli Paterakis, PLF's wartime comrade in the Cretan resistance to German occupation, came from the tiny mountain village of Koustogérako.
[3] Dunstan Curtis (1910–83), war hero, lawyer and civil servant, and his Australian wife 'Tony'.

fine sleet and hail that acted on the face like acupuncture, we crossed the stripling Wye and plowed uphill through the wind, pure Macbeth country, fit for little but mammoths, riddled with deep ravines and brooks running Guinness and foaming between huge boulders, with sudden fitful shafts of tearful sunlight and lingering patches of snow and boggy tracts like chocolate mousse decked with heather. Nothing but abandoned lead-mines and farmhouses in ruins and sodden flocks of sheep with pitifully bleating lambs who followed us in hungry and growing droves, mistaking us in those barren pastures for the occasional mangle-wurzel bearers that stand between them and starvation. We got half-lost on some high hills in wind, hail and rain and at last, reached a lovely cottage soaked: inhabited, when we knocked on the door for asylum, by a headmaster's wife and her pretty daughter, where we soon found ourselves talking about Greek and Egyptian archaeology over whisky-laced tea and cigars. The sun came out and we headed down the beautiful forested valley of Cwmystwyth, past the ruins of Hafod House, one of the first eighteenth-century gothic buildings to be built by a dilettante squire called Mr Johnes of Hafod. We got to a sad little town called Tregaron at dusk, and were so put off by the gloom of the aspidistras and lace curtains and the stifling deed-box fug of the rooms of the only hotel that we found a train to Aberystwyth. Rather a pretty little Victorian waterfront in a crescent between towering headlands, everywhere full of Welsh and Midland Easter holidaymakers; but we found twin beds in a lodging house and had dinner in the Marine Hotel, the best there; to the strains of *The Mikado* and *HMS Pinafore* from a palm-shaded string band. Dinner begins at 7 p.m. and ends at 8, so you have to look sharp. It was pretty awful and Robin and I were almost the only diners to wash down their meat with wine and not tea, administered by a *sommelier* in a pink tailcoat with white watered-silk lacings. We recovered in a pub till closing time. Next day, Easter Sunday, armed with full flasks, we strode north up the wild coast of Cardigan, sheer coal-black cliffs, winding grassy headlands and ferny cwms following each other for ever, billions of screaming gulls and rocks covered with cormorants perched with their wings hanging half-spread in that queer way they have, at last reaching the town of Borth, where we had rather good shrimps and Irish stew, lunch mugs of barley wine, then to the mouth of the Dovey river, a wide bleak estuary surrounded by fens full of waterbirds, and, at last, back to Machynlleth and the car, having covered about 70 miles in the last three days, and wild and hilly ones too. We set off South through Radnor and Breconshire, having dinner in a wonderful romantic valley in the Black Mountains at a pub built on the ruins of an Augustinian Priory, formerly belonging to Walter Savage Landor, where I might easily retire to scribble. It's called Llanthony, well known to Eddy & the Crichel boys,[1] and rather a find. Alas, there was no room that night, so we pushed on to Abergavenny, found rooms in the Blue Boar Inn, and, after looking at the Herbert tombs, went on, trudged under the trees for a couple of hours along the Usk, and reached Philip [Toynbee]'s house at noon. We had a hilarious banquet with him, Sally [Toynbee, Philip's second wife], Ben Nicolson[2] and three neighbouring squires in the main pub of Monmouth; then back to one of their houses where Philip kept filling his glass with whiskey, which I would swallow and top up with water when his back was turned, thus winning golden looks from Sally but getting pretty tight and noisy myself. Not that it mattered. It was all tremendous fun and you were bitterly missed by all. We stayed that night with Jim and Alvilde Lees-Milne in a ravishingly pretty Georgian house they have settled in near to Wotton under Edge.

[1] Long Crichel House, near Wimborne, in Dorset, shared by Eddy Sackville-West, his partner, the music critic Desmond Shawe-Taylor (1907–95) and the artist Eardley Knollys (1902–91). They formed what was in effect an all-male salon and entertained a wide variety of guests. Later they were joined by the literary critic, Raymond Mortimer (1895–1980), and, later still, by the ophthalmic surgeon Patrick Trevor-Roper (1916–2004).

[2] Lionel Benedict Nicolson (1914–78), art historian and author, elder son of Harold Nicolson and Vita Sackville-West.

Next morning, after looking at two lovely National Trust houses nearby, we had lunch at The Hole in the Wall in Bath,[1] which seemed to us as good and better than anything you and Graham claim for it. The best in England? The local National Trust man took us on a detailed antiquarian tour of the town. I insisted on going to see the Roman bath, which is oddly moving, the only Roman thing I've ever seen in England. Then, after a long hunt through the second-hand bookshops, where I bought the *Olive Fairy Book*,[2] on to Henry and Virginia [Bath]'s for the night, a very cheerful one, and back to London through the downpour next day. It was a wonderful trip, with not a disagreeable second, and Robin is an ideal and inventive cicerone and companion.

I found Cyril [Connolly] and Deirdre[3] there when I got back. They stayed three days, and I had a cheerful lunch with Magouche,[4] just back from tremendous Moroccan journeys. Did I mention in my last letter that we had a successful dinner at the Café Royal the week before: Cyril, Deirdre, Peter Q, Evan, Kate.

Graham[5] angelically asked me to the Mill House for the weekend, which I loved. Quiet, lots of work, music in the evenings, long walks in the afternoons. The daffodils we all planted look terrific – a great golden blur across the orchard, a real triumph of bulb-mastery. Ian Whigham came for lunch on Monday. So, back to London, and then here, the damp and rainy London weather suddenly becoming sunny and spring-like the moment St George's

---

[1] The Hole in the Wall restaurant, opened in 1951 by restaurateur and chef, George Perry-Smith, brought haute cuisine to Britain. Taking inspiration from domestic cookery books, Perry-Smith developed many of his own recipes, but was also keen to follow the suggestions of the influential food writer Elizabeth David. Perry-Smith developed a drive for uncompromising excellence and was always anxious to buy fresh ingredients from local suppliers. He became widely acknowledged as the father of the best of post-war English cooking.

[2] Andrew Lang, *The Olive Fairy Book* (1907), an illustrated collection of fairy tales.

[3] Cyril Connolly's third wife Deirdre, née Craig (b. 1931).

[4] Magouche Phillips, later Fielding – see dramatis personae.

[5] Joan's brother, Graham Eyres Monsell, had inherited the Mill House on the death of his mother in 1959.

channel was crossed. The first night, to Debo's confusion, I think, Sir O. Mosley[1] arrived unannounced. He has an alarming, perhaps unconscious, perhaps would-be hypnotic characteristic of suddenly lifting his upper eyelids so that white rim appears over the pupil. Thank God, no politics talked. A lot about French, German, Latin and Greek literature, in which, and in history, he seemed lucid and proficient. V. quiet, charming manner and style; but curiously a bit eerie. I'm glad to have seen him once, but don't want to do so again. Stoker[2] and a pal were here fishing for salmon; they have now gone and only Nancy, who arrived last night, Debo and I remain. Eddy [Sackville-West] comes to his house tomorrow. Otherwise, all is quiet. Long walks and rides, and a lot of work in a huge tower room I've never inhabited before. It's wonderfully peaceful, but it takes an effort to fight off Ireland's soporific spell. Andrew doesn't seem able to get away from the job[3] long enough to make the trip worthwhile for the moment. I wouldn't mind staying on till almost the day before going to Michael Astor's long heralded week-end on the 4th of May. All depends on when you get back, darling. Do send a telegram when you get this, and we will make some plans.

London seemed bloody with you away: worse still, all my other consulates were closed too: Janetta in Spain, Diana in Rome, Magouche in Morocco, Debo in Ireland, Nico & Barbara in France, only Annie in London. I dined there twice quietly with her and Ian *à trois*. Robert and Cynthia [Kee] were supposed to be here, but their little boy has got measles, so they aren't.

---

[1] Sir Oswald Ernald Mosley (1896–1980), politician, was married to the Duchess of Devonshire's sister, Diana. Leader of the British Union of Fascists, 1932–40, he was interned 1940–3. In 1951 he left Britain to live in Ireland, and later, in France. In a letter to Rudi Fischer (8 April 1983), PLF mentioned that he had met Mosley once or twice at Chatsworth: 'V. witty and civilised, but rather eerie and, to me, impossible to like. Diana has great charm and humour, and the remains of enormous beauty; but also something vaguely worrying ...'

[2] Peregrine Cavendish, known as 'Stoker' (b. 1944), then heir to the dukedom; now the current Duke of Devonshire.

[3] Andrew Devonshire was a junior minister in the Conservative government, appointed by his uncle Harold Macmillan, then prime minister. The Duke once referred to this and another such appointment as 'the greatest act of nepotism ever'.

Now. About the Horizon book on Greece.[1] Soon after you left I telephoned Cyril and put the whole question to him. We talked for ages about it. He was very tempted and undecided, but finally, and very reluctantly, turned it down on the strength of not being a sufficient ancient Greek expert. I said yes, like me, and then said what they needed, failing Maurice [Bowra], was (what I ought to have thought of at once, as you did on your card later), Rex [Warner]. We both saw that he was the ideal, and I determined to write to them suggesting Rex. Cyril rang again next morning and said he'd thought it all over and thought the £10,000 was too good to let slip – might take a sabbatical year off – and would like to take it on, if Rex refused, or was not thought suitable by Horizon. We talked over it a lot next week, he read all the correspondence, thought it over again and said, on third thoughts perhaps not. I want to forge ahead with my own stuff, so I've written to them, proposing Rex. Of course he's the ideal. We'll see what happens.

No more now, and please forgive this late and sprawling letter. Do let me know plans and dates at once. Love to everyone, and all Cretan news! And hugs and

tons of love from Paddy
X X X X

To Stephen Spender   Katounia
6 Nov 1963   Limni
               Greece

Dear Stephen,

This has just surfaced, so I thought I'd send it to you. See you soon and best love to all, Paddy

Wonderful about Seferis.[2]

[1] PLF refers to a project for the American illustrated book publisher Horizon, not the journal edited by Connolly.

[2] George Seferis had been awarded the Nobel Prize for Literature.

They Have Straightened the Tower of Pisa

They have straightened the tower of Pisa,
Solved the knots in the trees,
Drowned the rats in the Weser[1]
And switched the chalk and the cheese.

They stuff a lion by the Niger,
Stencil a leopard's pelt.
Experts are melting a pearl
And lining the 'cellos with felt.

A tractor shines in the apse,
A major is flying to Mars,
The condor blinks in a cage;
You can't see the bird for the bars.

'Lift the fish from the fountain,
The yeast from the daily bread
Wipe the tears from mountain
Ranges,' the stranger said.

'Mount my head on a charger,
Wrap my heart in a sleeve,
Square my blood with an ice cube
Shiver my bones through a sieve.

They won't be wanted at Christmas
At Easter, or ever again.
Close the account and the window
Fasten the door with a chain.'

[1] A reference to the story of 'The Pied Piper of Hamelin' (which PLF would have known especially from Browning's poem of that name), in which the piper lures the rats infesting the town into the river, where all but one drowned.

The trumpeter swan is dumb,
The farmer is deaf to the rooks
The hawks are blind to the world,
The words fly away from the books,

The fluting moults from the stone,
The pillow sobs on the bed,
A statue lies down in a quarry
And pulls down the rocks on his head.

To Ricki Huston   Paralia
5 November 1964   Kalamata
                                                                  Greece

Darling Ricki,

I've been meaning for ages to write and send congratulations, godspeed, wishes for luck and for happy omens and auspices about Allegra's arrival, and may they shower down on you both; indeed, on all concerned! Lovely Miltono-Byronic name.[1] Perhaps you ought to wangle a reflective little sister called Penserosa on to the scene,[2] who might bear the same relationship to Allegra that Tampoco, the less boisterous of those Castilian twins, bears to También.[3] Think of those moments of harmonious balance when they were *A. ma non troppo* and *P. ma non triste* …[4] I wonder what her married name will eventually be: Weintraub, Northumberland, Stripp, Chang, von Rantenstranch, Smith, Mendoza, Lupin, de la

[1] In August, Ricki Huston had given birth to a daughter, Allegra. Byron's daughter with Claire Clairmont was also called Allegra.

[2] A playful reference to Milton's romantic poems 'L'Allegro' and 'Il Penseroso', later put to music, for tenor and soprano respectively, by Handel.

[3] A play on words: PLF refers to the confusion between the word *tampoco* meaning 'either' or 'neither' in Spanish, and *también*, meaning 'too' or 'also'.

[4] An *allegro ma non troppo* is a musical passage played allegro, but not too much so; so a *penserosa ma non triste* would be one played thoughtfully, but not too sadly.

Bruyère, Assayian, Winthrop, Abdul Aziz, Brown, Bastable …?[1] It goes splendidly with all these shadowy suitors, and I hope they're nice enough for the little thing.

We've moved out of our tents at Kardamyli[2] into an odd and fascinating flat on the waterfront of Kalamata, above a tavern rife with delicious things. The windows overlook an avenue of jujube trees, which are giving rise to the following lines:[3]

On the quays of Kalamata
Where the shady jujubes grow
Dusky harlots stand and barter
Maidenheads lost long ago.

Blue-green jujubes, sigh and shade me
From the Dog-Star's cruel glow,
Shade and soothe me, say, what made me
Chase those maidens long ago?

Mullets loiter in the waters
By these rustling jujube trees.
Were the Mani's finest daughters
Born and bred for men like these?

Threadbare groves where sullen lurkers
Dog these dark-eyed maidens … Hark!
Kalamai's[4] unsmiling burghers
Rive their hymens in the dark!

---

[1] Allegra Huston, (b. 1964) daughter of Ricki Huston and John Julius Norwich, is a film-maker and writer. She lived for some time with Francisco (Cisco) Niño de Ortiz Ladron de Guevara, by whom she had a son, Rafael.

[2] PLF and Joan camped on the land they had bought while their house was being built.

[3] PLF's model is Edward Lear's nonsense poem, 'The Courtship of the Yonghy-Bonghy-Bo', which begins 'On the coast of Coromandel/ Where the early pumpkins blow'. He may also have been influenced, perhaps unconsciously, by Maurice Bowra's 'On the Coast of Terra Fermor' (see pp. 409ff.).

[4] An ancient name for Kalamata.

The <u>Drinking Room</u>, the <u>Scandinavia</u>
Mask their mangled midriffs now.
Who can stem their wild behaviour?
Ask not when and tell not how!

Ships from Bremen, ships from Rostock
Anchor by the jujube trees,
Lock-in-trade all gone and lost stock
Barrels broken on the quays etc. etc.

Least said, soonest mended. Here's a <u>NIGHT THOUGHT in a</u>
<u>FRENCH TRAIN</u>:

The Renaults rush to their rendezvous, the Rolls Royce's
    rhythm is deeper.
A lecturer sips his Evian, a cardinal sighs in his sleeper.
Nobody stops to hobnob with the lovely level-crossing
    keeper.

Every good and auspicious wish again, darling Ricki, and tons
of love
                                   from Paddy

To Jock Murray   29 Navarino Street
30 November 1964   Paralia
                                                 Kalamata
                                                   Greece

My dear Jock,
    Please forgive this awful delay. First, I'm dead against the BBC
idea for *A Time to Keep Silence*, either with an actor doing the
narrator or (and how!) the narrator doing himself. I think it <u>might</u>
make an interesting piece, but I would hate to be involved in it
by name. I felt at the time (still do) a trace of guilt, writing about
people who go to such lengths to achieve privacy. They didn't mind,

however, to my enormous relief. Perhaps they might even welcome a film piece about it, one never knows.

We have retired from our blue tents on the Kardamyli headland, not driven forth by cold, but by early nightfall and the uncertainty of daylight. Difficulties about bringing water from the village are slowly resolving themselves, also the complication of levelling a path through steep olive groves to allow the passage of building materials. I have built a sort of Doric kiosk on the site, floored and divanned with stone, with a cypress trunk in the centre and a beautiful giant compass with long spikes of rough marble inlaid in the floor; 16 cypress poles all round, a frieze of lattice work and roofed with mats: a cage for fair-weather work and meditation and a shelter from the blaze.

We are now settled a serpentine hour's drive away, in a flat on the waterfront of Kalamata, a large one with a sort of belvedere on the roof from which I am writing. The quay below is lined with jujube trees, the water beyond with caiques and two liners, the *Algol* from Bremen and the *Sperber* from Rostock, loading up with figs and raisins for West and East Germany respectively, while the sailors of each vessel gaze reflectively at each other over the bulwarks. Here we shall hibernate (inasmuch as winter exists here), dashing to Kardamyli twice weekly.

But the real point of this letter is to announce that good news impends and will be on its way to you as soon as respite and diligence can contrive. It's been a complicated autumn!

No more for the moment, except all the best.

Yours ever
Paddy

In 1965, a commission to write a piece about the Danube from the American magazine Holiday *provided Paddy with an opportunity to visit Romania, for the first time since before the war – and, more important, to be reunited with his former love Balasha Cantacuzène, whom he had last seen more than a quarter of a century before. Her life since then had been hard. The Cantacuzène estates had been confiscated by the communist government after the war. After trying and failing to escape from Romania in 1947, Balasha, together with her sister 'Pomme' and her brother-in-law Constantin, had been evicted from the family home of Băleni, with only fifteen minutes' notice, and resettled, first in Bucharest, and then in the unlovely town of Pucioasa, where they shared an attic studio. Although it was dangerous for them to be seen with a foreigner, they agreed to meet Paddy.*

Paddy was nervous about what he would find. Five years before, he had plucked up his courage to ask the Greek foreign minister if he might use his influence to help Balasha come to the West, as he explained in a letter to Debo Devonshire. 'She was over ten years older than me when I was twenty – so still must be! – which means over fifty-five (-six since last week). There was a faint chance of her getting out two years ago, but she didn't want to, because, after prison for two years (for trying to escape) and living in utter hardship as a pauper for fifteen years in forced residence & little to eat in a remote village, she said she dreaded seeing anyone again – painfully thin, teeth and hair dropping out fast. It's too awful. Poor Balasha! But I'm sure something could be done about all this, and thank heavens, there are several old friends who will cough up something to begin with. And indeed go on. She's a painter. She always adored Greece, and would probably want to settle here. How wonderful it would be if she did make it! We haven't met for twenty-two years. She used to be so beautiful.' A friend who had succeeded in getting out of Romania had told Paddy that, 'in spite of all these calamities, she's quite unchanged in character, just as funny and intelligent and charming as ever'.

To Ann Fleming   Mouth of the Danube
undated [April 1965]

Darling Annie,

It's very peculiar being in Romania again; in fact, nearly all the way it's been odd, revisiting places and scenes unseen for 2½ or 3 decades, many with a nineteen-year-old greenhorn's eye, now with a glance more mature than 23 summers. Castle on castle in S. Germany & Austria, where Joan joined me for ten days, marvellous stretches of the Danube, from Passau to Vienna, with wonderful meals at the Drei Husaren and Sacher's, culminating in the best performance of *Le Nozze di Figaro* that any of us are likely to see. I pushed on after that to Czechoslovakia, where Iron Curtain gloom and Slovak heaviness set in, redeemed, for me, in Bratislava, by an hotel full of the cast of a review on ice from Vienna: Len and Mac, two Scotch comedians, and above all, Duncan Whaley[1] (son of Whaley of Scott and Whaley, like Layton & Janson of our youth), marvellous funny half negro, half cockney comedian, dead spit of Paul Danquah,[2] living with the beautiful Czech leading lady, Tzvetanka. I'd never seen an ice show. It's pure magic. All those feathered and frosty & beautiful ice-maidens curvetting and sailing & floating, half-ballet, half-circus atmosphere. They took me under their kind wing for three days of light-hearted laughter & fun. We could forget about the Slovaks. How different the Hungarians! Looks, guts, high-spirits, style, in spite of the squalor of the region. The truth is, nothing can be the same since the 1956 uprising. It's knocked the stuffing and the conviction out of the régime. The 50,000 Russian tank-troops at Esztergom, and more elsewhere, only accentuate the precariousness of the status quo. Most of the counts & princes that I used snobbishly to haunt when v. young seem to have gone. How nice they were, and how earnestly they grilled one about the comparable merits of Lock, Lobb, Maxwell, Peel, Tautz, Swaine

---

[1] Duncan Whaley (1928–2000), ice-skating clown, star of the touring show 'Holiday on Ice'. His father, Eddie Whaley, was the straight man of the British comedy team [Harry] Scott and Whaley, who toured variety theatres for many years. He came from Montgomery, Alabama, and had been a minstrel show performer before coming to Europe.
[2] Paul Danquah (1925–2015), film actor, son of an English mother and a Ghanaian father.

Adeney and Champion & Wilton![1] I found myself instead involved in a fascinating, over-educated, Latin and Greek scholarly, counter-revolutionary middle class of great spirit & talent, thriving in leaky quarters all about thrice-battered Budapest: battered but marvellous, the river sweeping, hill-girt and [illegible] bridged. A hundred miles downstream I went for a twilight stroll, through the poplar woods along the banks at Mohács, back to the town through gypsy hovels wafted all the way by a gentle chorus of Magyár begging, and came on a lantern-lit barn where a nearly jet-black gypsy, surrounded by barges, tractors, drivers and herdsmen, was playing an elaborate gold harp two yards high. On the Hungarian plain and on in Romania, all sorts of forgotten phenomena kept softly exploding: odd costumes, rawhide moccasins, songs, the smell of dust laced with that of the omnipresent white drooping acacia flower blossom, lilac, huge irises and giant crimson and white peonies. Everywhere – the streets, paths, the river, smart hotels in Belgrade – was afloat with that miniature thistledown with which poplar seeds are winged, imparting an unsuitably dreamy air even to boot-faced and silently champing (silent as far as conversation went) commissars in restaurants. All this time, the Danube was rising menacingly, putting a stop to river boats, as none of their funnels could get under the low bridges at a gloomy Serbian town called 'Novi Sad' (*Bonjour Tristesse*[2]),which meant endless bus and train journeys swooping into the hinterland and back to the river at key points in Romania. Banat, the Southern fringes of Transylvania, were just as beautiful as I remembered, especially the last: deep forested ravines with winding rivers and wonderful birds – bee eaters, hoopoes, golden aurioles and rollers, a wonderful turquoise: storks on all roofs, and, further downstream, on domes and minarets.

From Bucharest I made a mystery visit on the back of a motorbike to those loved long since and lost awhile[3] – 26 years, indeed. V. moving, amazing. She – Balasha and her sister and family – have had a terrible time: dispossessed, persecuted, imprisoned, enforced

[1] All makers of quality products for gentlemen: hatters, bootmakers, shoemakers, shirtmakers [?], men's outfitters, manufacturer of luxury leather products, saddlers.
[2] A playful reference to Françoise Sagan's bestselling novel, published in 1954. *Novi Sad* actually means 'new garden'.
[3] 'And with the morn those angel faces smile,/ Which I have loved long since and lost awhile!', John Henry Newman, 'Lead, Kindly Light', 1833.

domicile in a strange village, no money at all – but oddly unchanged, morale intact, civilisation's flag flying high! Endless talk and laughter for 24 hours, then return after dark. After Bucharest, I came here: an endless waste of major and minor branches of the Danube, rustling growths of reeds ten feet high, opening on to long wooded river vistas like the Champs Elysées, widening into vast lakes covered with lotus and waterlily, narrow to corridors again, finally melting into the Black Sea. It's an amphibious world, inhabited by queer villagers in stilted houses among willows – Russian Lipovan heretics, Tartars, Romanians, Bulgars, Turks; but the real inhabitants are the cranes, ibises, bitterns, ducks, geese, swans, waders, spoonbills, avocets, curlews, pelicans and flamingoes: rustling, fluttering, squawking everywhere.

GREECE

This letter got set aside! Two weeks later now. I got away (just before the big floods began which now wreak havoc in Central & Southern Europe, poor people) through Bulgaria, then motored from Sofia across Macedonia & caught a plane from Salonika to Athens; and here we are in the Mani again. Marvellous to be in such a noisy and garrulous country after those tongue-tied republics. Joan has done wonders here, all cisterns and foundations dug, water gushing, masons sloshing mortar about … You know all about it! After all, even Chatsworth was once a few acres of holes in the ground. Today's Stoker's Coronation:[1] how I envy you all. Do please send a detailed description. I'll think of you all glittering and revolving under painted ceilings as we sit down to our fried sticklebacks and resin [small fish and retsina]! It took considerable moral fibre simply not to fly back for it.

Thank you so much, Annie darling, for being such an angel of kindness before I left. What a haven Sevenhampton was; I bet it's looking tremendous now. I must stop this now, far too long. But do write; & a billion thanks again!

Tons of fond love
Paddy
X X X

[1] Peregrine Cavendish, Marquess of Hartington and heir to the Duke of Devonshire, turned twenty-one on 27 April 1965.

To Balasha Cantacuzène   Kardamyli
undated [3 June 1965?]   Messenia
                                                        Greece

Darling Balasha,

I <u>am</u> a bad correspondent, and you are such a good one! Everyone I know is in a state of revolt and indignation with me at the moment, as a result of my appalling pen-paralysis; so do please forgive, darling. There is something so hand-to-mouth about living in a tent, (as I was till the early nightfall and occasional rain drove me into the village a few days ago), that militates against putting pen to paper; but I had to overcome this in order to finish the Danube article – only just done, much, much too long! – and write the last two chapters of my book on northern Greece, not quite finished yet, alas. There is, for some reason, something Herculeanly difficult about writing under these circumstances, with workmen coming and interrupting one every five minutes and dragging one to the slowly growing carcass of the house for consultation, with the result that one postpones writing from hour to hour, then from day to day, with the terrible result that you see! But now I'm under a roof again, and living a more regular and serene existence (!), this glacier will break up and I plan to become a model correspondent, in spite of the bullying letters and telegrams from English and American publishers that arrive full of reproaches almost daily. This, again, is not the proper letter I want to write, but the first on a list of apologetic missives to make amends for being so hopeless. In a few days' time I will go through your lovely letters again and write a real letter going into everything in detail.

I think I'll be here till almost Christmas, then back to England for a month, then here again. I want you to make a list of any books you want, also a prize parcel for you, and another for Pomme, of things that will be most useful. <u>Also</u>, please, do send me details of those hearing aid things – I mean, I think they vary from person to person, the type needed, as you <u>must</u> have one for when you want to listen to something nice – though I see the advantage of being partly incommunicado for a lot of the time! I'm so glad 'Fall of Constantinople'[1] arrived all right. I loved it, and knew you would too. Did Auden's four-volume anthology[2] ever arrive? It's a positive treasure chest of fascination. I hate being without it, and would like you and Pomme to have it handy too.

I got a <u>marvellous</u> letter from Ins[3] describing their time in the Loire. What a marvellous introduction to France! All Ronsard and du Bellay and the Pléiade;[4] and it seems like a miracle their getting jobs and somewhere to live. I'm about to write to her, and will see if I can help in their visit to London; and if I stop in Paris on either journey to or from, will get hold of them both. I do hope Pomme and Constantine don't miss her too intolerably.

I'm alone here at the moment – Joan's with a brother who has been rather ill in the country in the W. of England, but will probably come here in a week or two. I've settled in a funny little hotel on the edge of the village, with the sea splashing on the pebbles just outside the window, and the olive groves inland are full of black-clad women collecting olives on coloured blankets and beating the branches with bamboo poles. I go up to the rocky site of the ¼ built house every afternoon, feeling like Rameses or Cheops.[5] I'll tell you all about that in my next.

Meanwhile, darling B, tons of love and hugs from Paddy, and lots to Pomme and Constantine. Forgive delay!

P.S. A tremendous favour! Could you <u>possibly</u> translate, word for word, line by line, 'Mioritza'?[6] I would love to turn it into an English

---

[1] Steven Runciman, *The Fall of Constantinople 1453* (1965).
[2] W. H. Auden and Norman Holmes Pearson (eds), *Poets of the English Language* (5 vols, 1950).
[3] Ina ('Ins') Catargi (née Donici), Balasha's niece.
[4] La Pléiade, a name given to a group of sixteenth-century French Renaissance poets whose principal members were Pierre de Ronsard and Joachim du Bellay.
[5] Both Egyptian pharaohs: Rameses built the rock temples at Abu Simbel, and the temple at Thebes; Cheops (Khufu) the Great Pyramid of Giza.
[6] PLF was fascinated by this ancient Romanian folk-poem, which he would discuss at length in *Between the Woods and the Water*, pp. 235–8.

poem, but have forgotten many of the words in Constantine's anthology. '*In dosal stânei*' [behind the sheepfold] makes me think of Băleni after sunset so much.

Roumeli: Travels in Northern Greece, the follow-up to Mani, was at last finished, though it would not be published until 1966. This letter, about the photographs for the book, was written to Jock Murray's son, John, who had just come down from Oxford and was helping out at Albemarle Street.

To John Murray   Kardamyli
23 June 1965   Messenia
                               Greece

Dear John,

Thank you for your letter to Belgrade, which for some reason has been dodging me along the Danube till now.

I thought enclosed snap 546 – suggesting a bleak and blasted mountain landscape – might do for the Dilemma.[1] Joan has had very bad luck with her *Karayiozi*[2] snaps, but we are going to try again. What about 513, 575 and 587 for the Cretan part? When is closing time for photographs?

Do ask Jock to use the one of me in Cretan outfit. I know it's a bit absurd, but I rather love it and others seem to like it. The outfit is more elaborate and old fashioned than the sort actually worn, but dressing up like this and being elaborately snapped is a great tradition among Cretan mountaineers. This particular one was publicly on sale in Crete as a Christmas card after the war, so they think it's OK, which is all I care about; if anything, slightly underdressed for this type of snap!

---

[1] No doubt 'the Dilemma' was outlined in a letter from John Murray now lost.

[2] A form of shadow play practised in Greece, in which 'the actors are transparent silhouettes cut out of camel-hide, coloured, jointed and manipulated by the invisible puppet-masters on long rods which flatten and animate the figures against a stretched white linen screen lit from behind', *Roumeli*, p. 101.

I'm so glad all goes so well, and v. many thanks for taking so much trouble. When is publication date, do you think?

The Danube journey was tremendous, and I got away from it a week ago, just before the river overflowed everywhere, fleeing from the Black Sea to Sofia, then across Macedonia by road and then here, where our house is going up.

Yours ever
Patrick Leigh Fermor

P.S. Would you tell Jock that the Athens piece is in the current June *Holiday*.

Paddy had first met the Byzantine historian Steven Runciman (1903–2000) in Sofia in 1934. Afterwards he remembered Runciman and his companion Roger Hinks as 'impeccable in Panama hats and suits of cream-coloured Athenian silk and their bi-coloured shoes were beautifully blancoed and polished'. To Paddy, still only nineteen, their conversation seemed 'dazzlingly erudite and comic'. In contrast, Runciman remembered Paddy as 'a very bright, very grubby young man'. Their paths crossed again after the war, in Athens, where Runciman, Paddy's boss at the British Council, dismissed him, complaining of 'Paddy's little irregularities': too many parties, too few repaid loans. Though furious at the time, Paddy was not the kind of man to bear a grudge long.

To Steven Runciman   Kardamyli
24 July 1965   Messenia
Greece[1]

Dear Steven,

I've just finished *The Fall of Constantinople* and can't let the sun go down without writing to say how really wonderful I found it. I must have read the story in at least a dozen shapes, none of

---

[1] PLF wrote a note on this letter, commenting on his newly printed letterhead: 'huge heading for an almost non-existent house'.

them nearly as good. The compactness and non-fruitiness of the whole treatment brings out the tragedy, pathos, horror etc., far more effectively than anything more florid would have done. The Turkish background – Seldjuks, Rum, the Ghazis, the Anatolian provinces and their intrigues – was absorbing, and made Mehmet much more explicable. What an extraordinary creature. I was sad that there was no room for Djem;[1] it sounds so odd a tale; but of course he had no bearing on the story.

It's funny, among so unfeudal a people as the Greeks, what a strong hold the idea of Byzantine descent has on them. Here in the Mani, the villages teem with putative Palaeologi; Comnenes[2] and Medici as well, which is going a bit far. I wonder if there is anything in the 'Khan Timor' derivative of Dmitri Cantimir's name[3] (c.f. Callimachi from Kalmuck). There was an amusing portrait of him at Balasha and Hélène Cantacuzène's house in Moldavia, in armour, powdered wig and Louis XIV moustache, I suppose a copy of that one which always illustrated him, wherever that was, or is. Romanian reference books say he wrote a *Descriptio Moldaviae* in Latin. I've never come across it but would dearly love to. I saw B. and H. Cantacuzène in Romania last month, living in dire want near Tîgoriste (*Ô retour implacable de toute chose*[4]), and trudged round Mogosoaia[5] as a museum.

Anyway, what a marvellous book and a tremendous treat.

Yours ever, Paddy

[1] Djem, also known as Sultan Cem (1459–95), though a Muslim, spent five years as the prisoner/guest of Pope Innocent VIII in the Vatican. Djem was actually a pawn in the political game between his half-brother, the Ottoman sultan, and the pope.

[2] The Palaeologi and the Komnenos were noble families in the Byzantine empire.

[3] Dimitri Cantimir (1673–1723), Moldavian soldier, statesman, and man of letters, twice *voivode* (warlord) of Moldavia.

[4] 'And thus the whirligig of time brings in his revenges,' Shakespeare, *Twelfth Night*, Act V, Scene 1.

[5] The Mogoşoaia Palace, about ten kilometres from Bucharest, built at the end of the seventeenth century in what is called the Romanian Renaissance style. The property of the Bibesco family, it was confiscated by the communist regime in 1945.

Paddy closely supervised the construction of the house at Kardamyli, which occupied him for much of the rest of the decade. In this letter he expresses concerns about interruptions to his writing.

To Joan Rayner   Kardamyli
3 September 1965   Messenia

Darling Joan,

1) How marvellous about Turkey![1] I do think Aymer an angel to ask us, and feel very complimented: especially his leaving the two spare places in our gift. His letter set one by the ears and into an agonizing quandary of doubt about building. Everything is going on in lively style, but it's absolutely vital for a decision-taker to be on the spot in this phase where it's speak now or hold peace forever. Absence seems fatal, and I was just settling down, after a long wrestling match with temptation, to cry off by letter to you and Aymer, but urging you to go, when Junior arrived saying Hero would be undyingly grateful for 20 days' furlough in order to spread the gros béton[2] he has been promising to do since spring, and then come back to work harder and faster than ever, and what's more, all through the winter, doing indoor work – plastering, chimneys, etc., when it rains, carrying on with outer walls when it's fine. Also Paraskevas[3] had to kick off this Saturday (has now gone, he had always said he would have to), and Junior went on to say that they expected the first rains between 15–20 Octo[ber] (how do they know?), and would have to disperse to their olives ... All this being so, I tore up my gloomy letters and draft telegrams, and here we are!

2) What a shame Graham [Joan's brother] can't come. I can't think of a better five than it would have been. Two days ago, to my delight, Ian [Whigham] and Ralph Anstruther[4] suddenly arrived and we had a marvellous day of eating, drinking, swimming,

---

[1] Their friend Sir Aymer Maxwell was proposing a cruise in his yacht *Dirk Hatterick*.
[2] A concrete base, laid below the finishing screed.
[3] Paraskevas, 'Junior' and 'Hero' were workmen on the building site at Kardamyli.
[4] Sir Ralph (Hugo) Anstruther, 7th Baronet (1921–2002), army officer and courtier. As the queen mother's treasurer he had the difficult job of trying to restrain her spending.

talking, and, above all, going over the house and the plans. They were both full of enthusiasm and kind words for the former and marvellous and extremely helpful and sensible suggestions about the latter. More later about this. They had just come from Aymer (dossing down in the little house; the bigger is bursting at the seams with duchesses). Ian is wavering about coming, I think about 51% pro – longing to, but hindered by other commitments, none, I think, insuperable. My impression is that [he would] with a bit of urging, so do write to 88, Via Margutta [Rome]. What about Annie to take Graham's place? Janetta? It's far too small, alas, and strenuous, for us to return yacht hospitality by proxy to Diana. I've on purpose not written to Annie suggesting anything, so the ball is all in your court. I think, though he doesn't know her, Aymer is intrigued and would like J. It's not a tragedy if we don't get a 5th, but I think A. would like to as he is going, obviously, to so much trouble. Ian, quite apart from other reasons, knows the region a bit. He was very funny about Rosie Rodd's[1] life. I hope we don't see <u>too</u> much of her though. She's shacked up on the Turkish coast near Halicarnassus, I think, under extraordinary circumstances.

3) Darling, I've lost your telegram for the moment, about arrival dates, it sounded perfect, but do repeat them with details by letter, and I'll act accordingly; meeting, booking rooms, etc.

4) No word from Jock, though registered/airmailed the corrected proofs off days & days ago. Can you give him a ring?

5) I'm busy <u>typing</u> out the Danube outside. V. slow and laborious at first, it still takes ¾ of an hour a page, but I'm getting better every moment. With any luck, by the time it's finished I'll know how to do it as much as I'll ever need. I must be mad not to have taught myself earlier. If only I'd typed out each day's work from the ms at the end of each day, over the years, I would be a different person today, calm, rich, prolific, famous, rested, poised, perhaps even happier! But a change is on the way! The last bit is still unwritten, but when all this

---

[1] Rosie Rodd had divorced her husband and rented a dilapidated villa in Kusadasi, on the Turkish coast. There she met an American called Ken Baldwin, who moved in with her and whom she eventually married.

is typed out, I'll practice my new system, and all will be well, and I'll have something presentable to give a proper typist in Athens. After all, it's like having one's own private printing press. It's a late developing thing for me, like driving. Do urge me on about things like this and stop me being such a ghastly nuisance to everyone.

6) I've started doing some rudimentary cooking, kicking off with the following in an earthenware pot: lots of chopped courgettes, aubergines, tomatoes, several chopped and small, whole onions, lots of chopped and whole garlic cloves, water, 2 glasses of oil, a spoon full of butter, lots of rock salt, a great deal of Bucharest pepper, 2 dried red paprika pods chopped up. It was tremendous, so hot and vigorous that I hardly noticed when the last wasp of summer stung me on the elbow as I swallowed the first spoonful. I've done a lot of χυλοπήτες [tagliatelle], those pasta, egg-, macaroni-like squares that use up nearly all the eggs just now. Like pasta, it can be delicious. Junior has given me a couple of lessons. I've poached my first egg, made my first omelette! I asked Ralph & Ian about these, and they both said the secret is not to thrash the eggs up much before-hand – leave it runny – 'plenty of nose' as they rather disgustingly put it. Done, with splendid results. Lunch today, scrambled eggs, lots of butter with the nosey eggs in a waterless casserole floating in a bigger one, full of boiling water, is this the bain-marie principle?[1] Marvellous, I thought, though some stuck to the bottom. I plan to get lots of carrot, potatoes, etc., & make a vast *zuppa di verdure* …

7) I'm feeling a bit guilty about Johnny [Craxton]. I encouraged him to come when the yacht did, but not afterwards. I couldn't bear the idea of anyone hanging about or (rather jealously, per-haps) spending the whole day with the workmen, which I long to do, but resist, limiting myself to four inspections a day, if not, which normally happens, being summoned for advice about that often. It spoils everything if one has to talk, when one is in a proper working mood (as I am now), dawdle about, drink, be polite, utter, even, with anyone else but you. But I do feel guilty, as Johnny was

[1] A bain-marie is a method of cooking, in which the dish to be cooked is placed in a 'bath' of simmering water.

probably longing to come, and he's had such a rotten time (though he seemed absolutely happy about everything in Athens). But, if you can, when he arrives, <u>do</u> say how lovely I thought the cover and make him feel loved by me, which he is.

8) The violability of this place is a worry. Rodis Roufos's wife & two daughters[1] turned up the other evening, inopportune, but quite nice. Then Eileen Backley (Sam's ex-wife)[2] and a fearful journalist pal turned up, the Roufos's left, then stayed on till long after dinner time, asked me to dinner in K[ardamyli]. I refused, they finally buggered off, I said I was busy with deadlines. Yesterday, Sunday, was bad. Just settling down when, at 10 a.m., Chippendale[3] appeared, we talked window frames till 12.00; then Yanni Gouléas (boiling lupins [beans] on the stove, the only one) arrived with some correspondence to be translated into English, and ½ an hour's hobnobbing. I was smoking in the cellar afterwards, when a tall figure came in saying he hoped he didn't intrude (quite nice, David Something-Something, MP for Hereford,[4] married to a quite nice tall woman; ex-Hambro, whose brother has the shoot at Dumbleton, friends of Coote's & Letty's). This meant lunch – they kept saying no, they'd got a picknick, but it was 3 p.m. – eggs and bacon, which she cooked. Not sent by Coote, I hasten to say, but by Didi Serpieri,[5] who said I might advise about buying somewhere in Crete or the Peloponnese. (Quite nice, I repeat. Don't tell Coote!) They left about 5.00, and I was making a dash for my bathing dress when Leonidas and four Athenian kinsmen

[1] Arietta Scanavi, wife of diplomat and novelist Rodis Kanakaris-Roufos (1924–72). She had two sons, but no daughters. Roufos wrote a scathing review of *The Cretan Runner*: 'I do not doubt, not even for a moment, Mr Leigh Fermor's best intentions. It is his great love for Greece that made him translate and publish [sic] this book. In his introduction, he speaks with enthusiasm and admiration of the simple guerrillas that worked with him in Crete, for their courage, their cleverness and their selflessness. But that's how Kipling often spoke about the Indians, Lawrence about the Bedouins, Somerset Maugham about the Malaysians,' Rodis Kanakaris-Roufos, 'Philhellenism and Primitivism', republished in *Oi metamorphoseis tou Alachriou* (Athens, 1971).
[2] Unidentified.
[3] PLF's nickname for the carpenter.
[4] David Gibson-Watt (1918–2002), MP for Hereford 1956–1974, married Diana Hambro.
[5] Didi Serpieri, née Vlastou, from a prominent Greek family with mining interests.

appeared through the cypresses, he with a presentation bottle of Piperman [orange juice]. He arranged chairs in a ring, saying that he had promised them a first-hand account of General Kreipe's capture. It took an hour – not the telling, I gave a very abridged utility account, but the subsequent chat, so predictable that one could manage it half-asleep, but age-ing nevertheless. When they left I settled with a sigh to P. G. Wodehouse's *Uneasy Money* or sleep on the yellow chair, when I heard voices below and the murmur of oars. It was a boat-load from Kalamata brought by one of the young blacksmiths: quite a nice schoolmaster (I think), and his family. I made a dash for the typewriter, began a mad obligato, but there they were. I kept up the crashing till they were on me and received them standing. After half an hour, he said he saw I was busy and would come back when I was a bit freer and talk about all sorts of things. Their boat sculled back through the afterglow and I felt like cutting my throat.

We must have a high and forbidding wall at the vulnerable points. All – Niko, Ian, Ralph – say anything else is folly. I thought of putting a notice on an olive tree, down our turning – WORK IN PROGRESS – but this would only daunt the very few sensitive people, perhaps great friends, be ridden over roughshod by the others. It's not the locals; in spite of yesterday, they are discretion itself as a rule, it's Kalamata and, above all, England. My plan is to enlist all the locals on our side in keeping people away, saying I'm hard at work, not to be disturbed etc., when people ask the way, take them into our confidence in spreading the reputation that we're both fiends of agoroxenophobia, which I'm becoming. How right Larry [Durrell] and Graham are! Apart from these incursions, all has been perfect peace and quiet.

9) The work goes on splendidly. The two end rooms are now breast-high, and will soon be higher. At this very moment, Hero is spanning your room with its dividing arch, a beautiful white semicircle soaring above the walls. He now does them as perfectly, nonchalantly and almost as quickly as an expert blowing smoke-rings. Did I tell you the details of the room? Recesses for book cases on either side of the windows at either end, the two thirds part of the W. wall E. of the arch divided up into a recess for a

wide basin and for two wall-to-ceiling cupboards. I think it will be lovely. The only possible defect so far, I think (a very remediable one) is the lamp recess on the plan I made them do with a pointed top, as you said you rather like them, viz two slabs of Pelian stone. I don't think it looks right – merely Saxon or Carlovingian, instead of Romanesque, too uncouth, I think, for the suaver atmosphere upstairs, crying out for a roughhewn image of SS Dunstan or Swithin. I nearly had it filled in at once, but will leave it till you come for fun. It can be blocked in four minutes. This is a sort of impression:

The dotted line, except for the arch, now sailing up on its mulberry fan, slows the height of the walls now. They will probably be much higher this evening. Ictynus said the walls should be only 270 [cm] high, the same as downstairs. This causes general disapproval, strongly backed by Ian & Ralph, so they have been changed to three metres, which should be fine. I'm making Hero put a slab of wood among the masonry <u>everywhere</u> at picture hanger height, to avoid rawlplugs and general chaos; also two more on either side of the windows, just under the ceiling, for curtain-rods: You remember the hell at Kallirhoe [the Athens house]! This is what the room may be like in a few months: (looks far too long & vast) I've made a balls of it, of course; but never

mind. Judge true things by what their mockeries be.[1] You are looking in through the East window, fluttering in mid air like a seraph.

10) There has been a terrific amount of fuss about the shutters, and friction between Paraskevas & Chippendale while I was away for a night (see below). It's the old old story, the warlike music of saw on trowel. But cleared up now. They are simply not used to outside shutters folding back. I have persuaded Ian to send me [from] Cheltenham, via. Olympic Airways in Rome, the entire iron fastening and closing fittings of an outside shutter, to get the smiths here to copy; also, where the hinge comes if one wants to have this opening outwards <u>on themselves</u>, as in Italy and on the Danube, which are heavenly, viz [see overleaf]. They look marvellous, like the gills on a fish. <u>Why shouldn't we have them</u>? Now we are going to have all three: Shutters, wire netting against the wailful choir [mosquitoes], then the panes on the <u>outside</u> windows; on the verandah and corridors, I thought, wire first, all removable when unwanted,

[1] 'Minding true things by what their mock'ries be', Shakespeare, *Henry V*, Prologue to Act IV.

then shutters folding back into the reveal of the windows, inside the room; then panes, so as not to give the verandah and passage a too outdoors, shutter-smothered look. Then there will always be the curtains inside, if we want to ring yet another change in lighting, privacy, sound, temperature! etc.

11) The pistoletto man,[1] Vangeli of <u>Neochori</u>, above Stupa, told Junior his cousin was demolishing a lot of his old house to make a grocer's shop, there might be some *angonária* [cornerstones] going. Junior and I went, with the result that he is letting us have all the useful blocks of hard *poria* (OK by Hero) for inside, for plasterable building – somewhere between 300 or 400, I think – at five drach[ma]s each, 1 dr extra for mule transport to motor road, 250 drachs truck hire here – viz. 1 truck load – Among the other stones there are two nice old rough arches that might come in handy somewhere, also an amusing window frame. I tried in vain to dissuade him from demolishing the arches.

12) I very much wanted to try and get a few bits of raw, rough marble, for the cornerstones under the eaves (Ictynus was delighted at the idea. Something was needed, he couldn't think what), possibly

[1] A spray-plasterer.

with those small semi-circular knolls. Apparently the only place was a quarry at Pyrgos, so I drove there (1½ hours) one afternoon last week. It's an amazing place on the edge of a cliff over a huge wild gulf, a mile from the lovely old church of Charouda (do you remember? It's largely built of the local marble). All the workmen were Proastians, cousins of all our mob, friends of Hero's. They said I could take as much as I like free, as anything under a square ton they simply chuck into the sea, like shavings. The whole place was littered with blocks and slabs. So yesterday 2.00 p.m. (a day has passed since I began) I went off with Hero, Petro, one of the Georges, and little tough Panayioti junior following in a huge road building truck, hired for ½ a day for 800 [drachmas]. We took wine, ouzo & mézés for the workmen, and loaded up about 5 tons of the stuff, stopping for a drink and snack at [illegible], getting back and tipping it out in a glittering moonlit heap at 10.00 p.m … all very exciting. Rough and unpolished – treated like our own squared ashlars in fact – it is simply beautiful. Struck with a hammer, it makes an odd thud, like a bolster, not the clang of ordinary stone, and off fly huge snowflakes. I should think it's about £1,000 worth, all buckshee, and we can take as much more as we like. It might be lovely for the well, for the tops of the seats round the loggia, for lintels and sills, and the top of the low balcony wall; also, instead of wood, for the supporting pillars and the steps of the staircase; all treated in the same style as the capital of the two loggia arches. I took them into the old church at Charouda, and Hero at once said 'That's the sort of pillar we want for the verandah – I could make them easily!' He was in a state of great excitement. I think he may be right. They are octagonal, ending rather amusingly, like this [see overleaf], if you see the idea. One must, if we like the idea, get the width right for the proportions of the house – not too heavy, but not pencil thin, like the ones on Aymer's balcony – 8, 9, 10 inches? What about the big doors of the grave salon – & the fireplace? It might look lovely. I think the well should be v. simple, either a polygon or a cylinder. We all got back simply lacerated by the stuff – talk about stones wanting blood! – hands in shreds, & my back and shoulder zigzagged!

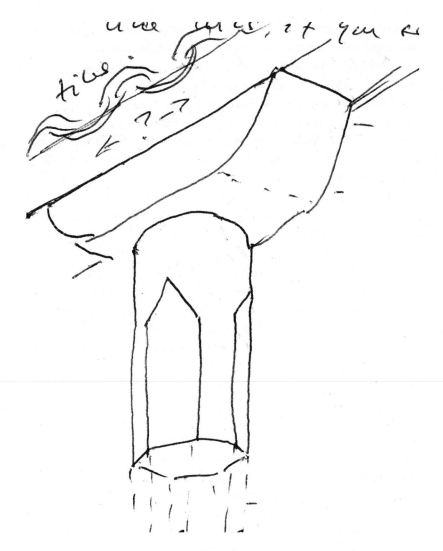

13) The thing is to stock up for the winter. With all this, the *angonária*, and our own piles of stuff, we are OK for materials. More ασβέστη [lime], sand and pebbles on the way. Chippendale OK for wood. Immediate programme: before everyone disappears: (1) to get

the two end rooms to roof height; (2) to get all the shutters & doors of the downstairs room ready for locking all our camping stuff in, when we have to strike it; (3) To clear all the earth away from the east cellar door ... so that the rains won't sweep the mountainside into the cellar; and (4) fling the grosbeton of the grand salon and the steps (I'm so glad you OK the idea. I think it will be fine) while we still have the chaps, so all is clear for work all winter. Everything is going fast and well, and with any luck, all this will be done when you arrive.

14) Ian & Ralph made marvellous suggestions about cupboard room, linen cupboards etc., which we need lots of – all being put into practice. Also loo advice, chimneys, shutters, all first rate. If Ian comes, we must take the plans with us.

15) I daren't mention the weather. It must be like this in Paradise. Smooth, warm (jacket, here in the evening), lovely magnesium shadows, clarity, kingfishers over the water ...

I <u>must</u> get this off, darling, otherwise no reason to stop. Do keep in touch with Aymer. Love to Graham, Elsie, Jim, & tons of love to you

from Paddy

P.S. Do bring the African [illegible]. Also any of those <u>doorknobs</u> we can find. They are not ideal, but might do for a bit. Chips were going to have these condensed milk [i.e. off-white in colour] & aluminium levers: another think coming![1] A couple of really good powerful torches might be an idea.

P.P.S. Your letter just arrived! Also the enclosed from Aymer. Not quite the same – but what do you think? I do hope yes.

X X X X

Just got J. A. Symonds life[2] – fascinating, & v. many thanks!

---

[1] A play on words.
[2] Phyllis Grosskurth, *John Addington Symonds: A Biography* (1964).

When visiting London, Paddy and Joan often stayed as paying guests of their friend Patrick Kinross, who owned a house in Little Venice.

To Patrick Kinross   Kardamyli
8 March 1968   Messenia
                                                             Greece

Dear Patrick,

Better late than never to write and thank you for all those London kindnesses – I've been meaning to for ages – viz., sumptuous shelter on arrival, moral support on that momentous snowy morning at Caxton Hall[1] and the splendid feast in the evening; and every quarter of an hour, I whisk a Papastratos No I[2] out of that pretty cylindrical box with the Maria Theresa thaler [silver coin] embedded in the lid. I enjoyed London like mad, much of it thanks to you, and to other Little Venetians. That's the place.

Janetta's was marvellous. That kitchen! It's the best I've seen in the world. The size and comfort of the rooms made us a bit discontented with our lot when we got back here. We found Kardamyli emerging from the worst winter in recorded history – snow a foot deep even on the island. We just missed this amazing vision, alas. Meanwhile, our old pals the workmen have taken possession again. I don't know what we'll do when they finally clear off, and the patter of hobnailed boots falls silent.

We long to know about the appalling invasion of Diana's house. She writes on a card 'can't write more this week all my thoughts are given to sheer enjoyment of my drugs raid'. First burglars, then peelers,[3] her house is becoming a sort of Brechtian stage. No 'chorus

---

[1] PLF and Joan were married at Caxton Hall on 11 January 1968.

[2] A Greek cigarette.

[3] Diana Cooper had been twice burgled in 1966. In 1968, for reasons never fully explained, the police ('peelers') descended on her house in Warwick Square in search of drugs. See Philip Ziegler, *Diana Cooper* (London, 1981), pp. 311–12.

of firemen', thank god;[1] but who will the next figurants [bit-part players] be? A Comus's rout[2] of encyclopedia salesmen?

See you later on, I imagine. Meanwhile, 1,000 thanks again for all and best love from us both

Paddy

P.S. Tell Freda[3] (with embraces) that that thick ratcatcher coat and the dinner jacket are at M. Astor's, 1 Swan Walk, should they be needed by her lads.

Building the house at Kardamyli dragged on much longer than expected. 'Oh, how I long for all this to be finished, darling!' Paddy would write to Joan, more than a year after the letter to Jock, below. 'I've got up twice at dawn, to clear the decks of letters, at least, but the moment people turn up, problems and distractions fall thick and fast …' He confessed to feeling 'inexcusably guilty about Jock', and apologised 'for being so frightful sometimes'. He was having a separate studio built, which he hoped would prove the 'solution to all sorts of worries'.

To Jock Murray | Kardamyli
10 May 1968 | Messenia
| Greece

Dear Jock,

Thank you for your letter. Your urgent but kindly worded plea for haste could not fall on less deaf ears. I'm at it like mad, all the

[1] PLF probably refers to *The Fire Raisers* (*Biedermann und die Brandstifter*), also known in English as *The Firebugs, Firebugs* or *The Arsonists,* written by Max Frisch in 1953, first as a radio play, then adapted for television and the stage (1958) as a play in six scenes, in which the action is observed by a Greek-style chorus of 'firemen'. Brecht often used the device of a chorus in his plays.

[2] In Greek mythology, Comus is the god of festivity, revels and nocturnal dalliances. During his festivals in ancient Greece, men and women exchanged clothes. He was depicted as a young man on the point of unconsciousness from drink. He had a wreath of flowers on his head and carried a torch that was in the process of being dropped.

[3] (Elizabeth) Freda Berkeley, wife of the composer Lennox Berkeley. They had three sons.

time, and have been for weeks. I've not moved from here since arrival. All Porlocians[1] have been kept severely at bay, the only visit has been Peter Q's and his new wife's which was no interruption at all, in fact a stimulus, as he knows the form and goaded from the touchline: only meeting at meals, while they led an amphibious life in the bay, or lolled dreamily under the olives with books. The only damnable interruption has been the constant presence of the builders. The trouble is we have no architect (we had one, but he has only been here five times in all), with the result that again and again during the day I'm reft from my table for orders and consult-ation; we have to hang on to the workmen, as everyone for miles is after them, and if we let them go for a month, I doubt if we would get them back for a year or more. They work fast and well, so that new conundrums are cropping up all the time, and one is constantly being summoned; compelled to doff one kind of thinking cap and take another down from the peg, then hailed to the site with paper, pencil, tape measure, protractor & compasses, or despatched for more materials or some vital emergency requisite by these eager but impossible and over optimistic artisans. Ironically, they are at work at the moment on the studio, or study – detached among the trees – where this last phase of the book should be drawing peacefully to its end:[2] a cool hothouse or smithy for the forcing/forging of many books to come. But this is no consolation to either of us, at the moment, for this infuriating slowness now. But I am working hard and well amidst these maddening difficulties – which I, too, had fondly imagined would be over by now – and as fever-ishly as if I were still the right side of the deadline, and will con-tinue to do so till it's all over; very soon, I hope. Stuck here, I've been not very lucky in typists; but I'm on to a good one, and think she might come here for the few days needed if one went all out. I'm tremendously contrite about all this; don't make any drastic changes of plans, as we may suddenly be in the clear earlier than all

[1] A reference to Coleridge's 'person from Porlock', who supposedly interrupted the reverie in which he was composing 'Kubla Khan'.

[2] 'The King's life is drawing peacefully to a close': an official statement released to the press on 20 January 1936, a few hours before George V died.

the foregoing might seem to indicate; above all, don't tell me about any postponements you might have in mind.

Do come here and inspect, later on in the summer – when those rival gerundives, the *cacoëthes scribendi* [an insatiable urge to write] and the *furor aedificandi* [craze to build] have passed their crises – if you are in this part of the world. It's not yet worth a special trip, but rather, like the Giant's Causeway in Dr Johnson, worth seeing but not worth going to see!

Back to work.

Yours ever,
Paddy

Love from Joan

Paddy was friendly with Michael Stewart, British Ambassador to Greece 1967–71, during the difficult period of the Colonels' rule, and his wife Damaris.

To Damaris Stewart   Kardamyli
20 June 1968   Messenia
Greece

Dear Damaris,

I can't let yet another sun go down without writing to say thank you to both for letting me come on that marvellous Samos-Asia Minor journey. We are both still under its spell; it was Open Sesame to the Hellenistic world, and, by leaving the great trampled sites for another day, reached almost through a secret entry. I've resisted sending Freya a card about the stark beauty of Nyssa; rightly, you will agree, on all counts.[1] One won't forget in a hurry looking down through the debris of Priene[2] at the Maeander twisting across the

[1] PLF is resisting a play on the word 'stark'.
[2] An ancient Greek city in Asia Minor, formerly on the coast but now inland, close to the Maeander (now known as the Büyük Menderes) river.

plain under the rising full moon in a river of green corn; or the sloping zig-zags of Mt Latmos like those mountains in Greco and Patinir[1] backgrounds, and the walls and arches below looping about among those freak rocks like masonry among a herd of elephants or a school of fossilized whales. As for Aphrodisias, short of Angkor, it must be the Mecca of ruin-pleasure; I wonder if Rose M[acaulay][2] ever went there? Aldous Huxley, sitting among the remains of Antigua, in Guatemala, checked himself on the brink of a fruity passage of thoughts on splendour and decay etc., by detecting with his mind's eye, a notice suspended by the Time-Spirit from a shattered cupola, saying NO MUSING, BY REQUEST.[3] He would have found it an even harder struggle among those bramble-choked lumps of architrave, spiral flutings, council chambers, floored with water weed, vast calidaria [thermal baths] shaded with walnut trees and columns standing in spinneys of Yonne-valley poplars. And what about that Corinthian capital with five long-legged stylites on top and the acanthus fronds crushed with a score of swifts' nests in the middle of 100 hovering birds? Not even the most extravagant epigonic stone-mason could imagine so wild an elaboration on his theme. No wonder one grows florid …

The beastly weather has stopped at last, and, apart from the poison of architectural ideas above one's station that our exposure to infection in Asia Minor have inevitably instilled, all goes well in the Mani; except, that is, for a terrible pot of dahlias that our maid Lela has given us: how to get it away from the place of honour on the balcony where she has proudly put it? It'll be bougainvillaea next. It would be hard to explain in Romaïc that, apart from the local vegetation, the only extraneous flowers one might think of planting would be those old fashioned roses with many petals like the rosettes on the shoes of Elizabethan courtiers painted by Hilliard.

---

[1] Joachim Patinir (c.1480–1524), Flemish landscape painter.
[2] A reference to Rose Macaulay's *Pleasures of Ruins* (1953).
[3] Huxley remarked on the architecture of the Spanish colonial city of Antigua in his *Beyond the Mexique Bay* (1934).

Very many thanks again to you both from Joan and me for a really marvellous treat.

Yours ever
Paddy

P.S. Charles de Noailles, the great gardener, when asked by P. Quennell, on return from a highly rarified horticultural conference, which plant had been most in favour among the delegates, looked quickly over his shoulder and then whispered 'Spurrrge'. I do see. There's lots here, luckily.

To Joan Leigh Fermor   Kardamyli
1 October 1968   Messenia
                                     Greece

Darling Joan,

How lovely to get your two letters, one waiting, and another just arrived. How exciting it all sounds, except the bloody weather. I know one only picks out the highlights in letters, which, compressed, sound like a Bacchic whirl with all the tamer intervals excluded. But it fills one with envy, all the same.

First: the Far Eastern plans sound glorious, and I'm very excited by them; so all absolutely OK as far as I'm concerned. Second, if you won't be too mis[erable], I think it's best if I come and pick you up in Kalamata rather than Athens, as it would make too soon a break in the work, which only starts on Wednesday, as it was/will be, a) too late in the week b) the day of the Referendum for recovery[1] and c) Tuesday is unlucky for a start, because of the Fall of the Πόλις [Polis, the City, i.e. Constantinople] in 1453. So I won't have had time to do much good or harm! I'll try and put off any

---

[1] Under a referendum held in Greece on 15 November 1968, voters were asked whether they wished to ratify a new constitution prepared by the regime of the 'Colonels'. It was approved by 92.1 per cent of voters, with a voter turnout of 77.7 per cent.

departure for Kalamata till then, and do all that has to be done before the plane arrives.

I'm <u>so pleased</u> you saw Pomme, darling; I knew she was longing to, but felt a bit diffident about saddling you with more visitants from my pre-War life: had, actually, thought of wiring you about her, when your letter arrived, saying you had met, to my great joy. I do fondly love her, and I'm so glad I went to France to see her.[1] I simply loved it – seeing her and Ina, I mean. Pomme and I slept at either end of a sort of attic-studio at the top of the house, so we talked for hours and hours. She spent every spare second of the day writing letter after letter to B[alasha] describing every outing, meal, picture gallery, person, scenery etc., so she could vicariously share this almost unbelievable reprieve. I felt that it was like squirrels storing up hazel nuts for the winter. Costa [Achillopoulos]'s house is very pretty and he was kindness itself. Though I feel that the endless cocktail parties at the houses of some of the most boring people I've ever met made Pomme quite bewildered, sometimes almost long for the silence of rustic isolation beyond the Iron Curtain; in fact, she, Ina and I went on strike after a day or two. The only one [sic] of those awful gatherings which was at all nice were dinner at a v. nice friend of Debo's called Mona Baring,[2] and Allanah's.[3] A. was v. excited and nice, as B[alasha] and Pomme came to her 'coming out' dance in the early twenties, and she and Pomme were able to exchange flapperish memories. There was a successful trip to St Tropez with a yacht trip and bathing and hours in the museum, and I took them and Costa and [a] charming violinist follower of Ina's called Roger Poirault (more of him when we meet) to a giant fish banquet on the waterfront at Cannes. We went for a long walk along the promenade, stiff with cars and yachts, the first time she had seen it for nearly sixty years! Once as a minute girl, they spent

[1] 'Pomme' Donici had obtained permission to visit her daughter, Ina, in France.
[2] Mona Montgomerie Baring, née Mullins (1909?–88), divorced England cricketer Amyas Evelyn Giles Baring in 1949.
[3] Allanah Harper (1904–92), one of the original 'Bright Young Things', editor and founder of the literary journal *Echanges*, who lived in Paris.

a winter there at the rather flashy villa of their (and Anne-Marie's!)[1] grandfather – all carriages; footmen, scarcely a car! (It was the first time she'd been out of Romania for thirty years.) It sounded almost like Constantin Guys but much more Edwardian, Boldini, really.[2] Isn't it odd? Anyway, the whole thing was a great, great success. Bless you for asking her to lunch at Wheelers. You're an <u>absolute angel</u>. One of the great blessings was that Michael [Catargi, Ina's husband] stayed away in the mountains somewhere near Besançon (he and Pomme don't get on, in spite of endless fruitless efforts on her side) until the night I was there, viz. my last. They saw me off finally at Cannes station, and off I went, by train. Three hours' soaking wait at Marseilles; then over the Rhône and N. to Nimes, where Xan met me in another cloudburst, and off we went through the dusk to the Galerie des Pâtres,[3] & Daph., then – there had not been time to get out of it – to dinner with a rather nice Languedoc she-squire in a pretty château, with a French painter couple, friends of D and X. It was rather fun, and a lovely change from the odious English-villa Sunningdale life at the Côte D'Azur, of which poor old Costa is king (I had often thought of what Amy said). The G. des Pâtres isn't beautiful, but it's not hideous by any means, and could, with planning and trouble, be v. much better. A bit chintzy – but very comfortable, and they absolutely adore it. I simply loved seeing them again, and was very touched by them, and a bit worried, too. Xan's brother-in-law[4] is either very crooked, or a lunatic, and this delay and worry over the cash – I think it <u>will</u> materialise someday – has driven Xan nearly mad; terribly nervy and frowning and

---

[1] See footnote on p. 21.

[2] Constantin Guys (1802–92), Dutch-born artist and illustrator for British and French newspapers. For Baudelaire, Guys was the quintessential artist of contemporary Paris, whom he obliquely referred to as 'Monsieur G'. Giovanni Boldini (1842–1931), Italian portrait painter, lived and worked in Paris for most of his career.

[3] The Fieldings were living in this house on the outskirts of Uzès, in the Gard.

[4] Anthony Crespigny Claude Vivian, 5th Baron Vivian (1906–91), impresario and restaurateur, who in 1954 had been shot in the abdomen by his lover, Mavis Wheeler (the former wife of the well-known archaeologist Sir Mortimer Wheeler and mistress of Augustus John), at a range of three inches.

anxious. The bugger-in-law's false promises have nearly landed them in terrible soup, from which Derek Jackson nobly rescued them two months ago; I think Diana's taking half the house has been a timely help too. Daphne, in spite of her several drawbacks and a dash of arrested development, is very good and calming and kind. They both work like blacks. Xan was so highly strung in London that he would jump at the sound of an exhaust, start shaking like a leaf, and had to take to sedation. Another thing that must have been upsetting was the discovery, on going through all the papers, wills, archives, etc., connected with the case, that his mother was not really his mother at all, but his grandmother. His real mother, a Miss Fielding, died giving birth to him, after being married in Calcutta to his real father, a Capt. Wallace in the Sikhs Frontier Force, who (retired and practising as an unsuccessful barrister), only died three years ago; so his many brothers are really his uncles, his father was never mentioned to him; and he was adopted into his gran's family and name in order to share in the legacy eventually. He has a whole sheaf of photographs and cuttings and tells the still only half-comprehended tale with considerable humour and bewilderment. In spite of all this, the stay was great fun, lots of drinking and laughter, and daily meetings with Larry [Durrell], who lives an hour's drive away from Uzès, at Sommières, in one of the ugliest and gloomiest Chas. Addams[1] houses I've ever seen, ingeniously uglified still further by all sorts of recent changes. But Larry was better than ever, not nearly as circular as they say, ebullient and full of beans and ideas, waiting when we arrived with a giant magnum; we even managed to triumph over the eternal presence of Margaret (who you didn't take to, nor me; anathema to X and D).[2] Lots of talk, drink, song, plans to meet in Greece next spring.

I stayed with the F[ielding]s a week. One day I gave a feast at that nice restaurant at end of the Pont du Gard; on another outing

---

[1] Charles Samuel 'Chas' Addams (1912–88), American cartoonist known for his dark sense of humour. His macabre characters often inhabited spooky old mansions.

[2] Margaret, Lawrence Durrell's younger sister. His second wife, Claude-Marie Vincendon, had died the previous year.

we went across the garrigue and along solemn gorges to the bleak foothills of the Cevennes, where we had a lovely picknick. On the last night, after calling on Douglas Cooper[1] and gazing glass in hand at his extraordinary collection of Picassos, Braques, Légers, etc., we all had a marvellous farewell dinner in Nîmes, and next day drove to Avignon and the Lucullus (𝄞𝄞 ♧♧!)[2] and I left by train for a rather dismal and lonely evening in Nice – it's an awful town – before catching the plane to Athens next morning (via Corsica, Elba, Stromboli and Calabria) where I luckily (as recounted in my last!) fell in with Aymer [Maxwell].

I got here just after dark, bargaining for old tiles in Tripoli and Asprouliana, to find all the lights twinkling in the arcade, everyone full of loving welcomes, olives doing fine, all cats OK (most of them were up at the roadside, thinking it was you!), clouds, sea warm as could be. The Jellicoes[3] turned up on Sat. and left on Sun. – I've persuaded them to house-hunt in Tzakonia. I began this letter in sunlight, under my lower shelter, when suddenly tar-barrel clouds assembled and then burst, blurring the first page of this. By the time I'd scuttled upstairs, it was all a grey deluge, splashing with rivers everywhere, and dark as dusk in December; a sea of Typhoo-coloured[4] moving slime outside, so one can't set foot out without Wellingtons. Felt rather glum and sad; wished you were here. So glad to think the days of the winter-swamps outdoors are numbered. We must tackle these bloody windows.

How lovely the Ghika stay was. I do miss them. N.B. They have left the key of the flat with the janitor, should you want to stay. Perhaps it would be more practical at the O.P.[5] for so short a sojourn. I'll reserve a room there for you (as I was turned out of mine for a night into a nightmarish hutch, because of a 'group' – it

[1] Douglas Cooper (1911–84), quarrelsome art historian and collector, who lived at the Château de Castille near Avignon.
[2] The Hiély-Lucullus restaurant in Avignon.
[3] PLF's close friend and wartime comrade, George Jellicoe (1918–2007), 2nd Earl Jellicoe, and his wife Philippa.
[4] i.e. the colour of tea.
[5] The Olympic Palace Hotel, a standby for PLF.

would have killed you). But <u>don't forget to cancel it</u> if you go to Kriezotou,[1] and call, in case I've sent any S.O.S. there.

Darling Joan, I do miss you and long for you to appear. Please forgive this rotten letter <u>and its lateness</u>.

With tons of fond love & hugs
from Paddy

Love to Lucy, Ian, Diana, Annie etc. I <u>pine</u> for more details.

X X X X X
X X X
X X
X

To Diana Cooper   Kardamyli
6 October 1968   Messenia
                                                 Greece

My darling Diana,

This is not a real letter – I'm going to write a proper one in the next few days – but merely an excuse to send the following verses, prompted by Hornibrook's *Culture of the Abdomen*,[2] which I am busy annotating. On the title page, Hornibrook quotes four lines from Pope's *Essay on Man*, viz:

In lazy apathy let Stoics boast
Their virtue fix'd, 'tis fix'd as in a frost,
Contracted all, retiring in the breast;
But strength of mind in Exercise, not Rest.

[1] The Ghikas' flat in Kriezotou St, Athens.
[2] F. A. Hornibrook, *The Culture of the Abdomen: the Cure of Obesity and Constipation* (1933).

These have just given rise to the following, which I hasten to send:

> See the soft Epicure's dull visage swell,
> Deaf to all Music but the Dinner Bell,
> While costive <u>Surfeit</u> a new captive holds
> And drowsy tinklings lull the Gluteal Folds,
> His languid tube <u>Hibernia's</u> tubers[1] clog,
> Sausage joins Mash in one <u>Lernean</u>[2] bog;
> Pork jostles Onion in the blindfold sty;
> Stagnant in Port, Roquefort and Stilton lie.
> See the wry Cynick with his hand on Hip
> – 'Tis Wind, not Wisdom, curls his nether lip.
> What inward <u>Actium's</u> uncivil knife
> Tears his wide frame with Intestinal Strife?
> Rumpsteak to Rump its torpid journey takes,
> – Sad Argosy and melancholy Jakes[3] –
> Cell clings to cell, below, before, behind,
> And empty Chambers echo but with Wind:
> Reboant[4] fanfares shock frail <u>China's</u> home:
> Where are the Troops should storm that flow'ry Dome?
> Leave wan Philosophy's delusive Lair!
> What boots their Dogma, what the Mystick's prayer,
> When Breath like Blowlamps wafts each pondr'ous Word:
> And fells the shrill Mosquito at a yard?
> Who, amid deafening sounds, can seize on Sense
> When each nice Saw[5] is drown'd by Flatulence?
> How can the reeling Novice, all aghast,

[1] Potatoes.

[2] The Lernaean Hydra was a serpentine monster in Greek or Roman mythology. It possessed numerous heads; each time one was severed, two new ones grew in its place. Its lair was Lake Lerna, reputed to be an entrance to the Underworld.

[3] A complicated play on words. 'Sad Argosy and melancholy Jakes' is a reference to Jason ('Jakes') and the Argonauts. A character in *As You Like It* is known as 'the Melancholy Jacques', pronounced 'Jakes', which is a slang term for a place to defecate.

[4] Resounding.

[5] Wise saying.

Sift Sages' <u>Canons</u>, under Cannons' Blast?
Or Maxims, belch'd like foetid Thunderbolts?
Or Doctrine, scanned by borborygmic[1] jolts?
Shun the blear Prophet and the Bedesman pale
With Codfish Eye, and Belly like a Whale,
Where murky <u>Jonahs</u>, huddling in the Dark,
Confound, like Mutineers, the luckless Barque,
And mask'd <u>Cabals</u>, to keep the Turnpike shut,
Swart <u>Catalines</u>[2] of the mœand'ring Gut –
Block the dank Highway with occlusive Gloom
And close the Appian road from Teeth to Bum.

Away! Away! At last the Pilgrim flees
To Woods and Dales more welcoming than these.
Cool Glades invite his step, and fragrant Bowers
Salute his Nostril with a myriad flowers.
Each gracile Nymph beside her slender Swain
Writhes on the verdant sward, but not with Pain;
Each peerless Breath, each Brow without Chagrin,
Spells outward Grace, and Harmony within.
Their twinkling Loins and suaver Limbs proclaim
Knowledge more blest than <u>Plato's</u>, <u>Zeno's</u>, fame.
Here Eighty-Summers – see th'elastic pace!
Treads the green alley with a stripling's grace:
Those hoary locks, that lucent Gaze bespeak
A Midriff that is flat and hard as Teake.
Who are these Gods? What rare Elixir's charm
Informs their shape and keeps the Waists from harm?
Pilgrims, advance! The inmost Grove embowers
The liquid Source of their cœlestial Powers;
Now new-born Wisdom woos the marvelling Ear
In soft but limpid syllables, for here,
Like Crystals glittering in their bosky Nook,

[1] Rumbling.
[2] Conspirators.

Spring the cool Waters of the HORNIBROOK!
Fall prostrate, traveller! Drink deep and long;
Then glide unchalleng'd in that heavenly throng.
Brisk PERISTALSIS![1] Let the Curtain rise
And universal MOTION[2] greet our Eyes!

Still delirious with the Muse's visit, I think I'll send Peter Q a copy, as a tribute to his impending book on Pope. What a terrible shame missing you at the Pastoral Gallery. I was convinced you were there, hence no letter, answering your beauty, to Zell am See, as I thought I'd be telling all viva voce. I loved the Galerie [des Pâtres], and seeing Daph & Xan. Poor X! He seemed positively fiend-ridden by that ghastly inheritance tangle.[3] I can't make out whether that bro-in-law/uncle is a fool or a knave: slightly, I think, the former. No more now, darling Diana, as I must pelt down the hill to the post.

Tons of fond love and hugs,
Paddy

To Diana Cooper   Raffles Hotel
29 February 1969   Singapore

Despatched in haste & unrevised

Darling Diana,

It's dusk in the loggia'd, swarded inner cloister of this hotel (presciently planted by the management with a rustling quincunx of Travellers' Trees), and Joan, Graham and Ian [Whigham] – all of whom would send love if awake – are locked in slumber upstairs after a late luncheon. Soon after nightfall, we take wing for Madras.

[1] Muscle contractions in the digestive tract.
[2] A play on words.
[3] See pp. 223–4.

I think of you hundreds of times a day in this town. I can't remember whether you loved or hated it – it might be either.[1] This hotel is rather run down, alas. The famous Long Bar doesn't seem to have fully recovered from its wartime troubles; it now looks like a parish hall temporarily decorated for a Women's Institute fête by an artistic squire's daughter, with lackadaisical Chinese waiters in uncrisp white drill who turn a deaf ear to one's wails for a drink. Ian took us to have a midnight drink in Boogie (?) St.[2] the night we arrived without a word beforehand to give the show away viz., the sudden *va-et-vient* [to-ing and fro-ing] between the tables, and as far down those lamplit vistas of leprous ideogram-hung streets as the eye could see, of amazing tarts – gleaming with sequins, rustling with frills, coiffed with towering hair-dos of jet-black and flaring chestnut and fluttering candy-floss, their eyelashes a yard long beating like gills. It took us a good ten minutes (Ian remaining mum) to tumble to the fact that they were really <u>chaps</u> to a man, if that's the phrase I'm after. The meanest of them would have made Danny La Rue[3] look like a landgirl.

This afternoon I was wandering about the cathedral, peering at the memorial slabs at the names of all the people that shipwreck, battle, mutiny and plague had laid low for the past two centuries, when a tremendous downpour began, turning the precincts outside into an English Cathedral close in December. Nobody in the dim interior except a Malay verger and me. Night began to fall, still no pause in the cats and dogs descending outside. The verger switched on the lights & I wondered which pew was yours and Duff's and how often he must have read the lesson from that flashing brass eagle. At last it stopped, and I pelted back to Raffles through the dripping twilight and here I am, scribbling away with a rajah peg [brandy and champagne] by my side.

<u>20th March. You see how it goes!</u>

<hr>

[1] Diana had accompanied her husband to Singapore in 1941, when Duff Cooper was sent there to report on the island's defences.
[2] Bugis Street.
[3] Danny La Rue (born Daniel Patrick Carroll, 1927–2009), Irish-born singer and entertainer, described as the 'grande dame of drag'.

But that's all shov'd be'ind me
Long ago and far away,[1]

and here we are – having moulted Graham in Madras and Ian, alas, in Bombay, one for Blighty, the other for Rome – in the Royal Hotel, Kathmandu, under the roof of your old fellow trouper Boris![2] Haven't seen him yet though we arrived yesterday morning: 'Mr Boris be resting,' say the smiling Gurka bearers, possessively and affectionately, mutely and collusively hinting perhaps, that some demon hangover has him in thrall.[3] We burn with longing and curiosity. Meanwhile, this hotel is one of the most fascinating I've ever set foot in, half magnificent – a late 19th century Royal palace, indeed – and half dilapidation and decay, a rambling and echoing Himalayan Cavendish: vast halls, branching staircases with pink marble columns, tall windows, contorted pelmets of carved teak, full length portraits of pearled and plumed potentates, sudden riots of foliating plaster work, plumbing more efficient than it looks by its Laocoön-like writhing, cupboards of varnished three-ply dust glowing like rime in the swags of curtains, indoor plants rampaging, slippered footsteps dwindling along Piranesi vistas of lofty arcaded corridor. There are signs of life here and there among the shadows, the slam of a door, a gramophone, a laugh muffled by distance; but little evidence otherwise, apart from the black-capped and sashed bearers in white linen tunics and jodhpurs. These have just given me breakfast on a lonely loggia, porridge, scrambled eggs and cold chicken, Nescafé from a vast tin. Underneath lies a large field lined with cherry trees, in the middle of which is a decorative pond with a life size leaden statue of a Boldini-like nymph (1900?) balancing a twirly handled urn on her shoulders. (At the

[1] From Rudyard Kipling's poem 'Mandalay' (1892), slightly misquoted.
[2] Boris Lisanevich (1905–85), founder and proprietor of the Hotel Royal (converted from a palace) in Kathmandu. A dancer with the Ballets Russes, he subsequently performed in the long-running play *The Miracle*, written by Karl Vollmöller and directed by Max Reinhardt, in which Lady Diana Cooper starred as the Madonna.
[3] A nod to Keats's line, 'La Belle Dame sans Merci/ Thee hath in thrall'.

end of the corridor where I'm sitting are two three-feet high equestrian statues on either side of a door. I have just inspected the inscriptions, they are Charles I and Oliver Cromwell.) Among the cherry trees three horses graze on daisies and clover, unridden for a year, the bearers say, now quite wild. In one corner two or three old motor-cars disintegrate (all with GB plates. The oldest of these, wheel-less and as triumphantly penetrated by vegetation as Angkor, the vehicle in which Boris first drove here of yore). The other side of a fence, among dockweed and cow parsley, lives a tremendous sow with her nine farrow. There is a pavilion with a staircase descending to a green mantled pool, weeping willows & ducks, then a gathering of tiered, thatched pagodas, taller trees full of cawing rooks at this early hour. Every hour there is a faint Anglican tolling from somewhere: otherwise, all is Buddhist and Hindu. When we arrived, a party of five Tibetan lamas were coming down the main staircase of the hotel, wrinkled as eskimos, fur hatted, soles six inches thick, prayer wheel in girdle and rosary on wrist and leaving the air afloat with the redolence of yak butter. In the street of the town, which is about the size of Dorking, pagodas, temples and carved balconies abound, painted wooden demons gnash along the eaves, Sherpa women trot past with tall, firewood-laden conical blankets slung across their brows on wide leather thongs (like the Woman of Shamleh – 'Lispeth' – in *Kim*) and every here and there an unlaundered beatnik couple from the West, with cascading locks of clogged flax and pale eyes wide with pot, mooches with the innocent aimlessness of the sacred kine that stray from lane to lane. The Himalayas surround all this in a jagged ring, snowy sierras appear; the furthest one in Tibet; and somewhere round the corner, invisible from Kathmandu itself, looms Mt Everest. Three chows and a fox-terrier alternately yawn and gambol about the building (whose?). A dozen Nepalese have just settled under the trees in a busy squatting ring round a big shallow tub. You'll never guess what they are at (I've just gone down to see): washing the drops, prisms & lustres of those enormous dismembered chandeliers in an ocean of suds. Constellations of damp diamonds glitter among the grass blades. There is a bird somewhere about called, I think, the Indian cuckoo or coppersmith[1] which goes bonk! bonk! bonk! bonk! nonstop.

I meant to give you a full account of our travels: Formosa, Hong Kong, Cambodia & Angkor (words fail), Bangkok which has turned into a tangle of Edgware Roads from a sort of tropical Venice in ten years; then Bali, the most wonderful place in the world, a criss-cross of green and blue bamboo shadows inhabited by angels. Then we flew across a rash of volcanoes and forests to central Java, & the great Buddhist stone-bell-cluster of the Borobudur; then zoomed at an acute angle across the equator again to Singapore & Madras, where we lost Graham, and then, after a host of southern temples crammed with Tamil votaries, to Bombay, where we lost Ian (he is returning to England and will tell you some of our adventures). J. & I went on to the great carved and painted caves of Ellora & Ajanta, followed hotfoot by the many temples of Khajuraho, whose carved walls wriggle in the midday blaze with the strenuous erotobatics of the entire Hindu pantheon. Dealing with us, the Indians have a chip on one shoulder, a bunch of forget me nots on the other; and so, we began to notice, have we … Moghul architecture swallowed us up in Delhi and Agra: tremendous domes like giant pointed pearls reflected in long parallelograms of water, battlemented walls with pavilions at every corner shaped like vast red sandstone solar topees on stilts; now here, far from the blaze and the dust of Hindustan, and only two hours drive to the Chinese border …

LATER. We've met Boris! Absolutely charming, lots of drink and laughter & happy memories of you. He's convinced Joan & I are four different people – no good explaining now. In an hour we swirl into the Himalayan passes in the motor-car of a smart and smiling Nepalese prince that Joan danced barefoot with in Bombay three decades ago. Back to Greece in one week!

[1] The Indian cuckoo and the coppersmith barbet are different species.

Joan sends love, and so do I, tons & tons, also hugs, darling Diana: Do write and put one in touch.

P

P.S. In Delhi we spent a whole evening with my fellow Duff prizewinner, Mr Chaudhuri.[1] Amazing! I adored him. He has a photograph of you on his desk locked in a chimpanzee's embrace. X X X

Janetta Jackson, née Woolley (from 1971 Janetta Parladé), was one of Joan's closest friends.

To Janetta Jackson   Kardamyli
3 August 1969   Messenia
                                                 Greece

Darling Janetta,

Well, that <u>was</u> lovely! The last of the Bisons[2] went up in smoke days ago, but my left hand holds a slice of brown bread with a lot of butter on it, and on top of that, cunningly interleaved, fragrant discs of alternating Catalonian chorizo and *lomo*,[3] with a big glass of Cretan wine handy. All this is going on under a rush mat shelter with a table where I write at 11.00 on Sunday morning with lots of cicadas grinding away and Joan's voice up above calling to her cats – two different sets of kittens, with their clans, who are not allowed to meet, so the house is sundered by a sort of cats' Berlin Wall, dividing the house into two mews flats, as Johnny C[raxton] (or I) might say.

Thank you 1,000 times, Janetta, for that marvellous end to my Western European holiday. I was filled with wonder and

---

[1] Nirad C. Chaudhuri's *The Continent of Circe: An Essay on the Peoples of India* (1965), won him the 1966 Duff Cooper Prize.

[2] A brand of cigar.

[3] *Lomo* is a Spanish term for tenderloin. PLF probably means cured *lomo* of some type.

admiration – envy too, I fear – at the progress of Tramores:[1] peace, ease, charm, grace, hearty proof against any half-hearted inroad of pylons vaguely marching (their transparent obelisks, if visible, rendered innocuous by a reflection-subjugating coat of paint) across the middle-distance. You will begin to count your blessings when you see what's happened here, viz. a string of horrible temporary huts sprung up along a nearby beach (<u>not</u> where we bathe, fortunately) with a squealing horde from a nearby mountain village, swarming for two months; also a pneumatic drill tearing up the road ¼ of a mile away, with a noise like machine gun fire, <u>all</u> deafening audible from the house. We must rise above it. Pylons, indeed …

Barcelona was wonderful. No room in the Oriente, alas, so I stayed at the Principe, nearly opposite, slightly hopeless but tolerable. It didn't matter as I was out nearly the whole time, revelling in the many wonders of the city, drinks in a dozen bars, dinner in a place called Celier in Calle de los Escuderos, where a nice queer pianist imitated lady opera singers and their bass partners, then to the New York Bar, where there was an amazing French erotic cabaret with spiralling and geometric psychedelic lights and a French running commentary of a very advanced kind. Then wandering about the Ramblas till very late; I found it impossible to keep away from them. Next day I spent in cathedrals, churches, galleries; in arranging for the transport of all my treasures to Greece – no chance of them catching the Turkish snail-boat, alas, but they will be here quite soon, it seems – and in hunting for tables in those lanes round the cathedral. Nice ones seemed to cost anything from 20,000 to 50,000 pesetas, so I had to desist. In the evening I drove out to Sancho's sculptor friend,[2] a very lively, eager, brilliant chap, looks like a high-caste Hindu or a gypsy, living in a ravishing farm-cum-manor house now embedded in the suburbs. We drank a lot – him, a pretty Catalan girl, a young v. intelligent

[1] The villa in the hills above Marbella where Janetta Jackson lived with the interior designer Jaime Parladé, Marques de Apezteguía.
[2] Xavier Corberó (1935–2017), Catalan sculptor renowned for monumental public works.

economist and a tall v. beautiful negress, *Harper's Bazaar* & *Vogue* model, also v. intelligent and funny. Argument, drink and laughter till daybreak, then a hair-raising spin in a car seeking out Gaudi buildings. Lovely. I forgot to say that at dusk the night before, after exploring the Gaudi Sagrada Familia[1] – surely one of the oddest buildings on the planet – I found my way into the crypt, where a Catalan vernacular Mass was in progress, with a dozen bats winging and squeaking over the heads of the faithful, more and more emerging from those freak vaults as time went on. Next day – Friday – was the feast of Santiago – no taxis! – when <u>at last</u> one was found, it got wedged in an endless and almost immobile traffic exodus which got slower and slower as it left the town, with the result that when it reached the airport, the bird had flown. A dreary wait for another in four hours' time … Bugger! Jaime had most kindly said I could settle up for my Tartana trophies[2] by post – but, thanks to un-bought tables, I still had lots of travellers' cheques, so changed what I owed at the Cambio [currency exchange], went to the post counter next door to send off a postal order – but, that part of the office was closed, owing to the Hol! <u>Bugger again</u>! Masses of unwanted pesetas on hand, but, as it turned out, <u>Thank God</u>! For on arrival in Rome, I discovered no T[ravellers] cheques; must have left them on the Cambio counter, so the pesetas, duly changed, saved my life, as I had to stay the night there! [DOES ALL THIS ADD UP TO A HANGOVER?] (The Amer. Express in Athens next day was marvellous. Nothing to show for how much I'd spent, but they offered an immediate refund, when the recovery forms were filled in.) Nobody I know was in Rome, so I went to a hotel called The Colosseum on the Esquiline Hill – quite nice – then a solitary dinner in the Piazza Navona, a nocturnal mooch along the Via Giulia, over the Tiber to Trastevere, back and up onto the Capitol where I wandered about for hours; dawn at last, over the

---

[1] The extraordinary cathedral-sized church designed by the Catalan architect Antoni Gaudí (1852–1926), still unfinished more than a century after construction began in 1882.
[2] La Tartana, on the road from Marbella to Ronda, where Parladé had a studio and sold antiques.

Forum, past the Colosseum and Palatine, then up the Esquiline and to bed. I took no risks next day! Hired a huge car out of some more of Jaime's merciful pesetas (now <u>lire</u>) off to Fiumicino [airport], and into Athens and a glorious lunch (not un-laced with chat about yesterday's muddles, as you might imagine) with Joan, Barbara, Niko [Ghika] and Geo. Katsimbalis, and here two days later. Niko and Barbara arrive tomorrow, and stay for ages, I/we hope.

The great excitement is now in your telegram, and the thought you'll all be here soon. Hip hip HOORAY! It will be marvellous, quite apart from all else that you will be inspecting the more or less completed abode for the first time, and Jaime altogether virgin, at last. You will be shocked by the amount of muck, loam, roughcast, limepits, etc., which still disfigure the place; but they'll all heal up one day. Now! Are you coming by car, ... or will you be needing advice about 'planes inside Greece? If so, do wire, and we'll send lots of instructions.

No more now, Janetta darling, except many, many thanks for all. What luck overlapping at Patrick's.[1] It made such a difference to the whole stay. Tons of love from us both and to Rose,[2] who I thought marvellous.

from Paddy

P.S. Please thank Sancho[3] for organising such happy times in Barcelona, and being such a help about shipping that lovely chair and its companion booty.

---

[1] Both were frequent paying guests at Patrick Kinross's house in London.
[2] Janetta Parladé's youngest daughter.
[3] Unidentified.

To Balasha Cantacuzène   Kardamyli
New Year's Eve 1969   Messenia
                                                          Greece

My darling,

    … You'll never guess where we are! I'll tell you later on: Now, to continue with the foregoing, Eddie Gathorne-Hardy came to stay for Christmas, I don't think you ever met him, a great friend of Mark Ogilvie-Grant's (who died last year, alas!) We were woken up in the dark on Christmas morning by a troop of village children who had trudged out through the snow to sing *kalendas* – the same idea as the *calînder* in Romania, not nearly as interesting or melodious, but rather nice nevertheless. At midday we had a huge feast – Joan, Eddie, Lela & Petro (the peasant couple who look after everything), their two boys, 10 & 14, Georgo and Stavro, and me: a huge turkey, plum pudding, masses of wine and lots of singing. It all went off gloriously.

    But it's been a ghastly winter so far. At the end of November it started raining and has been going on ever since almost nonstop, for 40 days and 40 nights, with dramatic and shattering thunderstorms several times every day and night. The noise is terrific, both the wind and the thunder and enormous waves crashing on all the headlands and resounding in all the caves that warren this coast, and leaping in huge fans of spray, and at times almost covering the little island (with a ruined house and chapel on it) which stands about ½ a mile out to sea. The noise goes on all the time, even penetrating one's sleep like trains shunting in the distance or, altered as things are in dreams, the roar of traffic. This onslaught is without precedent in human memory and all the old people in the village wag their heads with foreboding. This monsoon caused landslides all over the Taygetus mountains, and the road to Kalamata – thirty kilometres away – was cut in three places – road swept away or blocked by falling earth, bristling with torn up trees, and boulders, so for nearly two weeks we were cut off by road from the outside world. The next ordeal was that the deluge completely washed away the pipes that bring the water down from the mountains to supply the village, so for three weeks water was hurtling down outside all the windows, while, if one turned on a tap indoors, nothing but a startled centipede emerged. Of course, all the village people had abandoned the village wells once the water had been laid on just before the war, so they were foul and unusable. We were a lot better off out here, as there is an enormous cistern under the cellar and the downstairs arches, and buckets were eternally clanking down into the void through the well head. (I thought of you both and the icicle-crusted pumps of Pucioasa!) Then, in turn (me first briefly, followed by Joan), both of us got ill, Joan with this horrible flu that has been killing off people like flies. Three weeks in bed! As soon as she was a bit better, we drove helter-skelter to Athens through furious thunderstorms over the Peloponnese, on the sudden decision to change scene abruptly. The night we arrived we were both asked to dinner at our Embassy by Michael Stewart, the Ambassador, a charming man who started life as a painter and oriental expert who really lives (under a delightful rather tired Ld Melbourne exterior) for books, painting and music. Another access of coughing flu forced Joan to stay at home, alas (in the Ghikas's empty flat) so I went alone, & found Michael Stewart, a Greek friend called Yanni Georgakis[1] and A. Onassis and his ex-Kennedy wife, Jackie! I was shoved next to her, and we got on like anything. She's got a sister called Lee Radziwill who lives in London, who I know quite well, very similar eyes, yet very far apart, and speaks in a half childish, half rapt, rather mysterious kind of voice: lots of chat about books (she'd read lots of mine – if one can use the word lots – I was flattered to discover). It turned out to be rather

[1] Ioannis ('Yanni') Georgakis (1915–93), diplomat and political scientist, professor, Pantios School of Political Science, Athens, 1941–75 (Emeritus), rector 1963; Governor General, Ionian Islands 1945–51, Dodecanese Islands 1951; Greek ambassador at large, 1975–80. His first contact with the shipping magnate Aristotle Onassis was in 1965, when Georgakis was appointed president of the executive committee of Olympic Airways. After Onassis's death in 1975, Georgakis became permanent secretary to the Onassis Foundation, and in 1988 became its president.

a riotous evening, lots of argument, even singing and, when we departed, the two Os, Georgakis and I went to a nightclub for another hour of which I can remember little except a golden blur. Woke up next morning with a terrible headache, but we managed to get to the airport <u>just</u> in time and on to an aeroplane for Paris.

Douanier à Orly: *Rien à declarer?*
Moi: *Seulement ma gueule de bois …*
D. *Ça se voit, monsieur. Passez*[1]

It had been terribly cold in Paris too, constant clouds, fierce winds and rain, everyone said, but had suddenly changed. Lovely thin golden wintry sunlight made everything look wonderful, and up went our spirits. We settled into the Hotel Montalembert (known as the poor man's Pont Royal) in the Rue de Bac. Oh the bliss and excitement of French bourgeois hotel bedrooms! Brass beds, lace curtains, reproductions of *La Cruche Cassée* and *L'Escarpolette Mysterieuse* on the walls,[2] charming bogus Empire bed tables, serious, bulky Norman chambermaids. One found oneself going up and down in the creaky lift (made by the firm of Roux-Combaluzier) with provincial deputies with rosettes in their lapels, canons from Brittany, representatives of northern industries with their girlfriends, in smiling awkward silence, as always in lifts. The only disappointment was, no answer from Ina's telephone, in spite of constant ringing up (It turned out she was still in England, but learnt we were in Paris from Barbara, so got onto us the moment she and Michael got back.) It was marvellous, too, going into a rather swanky restaurant on the Quai des Grands Augustins and

[1] Customs officer at Orly: Anything to declare? Me: Only my hangover. Customs: So I see, sir. Go ahead.
[2] Two erotic paintings: *La Cruche Cassée* ('The Broken Pitcher') by Jean-Baptiste Greuze (1725–1803) of a scantily clad young woman at a well, and *L'Escarpolette Mysterieuse* ('The Swing') by Jean-Honoré Fragonard (1782–1806) featuring a young woman on a swing being watched by two lecherous suitors, one young, one old, the latter concealed in bushes.

ordering a dozen *belons*[1] each – they arrived on a vast dish of ice, covered with moss and seaweed, washed down with a bottle of cold, cold Sancerre – then a glorious tournedos and a fabulous claret; camembert, brie, coulommiers, Marc de Bourgogne … what a change from olives and goat's cheese (which I incidentally love). I'd better stop these gastronomic reminiscences, or we will all faint with nostalgia; me writing, you reading! We had other lovely meals at various bistros: Procope, in the Rue de L'Ancienne Comédie, haunted by Racine, Diderot & Voltaire, le Roi Gourmet in the Place des Victoires, with a statue of Louis XIV caracoling on horse-back in the centre of the round circus outside, seen through the small square windows, the Brasserie Lipp at St Germain des Prés, a labyrinth of mutually reflecting mirrors, tiers of flashing glasses as though painted by Renoir, reflecting the guzzling actors and writers below, the walls encrusted with Art Nouveau faïence of storks, waterlilies, bullrushes and pagodas made by L-P. Fargue's father.[2] It was tremendously exciting to be in a town again where so much has been built for pure aesthetic pleasure – not only cathedrals, churches, *hôtels particuliers* etc., but even the old shops seemed perfect in detail, and stuffed with wonders like Aladdin's cave. In Greece, apart from a couple of dozen ancient wonders and the mar-vellous sea and mountains – better than anywhere in the world – all the works of man are gimcrack jerry built, improvised and inco-herent and getting worse every day with cheap reinforced concrete. The contrast of this with a row of stone urns along the architrave of the Institut, a ribbed dome, or even the *espagnolette* [catch] of a window, can almost bring tears to the eyes! Our excuse for coming to Paris was to see the enormous retrospective exhibition of Alberto Giacometti sculptures, paintings & drawings: a wonderful feast. He died two years ago, and was a very old friend of Joan's and later of mine.[3] All was going well, when poor Joan suddenly had a mild return of the wretched flu we thought she had got rid of,

[1] Oysters from a river in Brittany noted for them.
[2] Léon Fargue, father of the French poet Léon-Paul Fargue, was an engineer.
[3] Alberto Giacometti, Swiss sculptor, painter, draftsman and printmaker (1901–66).

and had to take to her bed with the Duke of Wellington (if you see what I mean).[1] I wandered about on my own thereafter, buying second hand books on the quays, Cluny, Louvre, Carnavalet and the Musée Guimet to look at all the Indo-Chinese Khmer marvels there. Also went alone to a dinner party of someone called Cécile de Rothschild,[2] a tall, handsome, trousered, deep-voiced figure, whose prematurely white hair makes her look rather like Voltaire, rather lesbian, who sails about the Greek islands all the summer in her caïque, then a husky barefoot nautical figure, but here, surrounded by Picasso, Légers, Braques, Matisses etc., and extraordinary Greek, Etruscan and Hittite objects. It was rather fun: two extremely nice young painters, a burly girl called Marie de Broglie who has contrived to wander about in China, and Cecile's cousin Philippe de Ro.,[3] who owns and lives at Mouton, near Bordeaux, and had that very morning published a volume of translations of a large number of Elizabethan and English 17th century metaphysical verse, rather good. He was very excited about this and gave me a copy. I'll have one sent to you – though in your case the originals will have more point than the French renderings, as for Ins, who I gave it to as well. Well, it was an evening of *douceur de vivre* all right, *agrément*, as Aleko[4] would have said; and rather a stimulating one, lots of jokes and interruptions. Next day Joan felt a bit better, but not up to going out to Versailles to lunch with Nancy Mitford, so I went alone. She lives in a little house there, full of books, rather charming, but alas, still very pale and thin after an operation

[1] The first volume of Elizabeth Longford's biography of Wellington, *The Years of the Sword*, had been published earlier that year.
[2] Baroness Cécile de Rothschild (1913–95) was given Cézanne's *Les Baigneuses* at the age of thirteen, the foundation of her considerable art collection. She was a close friend of the notoriously reclusive actress Greta Garbo.
[3] Philippe, Baron de Rothschild (1902–88), racing driver, screenwriter, playwright, poet, theatrical and film producer, and wine grower, responsible for Château Mouton Rothschild. His memoirs *Milady Vine* (1984) were written in collaboration with his companion, the theatre director Joan Littlewood.
[4] Aleko Matsas, Oxford-educated Greek diplomat; it was at a party on his Athens roof terrace that PLF met Balasha for the first time.

for a benign tumour followed by flu, and nearly voiceless with cold, leaning on a cherry stick. I had been stricken by a temporary hoarseness so we croaked at each other over lunch *à deux* like two frogs. She's just finished a life of Frederick the Great, so was full of anecdotes of Potsdam and Charlottenburg. She says the real cause of the friction between F. and Voltaire was V's manner with kings, i.e., too flattering and subservient, then, when encouraged, too *frech* [insolent]; both of which made F. II and Louis XIV fidgetty and ill at ease. I do see. As always with her other sisters, the whole thing ended in jokes and laughter, recklessly improvised (and of a rather Baleniot kind[1]) till one was weak with tears and cacophonous with rival croaking. Owing to her ailments, she couldn't come up to the Château with me, as we'd planned, so I wandered through those extraordinary wintry rooms alone, seeing my own dim reflection again and again, then out into an afternoon of rushing clouds, nymph obelisks and fountains and yews topiaried into cone after cone, among quickly obliterated shafts of thin January sunshine. Back to tea with Nancy, then back to the Gare St Lazare reading *La Chartreuse de Parme* …[2]

***

The next leap on this glorious *aŭsflŭg* [trip] was Rome! Here again we settled in an old-fashioned haunt of senators and prelates, the Albergo Nazionale,[3] looking down on to the obelisk of King Sesostris and the vast hewn ashlars, the rusticated sills and broken pediments of the Cancelleria. There's another obelisk, on an elephant's back, just round the corner, a Column of Antoninus Pius, a little further on – companion to Trojan's, up which Dacian captives march in a spiral – and, almost next door, that huge hollow thing, the Pantheon. Here again, there was tireless and obsessional walking – forums, triumphal arches, ruin on ruin, colossal late mediaeval and renaissance palaces built for giants to live in twirling

[1] i.e. of the kind prevalent at Balasha's home Băleni.
[2] Stendhal, *The Charterhouse of Parma* (1839).
[3] The Hotel Nationale in the Piazza di Monte Citorio in Rome overlooks an obelisk of the Egyptian pharaoh Psammetichus II from Heliopolis.

baroque, tempestuous fountains gushing everywhere from riots of marble, a skyline bubbling with ribbed domes, culminating in S. Peter's; campanili, circular castles, miles of colossal city wall from the reign of Theodosius, the vast smashed concavities of Roman brick – baths of Caracalla and Diocletian – and pre-Christian bridges across the Tiber, the old Appian Way wandering off into the Campagna, through pines and cypresses and old sepulchres dilapidated and weed cloaked, as in Piranesi prints ... Phew! The only disappointment, I have always found, are the Romans themselves, especially the dwellers in those gigantic palaces – perfectly amiable and lighthearted, with magnificent names and beautiful features, but strangely vapid and provincial faces rather like coins and medallions of a bad epoch with the inscriptions totally effaced. The only ones of any interest seem to have French, English or American mothers: the rest are half-Brazilian, untouched by interests beyond fast motor-cars and starlets, their society – unlike the equivalent in N. Europe – unpolluted by the presence of writers or painters. It's a shame, because they are so nice to look at, and perfectly friendly, if one doesn't strain their poor old heads too hard. The women are much more interesting than the men. We saw several Roman friends here – exceptions to the above generalisations – several English, the writer Ignazio Silone & his Irish wife,[1] and the French painter Balthus who presides over the Villa Medici (Prix de Rome) with his pretty Chinese [sic] wife;[2] also an old pal of ours called Natalie de Noailles – light as a pretty, slightly mad jockey, and once, indeed, high jump champion of Italy – niece, I think, of the one you and Pomme knew as girls, married to and separated from a Roman, daughter of Charles de N., the famous horticulturalist, and Marie-Laure de N., the rather wicked art-patroness and amateur painter, who has just died.

[1] The pseudonym of Secondino Tranquilli (1900–78), author and politician, married to an Irishwoman, Darina Laracy.
[2] Balthus had moved to Italy in 1964, to take up a post as director of the French Academy in Rome. In 1967 he married Setsuko Ideta, a woman thirty-five years his junior whom he had met on a diplomatic mission to Japan.

When, about 10 years ago, I camped for six months to write in a semi-ruined Colonna[1] castle, uninhabited for two centuries, at a place called Passeranno, between Tivoli and Palestrina (I even persuaded Joan to come and share this rat, bat and owl-haunted wilderness for a month or two), she used to come out now and then with beautiful steeds in horse-boxes, and we went for wonderful rides through the Alban and Sabine hills and through the woods and valleys of the Campagna that still manage to look like the backgrounds of Claude and Poussin. She drove Joan, Balthus and me out to this extraordinary castle, where we had a happy time talking to the peasants who lived in cottages round the foot of the vast ruin, who had all been friends – we were very touched to find they still remembered one with affection. (I don't know <u>why</u> one should always be touched and surprised on occasions like this – I suppose rather conceitedly, one always imagines that one is the only one endowed with the faculty of memory!) The country round is very strange, and quite untouched – deep valleys with enormous trees, and streams running under them, fields with conical haystacks like the ones in Bukovina, towns like Zagarolo and Palestrina suddenly appearing on the tops of cones – walled cities with domes and spires, then range on range of tufted tufa hills with the roads chopped out of the volcanic rock, wild vegetation almost closing overhead like a tunnel to burst open suddenly and reveal the still snowy crest of the Sabine mountains in the distance. We had a marvellous lunch in the kitchen of a trattoria in the steep little town of Gallicano nel Lazio, surrounded [by?] the blackened hearths and brass cauldrons and listening to the thick Latian dialect in the room next door, none of which can have changed a lot since the Goths and the Lombards overran this part of Latium; then back Romewards with the dark bump of the dome of S. Peter's just discernable in the amber sunset as we approached the city. It was a memorable day, and our last.

[1] The Colonna family, also known as Sciarrillo or Sciarra, is the Italian noble family that owned the Castello di Passerano. It was powerful in medieval and Renaissance Rome, supplying one pope and many other Church and political leaders.

Please forgive this frequent change of ink! Both my pens – the blue for straight writing, and the red one, usually, for corrections, have been in a rebellious mood for ages, going on strike without warning and equally irrationally returning to work. It makes a sort of counterpoint!

***

One always returns here after an absence filled with a vague and nameless dread in case any creature should have died, but no, all was well, fire burning, lights twinkling, Lela the maid all smiles, Stavroula – a sort of electric woman who comes to help when there is anything special – paddling happily about in her black coiff – cats all nice and plump. The only worry was that the bloody weather was still wreaking havoc and so it has continued till three days ago. Rather gloomy. Soon after we arrived, we were joined by a strange friend called Peter Levi, S.J.,[1] a young, handsome and very gifted Jesuit priest who is a professor of ancient Greek at Oxford, translator and annotator of Pausanias, a poet and archaeologist, who spent most of his time translating the Psalms for the new Vernacular Mass, seated, like a lion-less St Jerome[2] in the loggia, surrounded by the Pentateuch, the Septuagint, the Vulgate, the Authorized Version and Luther's Bible behind a palisade of Hebrew & Greek Lexicons, & Latin, German, Aramaic & Chaldean dictionaries. He was followed by Cyril Connolly; Joan was in despair, as he's such a terrific gourmand, and there was nothing but beans, lentils, typical Greek Lenten fare, and a chicken or two. But it was great fun otherwise, with lots of reading aloud and conversations. Of course the moment he left, the weather changed completely, the caïques had started fishing again after their long hibernation, nets were bursting with delicious *barbounia* [red mullet] and *synagrida* [sea bream], and, best of all, three enormous lobsters (Cyril's

[1] Peter Chad Tigar Levi (1931–2000), poet, archaeologist, Jesuit priest, travel writer, biographer, academic and critic. He left the priesthood in 1977, and subsequently married Deirdre Craig, widow of Cyril Connolly. He was Oxford Professor of Poetry, 1984–9.
[2] St Jerome was often depicted with a lion, as he is said to have cured a lion by extracting a thorn from its paw.

favourite, alas). Then, suddenly out of the blue and just in time to eat them, came Michael & Damaris Stewart, so all was well. It was a charming two days, much of it spent poring over maps of Asia Minor, planning a great trip we are all four hoping to make at the end of May and beginning of June in a tough Landrover motor car, with sleeping bags if necessary, through ancient Greek and Seljuk sites in S.W. and Southern Turkey; Beethoven Last Quartets in the evening. They left yesterday. Now all is changed, it's beautiful cloudless spring weather, thrushes and blackbirds singing some-where, the sea gently lapping below instead of thundering and butterflies flittering about among the cistus and myrtle. Joan leaves for England in a few days, for three weeks or so; I stay on to build walls and outside staircases and hoping that my recalcitrant muse will shake off her winter catalepsy at last.

Tons and tons of love, darling Balasha, from Paddy (Ditto from Joan)

To Damaris Stewart   Kardamyli
mid–late June 1970   Messenia
                                                          Greece

Dear Damaris,

It's very rare that expectations, as high as ours have been for the past months, should be surpassed by so vast and triumphant a margin, but so it is! <u>Turkey, 1970</u>: a date to be marked with a white stone, or rather, with scores of them; each day was a succession of marvels and monster treats. I love the way our anabases and pilgrimages and Sprats- and Fellows-like[1] assaults and Dilettanti-Society[2] rambles, manuals and maps in hand, through all that

---

[1] Thomas Abel Brimage Spratt (1811–88), vice-admiral, hydrographer and geologist, who investigated the shores of Asia Minor, author of *Travels and Researches in Crete* (2 vols, 1865); Sir Charles Fellows (1799–1860), traveller and archaeologist, who led several expeditions into the interior.
[2] The Society of Dilettanti, founded in London in 1734 to sponsor the study of ancient Greek and Roman art, and the creation of new work in the same style.

stupendous wreckage, was scanned and, as it were, harmoniously broken up at the points of balance by cunningly placed liquid caesurae, and shady feasts beside brooks, all to end triumphantly each night in a golden haze of Kavaklidere.[1] These Turks had, if I may so put it, a supremely happy yolliday (on second thoughts, I realise that I can't), and we are about to piece it all together with maps and reference book and encyclopaedias before it clogs. (We haven't done so yet, because just as we feared, everything was in utter turmoil here – we weren't expected for over a week, and our warning message merely flung everything into hysterical chaos which will take some time to subside.) What all this rigmarole is clumsily heading for is, 1,000,000 thanks to you and Michael for this wonderful time. You were its only begetters.[2] We would never have seen half of those recondite marvels on our own – indeed, might have gone on postponing the journey for years. What luck to do it all under such expert guidance, and in that heroic vehicle that tackled canyons and craterbeds and landslides with the nimbleness of a polo pony and the speed – as the Asiatic textiles thickened underneath – of a magic carpet! In fact, instead of tame gulf-side slumbers here tonight, I wish we were all going to doss down at the dear old Göksu,[3] to be roused at dawn by the electric muezzin and then peer out of our cubicles at the storks gliding over the Barbarossa Plaj on the other side of the river. Everyone has been to Ephesus and Pergamum (except Joan and me a few days ago) – but what about all those secret theatres with cornfields flowing into the orchestra stalls colonnaded streams with the jungle closing in like Cambodia or Yucatan and imperial granaries sinking into the dunes and those higgledy-piggledy dancing figures scattered about the debris of Sagalassus? Give me an agora choked with capers and cowparsley every time, convolvulus twirling up the shafts of columns, stylite storks, an odeum full of frogs, with a Yürük [Turkish nomad] and a camel or two for scale in the middle distance while the slim bottles grow colder in mythical currents,

[1] Turkish wine from Ankara.
[2] Shakespeare's Sonnets are dedicated to their 'only begetter … Mr W. H.'
[3] The Göksu is a river on the Taşeli plateau.

poplars within poplars ... The Seljuk stuff, too, was brand new to us: those khans scattered about the plateaux like huge fossils, Sinbad-like shipyards the size of a cathedral, the tough and elegant bridges piled there for nothing, heavier than caravans and a few wooden siege-engines. (An occasional elephant, Ghaznavid loot from beyond the Indus?[1] I wonder ...) I'm glad we paid our devoirs to the ashes of Alaédin Keykúbad and Jalaluddin Rumi and Nasreddin Hodja,[2] delighted to learn that those polygonal conic *türbés* [tombs] are a sort of petrified memory of a nomad tent. I bet those nice old boys we hobnobbed with among the turbanned touchstones of Konya[3] were unfrocked Mevlevi dervishes,[4] Anatolian Renaissance men, i.e., splendid all-rounders if given the chance ... As an old Greek hand, I feel a bit furtive about the beginnings of a sneaking fondness for Johnny Turk, but reassured to learn that Fellows followed the same palinode [retraction].

Many many thanks again for everything – I promise it didn't fall on stony ground! Do please come here soon.

love Paddy

P.S. Please tell Michael that Danishmend is not a battle, as I thought, but a sort of rogue dynasty (descended from a 'teacher') centred on Sivas, for a long time a thorn in the side of their Konya cousins.

P.P.S: Definition of Seljuk Khan architecture: Cathedral Gothic with knobs off.

P.P.P.S. I'm relieved to learn that a figure in Seljuk history called Kadi Celebi is no relation of the character in Bleak House.[5]

[1] The Ghaznavids were a Persianate dynasty (977–1186), which at their greatest extent ruled large parts of Iran, Afghanistan, Transoxiana and the northwest Indian subcontinent.
[2] Alaédin Keykúbad, Seljuk sultan (it is unclear whether PLF is referring to Alaeddin Keykubad I, II or III); Jalaluddin Rumi, Sufi mystic and poet; Nasreddin Hodja, sage and wit: all three lived in the Seljuk Sutanate of Rum.
[3] The capital of the Seljuk Sutanate of Rum, in central Anatolia.
[4] The Mevlevi are a Sufi order, also known as the Whirling Dervishes due to their famous practice of whirling as a form of *dhikr* (remembrance of God).
[5] A play on the name Caddy Jellyby, a character in Dickens's *Bleak House*.

In the early 1960s Paddy had become friendly with Sir Aymer Maxwell, brother of the writer Gavin Maxwell. Sir Aymer had inherited an estate in Scotland, but he preferred Greece. He had a 'ravishing' house in Euboea, where he had allowed Paddy to stay while he was working on Mani. *Many years later, after Sir Aymer's death, Paddy paid tribute to his old friend. 'He was a sensitive plant, and the smaller the company, the happier he was.' Though he was shy and formal at first, 'his flair for the comic and the absurd could make tears flow, and with his kindness and hesitation, his cumulative backlog of shared laughter is certainly one of the things his friends will most miss.' His house on the steep shores of Euboea, 'with its pine forest and the ghost of Mt Parnassus beyond a sweep of sea [was] the background for much reading and late nights and endless talk …' Like Paddy, Maxwell liked to surround himself with books, and could recite whole pages by heart. It was he who came up with the line from Louis MacNeice that became the title* A Time of Gifts: *'he put me forever in his debt'.*

To Aymer Maxwell   Kardamyli
28 October 1970   Messenia
                                                                  Greece

Dear Aymer,

I feel very guilty at my long delay in writing to thank you (a) for the wonderful treat to my guests and me involved in those lovely journeys with Dirk Hatterick (b) for having Pomme and me to stay in the Negropont [Euboea], which she absolutely adored and (c) for the present of that dear little puppy, now called Troilus, after the dog that Petruchio shouts all over the house for, on returning home with his bride, in *The Taming of the Shrew*. ('Where's my spaniel Troilus?') Another name we thought of for him was Lailaps – 'Λαίλαπα', I suppose in the vocative – which was what Cephalus's hound was called, the delightful animal gazing sadly down, with a satyr doing the same on the other side, in Piero di Cosimo's *Death of Procris* in the National Gallery.[1] But the name sounds a bit silly, so Troilus it is.

He behaved beautifully on the way to Athens, wrapped in his splendid blanket on Pomme's lap, only getting mildly sick twice, and spent the night, fussed over by all, in the Embassy greenhouse. Next day I got him a collar and lead, a brush, flea powder and anti-flea necktie, a bowl, a travelling basket, and a huge sleeping basket at that luxurious dog-pampering shop in Karneadon Street, and set off together for Corinth, then across the mountains of the Argolid, towards Porto Cheli and Spetsai. He wouldn't <u>touch</u> the carrying basket but consented to lie glumly in the sleeping basket, but set up a wailing and barking of harrowing poignancy when we moved – the outrage was unbelievable to him – the smells, the traffic, the noise, the hairpin bends, the level crossings. At last he fell into a silent trance of misery on the floor, reviving again with howls of outrage on the stormy caïque trip across to Spetsai. It was a dangerous journey all the way – one hand steering, the other stroking … I felt like a murderer. But in Spetsai, all changed. Diana seized him like an infant redeemed from theft by gypsies, and her niece, grand-niece and grand-daughter and the other woman guest, took him in their embrace each night: (1st) Manners, (2nd) Paget, (3rd) Sackville, (4th) Lane Fox, (5th) Cooper, then back to the start – and these nights cushioned on so many well-born bosoms induced a mood of blissful complacency which was probably an unsettling preparation for the rigours of the Mani. However, he has been very good, sleeps in my room in his colosseum-sized house, is good about going outside, v. playful, shadow-boxes clumsily with the twenty cats here, who look on him with amiable amazement (to our relief) – one, Xanthus, even curls up with him sometimes – and frolics about the terrace with Mavrouli, Lela's little black puppy of

[1] In Ovid's story, the hunter Cephalus accidentally kills his wife Procris with a javelin. Since 1951 the National Gallery has recatalogued this painting as either *A Mythological Subject* or *A Satyr Mourning over a Nymph*.

the same age. Yesterday he fell over the cliff, but landed on a narrow ledge with a tuft of heather, [and] a death-defying B.O.P.[1] rescue with ropes and baskets was organised; this morning he knocked over a ladder. What yelps![2] Damaris Stewart – just left – says he's 'a very vocal little dog' but will grow quieter. Anyway, he has won all hearts, and is an honour to Turka's haughty line.[3]

We picked up Joan at Patras (she nursed T. all the way down) and two days later the Stewarts arrived, and Graham and Ian. They have all left now, after a happy week's stay, except Graham (Joan and he send love).

You must come and inspect progress the moment you get back. Meanwhile, dear Aymer, very many thanks again for old Troilus, and for many other kindnesses.

Yours ever,
Paddy

To Damaris and Michael Stewart   Kardamyli
undated [1971]   Messenia
                                 Greece

Dear Damaris and Michael,

Hardly had I written the above words this morning when in comes Petro saying we'd only got a few logs left – could we go in the car and dismember a couple of fallen olive trees on the road beyond Proásteion? So I dropped the pen with a sigh and off we set with axes, saws and crowbars and Troilus bounding through the asphodels. Only half of our task was down when the skies opened with a bang, shedding a deluge and forked lightning, and the three of us dashed for a conveniently placed grotto to shelter from thunderbolts, as Petro put it, where we crouched smoking and

---

[1] The *Boy's Own Paper*, a byword for boyish adventure.
[2] A nod to Joe Gargery's favourite expression in Dickens's *Great Expectations*, 'What larks!'
[3] Turka was mother of the puppy Troilus.

barking till it was over; got back just in time for a pre-luncheon swig, followed by a mess of marvellous pottage and a lot of resin [retsina], which Eddie Gathorne-Hardy kept nimbly on the move. Then of course, hoggish slumbers kissed one's eyes.[1] Now it's after tea and lighting up time, in front of a tremendous blaze in the studio … Something like all this seems to have happened <u>every time</u> I've settled down to write to you. I bet Lela will be over in a moment, as last week, saying that a kitten has fallen over a cliff and needs rescuing at a rope's end from its mewing-ledge half-way-down …

I wonder how San Zenone[2] seemed, now that that gold-lace cocked hat and rapier are all at rest in japanned tin (or flogged to a junior colleague?), until unborn grandchildren fish them out for dressing-up?[3] Marvellous, I bet, after that heavy social pounding of the last weeks in Athens. How nice the Nauplia meeting was, the overgrown ruins of Asini and the valedictory meal at Tolon. But we all felt very forlorn after you left. I hope the oil jar got home safely – or was it suddenly smithereens on the hard quays of Ancona?

I imagine you both in a fever of planting. On our way back after saying goodbye to you, we spent ages with a market gardener at Patras, and three days ago, he and a troop of chaps arrived with 7 enormous cypresses with vast globular roots done up in sacking. They are now cunningly placed in a sort of overflowing irregular quincunx in that rather bare bit between the circle-terrace and the studio wall, kept from being uprooted by the wind by a giant spider's web of ropes. I <u>think</u> we've got the hang of cypress planting at last, viz., <u>not</u> in a row in the Tuscan way – though they can look marvellous like that along an avenue – but in an irregular but coherent group, with at least two close together and a much shorter one springing up hard by, as though they had risen spontaneously from cones dropped from the tallest. I hope they'll look very telling.

---

[1] A nod to the poem 'Golden slumbers kiss your eyes', by Thomas Dekker (c.1570–c.1632).
[2] A village in the Veneto where the Stewarts had a house.
[3] Sir Michael Stewart's tenure as UK Ambassador to Greece ended that year.

I long for news of how our growth-boosting device succeeds. We've also planted some bay, box and lavender, and clumps of violets, stocks etc., with carefully planned nonchalance, and have been busy with wild irises and anemones, lovely purple and scarlet ones, dug up from the surrounding landscape. I wouldn't mind a few of those great globes of spurge, and there are some marvellous grey-green moonlit-looking sages among the ruins of Methoni. The best of these rather spectral rain-shrubs I've ever seen were at Selinunte. It's great luck having Eddie here at such a time; he's a great amateur botanist like Mark, and full of wise advice and knowledge.

I'm deep in Carrington's letters[1] at the moment – fascinating, compulsive reading. In an early letter to L. Strachey – 1916 – she writes (page 30) a lot about Combe House – I wondered if it is the same one as yours[2] (she was staying [with] her parents at Hurstbourne Tarrant). It had just changed hands and she thought the new owners were doing all sorts of things they shouldn't to the garden. She must have been a very attractive creature; she writes, about Ralph Partridge, in a letter to Gerald Brenan[3] in Spain (illustrating the farmer's over-caution): 'He enjoined me not to send you a plum-pudding in case it gets stolen on the way. But I'll defy him, and we shall see. If it vanishes, somebody is the happier. If it is never sent, nothing good can possibly come of it …' Unanswerable. Later she says 'The Wiltshire air is echoing with cuckoo's whistles. They give the air a great sense of perspective …'

It's pouring again, and the sea's thundering in giant waves. We wish you were both coming here soon, as at any time in the last two years or so. We've put all our eggs in one basket here; now half have gone, the other half being the Ghikas. But it will be lovely reassembling in Italy later in the year. *Viva San Zenone*!

With much love to you both,
Paddy

[1] Dora Carrington and David Garnett (ed.), *Carrington: Letters and Extracts from her Diaries* (1971).
[2] The Stewarts had returned to their house in Combe, near Newbury, Berkshire.
[3] Gerald Brenan (1894–1987), writer and scholar of Spanish history and culture.

P.S. A nice mealtime exchange:

<u>Eddie</u>: These pears are hard as rocks, my dear.
<u>John</u>: Don't fumble them all, Eddie, you'll bruise them.
<u>Eddie</u>: I'm afraid they're unbruisable, dear.

P.P.S. Troilus has completely lost his youthful Bismarckian look and, in repose, slightly resembles Holbein's *Erasmus*.

The Crete film – *The Castle of the Immortals*[1] – was literally beyond belief. But one need have had no fears on the score of anything being snide, slanted, chauvinistic in the sense of anti-Allied. It was a wild fantasy for ten-year-olds, although the place was packed with a whiskery audience of riper years. Not only are generals abducted, but strongpoints assaulted and carried, huge petrol and ammunition dumps sent sky-high, armoured columns annihilated and the enemy mown down in scores. The bursting of grenades and rattle of machine guns is nonstop. The General and I are the only characters called by their real names, and this the whole time. I came out of it as an intrepid, humourless Tarzan grasping a smoking tommy-gun, half-dead with metal fatigue, barking curt orders and gazing mysteriously into the *Ewigkeit* [Eternity] against a background of explosions and sunsets. My sincere disavowals, when questioned about it, are taken for becoming modesty, so what the hell … I only hope that people who know what was really happening – i.e. catching lice and reading *David Copperfield* under the stalactites well out of harm's way – don't think one had any hand in the production. Phew!

---

[1] A Greek film about the abduction of General Kreipe, released in 1971.

To Jock Murray   Kardamyli
20 September 1971   Messenia
                                                           Greece

Dear Jock,
    <u>S.O.S!</u> I woke up in the middle of last night with a frightful jerk, remembering that the letters I handed over for typing,[1] without re-reading, contained several bits about other people which really oughtn't to be seen by anyone but the addressee, as they talk very freely about other people in one or two places – nothing very damaging, merely private. Somehow, like a lunatic in the haste of departure, I forgot to go through them and do something about the few offending passages. I don't think it matters if the typist sees them, as Christian names blur the track to all but an initiate reader; but to anyone who <u>did</u> know, it would reflect very badly on my discretion – indeed, on common feelings of friendship (though quite OK written privately to Joan) to have risked letting these private things reach a wider circulation. I don't think there's anything at all damaging, as it only concerns friends: but my carelessness remains shamingly indiscreet. Please don't even <u>hint</u> to anyone that I have been so careless and callous. The kindest thing, Jock, would be for you to get them off the typist as soon as they are ready and charitably slip them into an envelope without scrutinising my tactlessly oblivious screed; and send it here, so that I can go through it carefully and prepare the text, for the final version, deleting anything that might give the slightest pain to the people concerned, or startle a reader with my lack of respect for privacy. It all sounds far worse than it is, I realise; there's nothing wicked or frightful, or exceptionable as a private communication to someone with whom one is on very intimate terms who knows everyone concerned very well; or particularly exciting, merely unkind-seeming and indiscreet and criminally careless not to have remembered. Thank heavens it's

---

[1] Letters PLF sent to Joan from an expedition to Peru with Robin Fedden. Edited versions of these would be published as *Three Letters from the Andes* (1991).

under your kind wing! I'd clean forgotten that it wasn't all straight reportage! Thank you so much, Jock, in advance, for rescuing me from my blunder, as I'm sure you will! I really need locking up.

Did you get a missing page that I left with the young lady in the glass confessional downstairs,[1] just as I was leaving? There are a few pages of the letter journal still to come (harmless, I think!) which I'll go through with a tooth-comb and send off tomorrow or the day after. Do send a line saying all's well, (or the worst!). MUM'S the word!

Joan's due back in London yesterday or today. Don't mention all the above, as she'd be justifiably horrified at my idiocy!

I found Xan and Daphne Fielding here when I arrived – now left for Cyprus, alas. They were both scribbling away hard, and, you'll be glad to hear, I'm, literarily speaking, back in the thick of snowy Bavaria in January 1934, and enjoying it.

The only thing that has overshadowed my return is the news that George Seferis is desperately – in bed, mortally – ill. Three operations on the stomach, tracheotomy, nasal and intravenous feeding, thin as a rake, and in a merciful coma for two months, during which time he has not recognised anyone. Only Máro [Seferis's wife] is allowed to see him four times daily. I talked to her on the telephone yesterday (having been warned by a kind letter from the Walrus,[2] which I found here). Alas, there's only one possible end to all this, and she prays for it as a merciful release.[3] It's absolutely shattering: Maurice Bowra[4] and George within a few months of each other is too much. Do tell Osbert about all this.

I read the two opening chapters of 'Departure-Holland',[5] and some of Germany out loud to Xan and Daphne, and, to my delight and surprise, their reaction was encouraging and enthusiastic.

---

[1] A reference to the glass booth, which still survives in the entrance hall of the John Murray building in Albemarle Street.

[2] George Katsimbalis.

[3] Seferis died on the very day that this letter was written.

[4] Bowra had died on 4 July.

[5] The first chapters of the book that became *A Time of Gifts*.

Morale has shot up. There are a few clumsinesses and ambiguities – most of the latter due to my bad handwriting with the typist – but I'm going to leave any trimming and polishing to the end.

No more at the moment, except apologies and thanks for the salvage operation implored above!

Yours ever
Paddy

To Diana Cooper   Kardamyli
24 September 1971   Messenia
                   Greece

Darling Diana,

Well, it <u>was</u> nice overlapping in London like that – I dreaded you might hang on in Austria, and so we'd have missed each other. I still smile when I think of the Mexican fox, and his nice compatriot head waiter. Best of all was lunch in that empty restaurant, with the breeze drifting through, and a lot of green leaves at one end; it was rather like eating in the riverside lane in a provincial town, and, considering the grub, a French one, e.g. Pacy-sur-Eure. I often think of that marvellous feast under the leaves there, with the Eure rushing by below us, an Ophelia-like tangle of green waterweed, when, after a couple of minutes' silence with fingers lightly tapping out the scansion, Duff wrote out the St George's Day telegram in verse to Daph. & Xan.

They were both installed here when I arrived last week (Janetta and Jaime too, to my added delight) and we had a marvellous few days before they had to go to Cyprus, to stay with other friends. Now comes a telegraph saying 'Household conditions farcically ghastly' – <u>I long to know why</u> – and suggesting a return to Greece instead, and, I hope, here. <u>I wish you'd come sometime</u>! Joan & Graham loom tomorrow and I can't wait to hear all about Tiflis, Bokhara, Tashkent and Samarkand, and wondering how golden the road proved.

I've just finished Pushkin's *Captain's Daughter*, a wonderful melodramatic adventure story about the Cossack revolt in the reign of Catherine II, and have started *The Queen of Spades*; otherwise I'm working like blazes at finishing the youthful *Journey* – those quickly masked reproachful glances, every time I return with the same hollow tale, are proving too much for me at last …

Please keep in touch
With fond love & hugs
Paddy

P.S. I <u>wonder</u> if you have any spare corner in an attic or a cellar? I've got all sorts of odd garments scattered about the capital, mostly hunting things – hard hats, harder boot-trees, boots, spurs, jacks, hooks, crops, stocks, breeches, broadcloth coats, a whole arsenal of vulpicide finery. I plan to assemble them all one day in one of those beautiful japanned tin trunks with one's name painted on in beautiful copperplate; lest moth and rust should corrupt. I daren't ask kind Patrick [Kinross], as every odd corner of his house is stuffed with the chattels of his friends, including mine. I'd absolutely understand if it was the most awful nuisance. I'm afraid this P.S. is dictated by cupboard-love …

To Diana Cooper   Kardamyli
27 February 1973   Messenia
                                                   Greece

Darling Diana,

I don't know what it's like in Warwick Avenue, but it's coming down cats and dogs here, and has been for three or four days, as from massed fire-hoses; except when it changes its wind into hail and rakes us with whiffs of grape-shot, all accompanied by blizzards and intermittent thunder and lightning of the most Wagnerian kind: olive-trees gesticulate for help, cypresses shudder and thrash together, waves come crashing in like Ney's cavalry,[1] cliff-high spray soars round the rocks and capes, and the noise in

[1] Marshal Ney led the cavalry charge at Waterloo that failed to break the Allied infantry squares.

all the caves as the sea hits them booms like running broadside, as though we were fighting back ... We are battened down, and in the ark (indeed, most of our passengers are four-foot, you're never heard such mewing), the fires roar – luckily we've got masses of neatly stacked wood in a sheltered place – and it's pretty snug considering. I'm delighted when this sort of weather sets in: a) because the walls and the roof we have shoved up keep it out so (touch wood) triumphantly, b) because all the things we've planted must be shooting out roots deliriously. Otherwise, not much going on. Before the rain started, a large marten used to sneak down from the mountains after dark, shit on the terrace, and sneak back to the mountains again. But for the last few days he must have been curled up resentfully in some lofty den. There's also a huge, grubby white tomcat from the village, Hagar's deadly foe, who prowls and prowls around, after some of our pretty and nubile Abyssinian[1] maids, no doubt; some of them, whose suspect white patches among the haughty Ethiopian grey tell their own tale, are almost certainly his daughters, or grand-daughters, for he's been hanging about for years. The tangle of incest hereabouts doesn't bear thinking of. Large formations of wild duck have been flying in from the sea, heading north. Harbingers of spring. The olive harvest is over, the oil safe in every cellar. Daisies, asphodels, orchids, scarlet and mauve anemones everywhere and spurge spreading in bigger and bigger globes. Orange trees heavy with oranges, snow all over the peaks of the Taygetus.

What I ought to have asked at the outset is: how is that wretched wrist? Not in much trim for writing yet, I expect, but do put a thumb-print on a P.C. What I'd like to know is: what are we all going to do without Annie at Victoria Square?[2] We'll all just gaze at each like baffled foxes and vixens with the last earth stopped.[3] I see your marvellous great niece has been delivered of a boy (or a

[1] A breed of domestic short-haired cat with a distinctive 'ticked' tabby coat, in which individual hairs are banded with different colours.
[2] Ann Fleming had moved to Wiltshire and given up her base in London.
[3] i.e. they have nowhere to take refuge.

girl?). Do please give her congratulations. It should grow up into a smashing stripling ...[1]

I'm afraid this is a hopelessly disjointed letter – I think I must be a bit dizzy from all the sloshing and thumping going on outside. Also, apart from work I'm deep in C.V. Wedgwood's history of the Thirty Years' War,[2] which is amazingly good, but enough to make anyone's head swim a bit. It's a terrible and fascinating tale of slaughter and destruction with strange figures appearing through the smoke: all the Habsburgs painted by Velasquez, the Winter Queen, Ferdinand II and III, Maximilian of Bavaria, Gustavus Adolphus, Urban VIII, Richelieu, the *Eminence Grise*, Piccolomini, Tilly, Christian of Brunswick, Bernard of Saxe-Weimar, the Princes of Orange, Condé, and Wallenstein: all with shoulder-length hair, moustaches and sometimes imperials, and wide collars of lace or starch, spreading over black armour inlaid with gold; except the Winter Queen, naturally.

No more now, no room, except for tons of fond love & hugs, darling Diana, from Paddy! (& Joan)

To Diana Cooper   Kardamyli
30 October 1973   Messenia
                                                       Greece

Darling Diana,

I can't remember whether you ever kept turkeys anywhere. We've had two turkey-hens here for the last month and they are delightful. We let them pick about the garden on the strength of their beautiful voices – quite unlike that [illegible] screech of their peacock cousins, equally not like the angry gobble of their

---

[1] Diana Cooper's great niece Louisa Lane Fox (married to the classicist and ancient historian Robin Lane Fox) had given birth to a daughter, Martha, who would become a businesswoman and philanthropist; in 2013 she was raised to the peerage as Baroness Lane Fox of Soho.

[2] C. V. Wedgwood (Dame Cicely Veronica Wedgwood OM, 1910–97), *The Thirty Years' War* (1938).

future husbands; they have a loud, lulling liquid trill that charms the air. Also they <u>look</u> rather nice, and they are shining examples of inseparable devotion: they are seldom more than a foot apart. Occasionally they come in through the French windows, walking and peering jerkily, like elderly lady-tourists advancing down the nave of St Peter's. When shadows fall they roost side by side on a mulberry branch, out of fox-reach. I can see their two plump silhouettes as I write. The cat situation is normal – viz., 20 to 25 I think, still splendidly captained by your old friend Hagar, who grows nicer daily. There are two chickens, a magnificent multicoloured and very tuneful cock; a few handsome rabbits. There were some ducks but they have disappeared down red lanes [i.e. been swallowed]. Lastly, there are two pigs belonging to Petro outside the garden walls; they have turned it into a sort of *wadi* by dint of gyring and gimbling[1], which is very good for the olive roots, every one says. It airs them.

Well, that's roughly our news. What's yours? Don't write, because we'll be at Patrick [Kinross]'s soon. I'm very excited, and long to see you and get up to date.

I've taken to writing like this [upright handwriting], as opposed to slanting, in the hopes of achieving legibility.

No more, Diana darling, except tons of love & hugs
from Paddy

---

[1] 'Twas brillig, and the slithy toves/ Did gyre and gimble in the wabe', from Lewis Carroll's *Jabberwocky* (1872).

To Balasha Cantacuzène   Chatsworth
25 November 1973   Bakewell
                                                 Derbyshire

Darling Balasha,

This is a joyful cry from the banks of the Valley of the Shadow![1] Yesterday there was a pheasant shoot here, and it was real northern Brontë-esque weather, brilliant blue sky, whirling clouds, red leaves flying past by the million, pheasants thrown all over the sky, guns twirling and banging as though in the hands of contortionists – all this among auburn bracken and tremendous old oak trees, which are all that remains of Sherwood Forest, about three miles from the house. Andrew Devonshire and I, being the only non-shooters, were standing talking under one of those tremendous oaks while the wind rose to a howl and suddenly there was a tearing and splitting noise overhead. We made a startled dash for it, and one huge limb of the tree came crashing down – we were just in time! Everybody gathered to survey the tons of timber that had fallen and took photographs of the two survivors among the wreckage. What an adventure!

3 weeks later. Same place.

What a disjointed letter this is! I've been moving about so much that this keeps getting interrupted, just as I think I'm going to settle down to it again. Do forgive!

Our main reason for coming to England now was for me to try and sort things out for my mother, who spends most of the time in a rather nice nursing-home in Brighton. I've been down to see her several times, and the tangle seems more or less cleared up. She still gets about quite a lot, we have had lunch out twice and the other day I took her to watch some performing dolphins in a huge tank with glass sides, a wonderful sight: they come when they are called by their trainer, leap hurdles, shoot several yards into the air to jump through hoops and make charming squeaks in answer to the trainer's whistle. Vanessa[2] (who sends her love) has been a great help in all this. During the week Joan and I stay with Patrick Kinross,

---

[1] A playful reference to the slaughter of pheasants.
[2] Vanessa Fenton, PLF's sister.

who lives by one of the old canals in the very pretty part of London known as Little Venice, beyond Paddington Station. He is writing an enormous history of the Ottoman Empire; the house is so full of books, there is scarcely room to move. A charming *vie du quartier* goes on here: next door lives Lennox Berkeley the composer, a charming man, and three doors away, Diana Cooper; round the corner, a painter friend called Adrian Daintrey, then John Julius Norwich, Diana's son, and then Barbara & Niko Ghika; so there is plenty of to-and-fro dropping in, apart from seeing friends further afield. At weekends, Joan goes to stay with her brother Graham in Gloucestershire – I went for two nights – and I come here or chez Annie Fleming – both friendly houses for Joan, but she feels impelled to go to Graham's by duty and inclination. The news in England is far from good, terrible crises impend;[1] but, as usual, it doesn't seem nearly so terrible when one is on the spot as when one reads about it far away. Joan, Patrick and I watched Princess Anne's wedding on the television in Diana Cooper's bedroom, as she has a coloured set. She was still in an enormous bed, so we all lay on it side by side drinking champagne, watching the procession and the service. It was a lovely bright winter day with red leaves falling, crystal coaches looking marvellous, the breastplates of the Household Cavalry flashing; bearskins, banners, muted words of command, presented arms; rumbling organs in the abbey, fanfares of trumpets from the vaults high above this white-clad girl and her dashing scarlet-clad dragoon.[2] Then a return procession, among cheers and thousands of waved handkerchiefs and all the city's bells pealing, and distant salvos of cannon. It was all very obsolete and indescribably moving; it is one of the few things – pageantry – that

[1] The National Union of Mineworkers had begun an overtime ban in November, leading to a shortage of coal to fuel power stations. Things would get worse: in mid-December the Conservative government announced that an 'electricity consumption reduction measure', which became known as the 'Three-day Week', would come into force at the end of the year. A junior minister advised responsible citizens to clean their teeth in the dark, only to have his house photographed by the press with every light ablaze.

[2] Princess Anne married Mark Phillips, a lieutenant with the 1st Queen's Dragoon Guards, on 14 November 1973.

the English are better than anyone (the only thing, it seems, at this moment!) It cheered everyone up. A lovely morning.

<u>Back to Chatsworth</u>. You'll never guess how I pass the day here: being sculpted! Andrew has got a sculptress pal – a scarlet-haired girl called Angela Conner,[1] very gifted and very nice – and he is getting various people sculpted by her; so far, uncle Harold Macmillan and John Betjeman and (out of turn, <u>not</u> in order of merit, but because I'm so seldom in England!) me. A lot of it – the head and bust – was done in her studio in London, but she has brought all the gear up here, and I sit on a sort of wooden platform while she thumps and gouges away at the clay, and the gramophone plays Scarlatti and Palestrina and I look fixedly out of the window at converging lines of enormous elm trees between which runs a long oblong lake with a group of stone tritons and sea horses in the middle, shooting the tallest fountain in the world up into the windy air so that it tosses and feathers like a plume. (It was placed there 150 years ago in honour of an expected visit of the Tzar. He didn't come, but this astonishing jet of water still hurls itself into the wintry sky.) Several swans, including a black one, swim above their reflection, also little flotillas of exotic ducks. Then enormous woods climb up hill on one side, and on the other the park flows away, dotted with oaks, with troops of fallow deer on the move in the middle distance by the banks of a winding river crossed by a columned Palladian bridge; and in the distance, the hills of Derbyshire interlocking along the horizon. It's a marvellous conjunction of wildness and sophistication, so convincingly done that, when one approaches the house through the woods the sudden apparition of this great palace, with its fountains and statues and urns, bursts on one like a fairy tale. It's a marvellous vista to fix one's eyes on when being sculpted. Apparently, one freezes into a fierce rictus, and occasionally, hovers on the edge of sleep. At these moments, Andrew or Debo are summoned, in the hopes that their lovely discourse will save the sitter's expression from total

[1] Angela Conner (b. 1935) made a bronze of Andrew Devonshire's head as well as of PLF's.

petrifaction. It's all tremendous fun. I can't get over the size of the trees in England: such a change after the olives and cypresses of Kardamyli.

A miraculous change has happened here. Two years ago, Andrew was getting into a fearful state through a love affair going wrong, i.e. our pal Janetta marrying Jaime Parladé, a charming Spaniard.[1] This brought on tremendous drinking bursts, and rash, angry and incalculable ways. Debo didn't mind about the love affairs, but was terribly upset at what looked like an approach to total disaster. It was getting really bad, when suddenly he gave up drink – of any kind, even beer or a weak sherry – altogether. The change has been <u>total</u>. It really was a heroic act and he has become an angel of goodness and kindness. It's like the lifting of some terrible curse and now both of them, so brilliant and remarkable in their totally different ways, seem to shine with equal radiance. What <u>is</u> amazing, is that he's an even better host than he used to be, pouring drinks for all the rest of us unredeemed ones, quite happy on a teetotal island lapped in with whisky, claret, port, champagne, brandy, etc., etc., quite unperturbed, and in ebullient spirits …

My darling Balasha, the moment has come <u>at last</u>, to finish this and get it off. I won't be so slow next time! Do send me your news, and Pomme's, as I long to know it; and forgive this abrupt ending to this untidy rigmarole; but if I don't follow my resolution to get it off <u>now</u>, I feel I may slip back again. All my love to darling Pomme too, and many, many masses of the same to you,

from Paddy xxx
and lots from Joan

[1] See pp. 283.

For almost ten years Paddy had been writing a book based on his pre-war walk across Europe. Though this had originated in a proposed magazine article of 2,000 words, it had now grown to such alarming proportions that Jock Murray was contemplating publication in two book-length volumes.

To Jock Murray   Kardamyli
20 May 1974   Messenia
                                                  Greece

My dear Jock,

I'm pondering deeply the question of 2 vols. Instinctively I'm against it, mainly because I feel something more substantial is needed than a first vol. of 90,000 words after this protracted silence. I hoped to jump into the arena again with something at least as long as the *Traveller's Tree* (172,000), which I think the whole of this book – I haven't counted it up – would certainly pass with ease. I have taken down and counted up two books which are separately published parts of a whole, viz, a vol ('Great Morning') of O. Sitwell's *Left Hand Right Hand* (133,000 words)[1] and Vol II ('Salve') of *Hail and Fairwell* (170,000 words).[2] (I hope all these calculations are right, more or less.) The first book you suggest would be about the same size of *Roumeli* (95,000). If this book is to be cut up into vols, I feel that the parts should be nearer *Mani* length (123,000?) (Note: Let us, for brevity's sake, use the working title *Parallax* for the whole undivided book.)

I repeat that I'm unhappy about cutting the book up for all sorts of reasons – the need to re-explain things, the loss of momentum, the feeling that, though I hope the finished undivided whole would be an imposing affair, its appearance subdivided might give the feeling of too much fuss about too little, a slight feeling of

---

[1] *Great Morning* (1947) is the third volume of Osbert Sitwell's four-volume autobiography, which began with *Left Hand, Right Hand!* (1943), and was followed by *The Scarlet Tree* (1946). The final volume was *Laughter in the Next Room* (1949).

[2] *Hail and Farewell*, by George Moore (1911–14), 3 volumes: *Ave, Salve* and *Vale*.

short-changing the reader, instead of overwhelming him with the contents of a cornucopia. But I do see your points of view: I'm delighted by point (1), respectful as a layman about point (2); not quite so swayed by (3).[1] My slowness in delivering the goods has been so atrocious that the slight <u>further</u> delay involved seems a venial sin by comparison, <u>if</u> the final result is what I hope it will be.

<u>But</u> I'm swayed in your direction by two things.

(I) Since getting your letter, I've had a look, for the first time at the remaining type, written years ago, and, even after reading the Romanian border, where the hurried style changes gear, I see that it needs a hell of a lot of work; it should never have been shown in its present ill-typed, ill-corrected form, divided up into jerky numbered subdivisions. In the light of the rewritten chapters that you now have (except for the first two chapters, which are not right yet), it needs a lot of topping and tailing, re-writing here and there, docking in some places, now and then expanding where opportunities have been missed, in fact, bringing into line with the revised beginning, which is on the right track. And all this, obviously, means a stiff spell of very hard work, including the completion of the last Constantinople chapter.

(II) Since the recovery of my fragmentary diaries in Romania, I long to write about the continuation of the journey from Constantinople: taking ship from the city, arriving in Salonika, spending a winter month in Athos, then accompanying the Greek Army on a borrowed horse through the two weeks campaign across Macedonia, abandoning the squadron I was with, and continuing alone into Thrace, then back through the Rhodope mountains – 1½ months on horseback – and continuing on foot southwards to Athens. But we needn't bother about these details – the first impact of Greece – now. <u>Certainly</u> the <u>present</u> venture should end at Constantinople – the book, or <u>a</u> book, should end there. But there might be a vol III; I have masses of notes on the region, made before *Mani* suddenly thrust its way to the fore, which will be of great help. The walk ended at Athens in May 1935, and the vol should end there.

[1] Murray's letter is lost; his points seem to have been in support of the idea of publishing the story of 'the Great Trudge' in two volumes.

Let's shelve this last paragraph for the moment, and think where 'Parallax I' should end. I am already across the Danube again, in Bratislava. From here, with a pal [illegible], I went by train to Prague, back to Bratislava, then on foot across S. Slovakia, staying with Baron Shey, then south to the Danube, reaching the big bridge near Komaron. I crossed this to Esztergom (Gran)[1] on Easter Day, at sunset, into Hungary, and suggest that Vol I should end on the middle of the Bridge. Vol II could start with a huge gathering of Magyar noblemen, all in fur and feathers, in the cathedral of the Cardinal-Prince-Archbishop, thousands of peasants, processions, peals of bells, setting the note for Hungary. This means the end of Vienna – being typed – and the above period afterwards, which I'm writing now; i.e. a half chapter and another long chapter, both of which follow on from what you have, to the natural break of the Hungarian frontier, which leaves the reader in mid air full of expectation. Now follows a passage of this letter wrapped up, I hope, in a lot of non-eye catching verbiage asking you, on my behalf, to inform the society of which the late David Carver was the head,[2] that your female colleague, who published the translation of *Mani*, has been roped into durance for some unstated reason, where she still vilely is: a kind, good person, always ready to help authors or anyone in trouble.[3] This occurred last week and there is nothing whatever one can do of course, except to inform the penmen who deal with such things, so that it should at least be set on record; the name is Nanny Kalianessi and it was mentioned in our leading newspaper last week – and here I can freely and voluminously ad lib for a line or two in the diversionary way that conjurors act when about to perform some feat of legerdemain![4] So prospects for a happy conclusion to all our *Parallax* questions begin to take shape.

[1] Esztergom is the Hungarian name of the city known as Gran in German and Ostrihom in Slovak.

[2] David Carver was general secretary of PEN.

[3] Athina ('Nana') Kalianessi, owner and publisher of the Athens publishing house and bookshop Kedros, had been arrested and charged under the laws prevailing under the military junta with spreading anti-national propaganda. She faced a court martial, but was acquitted after protests by British and French publishers.

[4] PLF disguised his meaning to evade the attention of the Greek censors.

I'm writing to Geo. Katsimbalis about Byron's Cephalonian letters to Solomos; if anyone can, he'll find out if they exist.[1]

I don't propose to look at the mass of stuff beyond the Hungarian frontier until I have finished with the stuff on hand, viz. 'Parallax I'; nor at the earlier chapters 1 and 2, which need attention. But I do hope you have handed my last lump of stuff over to the excellent typist who made the splendid fair copy in triple spacing, so that I can leap at them when the time comes – soon I hope. Please despatch when ready.

No more now, except all the best – also from Joan!

Yours ever
Paddy

To Balasha Cantacuzène
5 August 1974

c/o Lady Egremont
Cockermouth Castle
Cumberland

Darling Balasha,

Thank you so much for your sweet letter, and also to Joan, which I'll send on to her. My treatment ended three weeks ago.[2] I'd got off very lightly for most of it, but suddenly towards the end it became rather hell and worst of all when it stopped. I suppose it's cumulative. One was very sore and raw and unable to eat or speak: but it soon started to get better, and I compelled Joan to leave, against her will, as one of us had to be at Kardamyli; and I went to Annie Fleming's in Wiltshire[3] – an old haunt, no effort, great friends; a great sweep of lawns to a wild lake overshadowed by enormous trees full of waterfowl, lots of sleeping and nursery food and reading. Then I came up here. Pamela Egremont is tall, beautiful and an angel of niceness, a great friend of ours, who has travelled all over Asia and

---

[1] No letters have been found from Byron to his contemporary, the Greek 'national poet' Dionysios Solomos.
[2] PLF had been receiving treatment for cancer of the tongue.
[3] Warneford Place, Sevenhampton, near Swindon.

Africa, & ridden with the nomadic Baktiari tribe in two of their huge migrations across Persia. John Egremont died four years ago, a charming and funny creature, Macmillan's private secretary for years. He used to get so tight sometimes, that Macmillan had to put him to bed with his own hands. She, and three charming children, live most of the time at Petworth, a large and ravishing house in Sussex, where Turner lived for over 20 years among the woods and the deer he painted so often – also Cockermouth Castle … It is lovely here … I've got a lovely room, and a library nobody uses, where I write … the window in front of this desk looks out over a great loop of the Derwent river (in which I can see Pamela and two others fishing for salmon at this very moment, up to their thighs in the …

[The letter continued on a card, now lost]

Nancy Mitford died in 1973. In the last few years of her life, she had begun to assemble material for use in an autobiography. Illness prevented her from writing this memoir, but her close friend Harold Acton undertook to complete the work she had begun, which in due course would be published as Nancy Mitford: A Memoir. *The letter that follows was written in response to a request for help from Acton, and is one of several such letters Paddy would write over the years to biographers of those whom he had known.*

To Harold Acton
5 November 1974

Kardamyli
Messenia
Greece

Dear Harold,

How very nice to hear from you!

Now, about Nancy. I can't help about dates, but I'm sure the Mark-Nancy correspondence[1] will clear that up. Her first stay with us in Greece was in the mid-50s, I think, when Joan and I were living in Niko Ghika's house in Hydra. I've got a feeling

[1] The extensive correspondence between Nancy Mitford and Mark Ogilvie-Grant.

she came there twice, because I remember once we were alone with her (Mark would normally have come, too, perhaps did; in fact, I feel sure he did) and once when Niko made one of his rare descents into his borrowed house. It – they – were lovely time(s). She had brought Prof Alan Ross's pamphlet with her, which we read aloud, and were in fits over.[1] The thing was that she didn't take it <u>at all</u> seriously – though she thought the prof. had hit the nail on the head in most of his distinctions, if one <u>was</u> going to sort out those shibboleths – the point was the absurdity of the thing; and her article about it was v. much in this light-hearted spirit; I think she was astonished first, amused, and finally, bored by the fuss and the earnestness it provoked. We were looking after someone's beastly dog called Spot, who barked like mad at some visitors, and accepted others in silence. During a maddening call by some people we hardly knew, the wretch never stopped barking for a second ('Out, damned Spot',[2] I can hear Nancy wailing to herself with eyes rolled up dolorously), and when they left, she said, 'I'm afraid old Spot's an unerring Non-U indicator …' Bidden to some feast at Spetsai, we caught the steamer with Niko. He was praising Corbusier, and Nancy said, 'But I can't bear him!'; all the time, the steamer's gramophone was playing a deafening nonstop tune, rather like a roundabout's at a fair, which, to tease Niko, gave rise to an improvised song which we both sang mercilessly:

Corbusier! Corbusier!
Tout est si propre et si gai!
Les pannes d'ascenseur
Nous laissent tous rêveurs
Mais, quand même, vive Corbusier! [e poi da capo][3]

---

[1] Nancy Mitford's *Encounter* article, 'The English Aristocracy', had been prompted by an academic paper by Professor Alan S. C. Ross, of the University of Birmingham. Ross coined the terms 'U' and 'non-U', to indicate the different usages of different social classes in England.

[2] *Macbeth*, Act V, Scene 1.

[3] 'Corbusier! Corbusier!/ Everything is so clean and gay!/ The escalator failure/ Leaves us dreamers/ But, even so, long live Corbusier! [and then from the beginning].'

Lots of verses. For years, the phrase *'tout est si propre et si gai!'* surfaced whenever a particularly squalid or mournful scene came in sight. She couldn't bear the lateness of meals – 'nearly as bad as Spain!' – 'It's all right for <u>you</u>, reeling drunk all of you, but what about poor abstemious <u>me</u>?[1] Well, inner resource, I suppose … I'll just think about Voltaire,[2] or Madame de Boigne,[3] till a crust appears …' She was very good about being teased; the strongest remonstrance was: 'Dear boy, do try to be nice.'

After Mark ('Old Gent'), her favourite Anglo-Athenian was certainly Roger Hinks (Quite right! Charming, civilised, affectionate, pessimistic man! He's a terrible loss) who was head of the British Council at the time, and suffering bitterly from anti-us emotion during the Cyprus troubles. One day he said, 'I'm off to Italy to see some proper painting, and by <u>painting</u> I don't mean the daubed planks that masquerade under the name <u>here</u>! They haven't an inkling of *chiaroscuro* or *morbidezza*!' (This occasioned a song to the tune of 'Giovinezza', which went:

Morbidezza! Morbidezza!
Chiaroscuro! Che belezza!
Carlo Dolci! Dosso Dossi!
Caravaggio, come va?
Lippo Lippi! Baldovinetti!
E Beccafumi di qua e di là!

Voglio putti
E tutti frutti
E un stupendo 'tutti'
A la <u>Scala</u>.

---

[1] Mitford was a light drinker, abstemious by comparison with PLF.

[2] Nancy Mitford wrote *Voltaire in Love* (1957).

[3] Adèle d'Osmond, Comtesse de Boigne (1781–1866), French aristocrat and writer. As a child she lived at Versailles, where her mother was lady-in-waiting to Louis XV's daughter Marie Adélaide. Nancy Mitford drew on her volume of memoirs in her biography *Madame de Pompadour* (1954).

Serata di gala-
Forse domani! Qui lo sa?

Not v. good, but an instant birth (from me, I think); taken up eagerly by N. Roger took it in v. good sport. Nancy's nickname for him was 'The Old Turkish Lady'. Another old friend, from bookshop days and long before, [was] Eddie Gathorne-Hardy. They were v. funny together.

Later, on another visit, we were living in a rather wretched house at Limni (on the W. coast of Euboea, with an amazing view over the sea to the snows of Parnassus). There was no room for a guest that you could call a room, so Mark brought her to stay with our neighbour Aymer Maxwell (Sir A. Maxwell of Monreith, Bt, elder brother of Gavin's, but I believe – I never met him – much nicer), a delightful Galloway laird, v. civilised, rather eccentric, very amusing, an angel in fact, always in a bit of a stew about what he gravely calls 'my staff' – rightly, I must admit. It was an immediate click – 'I adore Sir Aymer; and I love Bleak House' – it was the former English overseer's house of a nearby, abandoned, magnesite mine, not beautiful, but full of charm, only petrol lamps and candles, with a touch of the dark bungalow about it, only bigger and more rambling. There are several other English there,[1] all nice; but minor feuds rage and gossip, complications which they all revel in without realising it; not to mention labyrinthine complications, slander and conspiracy among the local Limniots, and subtle playing of one foreigner against the others, then vice versa in every possible permutation. Nancy was fascinated: ('I quite see. A Euboean *Cranford* ...') We had most of our meals in an outdoor taverna among the trees, which is always full of shaggy resin gatherers from the mountains in summer, pals of Aymer's, and of ours, and often tight. There is a great deal of unsteady dancing in the evening, lurching and retsina-spilling and not very tuneful song. At one moment when a stumble had

[1] Philip Sherrard lived nearby, as did the retired politician, diplomat and athlete Philip Noel-Baker.

brought down a whole Indian file of dancers in a sottish and Breughelesque heap, Nancy murmured, 'Arcady', heaving a sigh of mock rapture, followed by her round-eyed pitying look, then a bell-like peal.

Aymer took us for idyllic sails in a charming yacht he has called *Dirk Hatterick* (after the Galloway pirate in *Guy Mannering*), down to the Euripus in the Straits: to Francis Turville-Petre's former 'Down-there-on-a-visit' island[1] to the Boeotian shore, up the coast towards Mt Pelion and the Gulf of Volos, to a small island with a tumbling monastery that he was thinking of buying, dropping anchor in deserted and brilliant blue green bays, bosky to the water's edge with cistus, rosemary, lentisk and thyme under reflected emerald green pines and the tall spurs of Mt Candili: always with Parnassus afloat and glimmering in the west. She loved it. They were very happy days. But once, on a short outing when due back for luncheon on shore, for some reason, instead of on cushions on the deck, it grew later and later ... Nancy closed her eyes with a sad sigh, and made the French sawing gesture across her tummy with the flat edge of her hand. ('Nancy, you think of nothing but meals', 'Try to be nice'); then: 'Early and light, early and light, are the luncheons the Limniots love.'[2]

Aymer is coming here in three days' time, and he has a wonderful eye and ear and memory for the sonic and the odd, so I'll make him cast his mind back.

She came down here with Mark soon after we had finished building the house, and liked it very much, I think. It must have been six or seven years ago. I can't remember any separate fragments

[1] Francis Adrian Joseph Turville-Petre (1901–41), archaeologist, known to his friends as 'Fronny'. In 1931 he took up residence on his private rented island of Agios Nikolaos (St Nicolas) near Euboea. His friend Christopher Isherwood visited him there in 1933, and later portrayed him as Ambrose, the mad king of a small Greek island, in his *Down There on a Visit*.
[2] 'Far and few, far and few,/Are the lands where the Jumblies live', from Edward Lear, 'The Jumblies' (1871).

of chat: only endless talk on the pebbles in the bay below, and lying on the terrace; and a journey down the Mani to look at the San Gimignano-like towers, and a picknick on a flower-covered ledge in the masonry, of the Arcadian Gate in the ancient ramparts of Messene, which undulate across the valleys under Mt Ithome like the Great Wall of China. Sleep under the branches was broken by voices: a carload of Germans looking at the titanic fallen lintel that half bars the great Portal. We watched them unseen in our eyrie and unspeaking till they drove away. A wild and marvellous spot.

Other memories of Nancy revolve around the Rue Monsieur and the Rue D'Artois at Versailles; Paris; Chantilly; London; Chatsworth; and Lismore; but this is all familiar territory. But I've got in the mood of thinking about Nancy, so here are some random fragments as they crop up in my mind. Chez Diana Cooper at Chantilly once, Nancy came to luncheon, and Diana showed her – with justifiable pride, because they looked ravishing – scores and scores of tulips springing up in random clumps and constellations among the trees on the lawn that slopes down to the lake. This evoked a wail of anguish from N: 'Diana! Oh how <u>could</u> you? Confetti!' …

I once went for a long walk with her in the woods above Chatsworth – all bracken, foxgloves and gigantic oaks, the last remains of Sherwood Forest. We agreed that little could have changed since Robin Hood. 'I can just see Gurth and Wamba!' – the two Saxon swineherds in *Ivanhoe* – 'pasturing their herds on the acorns!' All was well, until, further downhill, vast clumps of rhododendrons hove into view, in full bloom. 'Oh <u>look!</u>' Nancy cried: 'The <u>rhodies!</u>' – one could hear the inverted commas hovering in the air. 'I don't think Gurth would have liked <u>them</u>! Not at all! Nor Wamba! He'd have highly disapproved …'. Years later, in Ireland, Debo drove us over to Mr Congreve's at?[1] (he has the most varied and colourful debauch of rhodies you've ever seen). As we drove up through this dazzling explosion, she leant back to me and said: 'I

---

[1] PLF put a question mark here, no doubt because he could not remember the name of the gardens at Mount Congreve, Co. Waterford.

say! Lucky Gurth and Wamba aren't here!' in awed tones. A lot of
Nancy memories are connected with joint sojourns under Debo's
and Andrew's roof at Lismore: the first time for a week or two
with Debo, Nancy, Woman[1] and Kitty Mersey ('my wife' D. says).
Nancy: 'Now just because he's the only man here, there's no need
to pander to him.' It was tremendous fun being with three of those
sisters together: they would gang up by twos against the remaining
one for teasing purposes – more in pious commemoration of
schoolroom usage and custom than anything else. When it was
Debo and Woman against Nancy, 'The old French lady,' or 'Poor
Nancy, she's a frog, you know!'[2] If Nancy should ever use a French
word in conversation, absolutely automatically and expression-
lessly, Debo would say, 'Ah oui!' or quelle horrible surprise!', often
both, e.g. Debo: 'Come on, old French lady!' Nancy (appealing to
a third party with a sigh): 'Poor child![3] She's wanting, you know. Un
peu toquée [a little cracked] ...' Debo: 'Ah oui. Quelle horrible surprise.' When she and Debo combined against Woman, both would
imitate her rather idiosyncratic way of talking, which I think she
loved. It was very funny. The basis of Nancy's onslaughts on Debo,
when her turn came, were accusations of illiteracy – unfounded.
(It's my theory, because, though never seen to read, she's so full
of surprises that Xan Fielding and I determined long ago that she
must be a secret reader: cupboards full of empty books discovered
after decease, we suspect, like all the empty bottles found after a
secret drinker dies.) When very young – but I expect Debo had
told you all this – the great thing was, by appealing to Debo's love
of animals, to wring her heart until tears rose to the eyes – 'welling
up' was the expression used, just as 'mantling' means to blush ('Did
you well up?' 'I'm not sure, but I think I mantled'). I expect D has
told you how Nancy would wring her heart and make her well up,

---

[1] Pamela Jackson, née Mitford, second of the six Mitford sisters, known as 'Woman'.
[2] She had lived in France since 1946.
[3] Debo was the youngest of the Mitford sisters; Nancy, the eldest, was more than fifteen
years her senior.

and, indeed, overflow, by plucking her heartstrings about a poor little spent match, alone in a matchbox, all unloved, etc.

Lismore, again. Nancy arriving from the village shop with a postcard, depicting, in sombre colours, an old Irish peasant, sitting sadly and pensively on the right side of a grate. Nancy: 'Look! Whistler's Father!'

It was wonderfully apt, colouring-style, position etc. She promptly sent off a score or so to various friends. (So did I, copycat.) It was nice hearing Mitfordese in so unpolluted a flow – 'When do they loom, the fiends?' 'No sewers to dinner to*day*, I trust.' 'It'll all loom in the wash, I dare say.' The fire was getting low. Nancy peered in the grate and said bleakly, 'I note no bellows.' There were several expeditions: to Elizabeth Bowen at Bowenscourt, just before it was sold and pulled down, and a lot of toing and froing to Eddy Sackville-West at Cahir, in Tipperary,[1] after he had left Crichel. Raymond Mortimer was staying, and they came over to Lismore for a marvellous picknick, arranged by Andrew, on the edge of a wood (Andrew, Debo, Nancy, Eddy, Raymond, Clodagh Anson,[2] Bill Stirling,[3] Rory More O'Ferrall). A huge fire was built. Nancy gathered a small handful of sticks, threw them on and sat down firmly, saying 'No Mohican me.' Luncheon at the D. of St Albans[4] in a tumbledown house which had just been further reduced by fire, so the feast was in the kitchen, I think. D of St A: 'Nancy, I'm very sorry to say, [you're] a literary prostitute.' N: 'Obbie! How can you be so cruel?' (He lent me two vols of memoirs of the Pss Palatine – still unreturned, alas; and too late now …) She was spellbound by a wax dummy in a dress-shop window in Fermoy, Co. Cork: discoloured, flyblown, with horse-hair shingle moulting, wearing a 1925 cloche hat and a low-waisted short skirt of the period, and half melted,

[1] Eddy Sackville-West lived at Cooleville House, Clogheen, Co. Tipperary.
[2] Lady Clodagh Anson, a neighbour of the Devonshires at Lismore.
[3] William (Bill) Stirling, Scottish landowner. Debo enjoyed the shoots at his estate in Perthshire.
[4] Osborne de Vere Beauclerk, 12th Duke of St Albans (1874–1964), had married the Dowager Marchioness of Waterford.

so that the figure was stooping over in a drunken lurch. Whenever plans were discussed, she said '<u>Do</u> let's have another look at that lady in Leigh Fermoy!'[1] She and Eddy S.W. and I went to see a marvellous garden, belonging to Mrs Annesley of Ann[es] Grove (Cork). There was some giant gunnera in the water garden, like mammoth rhubarb, dangerous man-eating looking plants. Later, when someone came under unfavourable comment, N said, 'The fiend! Let's throw him to the gunnera!' In the same garden, I sat on a bench which promptly came to bits. '<u>Look</u> what the boy's done <u>now</u>!' N said. I pointed out that both legs were rotted hollow. She looked and said 'Ah well, perhaps there <u>were</u> faults on both sides …' You know how fond she was of the idea of bad hats. Sade was being discussed. N: 'The Marquis de Sade? Such a dear old soul, I've always thought …' <u>Greece</u>. She, Joan and I were asked to luncheon by a very socially minded lady at another island. Just as the steamer was leaving, a motor-boat came whizzing after us. The boat stopped, and a servant came aboard, with a gold bound guest-book (that awful American habit of making guests for a meal sign). Nancy duly signed, and off we sailed. N 'The Madame Verdurin[2] of the Archipelagos!'

Well, that's the lot, I think. I'm sorry about the confusion of the page numbering, but hope it's clear; and sorrier still about the smudged condition. I had put a glass of whisky and soda on my desk (during a thunderstorm), then all the lights went out, as they are prone to here. Fumbling for matches, I knocked the glass over, hence the frightful mess. ('A likely story!' I can hear a teasing *voix d'outre tombe* [voice from beyond the grave] saying …) I've done my best to repair the damage …

I do see that it <u>must</u> be a hard task! I'm sure you'll do it beautifully. I'm alone here at the moment – Joan has gone to Blighty to help look after Cyril, who is desperately and dangerously ill, alas,[3] until Aymer Maxwell comes.

[1] A play on PLF's surname.
[2] A character in Proust's *À la recherche du temps perdu*. An autocratic hostess, Verdurin is determined to rise to the top of society.
[3] Cyril Connolly died later that month, on 26 November.

Do please come and see us, if ever you come to Greece. Raymond M[ortimer] and Dadie Rylands came for three weeks, and left a fortnight ago; since then, all calm.

Best of luck with the great enterprise!

Yours ever

Paddy

Belated congratulations on the K![1]

To Balasha Cantacuzène   Kardamyli
1 February 1975   Messenia
                                             Greece

Darling Balasha,

I'm so ashamed of myself, being such a slow correspondent, compared to Joan! She's busy making marmalade in the kitchen, so I went down to the village, to post her letter to you; and here I am at my desk, in a mad rush to catch up. Not really, of course! I kept meaning to write a long letter while we were in Spain; but, what with finishing a chapter in a hell of a hurry, and correcting others, typed, and moving about, didn't manage. If there wasn't a two-way rule about apologies for shortcomings about correspondence, I'd pile ashes on my head at this point ...

How funny your mentioning Brian Howard! I got to know him much better later. He was always impossible, but very complex and extraordinary, viper-tongued through failure, but with, nevertheless, a touch of something v. exceptional and extraordinary that made him quite unlike anyone else. He became rather a friend – and much nicer – in the end, was also an old one of Joan's from many years. He and his boyfriend Sam [Langford] died within three days of each other in Villefranche ten years ago, half drugs, half suicide. An awful case of squandered gifts. He is very well caricatured in some of Evelyn Waugh's books, notably as Anthony Blanche in

[1] Harold Acton was knighted in 1974.

Put Out More Flags,[1] and a book *(History of A Failure)*,[2] to which many contributed – I was supposed to, but didn't, I can't remember why – came out later.

Joan and I write to you independently but share answering – much better, in spite of the danger of covering the same ground – so I'm not quite sure how much she recounted, so will do it as it comes. We were met at Málaga airport (though we arrived by an earlier plane than we thought, so wandered about the town first) by Janetta Parladé, in a great tough truck-like car, suitable for rough terrain, in pouring rain. She's a tremendous friend of both of ours, and very difficult to describe, but I'll try. The factual details are easy: a distant relation of Prue [Branch]'s, only worth mentioning because there is some indefinite similarity somewhere, the same spontaneous, un-forced freedom from convention, and unconscious poetical aura. Nancy Mitford based 'The Bolter' in *Pursuit of Love* half on Dina Haldeman,[3] and half on her [Janetta's] grandmother (neé Ruthven),[4] whose frequent fugues shocked the 80s and 90s. From a brief Orr-Ewing marriage, J's eccentric mother was born. She married a Colonel Culme-Seymour, who commanded the Rifle Brigade in the first War, had two children, and was killed on 'Hill 60' in the Ypres Salient, whereupon she

[1] Howard is often thought to have been the model for Anthony Blanche in *Brideshead Revisited*, but Waugh himself suggested that the character was a composite, part-Howard, part-Harold Acton, 'who is a much sweeter and saner man'.
[2] Marie-Jaqueline Lancaster, *Brian Howard: Portrait of a Failure* (1968). Howard is credited with coining the phrase: 'Anybody over the age of 30 seen in a bus has been a failure in life.'
[3] Lady Myra Idina ('Dina') Sackville (1893–1955), a member of the 'Happy Valley' set. She married, first, Captain Euan Wallace; then, in succession, Captain Charles Gordon; Josslyn Hay, 22nd Earl of Erroll; Donald Carmichael Haldeman; and William Vincent Soltau.
[4] The Hon. Beatrice Mary Leslie Hore-Ruthven, daughter of Walter James Hore-Ruthven, 9th Lord Ruthven of Freeland, and Lady Caroline Annesley Gore, married Charles Lindsay Orr-Ewing in 1888. They were divorced in 1894. Their daughter, Janet Beatrix Orr-Ewing (1890–1974) married Captain George Culme-Seymour, who was killed in 1915; and then Geoffrey Harold Wooley, VC (1892–1978), later the Reverend Wooley.

immediately married his second-in-command, who had won the VC saving the same hill: offspring, a boy called Rollo (promising poet) who was killed in the RAF in 1940; and Janetta. He became a clergyman and classics master at Harrow, separated from his wife, and, for some reason, hatred reigned between Janetta and him. (He sound[s] a terrible conventional bigoted prig.) So J. was v. much in her mother's camp, then on her own until Ham Spray and the Partridges, and the whole Strachey-Carrington aura and the dying breath of Bloomsbury became her mental and physical habitat, and with writers and painters for friends. She used to be tremendously farouche, but not now; v. quiet and thoughtful and v. beautiful in a way that grows, rather than bursts on one: slim and light 'un-opulent' – as a girl or boy of 15 with a lovely clear look: fine bones, blue-grey eyes, skin and straight floppy hair the same light colour, usually tied back at the nape to keep it out of the way, like one of Nelson's midshipmen, and a slightly sad or solemn expression, lit with frequent laughter. No vanity at all, and blessed (or burdened) with an involuntary knack of inspiring love, which she always retains as friendship (three marriages & three daughters). The one which for years, might have threatened the worst complications has been Andrew Devonshire, who longed to chuck everything for her. Thank God, although v. fond of him (he still adores her to desper-ation) it was the last thing she ever wanted or thought of. (It was an agonising time for me, as I love both her and Debo.) A good ama-teur painter; but her real passion is cooking, which she does bril-liantly, quietly and with a miraculous lack of fuss: one always seems to be sitting in [a] beautiful tiled-floored kitchen, with a large green parrot in a cage – or out – two dogs and a cat asleep in a basket, with hams and onions hanging from the beams; glass in hand, talking and laughing, while she unhurriedly chops, bastes, stirs and talks (helped by Zora, a nice fat Moorish maid from Ceuta or Tetuan), till suddenly she pulls something out of the oven, and, in a moment, we are all round a table at one end, with candles twinkling and one's knees under a thick scarlet table cloth, toes warmed by one of those bronze charcoal *braseros* underneath, eating something glorious; and only breaking off now and then to draw another cork. Jaime

Parladé – they've been married five or six years, but together much longer – spends much of the day in Málaga or Marbella, or along the coast, building and decorating houses, and laying out gardens – he has a sort of imaginative genius for botany and horticulture. Though his hair is chestnut, he is a sort of Spanish version of Janetta in lightness and harmony and charm, so that they look very akin; a Bohemian breakaway from smart, prosperous, v. anglophile, bridge-playing parents. (His mum, Doña Paloma, was a famous beauty, by all accounts.) He's also v. funny, loves history and painting, and knows a great deal. Bisexual in an effortless Mediterranean way – a bit like Napier Alington[1] was – but worshipping J., as she does him. Also staying were Frances Partridge, busily translating a book from Spanish into English, and Xan and Magouche (who you know all about),[2] then, a few days later, Robin Campbell,[3] also an old friend; he used to paint, is now on the Arts Council; gets about very slowly, as he was one of the officers on the famous commando raid on Rommel's desert headquarters, when nearly everyone was killed, including Geoffrey Keyes, the leader.[4] Only Bob Laycock got back to our lines after three weeks, disguised as a Bedouin; poor Robin caught a whole burst of machine-gun fire, which took his leg off just below the thigh, difficult for an artificial leg. The Germans were v. decent to him. (They had landed from a submarine.) A few people came to meals, now and then: Rosemary Strachey (painter) who lives near, quite often, also Gerald Brenan and his girl Linda,[5] who translated all S. John of the Cross's poems for Gerald's Life of the Saint, and is now teaching herself Greek. Xan and I were made

[1] Napier Sturt (1896–1940), 3rd Baron Alington, a friend of Balasha's, who lived at Long Crichel House; PLF stayed there several times before the war.
[2] Xan Fielding had left Daphne for Magouche Phillips – see pp. 287–8.
[3] Robin Francis Campbell (1912–85), CBE, DSO, soldier and painter, married to Lady Mary Sybil, née St Clair-Erskine, daughter of the 5th Earl of Rosslyn (and sister of Hamish).
[4] Keyes won a posthumous Victoria Cross for leading this botched operation, intended to kill or capture Rommel.
[5] Lynda Nicholson-Price (1943–2011), poet and translator, who had been Brenan's companion since 1968.

to do a lot of reading aloud from Sappho and Æschylus. There were some gay and amusing Spanish friends of Jaime's on Christmas day lunch – which was out of doors, on a leafy terrace, one of whom was called Escobar, which, remembering frequent mentions of your friend Willy E., made me prick up my ears. He was about 70, with a beaky nose and Habsburg jaw, quite a well-known playwright, v. proud (Jaime says) of a title he'd just inherited from an uncle, viz. Marqués de las Marismas del Guadalquivir – the Guadalquivir lagoons![1] (I don't blame him.) He had had a diplomat brother, but [also] called Luis, who had been *en poste* in the twenties in Belgrade, he wasn't sure about Bucharest – he died about then. It's probably a different one.

The house was built by Jaime from a tumbledown farmhouse and an old Moorish tower, high up above a green valley of overlapping pine-clad hills, (not another house in sight), down which flows a swift rocky stream, the Guadalmina. There is so much water that the garden, descending in steep hillside in layers, is a wilderness of trees and flowers and marvellous strange evergreens and cork oaks – it made us waterless Maniots very *rêveurs* [dreamy] … The day after Christmas we went to a remote village just north of Málaga, where people from all the surrounding villages – shepherds, ploughmen etc. – gather every year for strange competitions of music and dancing – only men, wearing amazing hats like tea-cosies entirely made out of flowers – to the tunes of lutes, violins, African-looking drums and brass discs – like the ancient crotala – not castanets – clashed together at high speed between middle finger and thumb. The dances were sort of rustic *malagüeñas*.[2] Everyone was drunk and happy. When it was over, we had one of those late Spanish lunches at a *guinguette* beside the sea, haunted by sailors: *angulas* [elvers], those tiny eels by the thousand, and delicious soles; then looking at the carved choir stalls in the cathedral and the archbishop's palace and home. In the evenings, lots of music, then dictionary-game

---

[1] Luis Escobar Kirkpatrick, known as Luis Escobar (1908–91), 7th Marqués de las Marismas del Guadalquavir, author, playwright and theatre director.
[2] A dance native to Málaga, Spain, that is a variety of the fandango.

and *bouts-rimés*[1] and talk by a huge fire. I had a lovely room with a writing table and managed to get a lot of correcting work done, and felt virtuous. There were long walks in the hills, some of it through forests of pine and oak, streams running along deep gorges, on the edge of great thickets of *maquis* and *garrigue*. In one of these I came on five wild boars, two of them huge, with great ridges of bristles, rootling in the undergrowth.

For New Year, we all set off westwards in two cars, stopping at various *tiendas* and *fondas* on the way for drinks and tapas – usually chorizo, in my case (I've a passion for it): along the coast, past the rock of Gibraltar, looking enormous and fierce, with the Moroccan coast looming the other side of the straits, down to Tarifa, the southernmost point of Europe, exactly half a mile S. of Cape Matapan, the tip of the Mani! It's still a flat-roofed semi-Moorish town with a constant wind blowing. Jaime explained that the inhabitants are all slightly insane from this, and are known locally as *los aventados* [winnowing forks] – they look it! *Le vent qui vient à travers la montagne me rendra fou …*[2] We drove to the top of a great ridge and looked down on Cape Trafalgar, and got to Cadiz about sunset, where we heard the New Year being rung in by all the bells of the town – the oldest continuously inhabited one in Europe, some say – in the Cathedral Square. A marvellous town, jutting out into the Atlantic in a great ring of ramparts, full of domes and belfries and huge tropical trees grown from seeds planted by conquistadors returning from the new world. Lots of Roman remains in the museum, but, above all, many Zurbaráns[3] – I love him. We stayed there two nights, going next day along the coast to Sanlúcar at the mouth of the Guadalquivir, full of New Year crowds holidaymaking and very nice, and ate delicious shrimps and eels and *percebes* [goose barnacles] in a riverside booth, and

---

[1] A game in which players construct a poem by being given a rhyme and inventing the line that precedes it.

[2] 'Le vent qui vient à travers la montagne/ Me rendra fou!', from 'Guitare' (1866) by Victor Hugo.

[3] Francisco de Zurbarán (1598–1664), artist nicknamed the 'Spanish Caravaggio'.

watched a liner steaming upstream towards Seville in a great cloud of gulls, while a school of dolphins curvetted out to sea. On the way back we stopped to look at some lovely stables of a Madame Thierry – one of the great sherry growing dynasties in those parts – filled with scores of beautiful grey horses, slightly dappled, cousins of the Lipizzaners of Vienna, and groomed like ballerinas.

Our return journey next day took us inland to Jerez, where we went and looked – only the men, because the *Cartuja* is severely enclosed – to the Gothic Carthusian monastery where the Cadiz Zurbaráns came from; then on to Arcos de la Frontera, built on a spike on an enormous and dizzy cliff, one of the outposts of the *reconquista*, before Ferd. and Isabella finally recaptured Granada (Darling, I know you know much more about all this than I do![1] So do forgive any involuntary teaching to suck eggs!) There is a nice old English Duquesa de Arcos here, that Janetta and Jaime and I went to see a few years ago. We hadn't time now, so we slunk about the little town rather furtively, for fear of being espied from the battlements. Then on to Ronda, which I know you know well. (I first got to know it 20 years ago, when I went to stay with an anthropologist friend, Julian Pitt-Rivers, who was living at Grazalema, in the Sierra Rubeia a few miles off. He wrote a book about it, v. good, called *People of the Sierra*.[2] He finally eloped with Margot Primo de Rivera, the Spanish ambassadress in London, and settled in the Dordogne; now chief professor of Anthropology at London University. We went to see the de la Cerda palace there, belonging to relations of your friend with the bristle, the D. of Parcent. I think I first heard about the Knight of Ronda from you. There's a marvellous secret staircase going right down through the rock to the river that gushes along the canyon below.) This time we looked over the old palace of some friends of Jaime's called the Marqueses de Salvatierra, built on the lip of the gorge, full of rather clumsy touching portraits, with marvellous patios and suitably gloomy salons, of the type you must know v. well. We left Xan and

[1] Balasha's husband had been a Spanish diplomat.
[2] Published in 1954.

Magouche here, and so home to Tramores, J&J's house, which is not far off – one hour – and still in the Sierra de Ronda.

But we were back near Ronda in a few days, to stay in a farmhouse belonging to Jaime's father (he has them dotted all over the place), more like a charming country house, so noble is the Andalusian village style of building. Joan and Jaime and I went for long rides through the rolling country and forests of cork oak on rather palomino-like horses with long blonde manes and tails, heavy Spanish saddles and tin box-stirrups, and that lovely and tireless Andalusian gait. It's the most beautiful, rolling, russet-coloured country, each skyline ending in fold on eccentric fold of sierra, every plain and mountain range gridded with beautifully planted olives so that everything is striped and crisscrossed, except where spinneys of cork-oak cloud the hill tops. It was lovely to see huge flocks of sheep grazing – much bigger than any in Greece – and herds of black and dark brown pigs rootling under the oaks. Huge expanses of sky and racing clouds. Lovely, too, to be in a horse-civilisation again, with farmers and shepherds and swineherds all riding beautifully, legs almost straight on long stirrup-leathers and black sombreros, occasionally, if they are herding *vacas bravas* [wild cattle] for bull-breeding, equipped with long Quixotic lance-like poles. The villages were all on hilltops, all snow white as if a flock of doves had settled there, each with a belfry, a dome or the wreck of an Almoravid fortress. At Ronda la Vieja, there is an old Roman theatre on the edge of a windy gorge. We drank and sang a lot by the fire, after a great feast in the farmhouse kitchen.

On the morrow, we went over to the other side of Ronda, while Magouche, aided by Xan, is turning another farm into a charming rustic house – all thick white walls and tiles, the same style as Tramores. It's not inhabitable yet, except for their quarters. (There's been rather an upheaval re. Xan and Magouche finally falling into each other's arms, after nearly doing so for a year or two; which leaves poor Daph alone. It hadn't been going well for some time. Once again, I – we – are terribly fond of all concerned. It all spells unhappiness for Daph, I'm afraid, though it's all taken place in a friendly and unexplosive way ... but still. At least X and M seem deliriously happy …) Magouche and Xan gave a great midday banquet on the terrace: all of us, and Bunny (David) Garnett[1] and his daughter. They had driven over from Gerald Brenan's, where they were staying. Gerald and Bunny are old friends and rivals, both 80-something. Bunny had first married Frances Partridge's sister, then Angelica, Vanessa Bell and Duncan Grant's daughter, and, for the last two or three years, has had a rather possessive, quasi-paternal crush on Magouche (they are splendid old boys!) – so, of course, looks on Xan with rather a questioning, not very good-tempered eye. Anyway, it all went off well and was great fun. Joan and I stayed on with X and M for two nights, the first guests, in a still rather wet room and a fire smoking like anything but v. cheerful, nevertheless, the house looking v. romantic with kerosene lamps.

When we got back to Janetta's, we thought we might be staying a bit too long (the other guests left); but it seemed all right, luckily, and J and J formed a marvellous plan of motoring to Madrid with us, v. slowly, as that's where we had to return from; and *ainsi fut dit, ainsi fut fait!* (if that's the phrase I'm after!). It was the most lovely journey. I forgot to say that Joan, Magouche, Xan and I drove over to Gerald Brenan's for luncheon. He lives with Linda the poetess in non-sexual cohabitation, in a charming little house, full of books and Carrington pictures outside an inland village called Alhaurín, not far from Malaga (Bunny had just left). We sat on talking till long after dark …

Tons of fond love, darling Balasha – and to Pomme – from Paddy

XXXX

---

[1] David Garnett (1892–1981), writer and publisher. As a child, he had a cloak made of rabbit skin and thus received the nickname 'Bunny', by which he was known for the remainder of his life.

Paddy wrote this letter of thanks to his friend Pamela Egremont, while staying with Michael Astor at Bruern Abbey in Oxfordshire. He had been Lady Egremont's guest at her house outside Cockermouth, and together they had made a tour into Scotland, described in the letter that follows the one below.

To Pamela Egremont   Bruern
14 August 1975   Churchill
                                       Oxford

Dearest Pamela,

À propos of those children in the churchyard, one has to give people that age full marks for enigmatic directness. I was sitting beside a cedar tree in the quiet eventide last night – in fact, after dinner – when I was joined by a naked little girl – Michael [Astor]'s daughter Judy,[1] aged four – dragging a teddy-bear Hector-like[2] by one of its hind legs – who said: 'What's your name?' I told her, and she said: 'Well, Paddy, you've got to lock Sylvester out, [illegible] tomorrow morning. He's had another bird and Tessa won't leave that horn alone. She's been playing with it all day.' Sylvester turned out to be a huge and rather sinister black and white cat, who was even then stealing across the middle distance: Tessa, a Labrador bitch, hard to discern further off in the shadows, clattering an old ram's horn on the flagstones by the lake, as though in search of any lingering goodness within. With these words, this small night-walker went off stage again, followed by her dragged victim.

I dread the thought that this untidy letter won't reach you before you set sail for Canada on Saturday! The thought of you hobnobbing with Hurons and Blackfoots without having had an <u>inkling</u> of how grateful/braced/haled/consoled/amused/charmed and filled with delight I was and <u>am</u> by that lovely northern sojourn and journey, is – a deep breath! – not to be borne. I'm still psychologically sitting

---

[1] Her name was in fact Polly; her mother's name was Judy.
[2] PLF alludes to the body of the vanquished Hector being dragged in the dust by Achilles.

at that inspiring Cockermouth desk, peering out at heron-level over the Derwent and the woods as the heaps of corrected MSS mount up, with one ear pricked for the click of the slate next door, wondering what new axiom will be chalked there. Happy days!

So strange to think that our Scottish journey was the first time I had crossed the border since landing from a Middle East troopship in 1945![1] I loved Bardrochat[2] and all the ebullient life seething so joyfully there – a rare experience in the last de-tribalised (half? quarter?) of the 20th century. As for the Alain-Fournier experience of our invasion of Monreith[3] – those butterfly-haunted upper reaches of the Limpopo – and the eerie concatenation of coincidences they unloosed – *je n'en reviens pas*.[4]

Mr Sponge[5] has fallen on his feet again! A quiet room with symmetrically striped lawn soaring away into distant woods, diminishing ranks of cedars, a *pièce d'eau* [ornamental lake] tapered by linear perspective, the whirr of a mowing machine somewhere, and the voices of wood pigeons trying to put everyone to sleep. I went for a long sylvan stroll with Michael before dinner last night through glades rank with willow herb run to seed and clumps where, only a month ago, all the Heythrop foxes could have been decadently gloved in magenta,[6] but no longer. Issuing from these woods, with Tessa the horn-fancier pounding among the Friesians, we followed reedy loops of the Evenlode, and it occurred to me that, were one writing a smart Edwardian novel, two of the characters might be the bluff Earl of Windrush, and his son, Little Ld Evenlode, shy and tortuous on the surface, full of hidden depths when you know him …[7]

---

[1] PLF had disembarked in Glasgow.
[2] Bardrochat House, Galloway, owned by the McEwen family since the mid-nineteenth century; now a hotel.
[3] See next letter.
[4] 'I can't get over it'.
[5] PLF refers to R. S. Surtees's novel *Mr Sponge's Sporting Tour* (1849), but also to himself as a 'sponger', able to exploit the hospitality of friends.
[6] A play on the word 'foxglove', found in several of PLF's letters.
[7] The Windrush and the Evenlode are nearby rivers, both tributaries of the Thames.

No more now, dear Pamela, as this will never catch you before take-off: only, let's have a great feast when you return; 1,000 thanks again; and

tons of love
from Paddy

P.S. Just at this point, enter an old-fashioned housemaid in a goffered cap, bearing a neat parcel from you, rife with pills and scarlet slumberwear!

On his Scottish tour with Pamela Egremont, Paddy had stopped to look at his friend Sir Aymer Maxwell's house in Galloway. Sir Aymer was a neglectful laird, who had continued to live in London after inheriting the estate from his grandfather in 1937. By the time it passed to his nephew after Sir Aymer's death, half a century later, Monreith House was in a state of disrepair, and many of the rare trees and plants on the surrounding estate had disappeared.

To Aymer Maxwell   c/o Patrick Kinross
2 September 1975   4 Warwick Avenue
                                              London

Dear Aymer,

How appropriate both those northern postcards arriving together! It <u>was</u> an adventure and a treat, surreptitiously boxing for you at Monreith while you were coxing for me at Kardamyli. We were in two cars, divided between Pamela [Egremont] & her son Harry[1] – v. nice looking, like a young Nicholas Hilliard Elizabethan – and, apart from me, an amazing man aged eighty called Sir Hugh Boustead,[2]

---

[1] The Hon. Harry Hugh Patrick Wyndham (b. 1957), second son of John Edward Reginald Wyndham, 6th Baron Leconfield, and Pamela Wyndham-Quin (1925–2013), styled Lady Egremont.

[2] Colonel Sir Hugh Boustead (1895–1980) represented Great Britain in the Olympics, explored the Western Desert, won the Army lightweight boxing championship, and participated in the 1933 Everest expedition with Eric Shipton. He published his autobiography, *The Wind of Morning*, in 1971.

who deserted from the Navy as a snotty [midshipman] when the first war broke out, enlisted in a highland regiment, was awarded the MC and arrested for desertion on the same day, boxed for the army three times, went thrice up Mt Everest, commanded the Sudan Camel Corps, reconquered Ethiopia in 1940 more or less single-handed, governed various places since, beloved by all the Sheikhs and Emirs of the Trucial States, small, wiry, unmarried, mad blue eyes, rather shy and old-fashioned (e.g. 'I say, Pamela, I hope you won't think it offside if I say that your dress looks ripping?') We picknicked somewhere near Clatteringshaws Loch, and got rather lost after Newton Stewart, picked up the trail near Whauphill, and were instructed to go on till we came to 'a beachy head' – so we understood 'but it's been cut doon', i.e. that beech hedge. We found a silent lodge and drove down that amazing avenue of enormous trees, all gasping with wonder. Glimpses of the lake on our right made us feel we were on the upper reaches of the Limpopo. It was a marvellously hot, silent, windless day. We passed a smart building with a parked car on the left, a venerable ruin hard by, then downhill to the House,[1] which looked inexpressibly romantic, though close-pressed by vegetation, as though all the trees and shrubs had been playing grandmother's steps, closing in. Apart from the cannon from Dirk Hatterick, we were very intrigued with that large unshaped stone, inscribed with primitive lettering – runes? ogham? – standing on the grass.[2] We construed the welcoming Latin inscription over the door, but alas! all was locked. The cupboards beside the doors yielded dismembered fishing rods, cricketing gloves, and the like. So we gazed indoors with our noses flattened against the glass, translating the names over the doors, wondering who had put the buddleias in the vases on the consol tables, peering at the painted gentlemen in breast-plates and full-bottomed wigs. Pamela thought one lady on the right in the gallery might be Arabella Stewart.[3] When we had feasted our eyes

[1] Monreith House, Aymer Maxwell's seat as Laird of Galloway.
[2] Probably the Monreith Cross, a stone inscribed with carvings dating from the tenth century.
[3] Lady Arbella (or Arabella) Stuart (or Stewart) (1575–1615).

there, we went round to the front and up the iron spiral – all locked again – but gazed in over the piano, the books, the typewriter, the hanging stuff on the wall, books beyond; downstairs, into domestic regions, upstairs into rooms charmingly painted with gold piping on the panels and shutters. Even round by the stables, there was no entry, but it was perhaps more tantalising and fascinating that way. The *Grand Meaulnes* comparison was absolutely right. Nothing could have been more romantic and memorable. There were quantities of butterflies everywhere, also birds, and Pamela was very clever at identifying all the rare shrubs which had broken loose and seeded themselves. We explored beyond those almost jungle-swallowed balustrades, descending in terraces and would have liked to have wandered and lingered much more. The surroundings made a marvellous impression of an enormous primeval forest, under a strange and secret spell. It made the outside world, when we tore ourselves away, seem very commonplace.

We spent about five days at Bardrochat chez Rory [McEwen] and Romana,[1] full of pretty, amusing and intelligent children, also [his brother] David and an amusing girl called Caroline Cholmondeley[2] & Karl Miller & his wife & son.[3] It was very noisy and cheerful. Just as we passed the Monreith turning, on the way south again, and talking about our invasion, Pamela turned on the car wireless: a long talk was beginning, entirely devoted to Jane Maxwell, Duchess of Gordon, talking about Monreith, hers and her sister's studies, marriages, etc., and how she managed to recruit nearly 1,000 redcoats by alluring them to take the King's sovereign (I thought it was a shilling) by kissing it from between her lips. Sounds rather fast. And to end up this day of coincidences, there, at Cockermouth, when we got there, was your letter. We drove to London next day and Pamela pushed off to Canada next evening, after a midday feast with Diana Cooper. How nice she is.

[1] The artist and musician Rory McEwen (1932–82), married to Romana von Hofmannsthal.
[2] Caroline Cholmondeley (b. 1952), daughter of the 6th Marquess of Cholmondeley.
[3] Karl Miller (1931–2014), critic, founder of the *London Review of Books*.

I spent the next week at Michael Astor's[1] scribbling away, correcting & pruning. I am in the middle of what I call Mr Sponge's Revising Tour, taking in Chatsworth & Annie Fleming's first, then Cockermouth, Bardrochat & Bruern, now here: I think the blow may fall on Bolton Abbey[2] next ... I was in hospital last week, where they were striking a final blow by turning one's poor old tongue into a sort of hedgehog of radioactive needles for several days, which makes one feel a bit groggy afterwards, but nothing fiendish.[3] Joan, Graham & I have just been for a walk through the woods above Dumbleton, full of scurrying pheasants, elderberry, ragged robin, & willow-herb. Delicious redcurrants, blackcurrants, gooseberries & blackberries, with masses of cream at the end of all meals.

Sachie Sitwell was sitting next to a girl of 8 at luncheon recently. During a silence, the following was overheard: <u>Sachie</u>: 'Do you drive?' <u>Small Girl</u>: 'No.' <u>Sachie</u>: 'You're so wise. Nor do I.' Later, a woman who had been talking to him nonstop, suddenly paused and said, 'But perhaps I'm boring you?' Sachie (testily): 'Never mind! Do go on.' (We had lunch with Sachie at Weston on the way down.) We're not quite sure of plans, but back to Kardamyli within a month, I think, so do come – Graham too, I think. Joan sends *tant de choses* [her love], and thanks for your letter, & is writing.

¡Hasta la vista! Paddy

To Balasha Cantacuzène　　　　　　　c/o Lord Kinross
9 February 1976　　　　　　　　　　　4 Warwick Avenue
　　　　　　　　　　　　　　　　　　London, W2

Darling Balasha,

I've been meaning to write for days, but suddenly everything got into a terrific rush! Towards the end of the month, that is. Xan and Magouche motored up to Athens, I stayed on to get some writing

[1] Bruern Abbey, Oxfordshire.
[2] An estate in Wharfedale, north Yorkshire, owned by the dukes of Devonshire, which takes its name from a ruined twelfth-century Augustinian monastery.
[3] PLF was again being treated for cancer of the tongue.

finished, and flew up next day. They told me they had spent the night at Andritsaina, and climbed up to the Temple of Epikourios Apollo at Bassae under a metre of snow! I wished I had been there. The whole Arcadian landscape was white, the floor of the temple smooth white, only marked with their tracks, and those of crows, hares and foxes!

Next day was a red-letter day. Xan and I flew to Crete, where our old wartime friends had been preparing a banquet in our honour for days. We got out at Canea, where we were met by a swarm of old guerrilla pals, and, after a morning of doing the rounds in the capital, we set out in a fleet of cars for Vaphé in the foothills of the White Mountains, a great lair and stronghold of ours during the resistance, where we were awaited by the Vandoulakis and Petrakis clans. We stopped again and again on the way up the steep stepped village street for *tsikoudia* [raki] and *mézé* – all waiting on tables outside the doors! – swallowing about twenty of the former by the time we got to the scene of the banquet, in the terrace outside the peasant farmhouse. As we came under the archway, there was a great outburst of rifle and pistol fire in the air, and there was sporadic *feu-de-joie* all through the following hours. There were white-haired and whiskered chaps, some of whom we hadn't seen for 33 years – tremendous greetings, embraces, hugs, laughter, reminiscence. It was a blazing sunny day, with a long table – or tables – and blinding white table cloths, stretching away under a bare vine trellis, with olive trees and orange trees all round, all the tumbled tile roofs of the village below, and the glittering snow-white upheaval of the tall mountains above, and a cloudless sky. We had *mézés* again, pillaff of chicken, the lambs roasted on spits, then delicious Cretan '*kaltzounia*' – crescent-shaped cakes of feather light pastry, with white *mizithra* [ricotta] inside. Three different kinds of strong amber-coloured Cretan wine. We were sixty at table, and there was lots of wonderful singing, both '*rizitika*' – foothill songs – and *mantinades*,[1] or couplets, of which X and I remembered lots, to great applause. No speeches, thank God, but endless clashing of glasses, songs, laughter, all [illegible] by gunfire and shouts. Everyone pretty tight

[1] Narratives or dialogues, sung in the rhythm of accompanying music. Often one verse elicits another, and so on.

and very happy. It was nearly dark when tearful farewells came. One and half hour's sleep, then another, smaller feast in the old Venetian harbour of Canea, sleep, and back, feeling rather strange but absolutely OK, to Athens next morning. Phew!

In Athens we saw Barbara and Niko Ghika, also George Katsimbalis, & Eddie Gathorne-Hardy and had luncheon at the Embassy (nice people called Francis & Hazel Brooks-Richards[1]). Then, last Wednesday, we left: motoring from Athens to Patras, across the gulf at Rion-Antirrion, then across Epirus to Igoumenitza, caught the Corfu ferry, dined with an old friend called Marie Aspioti,[2] got up next day in the dark and caught the motor ferry which carried us up the lee of the snow-covered Albanian mountains and across to Brindisi at sunset, where we landed in time to motor to the airport and meet Joan who had left London that morning. A joyous feast in a fish restaurant, then, after looking at a couple of Norman churches and the pillars which mark the end of the Appian Way, we drove to Lecce – made vermiculated palaces and churches – then across white and green park-like Apulia to Otranto. The floor of the Byzanto-Norman cathedral there is a marvel – huge, inlaid with Bayeux tapestry-like mosaics dealing with a mad confusion of pagan & Christian scriptures, philosophy & mysticism – Adam and Eve, Solomon, the Q of Sheba, Alexander the Great, Christ, King Arthur, Jonah and the whale – half-classical, half-Dark Ages, half-Norman, half-Saracen … It was turned into a mosque for 13 months by Mahomet II, the capturer of Constantinople. There is a wonderful crypt, countless different-capitalled columns, like the mesquita at Cordoba. At dusk we went

---

[1] The British ambassador, Sir Francis 'Brooks' Richards (1918–2002), and his wife Hazel. During the Second World War, Brooks Richards had been a director of operations for SOE in North Africa, and in the autumn of 1944 he joined the staff of Duff Cooper, minister-resident charged with re-opening the British embassy in Paris. His wife was the daughter of SOE officer Stanley Price Williams.

[2] Marie Aspioti (1909–2000), writer, poet and publisher, who ran the British Council Institute in Corfu when PLF and Joan came to stay with her in 1946. According to one of those who knew her, Aspioti 'loved England', and 'gave her whole life to the Institute'. Like PLF, she would be dismayed by British policy in Cyprus in the mid-1950s.

to Kalimera, the chief village of the Salentine Greeks, who have been there either since Magna Grecia, or since Nicephorus Phocas, and Xan and I had long talks over wine in their extraordinary dialect. On to Taranto, in the tracks of Normans, Byzantines, Frederick II of Hohenstaufen, Hannibal and Fabius Cunctator ... Next day we drove to the old Doric temple of Metapontum, on the instep of Italy, on the Apulian-Calabrian border; then turned inland and north, over wave on wave of mountains, ending up at dark in the Samnite-Campanian town of Avellino, rather dismal, but fun because we were all together. Then – yesterday! – we drove over several more airy and beautiful mountain ranges to the lofty village of Caserta Vecchia, where we gazed down like eagles on the huge Bourbon Palace and fountains, far below at C. Nuovo, with Vesuvius on one side, Naples on the other, then the Tyrrhense sea, Procida, Ischia and Capri ... We gazed at scores of misshapen Pre-Roman tufa carved earth-goddess seated statues, each nursing ten or fifteen swaddled papooses ... rather eerie, in the Museum at Capua. We picnicked off wine, bread, sardines & Cretan cheese, leaning against a ruined tufa wall by a gleaming plantation of poplars on the banks of the Volturno river. (A few miles away, we saw where it is crossed by the railway bridge, from which Lafcadio, in *Les Caves du Vatican*,[1] pushes the unoffending stranger from his railway carriage.) We stopped at several more churches in the afternoon, driving between the Volscian, then the Alban and Sabine Hills – avoiding Rome as money is running low! – and north to Orvieto, getting here at midnight, where (having telephoned earlier) a delicious *zuppa de verdura* was waiting. This is a Tuscan farmhouse a few miles from Siena, inhabited by Magouche's daughter Maro Gorky, who is married to Matthew Spender, Stephen's son, both painters, and young, enthusiastic and charming. Two daughters (Saskia and Cosima). Matthew makes his own wine – delicious, and is adored by all the local Tuscan peasants and villagers, and even plays the clarinet in the local band. It's morning now, and I'm scribbling this in a glassed in loggia overlooking a dilapidated Tuscan farmyard

[1] See footnote on p. 103.

and trellis, then wave on wave of Chianti vineyards and olive groves, with a castle here and there. It's terribly cold, but sunny. We've just discovered – *ô maleur*! – that we've left all our passports in Avellino … Never mind. Must stop now, darling Balasha and darling Pomme. Please send all your news to London. I'll write more later on.

Meanwhile, 1,000 tons of fond love from both of us, Paddy

To Xan Fielding   Kardamyli
last days of March 1976 (perhaps *the* last day)   Messenia
                               Greece

'Άγαπητὲ Σύντεκνε' [Dear God-brother],

I've been meaning to write for ages, too, and now yours puts me to shame. What a lovely time that was, and what a comic and disjointed one too – here, and on the road, and at Anane,[1] and in Venice. You and Magouche <u>were</u> sports to switch plans on the way to Venice like that, and on the spur of the moment – 'Done in the smack of a whip, and on horseback too!', as Sir Benjamin Backbite says[2] in *The School for Scandal* – and I was so impressed, I'll never forget it. That's the way to live.

First things first. I'll get down to *Monte Carlo*[3] the moment I'm free, and it shouldn't be long now. I've got your deadline firmly in mind, and you know they call me Deadline Dick … I do vow I won't cause anxiety. Jock Murray's managed to goad me into a state of fidgetty literary immediacy – he's busy doing to my text what I'm going to try to do to yours, viz. raking it with the eye of a friendly hawk. Meanwhile, final tasks crowd in amazingly. I'm finding it almost impossible to get back to work, too, but have managed at last. What a sigh one heaves when that barrier is passed! It's like going through the Looking-Glass, and all looks

[1] Unidentified: possibly the name of a house.
[2] It is Crabtree who says this: *School for Scandal*, Act II, Scene 2.
[3] Xan Fielding's book *The Money Spinner: Monte Carlo and Its Fabled Casino* was published in 1977.

different. I wish I were a better concentrator: feel like a grasshopper harnessed to a plough.

I enjoyed London,[1] but I wish you and Magouche had been in Chapel St. That marvellous earth was stopped.[2] But the great thing was that Janetta was there and I don't know what I would have done without her; she <u>does</u> make a difference, as one's few friends do. The visit to the hospital went triumphantly well – I touch wood lest hubris bring down nemesis! – and Drs Lederman and Clifford kept patting me and each other on the back and grinning like turnip-lanterns. Patrick [Kinross] looked rather thin and peaked, but got visibly better. I bet he would look better still if he ate something nicer than those tired old nondescript 'Monty'-esque dogs' brekkers[3] that seem to be his staple. I must say, after nearly a month in London, it is marvellous to [get] back to the food here – I don't mean its gastronomic elaborations, but the simplicity and the freshness. It's a treat to see Lela, at a quarter past five, coming up from below with a colander full of green things just plucked up. Lentils tomorrow but not too much: I must have gorged like a hog while away, I daren't name the figure the scales showed on return, but I'm 'going down fast sir', as the imaginary Dickensian O. Twist scale-side lift boy murmurs, taking over from his gloating Pickwickian Fat Boy colleague as I step naked onto the device. There's a slim man trying to climb in,[4] and it's all his.

I envy you both the planting fever, and all the goings and comings and municipal larceny! My advice is, don't look on all this

[1] During this stay in London PLF wrote to Joan about a visit to Diana Cooper, who had been in bed when he arrived, 'but leaped out of it when I suggested dining, so we had a lovely time at an empty Didier's where a v. drunk unknown young woman, after gazing all through the meal, said to Diana on the way out, she was so beautiful she had to kiss her, and did so'.
[2] i.e. PLF no longer had a bolthole in Chapel Street.
[3] Field Marshal Bernard Law Montgomery (1887–1976) was famous for insisting on a full English breakfast, hence the expression 'The Full Monty'. Anything less – such as cereal or porridge – was a 'dog's breakfast'.
[4] 'Imprisoned in every fat man a thin one is wildly signalling to be let out,' Cyril Connolly, *The Unquiet Grave* (1944).

as Freudian displacement activity, which thought seems to exercise you, but charge in full tilt! Now's the time, with momentum, excitement and steam-up! It wanes later, and is hard to revive, but while the heat's on, you are a life force – horticulturally, architecturally, hydraulically and aesthetically irresistible – and everything goes down before you. It's odd, but so; people recognise the state and seem to welcome one's roughshod trampling. At such moments, a couple becomes an amalgam of Rameses, Hadrian, Pomona, Ceres, Balbus, Babel, Sardanapalus, Priapus, Contrary Mary, Flora and a steam-roller. 'Δύναμι στα χέρια σας!' ['Strength to your hands!'], as they say here.

I wish I knew why my writing gets smaller and more cramped and illegible as the page goes on. I think it's a subconscious intention not to write long letters – in order to get back to work – which limits me to a page, onto which I then try to cram more than it can hold ...

Poor Balasha died last week, the result of a ghastly operation two months ago – a long letter from Pomme was waiting, a marvellous one, which I'll show when we next meet. She drove off with her in a truck all the way to Băleni, to put her in the Cantacuzène vault there. The whole village turned up at the church, all in floods and kissing Pomme's hands and cheeks ... I have written a most inadequate short tribute for *The Times*, and sent it off but they probably won't print it. I can hardly believe it. We corresponded about 2 or 3 times a month, Joan too.

I stopped at Venice on the way back, and missed you both dreadfully as I clocked into the Accademia.[1] I got a marvellous corner double room for the price of a single – 7,000![2] They are nice. The table looked lovely, not quite finished, but all in train. I went out to the Arsenale to look at the Greek Lion Fr. Morosini stole from Piraeus, with runes on its shoulder

[1] A *pensione* on the Dorsoduro, near the Grand Canal.
[2] About £40.

scratched there by Harald Handrade.[1] Had dinner with A-M. Cicogna,[2] prompted by M[ichael] Astor. I let out a great big but silent Boo as I went past Florians,[3] and sighed in the bookbinders. Morin, the nice trat[toria], was shut. Slunk off to The Danieli for a late swig, there was the solitary figure in the check hacking-jacket in the same chair the pianist playing Granados …[4]

Joan sends lots of love, and lots from me to you both! Paddy

To Jock Murray   Kardamyli
undated [August–September 1976]   Messenia
                                                    Greece

Dear Jock,

I think, subject to your agreement, that a marvellous solution to the title question has descended on us, viz. *A Time of Gifts*.[5] You will see the relevance in the attached poem of Louis MacNeice's, my old pal.[6] It gets over my growing feelings against the down-beat note of *Winter Journey* and all your objections to *Parallax*; and if the title is printed in two lines, it would be easy to make the O of 'of' the loophole for Johnny [Craxton]'s sunburst. I do hope you like this. I think it is just what we were searching for: indefinite,

[1] The massive stone lion, which stands three metres high, dates from about 360 BC. From the first or second century it stood in a prominent position in the Greek port of Piraeus, becoming a landmark there until it was looted by the Venetian naval commander Francesco Morosini in 1687. The shoulders and flanks of the lion are covered in runes, carved in the eleventh century. It is generally held that these were carved by Scandanavian mercenaries in the services of the Byzantine Emperor; attempts to link these runes to the last great Viking King Harald Hardade (c.1015–66) have not gained widespread acceptance.
[2] Countess Anna-Maria Cicogna, a friend of Nancy Mitford's.
[3] Caffè Florian, in the Piazza San Marco: established in 1720, it claims to be the oldest coffee house in the world.
[4] Enrique Granados Campiña (1867–1916), Spanish pianist and composer.
[5] 'For now the time of gifts is gone', from 'Twelfth Night' by Louis MacNeice (1948).
[6] PLF had come to know MacNeice in Athens in 1951, when he took up a post as British Council representative there.

a poetical quotation, susceptible to many interpretations, and all of them lucky and charming ones; euphonious, balanced, looking well on the page, memorable, and agreeable to say. An explanatory subtitle would convey the book's more specific contents. Everybody we've tried it on is transported by it, as though it were the *titre juste* which has been waiting for us to discover it all along.

What I suggest is <u>not</u> to print the relevant verse of Louis's appended poem, with the others, before the Introduction, but to make a readjustment of the end of the penultimate section – Christmas morning in Bingen – and attach a footnote.[1] See overleaf for the copy of the poem. I have changed 'the' to 'a' in the adapted title, as 'the' would be too like 'the forgotten years' 'the productive years' 'the year of hope' and 1,000 other dog-eared literary stand-bys. And I think the contrast with *A Time to Keep Silence* all to the good!

Full of hope,
Yours ever
Paddy

V. many thanks for the bank-transfusion.

Having finished work on the first volume of his account of 'the Great Trudge', Paddy accepted an invitation from his friend Robin Fedden to join an expedition to the Himalayas.

To Jock Murray   Tos Mts
5 October 1976   Himachal Pradesh
                                                    India

Dear Jock,

This is a hurried note, as one of our party, Myles Hildyard,[2] is going down to Kulu with a sherpa tomorrow – to meet us later on – and will be near a pillar box in two days.

---

[1] This suggestion was not adopted.
[2] Myles Hildyard (1914–2005) had fought in Crete in the war and won the Military Cross.

We've been trudging for a week now – up to the terminal moraine of the Parvati river and back, and left two days ago up the Tos Valley. We are encamped among giant boulders, a ledge on one side of it, horses grazing above, for the last time, as we are sending them back tomorrow (too stiff going) with most of our stuff except bare essentials, and carry on – 5 of us and 5 sherpas. The peaks all round us are deep in snow, but not quite as deep as the mountaineers would like, but never mind. We are striving towards the pass that will lead us into Lahaul, all Buddhist and Tibetan speaking – when one gets down to inhabited regions. We are 13,000 feet up – not v. high – v. tired and it's pretty cold, hence the badness of my writing, on a map case, in mittens. We are acclimatising as fast as we can, all felt pretty awful to begin with but, touch wood, all seems to be coming right.

We'll be back in Kulu on the 18th, then Delhi via Chandigarh, so % Imperial Hotel there is the best address, if needed. I do hope the book is going well, am v. excited about it. Mr Keay's book on India[1] is splendid, and is going from hand to hand like a hot cake and mining golden opinions.

No more for the moment. Getting dark – 6 p.m. – and we are about to assemble for our nightly double whiskey, then rice, dal, potatoes and chapatis and to bed about 8, which seems like midnight.

All the best, and love to all
Yrs ever
Paddy

[1] Probably John Keay's *Into India*, published by John Murray in 1973, but perhaps a proof copy of his *When Men and Mountains Meet: The Explorers of the Western Himalayas, 1820–75*, which Murray would publish in 1977.

To Diana Cooper   Puri
1 January 1977   Orissa[1]

Darling Diana,
    Happy New Year <u>and with knobs on</u>!
    Joan and I are in a charming hotel on the slopes of the Bay
of Bengal, resting for 3 days after our many travels which, on my
side, began immediately after that lovely feast at [the] Ghikas,
just over 3 months ago. What glory to be able at last to tackle the
great jam – of which this is the first log loosened – which has been
mounting up.
    I won't tell you about our Himalayan adventures in detail, as
I kept a sort of diary in my instalment letter given to Joan, which
she has typed out and of which I'll send a copy in the fullness of
time – only to say that it was amazing, and, I think, enjoyed most
of all by me, as being a greenhorn to the game, compared to all the
other old hands. The expedition was overcast for a spell by poor
Robin [Fedden] feeling rotten – we all did at various moments –
but it struck him at a horrible time, in the Sara Umaga La pass –
v. high,[2] deep in snow and ice; but he rose above it like a hero, and
all was well. I'd never camped on a glacier before. Beyond this pass,
the skewers that pegged down our little tents had no grip in the
fresh and falling snow, so the 6 Sherpas in attendance – marvels!! –
talk about Peaseblossom, Cobweb, Moth and Mustard-seed![3] –
had to weigh the sides down with great lumps of granite and
quartzite: we lay zipped up inside our shrunk prisons from 6 p.m.
to 8 a.m., flakes mounting up, till one dug oneself out when day
began to glimmer … The descent from the north side was stepping
down from glacier to glacier, through great snowfields covered with
those caked ice-tables, which the others took for granted, but not
me: vast lumps of rock that is, some twice the size of a London bus,

[1] An Indian state on the Bay of Bengal, now known as Odisha.
[2] About 16,000 feet above sea level.
[3] Fairies attendant on Titania in *A Midsummer Night's Dream*.

poised on pedestals of ice, blue green and diaphanous as lalique when sunbeams fought their way down into this wilderness, some as small as the toadstool marking the Lost Boys' chimney, on which Capt. Hook singed himself. We worked our way down into the wild and empty provinces of Lahaul, inhabited by a few Tibetan-speaking Buddhists, and their yaks, with a few lamaseries cowering under snow in the clefts; down, down, to the thunderous and jade-green Chandra river at the bottom of its canyon, with taller and taller ranges soaring above. (Eventually, it turns into the Chenab and flows into the Indus, and joins the Arabian gulf ...) Three mountaineering weeks ended with a climb to a remote eyrie of a village where all leather is forbidden, involving a lightning change into gymshoes, rope belts, hidden watches, where all is sacred to a mysterious, pre-Aryan god called Jumloo. One of the eeriest places on earth ...

We all separated at Delhi, and I went to Simla for a month – scarcely a white face in those airy lanes, but haunted by many a parental ghost and by Mrs Hawksbee, the Phantom Rickshaw, Kim, the Gadsbys and Lurgan and Sheila-land Sahibs.[1] Except for Vice-regal Lodge – now a sort of Hindu All-Souls – and some surviving four-posters above the clouds – the architecture is not distinguished: lots of half-timbering, pebble dash and spiky turrets of dark red corrugated iron and frills of fretted woodwork; but atmosphere extraordinary, air intoxicating, and scenery – topped by deodar-clad Jakka Hill and processions of Bandarlog[2] holding each others' tails – breathtaking: hundreds of mountain ranges flowing away in every direction, sierras with thin level strata of pale blue vapour up to their shoulders, like the bones of a half-created world shaking themselves out of primordial smoke; with the snowy peaks we had just been swarming – Laboul, Spiti, Kulu – floating and glittering on the north and eastern skyline, and the whole of the Mid Himalayan Chain, the threshold of China and Tibet. I managed to wangle my way into staying in the former Hot Weather Govt.

[1] All figures from Kipling stories.
[2] A term used in Kipling's *The Jungle Book* to describe monkeys of the Seeonee Jungle.

House of Governors of the Punjab, under Jakko Hill; lawns, flagstaff and bandstand poised over the void, deodars ascending, and a huge weeping-willow growing from a shoot of the one over Napoleon's grave at St. Helena; and next to the arbour where I worked, a tomb-stone saying: 'The grave of/ COONAH/ the faithful dog/ and affectionate companion/ of/ Lady Gomm/ through 12 years/ May 11, 1851'. Only six years pre-Mutiny ... From Simla I went to Lahore, now in Pakistan, which seemed pure Arabian Nights. From the Zam-Zammah gun there, I followed the Kim and lama trail[1] to Amritsar, Amballah, Saharunpur, then up into the Hills again to Dehra Dun and Mussoori, down through Meerut to meet Joan, who fluttered down at Delhi from Kardamyli on the 15th Dec. We went off to that huge Rajput fortress at Gwalior, the early Buddhist ruins at Sanchi, and by train to Lucknow. Oh, the Residency! It must have been one of the finest Regency buildings in the world before the siege. The Moslem part of the town is split between the Shia and the Sunni sects of Islam (Imaginary Guide: 'This is where the Shi'ites live'. Traveller: 'Really? Then give me the Sunni side.') Benares for Christmas: Father Krishna's sleigh drawn by white oxen ... Carol-singing in St. Mary's Church there: 'Good King Wenceslas', 'Once in Royal David's City' etc. Congregation 5 English, 10 Eurasian, 15 Indians. An elephant passed the lychgate on emerging, hayload stuck well back out of trunk reach, then camels with burdens in sacks, perhaps myrrh or frankincense! ... Calcutta is near here. Bangkok next week. Please send news.

Tons of fond love,
Paddy

... Phew!!

---

[1] In Kipling's novel *Kim* (1901), the vagabond hero carries a message up the Great Trunk Road, accompanied by a Tibetan lama. The journey begins by the Zamzama gun outside the Lahore Museum. PLF planned to write a long article, similar to the one he had written on the Danube, following in Kim's footsteps.

'Feeble and I have been reading outloud A Time of Gifts,*' Betjeman wrote to Paddy on 24 April 1978. 'We are very sorry to have finished it for it is a life-enhancer, a poem and an adventure story.'*

To John Betjeman   Kardamyli
14 July 1978   Messenia
                                                          Greece

Dear John,

Just hobbled back here and found Joan and Graham, and also your marvellously bracing letter about *A Time of Gifts*. Thank you so much for letting me doss down in No 29. I <u>did</u> enjoy it and can't tell you what a boon it was; and please thank Feeble[1] from me for that jolly valedictory feast. I can't get over meeting Mrs T. S. Eliot. Was there just a touch of a portlier Mrs Thatcher? Anyway, it was splendid and Mark was in tearing form.

I forgot to leave three quid, about right for a short Athens call made after dinner, but not loquacious, so it's among the addenda. The other items are a slightly topped-and-tailed Eddie obituary,[2] – which *The Times* doesn't seem to be using – in case Alan[3] wanted it among others for the *London Magazine*. I think you ought to do one as well, more chatty and with a bit of *oratio recta* [direct speech]. The other addendum is something I cut out of *The Spectator* 24 years ago. I came across it recently and it seemed so remarkable that I got it copied, also with a translation of Helfrid Uggins's 'Helbatrawss', in case Baudelaire isn't handy.[4] I wish I knew who Anselm Chilworth was, whether it's his real name, and whether he's still alive. A king among men …

Love from Paddy

[1] Betjeman's nickname for his 'beloved other wife', Lady Elizabeth Cavendish. Her sister-in-law Debo dubbed her 'Deacon', a reference to her pious Anglicanism.
[2] Edward Gathorne-Hardy had died on 18 June 1978. PLF's obituary remains unpublished.
[3] Alan Ross, editor of the *London Magazine*.
[4] A translation-cum-parody of Baudelaire's poem 'L'Albatros', presented as the work of the cockney poet 'Helfred Uggins', published in *The Spectator* in 1954 in an article entitled 'The Cockney Renaissance' by Kingsley Amis, writing under the pseudonym 'Anselm Chilworth'.

Magouche Fielding had introduced Paddy to Bruce Chatwin in 1970. Chatwin, then only thirty, was trying to write a book about nomads. In August of that year he came to Kardamyli to stay with the Leigh Fermors. Chatwin admired and envied Paddy, who recognised in the younger man a kindred spirit. The two had much in common: erudition, energy, loquaciousness, interest in and knowledge of an extraordinarily wide range of subjects. Towards the end of 1977 Chatwin's first book, In Patagonia, *was published. He received several appreciative letters from established writers, including Graham Greene, who wrote to say that it was 'one of my favourite travel books'.*

To Bruce Chatwin   Kardamyli
18 January 1978   Messenia
                                               Greece

Dear Bruce,

By an awful string of postponements, temporary loss, movement etc., it has come about that I've only just read *In Patagonia*: finished it this morning, and don't want to let the sun go down without writing to say what a marvellous book it is. Learned, amusing, the aestheto-polymath glance, beautifully written, enterprising and fascinating all round. I wish it was half as long again – not, here, for an extension of these particular travels after the last page (though of course one would like that too), but I wish you had let it off the leash a bit more, to luxuriate and ramify. I think you are too strict with yourself, out of a totally baseless dread of boring; and chop it up into <u>too</u> short sections, so that one feels a bit like a child being rushed through a picture gallery, and always lagging behind, longing to dwell … How splendid it is, when you forget the salami discipline, and let it rip! I think, out of avoiding sloppiness, you sometimes give things you are worried by and things that leave you cold, the same deadpan or poker-faced treatment. This looks like criticism, but is the opposite by corollary! It's a splendidly original book and I've got a very clear impression of P. and your adventures. What about Great-Uncle Charlie's memoirs?[1] They are so fascinating – surely they could make a whole book? In our 4th edition of the E. Britannica, it toys with the idea of the Mylodon[2] being still extant in Patagonia; as they could have just then.[3] The Hesketh Prichard you mention[4] must have been the father of a pal of mine called Alfgar H.P.[5] I knew that his father was a great traveller, and, when a soldier, founded the [illegible] school at Hythe.[6] Alfgar's mother was a sort of lady-in-waiting, re-married with the amazing name of Lady Elizabeth Motion.[7] Alfgar was an SOE pal, v. reckless and dashing, parachuted to the 'resistance' in Hungary in 1942, and vanished from human ken under probably frightful circumstances.

Parts of the book were so funny I read them aloud to Joan – who'd already read and loved the book – and there was much laughter. *Qué genio!* etc Jam all through!

[1] Charles Milward, a cousin of Chatwin's grandmother Isobel, had run away to sea at the age of twelve, and kept a journal of his adventures. Shipwrecked on Cape Horn, he settled at Punta Arenas in southern Chile and became British consul. Early in the twentieth century he had sent Isobel a tuft of skin from the body of an animal found in a cave, believed to be a brontosaurus.
[2] A genus of giant ground sloth that lived in the Patagonia area of South America until roughly 10,000 years ago, now generally accepted to be extinct.
[3] The fourth edition of the *Encyclopaedia Britannica* was published in 1810.
[4] Major Hesketh Vernon Hesketh-Prichard (1876–1922), explorer, adventurer, big-game hunter, writer, journalist and marksman. In 1900, he travelled to Patagonia, funded by the *Daily Express*, to investigate rumours of a hairy beast roaming the land, conjectured to be a living example of the Mylodon.
[5] Alfred 'Alfgar' Cecil Giles Hesketh-Prichard (1916–44), SOE officer and first head of its Czech Section, trained agents to conduct the assassination of Reinhard Heydrich. He died on active service in Austria on 3 December 1944, for which he was posthumously awarded the Military Cross.
[6] In 1915 Hesketh-Prichard founded the First Army School of Sniping, Observation, and Scouting at Linghem in France.
[7] Hesketh-Prichard's widow Elizabeth became Woman of the Bedchamber to Queen Mary, and in 1927 married Major Thomas Augustus Motion, Master of Foxhounds.

We've been back two weeks from Christmas with the Ghikas [on Corfu] & Xan & Magouche – and Miranda and Da'ad,[1] both in a bit of a state. X & M and I did some tremendous walks, on the last day from the top of Mt Pantokrator to nearly home, at tremendous speed for fear of the dark. It was a marvellous trek; but nothing compared to the marvellous beaver- and condor-haunted journey from Haberton to Viamonte![2] I was lying on a ledge in Lahul last year when a lammergeyer [bearded vulture] must have thought I was carrion, and swooped just like your birds; when he returned I whirled a terrified ice-axe, and he buggered off.

V. many thanks again for a <u>major treat</u> – Do let's have plenty more, and let it rip: Joan sends her love to you both, and so do I.

Yours ever, Paddy

---

[1] Miranda, daughter of Barbara Ghika by her first husband Victor, 3rd Baron Rothschild, and her daughter Da'ad.

[2] Bruce Chatwin, *In Patagonia* (London, 1977), pp. 178–81.

Following the publication of A Time of Gifts *in 1977, Paddy received a letter from a stranger living in Budapest: Rudi Fischer, a naturalised Australian of Transylvanian origin who worked as a languages editor for the* New Hungarian Quarterly. *Fischer's letter was appreciative, but not uncritical, and he drew attention to several mistakes in the text. It was obvious from his comments that Fischer's wide knowledge was matched by a meticulous attention to detail. Paddy determined that the book's sequel should not be published without Fischer's scrutiny.*

To Rudi Fischer   Kardamyli
April Fool's Day 1979   Messenia
                                                                             Greece

Dear Mr Fischer,

Thank you very much for your letter and the postcard of the beautiful Mostar bridge.[1] Indeed I know it, and last time I saw it, half a dozen little Herzegovinian boys were jumping off it in turn, holding their noses: all Moslems now, probably of Bogomil[2] descent, after being Orthodox and Shamanists at the start, I suppose.

Thank heavens, George Ps[ychoundakis] is all right now. He's got a decent job taking care of one of the German war cemeteries in Crete, through a very nice Cretan resistance figure who has become German Consul in Canea. I wish it was the English one, though. He comes here sometimes with his wife and makes us all laugh. He has spent the last few years translating the whole of the *Odyssey* and the *Iliad* from a modern Greek version into the dialect and the 15-foot metre of the *Erotokritos*.[3] It's splendid, and we hope to get it published soon …

[1] This sixteenth-century bridge was destroyed in 1990 during the Bosnian war, and rebuilt in 2005, and is now a UNESCO World Heritage Site.

[2] Bogomilism, a Christian neo-Gnostic sect particularly strong in Bosnia-Herzegovina. It had been founded in the tenth century by the priest Bogomil.

[3] *Erotokritos,* a romance written in the Cretan dialect of Greek, composed by Vikentios Kornaros in the early seventeenth century, consisting of over 10,000 fifteen-syllable rhymed verses. It remains a popular work to this day, largely due to the music that accompanies it when recited in public.

I'm very glad you were stern about Dracula to my old friend Iain Moncreiffe.[1] I hope it isn't a nuisance, my having willed him on to you. Please be kind to him if he gets in touch, which I'm sure he will do. You must be patient if he tells you his descent from Charlemagne, Hannibal and Haroon'al-Rashid within five minutes of meeting. It's not really snobbery, it goes far beyond it and becomes something very <u>strange</u>: historical romanticism really, which has landed him in that Dracula rot. He used to drink like a fish, but no longer. But he used to talk so much, people used to get out of cars and walk. He <u>can</u> be very funny. I'm v. fond of him. He and I were in the same squad at the Guards Depot in 1939. He's not at all strong, and looked like collapsing after every drill at that fiendish place, but stuck it, and did v. well in the Scots Guards, where he got a commission. To balance his drawbacks, he has a heart of gold …

All your notes about drinks are <u>gratefully noted</u>, and may well stop me from putting my foot in it in Vol 2! No more now, as I want this to get off. I'm sure Jock Murray my publisher would be <u>delighted</u> if you called. I'll tell him.

With kind regards
Yours
Patrick Leigh Fermor

I'm also sending I. Moncreiffe to my old Máros-dwelling friend, Elemér Klobusiçky.

---

[1] Sir Rupert Iain Kay Moncreiffe of that Ilk, 11th Baronet (1919–85), genealogist. 'He told me that, in spite of his passion for tracing descents, there was one quite recent one on his distaff side that he couldn't follow for lack of documents … Then one day, years later in clubland, I found him beaming. He took me aside with a drink, and the news that research had made a triumphant breakthrough … via what he called a legitimacy hiccup and a Croatian serf, the lost line had been traced. It led straight back to all that was most resonant and august in Hungarian history, and, among others, to the great Transylvanian house of Báthory, which had reigned in Transylvania and Poland. "And what's more," Iain went on with a rapturous expression, "we descend directly from Elizabeth Báthory, the Monster of Csejthe, sometimes known as 'The Blood Countess'! This fiend of wickedness or folly," he explained, "was convicted in 1610 of the slow murder – in order that their blood might

(cont'd opposite)

To Jock Murray   Kardamyli
late June 1979   Messenia
                                                        Greece

Dear Jock,

Thank you so much for your letter, and all the kind words about the car.[1] Alas, acts of malice are not covered by insurance; but perhaps the Greek Government may do something about it, so fingers crossed. Lots of letters of commiseration came, and the best of all was a telegram from Canea that Joan and I found so moving that I can't resist sending a translation, though perhaps I shouldn't.[2]

I'm <u>delighted</u> at the idea of my Malana piece in the *London Magazine*.[3] Would you ask Alan Ross to send me a proof, as I want to add half a dozen words, mentioning Dervla Murphy's[4] journey there?

I enclose a gloomy little note from the St Martin's Press in New York. What a shame! Perhaps it would be nice to have one or

magically preserve her beauty – of more than six hundred girls. Her servant-accomplices were tortured to death and she perished in her grim castle after being four years immured in the dark." Iain's eyes were sparkling as if he were leading in a Derby winner.'

'Anyone who knew Iain even slightly was aware of the warmth of his character and his deep kindness, and if he seemed to relish the deeds of monsters like the horrible Countess, or of Vlad the Impaler (whom he insisted on calling Dracula), this was not due to any answering streak in his own nature. It was the survival into riper years of the sort of boyish gusto that revels in the rack of historical novels, the Thumbscrew and the Scavenger's Daughter, and the torments that Sioux and Hurons inflict on captured palefaces ...', from PLF's contribution to *Sir Iain Moncreiffe of that Ilk: An Informal Portrait*, edited by John Jolliffe (London, 1986), republished in *Words of Mercury*, pp. 173–85.

[1] PLF's car, a Peugeot 404, had been blown up by Cretan communists on Easter Day. 'Perhaps they got it confused with Ascension Day,' he joked in a letter to Rudi Fischer.

[2] For the text of this telegram, see *Dashing for the Post*, pp. 329–30, n.4.

[3] Malana, an ancient Indian village isolated from the rest of the world. 'Paradox in the Himalayas' was published in the *London Magazine*, December 1979–January 1980.

[4] Described in her *Tibetan Foothold* (1966).

two copies.¹ What do you advise in such cases? I haven't answered this yet – could you for me?

How lovely your India journey sounds! I do love that extraordinary place, and the inhabitants too, in spite of their sometimes exasperating traits. Our journey,² too, was a delight. We met Janetta on the plane, and based ourselves in the shaky, old-fashioned rather charming Philadelphia Hotel in Amman, bang opposite the enormous Roman theatre. From here we radiated all over the country in a hired motor-car, strolling along the pillared streets of Jerash, peering at dancing-girls painted on the walls of desert castles and hunting lodges for the earliest Califs, before the dismal Islamic veto on representation of the human form came into being; clambered about in windy Saracen and Crusader fortresses, dived into the Red Sea at Akaba, and bounced off the Dead One. We thought of Lawrence and Freya in Wadi Rum,³ and had picnics in other Wadis which were minor Grand Canyons, slumbering afterwards among oleanders, while hardy camels milled past. Petra is even more surprising than one thinks: brand new looking Kedleston facades⁴ carved – yesterday, it looks like – out of the reddish purple rock, streaked inside, as though one were in a hollow cornelian or bloodstone. 'And the dukes of Edom shall be <u>amazed</u>!' it says in Exodus;⁵ and I bet they were.

Jerusalem, where we finished up, was a fascinating warren of marvels and oddities. I found it hard to tear myself away from the Wailing Wall, spellbound by those astonishing transports …

¹ Presumably St Martin's Press had written to inform PLF of their decision not to reprint one of his books – probably *The Violins of Saint-Jacques* – and offering him the opportunity to buy a quantity of the remaining copies.
² i.e. to Jordan.
³ Wadi Rum, otherwise known as the Valley of the Moon. T. E. Lawrence passed through Wadi Rum several times during the Arab Revolt, and much of the 1962 film *Lawrence of Arabia* was shot on location there.
⁴ See footnote on p. 99.
⁵ Exodus 15:15 (without the exclamation mark).

I'm so sorry to hear that you haven't been too fit, and hope that all is well now. I've got to come to London sometime for my overdue check up, and am toying with the idea of next month.

Joan sends her love, and hers and mine to you both.

Yrs ever
Paddy

To Rudi Fischer   Kardamyli
1 October 1979   Messenia
                                   Greece

Dear Mr Fischer,

I didn't know about *'fliegen die Schwalben furt'* [the flight of the swallows south] on Lady Day. They are still knocking about here, but will be off soon I expect ...

'Leigh' is etymologically the same as Lea, in the Oxford book of surnames, so I think 'Pratus' will do; and Fermor = Farmer originally. In fact, where we all come from originally in Northamptonshire and Oxfordshire, the name is spelled Fermor, Farmer & Farmor, when writing was largely phonetic. It must originally have been pronounced the same as 'farmer', and probably should be still. I wonder when the modern pronunciation – as written, with rather more 'er' than 'or' – came in? Probably a 200-year-old vulgarism, like Clurk and Durby in America, or among cockneys – unless they are the correct ones? ...

I would have felt sure Wystan Auden must have seen the church at Loipersbach, before the rather convincing reasons you adduce. It's a bad mistake about the poor Crim[ean] Tartars;[1] there's one very nice one living in London called Azamat Giray, one of the ousted ruling line. No danger of his ever seeing it – he's never off a horse

---

[1] Fischer had been angered by a line in Auden's poem 'Whitsunday in Kirchstetten', especially the identification of Crimean Tartars with Stalin implicit in the use of the term 'Crimtartary'. Fischer wrote of the Tartars that 'they were Stalin's victims, deported from their homes as a nation, and still not allowed to return'.

long enough to open a book. Auden was rather a friend of ours during the last years of his life. He'd settled for a long time in Ischia, then got fed up with the south ('Farewell to the Mezzogiorno') and settled in Austria.[1] He had an extraordinarily furrowed face, someone said a fly walking across it would break his leg. I like some of his things, and you ought to like ...[2] But the one you quote about 'our habits end' does seem arrogant and unimaginative.[3]

Yes, I <u>did</u> go back to Esztergom last year, and noted the forlorn state of the Bridge. I had already written the next bit — also Esztergom — before going there, and certain details had changed, both in fact and in my memory. I don't think I'm going to change them, certainly not the <u>actual</u> changes, which not only don't matter, but nor will I clean up the inaccuracies of memory, unless they become ridiculous and flagrant. One's first glance at something, one's age, and make-up at the time, have their rights too, and also the way the first glances have matured since or even gone off the rails here and there, have claims which might make later rectifications tantamount to doctoring! It's a delicate point; but there is a case to be put ...

I've read Ignotus's Hungary[4] and found it very good, well written, readable and honest. I found it rather upsetting too. Purely by chance I found myself in Budapest in just the kind of smart Hungarian circles he makes such telling and destructive fun of: indeed, swallowed whole the rather stagey, Gypsy-music, horsey and it seems, rather bogus world of landowners of different kinds who were kind to me. I didn't find the country-dwelling ones as vapid as he makes out. Especially in Transylvania, there were lots of original, odd, well-read, good and real people who escape from Ignotus's stereotype. But it's true enough, all the same, for me to recognise its validity as a generalisation ...

[1] Auden summered in the Austrian village of Kirchstetten in the final few years of his life, and attended Catholic Mass there.
[2] PLF here quotes the same lines as in his letter to Seferis (see p. 105).
[3] Another line from Auden's 'Whitsunday in Kirchstetten', referring to the absence of Christian worship in the communist bloc.
[4] Paul Ignotus (1901–78), a Hungarian writer imprisoned by the communists in 1949. After the failed uprising in 1956, he was in exile in England. His book *Hungary* was published in English in 1972.

[Among the] people who were extremely kind to me [was] Count Paul Teleki[1] and his wife [Jo]Hanna, who was PM later and committed suicide. I'd been sent to them by a cousin – if you remember the castle near St. Pölten in *A Time of Gifts*, where the wife was a Greek from Trieste? It was called Pottenbrunn … Anyway, he was very decent to me, and it's thanks to him I had such a lovely time in Transylvania. But I hate to read about the anti-Jewish laws during the war. His suicide seems prompted by very respectable reasons. Needless to say, most of this world looked back with hate on Karolyi,[2] Kun,[3] etc., and the White Terror was very underplayed. Books that were knocking about in these houses were those by Jean and Jérôme Tharaud,[4] *La Chute des Habsbourg, Quand Israel est Roi*,[5] etc. Why were they, one a French academician later, so bound up with Hungary?

I find Hungarian history fascinating, but terribly sad, with all the stupidity and oppression and inhumanity, as well as the glories …

Is there a good account of the Siege of Buda? I think Berwick, James's illegitimate son, was there. Also, at the storming of Esztergom in 1595. Elizabeth's favourite, Ld. Arundell of Wardour 'captured the Turkish banner with his own hands whilst forcing

---

[1] Count Pál Teleki de Szék (1879–1941), prime minister of Hungary 1920–1 and 1939–41, tried to preserve Hungarian autonomy from the Nazis by enacting far-reaching anti-Jewish laws, and committed suicide when German troops entered Hungary on their way to attack Yugoslavia.

[2] Though an aristocrat, Count Mihály Károlyi de Nagykároly (1875–1955) espoused progressive and socialist causes. He was Hungary's leader during the short-lived First Hungarian People's Republic (1918–19). Following its collapse Károlyi went into exile, first in France and then in Britain. In 1946, Károlyi returned to Hungary, and from 1947–9 served as the Hungarian Ambassador to France. In 1949, he resigned in protest against the increasingly repressive acts of the communist government, and spent the remainder of his life once more in exile in France.

[3] Béla Kun (1886–1938), de facto leader of the Soviet Republic in Hungary that overthrew the government led by Károlyi in 1919. Following the failure of the Hungarian revolution, Kun emigrated to the Soviet Union, where he was an active participant of the Red Terror in Crimea (1920–1). During the Great Purge of the late 1930s, Kun was arrested, interrogated, tried and executed, in quick succession.

[4] The writers Jérôme Tharaud (1874–1953) and his brother Jean (1877–1952). Jérôme Tharaud was elected to the Académie française in 1938, and his brother in 1946.

[5] *La Fin des Habsbourg* (1933), *Quand Israel est roi* (1921).

the water-tower'.[1] Bravo, sir. I rather like these Anglo-Hungarian overlaps. István Gál wrote a very nice paper on Sir Philip Sydney in Hungary.

The 'Liberation' of Hungary by Eugene of Savoy, for the rest of Europe, has some of the glamour of a crusade – 'the infidel being thrown back'! – for all but the poor Hungarians. Leopold I sounds a hopeless man …

All the best! I want this letter to be particularly legible; but I see it's as bad as the rest!

Yrs ever
Patrick Leigh Fermor

To Janetta and Jaime Parladé   Kardamyli
2 February 1980   Messenia
                                                 Greece

Darling Janetta & Jaime,

Thank you so much for those glorious and happy sojourns. It was perfection, as it always is except that it gets better every time. It always reminds me of the Abbey of Thélème[2] – no religious non-sense about <u>this</u> particular one, I hasten to say! – 'where *fay çe que vouldras* [do what thou wilt] was the whole of their law'.[3] I wish we'd played a bit more Dictionary; it's the perfect place for it, but we only thought about it that last night! We clean forgot to play any Word Making and W. Taking – the rich man's Scrabble – at

---

[1] Thomas Arundell (*c*.1560–1639), eldest son of Sir Matthew Arundell of Wardour Castle, Wiltshire, took service under the Holy Roman Emperor Rudolph II, and was made a Count of the Holy Roman Empire after storming the breach at Esztergom. His assumption of this title displeased the Queen, who had him imprisoned in the Fleet. He was made Baron Arundell by James I in 1605.

[2] The 'anti-church' in Rabelais's *Gargantua* (1534).

[3] This is the principle underlying 'Thelema', the philosophy developed in the early 1900s by the occult writer Aleister Crowley (1875–1947), denounced in the popular press as 'the wickedest man in the world'.

Ronda, too, though Joan and I had been planning some pretty fierce set-tos. What I can't make out is that, in spite of all those delicious meals and the steady procession of *copitas*,[1] only one kilo had been put on by the time I mounted the home-scales in trepidation. I'd counted on <u>at least</u> double, get rid of that in no time, and back on the uphill path to sylphdom – not as easy as it should be, owing to Joan's delicious things, but it's not bad, after munching a path across the [Iberian] Peninsula nonstop.

It was very exciting seeing Portugal again after thirty years, and <u>then</u> only [for] a few days. You've never seen such prawns and such crabs as the ones we ate at Nazaré – so big and horny, we were given great mallets to break our way in like burglars, and prawns went down the red lane by the bucket-load. I must stop talking about grub. (Lunchtime looms here …) Portugal seems strange, wild and remote after Spain: almost like a trip to Wales. That French place Jaime recommended in the castle at Lisbon was <u>tip-top</u> (*Chez Michel*). Marvellous wild boar pâté with pistachios …

We had a happy time at the Tile Works. What nice men, and what pretty tiles. We found some beauties for their kitchen, and spent hours arranging them on the ground, rather as we did in that nice yard in Seville about 10 years ago, and which have been our delight ever since. We adored Alcohacy and Batalha and wandered inland and up the Douro into that rather dreamy Quinta country, then Braya and Santiago de Compostela, where we sadly parted after a lovely journey. We stayed at the dear old Victoria in Madrid. Joan went to bed after dinner at Botin the first night, I wished I had instead of going to *Apocalypse Now*, which I loathed and despised.[2] Spent evening and drinks next day with the two elderly members [of the same family] (Lily Prat and Julie Ghyka), who belonged to same Romanian turtle [circle?] of old, in Bucharest. Then had a snackette or last supper at the Jijón, which was rather a good idea, if one doesn't want a slap up feast ….

[1] Small glasses, usually of sherry.
[2] Francis Ford Coppola's film *Apocalypse Now* had recently been released.

We waited for ages to be called to our flight, sitting over coffee at the airport in Barcelona, only to discover it had flown away. We were in the domestic flights part (no café anywhere else. NO ONE TOLD US!), where no international flights were announced. Only Canary Isles, etc. We were furious, till we – or rather Joan – realised it meant a lovely day and night in Barcelona. We spent hours in the Picasso exhibition, which is really marvellous; then prowled all round the twilit Sagrada Familia. Only the crypt was open, dimly lit. They have got rid of the bats. Ten years ago I went to Vespers there, and they swooped and shrieked overhead by the hundreds, while the priest intoned the office in Catalan, first vernacular liturgy I'd ever heard: *Priej, hermanos* instead of *Orate Fratres.*[1] It was like something out of a late 18th century Gothic novel.

After a smashing dinner at the Amaya, I had a very rum adventure in the lanes off the Ramblas. I described it in my B. & B. letter to the Fieldings a few days ago,[2] while it was still brand new in my mind, and feel I'd make a hash of it if I repeated it now: so <u>DO</u> ask them to bring it over when they next come.

I wonder how the Egyptian journey goes, and envy you frightfully. I wish I'd spent some of those very generous leaves from Crete which we were given in the War, by going up the Nile, and seeing something more of ancient Egypt than the Sphinx and the Pyramids. But, with the excitements of Cairo and parties and love-affairs, it simply wasn't in the running. Do give my love to Frances [Partridge] and my salaams to Stanley.[3] I do hope you come here

---

[1] *Orate fratres* is the incipit of a request for prayer that the priest celebrating Mass addresses to the faithful participating in it before saying the secret or Prayer over the Gifts. The full text of the priest's exhortation is: *Orate, fratres, ut meum ac vestrum sacrificium acceptabile fiat apud Deum Patrem omnipotentem* ('Pray, brethren, that my sacrifice and yours may be acceptable to God, the almighty Father').

[2] PLF set out 'to rove the town' after Joan had retired to bed, and became embroiled in one 'hell of a row' after being overcharged in a bar. Afterwards, in another bar, 'a rather splendid looking girl' pointed at her 'very tough-looking pals who were standing on either side of her and asked, "Which do you want? Him – or him? Or me?"' See *Dashing for the Post*, pp. 332–5.

[3] Stanley Olson (1947–89), an American who lived in London, the biographer of John Singer Sargent.

soon. You (Janetta) have at least been recently but you (Jaime) haven't for a century! So do try.

With many, many thanks again and fond

love to you both,
from Padd.

P.S. The letter <u>still</u> hasn't turned up here, but we haven't absolutely given up hope, as things posted in November are beginning to arrive. What a sad decline our planet has gone into.

I had a long thing about climbing in the Himalayas in the Dec[ember] *London Mag.*

Like Paddy, Philip Sherrard was a philhellene, who chose to spend the latter half of his life in Greece. The two men had met soon after the war. Like Paddy too, Sherrard was friends with some of the most prominent figures in Greek letters, Seferis and Katsimbalis, for example. In the early 1950s Sherrard had been baptised into the Greek Orthodox Church. 'His tall, bearded figure and his bearing gave him the air of being a satrap or an archimandrite, but there was nothing remotely pietistic about him,' Paddy wrote after Sherrard's death in 1995. 'There was neither electricity nor telephone in his house, and neither were missed,' he recalled. 'Cheerful winter sojourns stick in the memory, with snow outside and intricate literary paper games and stylistic pastiches inside. Philip would throw more logs on the fire, turn up the wick of the lamp and read out newly found passages from de Quincey and Hazlitt – and the racy sequences from Boswell – until very late.'

To Philip Sherrard   c/o Mrs Robin Fedden
undated [May 1980]   20 Eldon Road
                                                       W8

My dear Philip,

It was very clumsy and insensitive of me to quote Diana Cooper's comment and I would never have dreamt of doing so if I had realised how closely you felt bound up in Bloomsbury.[1] It was said very amusingly and lightly and in passing, and only to me, and we both laughed before moving on to other themes. There was nothing denigratory about it, and the words I think were distinctly touched with the sort of ruefulness that someone in a starched pinafore might feel at the sight of others having a glorious time dressed up as Red Indians, i.e. absolutely harmless and comic as it came out; and it was in the hopes of a smile, a laugh even, that I put it in as a marginal afterthought before closing my letter. I must have done this very maladroitly and would that I hadn't. It's fatal when the correct tone of voice is not conveyed in reported speech. So many apologies!

I agreed with all of your noble defence, but I do think you omitted something in your account of Bloomsbury sufferings and trials, viz., fun and the pleasure principle, with quite a dash of Thelema and *fay çe que vouldras*, thank heavens. Perhaps I've not got the hang of it; but I didn't think they would have minded a bit about Diana's comment. There's so much teasing and mockery in, for instance, conversations between VW [Virginia Woolf] and Lytton S[trachey], and many others, that Diana's remark would be thought pretty innocuous stuff. When one thinks of VW on her friends and foes, or in between – Sibyl Colefax, Ottoline M[orrell] etc. – it becomes more innocent still. I'm rather pro the sort of *sprezzatura* or unguarded speech, that Castiglione thinks the stamp of a civilised person,[2] which obviously the Bloomsbury people practised and D. Cooper still does, in a fairly similar way. But this

[1] PLF had quoted Diana Cooper's disparaging remark that Bloomsbury was 'a barnyard'. Sherrard's mother, Brynhild Olivier, had been a close friend of Rupert Brooke and Virginia Stephen (later Virginia Woolf), and his half-sister was married to Quentin Bell, son of Clive and Vanessa Bell.

[2] PLF often referred to this quality of *sprezzatura* ('nonchalance', 'careful negligence' or 'effortlessness and ease'), described as one of the most important, if not the most important, attributes of the courtier in Castiglione's *Il Cortegiano* ('The Book of the Courtier'), published in Venice in 1528.

doesn't let <u>me</u> off! I've just sent the Békássy proofs[1] to Quentin Bell, also a small contribution to the Charleston fund, half as a sign of admiration and gratitude to all that world, and half a self-inflicted fine for misplaced levity.

Much to say, but no more now, as Aymer says you are about to come here, and I want this to get you before you leave,

Paddy

To Aymer Maxwell   Kardamyli
22 April 1980   Messenia
                                                                Greece

My dear Aymer,
  Many apologies for delay in writing.
  How very exciting about your coming on Matila Ghyka's Documentary Chronology of Romanian History in Peter Eatons.[2] You very nobly append to this a tentative murmur of 'Quis', to which an excited 'Ego' comes ringing back! I've never seen it & would simply love it.
  Joan and I are in despair. Our neighbour Boutos has had a road bulldozed right down from the main road past the bottom of the garden wall to the very pebbles of the beach – or rather they plan to complete the last few yards of destruction unless I can

[1] PLF was interested in the Hungarian poet Ferenc Békássy (1893–1915), the brother of his Kardamyli neighbour Eva. In the early 1900s Békássy and his five siblings had been sent to England to be educated at Bedales; subsequently he read history at King's College, Cambridge, where he became friendly with John Maynard Keynes, and was elected a member of the Apostles. Békássy's letters to Keynes (edited by George Gömöri) were published in the autumn 1980 number of *New Hungarian Quarterly*, and it may have been proofs of these that PLF forwarded to Quentin Bell. Békássy returned to Hungary at the outbreak of war in 1914, and was killed fighting on the Russian front. A collection of his poems in English, edited by F. L. Lucas, was published in 1925 by the Hogarth Press.
[2] Peter Eaton (1914–93), second-hand bookseller, had a shop in Holland Park and another, much larger, at 'Lilies', a Victorian mansion in Buckinghamshire.

wring their hearts. A bulldozer with a 5 metre wide blade. Can you imagine the havoc and desecration? Not a word of warning or confabulation about it beforehand. I can't bear to dwell on the subject further ...

I've been involved in some literary correspondence with Philip[1] – rather fascinating. I'll tell you all about it when we meet. But why I mentioned this was that I had the sudden inspiration – or rather I hope it is one – of asking him to get some friend with a truck to transport the dear old painted table to the Ghikas's house in Athens.[2] The Ghikas seem excited about it, and it would be nice to think of it ending its days on the terrace in Corfu.

We <u>hate</u> the idea of your drawing stumps in Greece. Do come here a lot, nevertheless.

We were up to the neck (thanks to the Onassis Foundation to which, for some reason, I belong to the prize-giving committee) in Mr. Macmillan's visit here to collect one of the prizes.[3] Joan & I were flown to & fro buckshee, we had a huge suite at the GB[4] etc. It was all rather fun. H McM.'s speech in the old parliament was brilliant & charming – infinitely better than the cut-&-dried rigmarole of Simone Weil,[5] a co-laureate, i.e. easy delivery with one or two Greek quotations, rather like Fox, Derby or Ld. Grey speaking. All extempore, only once peering at what looked like a piece of crumpled rear bumf, level with the tip of his nose. There were endless banquets, receptions etc., all hell, except a stately one at the President's palace, where after dinner I heard Mr. Macmillan on a sofa explaining the War of Troy to some amazed Greeks: 'Of course, it was nothing to do with Helen at all. The Trojans wanted

[1] Philip Sherrard lived near Maxwell's former house at Katounia.
[2] A tabletop commissioned and painted by PLF as a thank you to his host Aymer Maxwell in the early 1960s; when Maxwell gave up his house in Euboea, PLF had the table transported to the Ghikas' house in Corfu.
[3] Harold Macmillan, chairman of the British Acropolis Appeal Committee, had been awarded the Onassis International Prize.
[4] The Grande Bretagne, a luxurious hotel in Athens.
[5] Simone Veil (1927–2017), lawyer and politician, First President of the European Parliament.

to get hold (of) a young Greek <u>filly</u> as their own bloodstock was probably rather poor, & sent Paris over to pinch it, which he did. That passage of the old men on the Skaian gate admiring "Helen" as she passed' – οὐ νέμεσις' ['no cause for anger']¹ – here followed a rumble of hexameters – 'has never been properly understood. Can't you see it, somebody trotting this beautiful young brood mare past – probably a chestnut with flowing mane & tail, a blaze on the brow and four white socks – she must have been charming …'

'But what about the wooden horse, Mr Prime Minister?'

'They've got <u>that</u> all wrong too! The Trojans were a wily & intelligent lot – they wouldn't have been fooled by such a transparent device, not for a moment. No, it must merely have been the horsebox sent to fetch the stolen steed back in, something of that kind, don't you know …'

They looked very surprised.

We flew to Olympia, bear-led (herded) round the ruins by a very nice archaeologist, with splendid interpolations & quotations by Mr. McM – It was a very hot day. We halted under a pine tree and he removed his battered panama, and mopped his brow with a bandana. He was wearing an old cardigan, a Brigade tie one day and a faded O[ld] E[tonian] one the next, and, 'as the Governor of North Carolina said to the Governor of South Carolina, "It's a long time between drinks",'² – and some ouzo was found, which unloosed some delightful reminiscences under the pine-needles.

Next day we drove to Marathon & Vavrona (Mr. McM, a grandson, Adam – v. nice, son of Maurice & Katie – Michael Stewart, Yanni Georgakis, us), & the day after they borrowed a

---

¹ In Book 3 of the *Iliad* seven old men, elders of the people, sit by the Skaian gates of Troy, and offer their opinion that Helen should be returned to Greece. Their complaints are softened however when they see her: 'Surely there is no blame on Trojans and strong-greaved Achaians if for a long time they suffer hardship for a woman like this.'

² In fact the governor is supposed to have said: 'It's a damn long time between drinks.' This story, well known on both sides of the Atlantic in the late nineteenth and early twentieth century, is generally believed to have been apocryphal.

yacht to the Temple of Aphaia on Salamis[1] and then lobsters in a tavern. I've never seen anyone enjoy himself more.

We go to the Ghikas in Corfu next Saturday, stay ten days, then back here for a week, then to Blighty here or there, we'll see you soon.

Yours ever,
Paddy

I wish I were more legible.

The following letter was written after both the Spenders and the Leigh Fermors had been guests of the Ghikas on Corfu.

To Stephen Spender   Kardamyli
5 August 1981   Messenia
                                                              Greece

Dear Stephen,

Very many thanks for the ravishing snaps – they're <u>just</u> what I was after, and I think the table looks very handsome. I wish it were a bit smaller! It was made to go on a millstone table, on top of a round tower in Euboea, in order to reach the seat going all the way round; and of course it's too big for any mortal needs, and may be a bit of a white elephant. So it's just a keepsake really, though on the large side.

The water crisis got worse. Nothing but a hollow gurgle when one turned on a tap, and occasionally a few auburn drops or a centipede. But a fault was discovered and put right, thank God, and now it gushes as if Aaron had struck the rock with his rod – and nobody's here to wallow in this sudden plenty! It has all at once become very hot – a time for work in the penumbra of shuttered rooms, long sunset swims and late-night feasting under stars.

---

[1] The Temple of Aphaia, on the Greek island of Aigina, was a favourite of the neoclassical and romantic artists such as J. M. W. Turner.

I went for a long walk in the mountains yesterday, and came upon a group of nearly full-grown kids (four-footed), beige and snow-white, standing among the rocks. They must have thought I was their shepherd, for they followed me, and every time I stopped, they stopped too, gazing raptly. It was like Grandmother's footsteps. After about a mile, I was rather worried, but at last managed to steal away without them doing the same. I could almost hear the pennies dropping in those little horned pates.

I hope China goes well, you must be in full spate.[1]

I think we shall only realise much later on, and increasingly, what a terrible gap Annie has left.[2] Debo went to the funeral, and thought afterwards, as they all had drinks and things at Sevenhampton, gazing at the vast disparate throng of rather fascinating people, that she'd never see any of them again, and the same among themselves for all the rest, as the factor that had brought them together had been removed. Oh dear.

Joan's going to write.

Love to you both, Paddy

P.S. *The Times* obituary [of Ann Fleming] was by Martin Charteris. There was rather a good one by Raymond Carr somewhere. Caroline Blackwood's piece was tip-top, & v. funny.[3]

---

[1] See next letter.
[2] Ann Fleming had died of cancer on 12 July.
[3] Ann Fleming had introduced Lady Caroline Blackwood to the artist Lucian Freud, with whom she eloped and whom she later married.

To Rudi Fischer   Kardamyli
2 February 1982   Messenia
                                                          Greece

Dear Rudi (I haven't yet had your sanction of this familiarity but I'll soldier on.)

I am very behindhand. I have a splendid array of Fischeriana before me. I'm deeply grateful for this marvellous help, and I will try and pat the balls back in more or less chronological order. I am also going to attempt to write more clearly, as I have nothing but complaints. Greek 'ε's are a help when I can remember as it stops words melting into a tangle.

I'm assembling a wonderful array of Hungarian stamps. I'm not a philatelist, so I wonder who the eventual lucky collector will be? Csontváry's Acropolis[1] is still my favourite of his among the minor p.c. gallery, which is also assembling. Yes, of course it was in Baron Herzog's house that I saw the Grecos.[2] I didn't mention it because there are too many barons already in the book (not to mention grafs) and I don't want to ram [names?] down the reader's throat unless they are intrinsically interesting. It's rather the same pattern in Translyvania – except they are, of course, all very different. I don't really get back into the peasant world until I cross the Danube into Bulgaria. I wish I'd had a wider Hungarian spectrum. It wasn't as I'd planned it at all. But it's too late now. Herzog was a very tall, tweedy young man. I don't think he knew much about these particular possessions. He muttered something, and left us in a long room which had nothing else in it, except a long divan-seat right along the opposite wall. The more I look at the Courbet wrestler, the more convinced I am that this is what I have in mind. The field and the Grandstand are just as I remembered them. The point was, the picture struck me as utterly unusual for Courbet, as this is. (There may easily be some subliminal Manet-Monet-Rousseau

---

[1] Tivadar Csontváry Kosztka (1853–1919), Hungarian artist.
[2] In the inter-war years the Hungarian banker Baron Mór Lipót Herzog assembled one of Europe's great private collections of art.

switch at work.) Thank you for putting me right about Café Gerband near the Vövösmarty statue. I was confusing it with a very similar place called Beaudrot in Alexandria, as opposed to smart Groppi's in Cairo, great haunt of staff officers, who were known collectively by the rest of the army as 'Groppi's Horse'. I'm <u>delighted</u> to have the words and tune of Erika.[1] I've picked it out, but still can't get it by memory: a sort of block; it's not bad for tunes on the whole.

I quite agree with your thoughts about these chapters in general. There <u>is</u> something missing, and I hope it will come right. I am hoping the other question – sexual involvement etc. – will solve itself, because of course there was some, especially in Transylvania, and I'll have to do something about it. But unless they are well done, these sort of recollections have a terrible knack of sounding silly, fatuous or complacent or mock bashful or jocose or maudlin. I'll have to wait and see how it goes. *Solvitur ambulando*, perhaps ...[2]

I'll take your advice about leaving Hungarian words to be vetted at proof stage ... I'm delighted to have such clear rulings on place names or districts, and will correct them all – Pilir, Bákory, Börzöny etc. V. useful indeed.

I am rather worried about my Esztergom-Visegrád journey. My diary entry is extremely summary – I suddenly slacked off, for some forgotten reason, when crossing into Hungary, just where I need it most. Perhaps I did lose my way! The way I wrote it is all I can remember. I think I'd better insert a footnote, since it doesn't quite fit in with times and distances. I didn't miss the village of Visegrád and I did get an impression of some ruins, but didn't dawdle there unfortunately. Of course I have since seen those splendid things which, there, as at Esztergom, have only seen the light of day since my journey, and I was very keen not to get the two confused. Your idea that I must have overnighted somewhere

[1] 'I found the song impossible to get by heart. It tells of a swallow flying low over a field of ripening wheat', *Between the Woods and the Water*, p. 39.
[2] 'It is solved by walking'.

near the Papret, then walked 10 miles, sounds rather inviting. Yet I seem to remember dawn light along the valley when I got to the river …

Re. blackthorn-sticks in the Irish Guards.[1] I'm not exactly the horse's mouth, but near enough. I joined 'the Micks' in the ranks in 1939, same day as Iain Moncreiffe and other friends, though he was in the Scots Guards. It was the first time future Guards officers went through the ranks, and a very good idea, though it was tremendously tough. We were all from the five Guards regiments – Grenadier, Coldstream, Scots, Irish and Welsh – trained in a squad of 30 at the Gd's Depot at Caterham by the Coldstream. All had been fixed up before joining through mild pull, I'm sorry to say. When I was finishing my recruit time at the Depot, I had tempting promises of future exciting intelligence work in Greece, and like a fool, talked about it. The Col. of the Micks, who I knew quite well (Tom Vesey), had me up to Birdcage Walk (Wellington Barracks) and asked me if this was true. I said it was, and he was very cutting about it. 'What's the point of us training you as an ensign if you go buggering off on some ghastly Intelligence rubbish?' I was given a week to decide. If I hung on with the Micks as an officer, I would, morally, have been bound to eschew all tempting 'I[ntelligence]' offers. So, most reluctantly, I went into the Intelligence Corps. Very unhappy, because I loved the Irish Guards. But I was much more use where I went, as it turned out, than I would have been as an ensign in the Brigade. We remained great friends. All this didn't stop me always carrying a blackthorn stick! Yes, they are full length, either with a knob at the top (sliced and polished) occasionally with a crook: shiny, jet black, and with as long thorns as possible. If you want a really good description of an interview in Birdcage Walk, see Basil Seal in *Put Out More Flags*. (B.S. is based on Peter Rodd, Nancy Mitford's very harum-scarum husband, now dead poor chap.[2])

---

[1] Officers in the Irish Guards traditionally carry blackthorn sticks, known as shillelaghs.
[2] Peter Rodd (1904–68) is generally thought to have inspired the character of Basil Seal, the protagonist of Evelyn Waugh's early novels *Black Mischief* (1932) and *Put Out More Flags* (1942) and his last short story, 'Basil Seal Rides Again' (1962).

How very interesting about the domestic sows and the wild boar. Love laughs at locksmiths.

On to Next Letter. 5.12.81.

Topography round the Kakuk now clear. I remember the Prince of Wales plaque. I also remember one at the Arizona[1] or was that on a later visit? Perhaps <u>he</u> went on one earlier than the time he was given the signed score by Miss Arizona. I remember her ....

Very glad of the feminine endings rulings. They exactly tally with Eva Békássy's rulings.[2] (I read her the Alföld bit last autumn, and it made her laugh.) She didn't know any of those people very well as all her acquaintance were either (through her marriage) Transylvanians or Transdanubians from her home ...

I've been slow in answering because I have been fidgetting about Greece. I went to Crete for the 40th anniversary of the Battle – the last that will be celebrated until the 50th – and it was very moving. Lots of Australian and New Zealand veterans, also British, and the Aus. & New Zealand foreign and defence ministers (and, unexpectedly, the German ambassador, as well as all of ours) ...[3]

Corfu, yet again, was the next sojourn, with the Ghikas. Yes indeed, they once lived in a charming old island family house in Hydra, which my wife and I had lent to us by them 20 years ago, for two years. I wrote a long thing about his painting which I could get xeroxed, my new passion. (It gives me a Caxton-Gutenberg feeling.) Here we were joined by Stephen Spender, hotfoot from East China, where he had just been everywhere, preparing a book with Hockney.[4] When we left Corfu, they came here with us

---

[1] A nightclub in Budapest, where 'Miss Arizona', wife of the proprietor, sang her husband's songs, including 'Fekete pillangó' [Black Butterfly], a signed score of which was handed to the Prince of Wales after he visited the club in 1936. At the age of seventeen, under the name Mici Sagár, she had danced at the Casino de Paris.

[2] PLF's neighbour in the Mani, sister of the Hungarian poet Ferenc Békássy.

[3] For a description of the celebrations, see *Dashing for the Post*, pp. 348–9.

[4] Stephen Spender and David Hockney, *China Diary* (1982).

(he and his pianist wife Natasha, that is) and left a few days ago. He's an old friend. We were suddenly rung up by the Observer, with the horrible news that Philip Toynbee, another v. old friend, had just died. We had an hour to write something and dictate it back, and I think I sent you the upshot. A horrible loss. Stephen used to know M. Karolyi well (bête-noire, of course, to most of my journey-associates) and liked him very much, and his wife Catherine (still alive),[1] even more. He was v. interesting about both; also said that he (S.S.) had managed to get Auden and Mary McCarthy to Budapest at a moment when the PEN club could do a lot of good for writers. He also likes Ignotus[2] very much, and told me a strange tale of him and his wife, meeting in [illegible] of the two fires at his London flat and her death in the last. The reaper has been very busy. One of my greatest friends, Ann Fleming, was v. ill (cancer, like Philip T.), Ian's widow; and I was going back to England to catch a last glimpse of her; but today's papers are full of her obituary, so it's too late.

I'm not going to go into political problems[3] at all deeply, for the reasons you suggest – the fairer one tries to be, the more trouble one is in. But it is possible, I hope, to write a dispassionate paragraph or two saying what the two cases are, and why certain neighbours are on bad terms, without giving any sort of verdict, which I'm utterly unqualified for. What I am trying to do, with your kind and generous help, is to build up the submerged 9/10 of an iceberg, of which only 1/10 will show, but if the 9/10 are rubbish, so will the 1/10 be! All kind wishes & thanks!

Yours sincerely,
Patrick Leigh Fermor

[1] Károlyi's wife Katinka (née Andrássy) died in 1985.
[2] See footnote on p. 316.
[3] PLF refers to the problem of reconciling Hungarian and Romanian territorial claims.

To Diana Cooper   Kardamyli
4 August 1982   Messenia
                                         Greece

My darling Diana,

I've just heard that you've had a horrid fall and bust some ribs.
I <u>am</u>, we <u>are</u>, sorry, and do hope it hasn't been too wretched. The
only thing is you have a more resilient capacity of recovery from
slings and arrows like this than anyone I've ever met, and I feel confident that you will be as good as new in an incredibly short time.
Do please send news.

Soon after I wrote last (after Hungary and Romania) Joan and
I took the car over to Crete with a convenient nearby car-ferry,
and spent ten days. It was terrific, late May, blazing skies, flowers
all still out owing to a very wet winter. We went to all the villages
where we hid during the war, right up in the mountains like nests
and the welcome was amazing – tears, hugs, whiskers, feasting,
dancing and blazing off into the sky with rifles and revolvers. Some
of the really remote ones I hadn't seen for 38 years. Everything
seemed miraculously unchanged. The only difficulty was getting
through fifteen meals a day: we had to eat and drink in every
house of every village we visited, otherwise they would have pined
away. When we arrived, people said 'How <u>thin</u> you've got,' but,
by the time we left it was 'Tsk, tsk, tsk! We <u>have</u> put on weight!'
Joan's conduct was heroic throughout. She loved it. It was marvellous drinking <u>absolutely pure</u> wine (without any chemicals
in, like ordinary ones) under the vineyards where the grapes had
been grown and trodden. We saw lots of little girls I had baptised
during the war, some of them grandmothers now. I only stood
godfather to girls, as if there had been any god<u>sons,</u> and they had
fallen in love with the girls, they wouldn't have been able to marry.
God-brotherhood & -fatherhood is considered a stronger bond
than blood, and such matches – which never happen – worse than
incest.

We clambered into stalactitic caves where we cowered of yore,
and revisited haunt after haunt. When we left, the car was full of

presents, great demijohns of wine, red and amber-coloured, wicker covered gallons of mulberry-raki, marvellous cheeses the size of chariot-wheels, sacks of raisins, strings of threaded figs, baskets of walnuts, a goats hair cape and two tall and wiggly shepherd crooks. We came back in a sort of trance.

Steven Runciman is recumbent under a tree the other end of the terrace, with lowered lids. Graham and simpatico Ian Whigham were here a week ago. Did we write the joint p.c. we were always talking about? Ian took wing for Bangkok and his pagoda under the coconut palms of his Malaysian creek. We hope Janetta and Jaime are coming at the end of the month. <u>I wish you were too.</u> <u>Why not</u>? Just the place. There is a damn road now at the bottom of the garden which could make itself useful for once, by letting you hobble straight indoors without any wandering in the rocks. Do ponder this, <u>we'd simply love it.</u>

> tons of fond love, darling Diana
> from Paddy
> OXO

P.S. Please send news.

On 20 April 1983 Paddy wrote to his American editor, Elisabeth Sifton, to tell her that he had been invited by the Cretan Association of New York to be a guest at the celebration of the forty-second anniversary of the Battle of Crete. 'I've never been to the United States and these three days in a sort of Cretan ghetto will be a very strange first glimpse. But if I can make a break for it for a few hours, it will be lovely to meet briefly and feast,' he wrote. 'Please steel yourself for confrontation with a raffish figure half-stunned with the raw Cretan mountain spirits which they pour down one's throat almost without a break.'

Paddy was accompanied by 'my old Cretan guide and pal' Manoli Paterakis, 'a whiskered, eagle-browed mountaineer who has only once left his goatfolds in the Cretan sierra'. Paterakis was unimpressed by the skyscrapers and the ballyhoo of New York. 'I found him looking pensive one evening, and asked why? He said – "It's just about milking time for my ewes up at Koustogérako," – his sheepfold in the White Mountains.'

To Xan Fielding   Kardamyli
12 June 1983   Messenia
                                                              Greece

Darling Magouche, Xan παιδί μου ['dear boy'],

Magoush, you <u>were</u> a saint to respond so swiftly to my cry. Alas, I only got your <u>letter</u> on return here – I wrote too late, and it must have got here the very day I left – I long to go back, letter in hand, and follow its guidance to the letter! Anyway, even so, via you and Mrs Sifton I at once got in touch with Jane Gunther[1] (at least, when I was on leave from Cretan pals in a pan-Cretan enclave of Long Island, near Baldwin and Belmore – which you probably don't know – after nearly a week). She was tremendously nice and welcoming, and had Glenway Westcot & Munroe Wheeler[2] to drinks, which was lovely, as well as Natasha,[3] on the brink of departure and looking splendid. I was gassing away after they had left, and

---

[1] Widow of the American journalist and author, John J. Gunther (1901–70).
[2] The novelist Glenway Wescott (1901–87) and his companion Munroe Wheeler.
[3] Probably Natasha Spender, pianist and wife of the poet Stephen Spender.

suddenly looking at a new digital wrist-watch – as difficult to set as flying a jet plane – that a Cretan had just given me. I saw it flashing '10.30 – 10.30' and jumped to my feet, apologising profusely for staying so long. As it was just past 8, only, and broad daylight, Jane Gunther must have thought I was a wild looney.

Manoli and I pushed off from Athens, and, the pilot being a pal, we were whisked up to the otherwise empty luxury class and feasted on champagne, caviar and *foie gras*, and, in the fullness of time, let out at Kennedy airport, where lots of Cretans met us, and whisked us off to a Cretan gathering, then a sort of sea-side banquet, and finally dossed down: Manoli with his Koshilakis cousins, I with George Doundoulakis, student head of our intelligence network,[1] now an eccentric inventor who is about to launch a new kind of internal combustion engine which will use 90% less fuel than the modern ones. The days were endless hobnobbing, a bit exhausting on top of jet-lag, which, because of this, took ages to disperse. On Sunday there was a great gathering, followed by feasting, and terrific Cretan dancing in full jig by young folk, some of whom have never left the USA. We were given a great welcome, and both made speeches (mine a re-hash of the monument one three years ago,[2] Manoli's a fruity ramble about the Battle and shooting Germans). It was terrifically moving seeing lots of old pals, or their relatives. Masses asked after Xan and sent their love. All this was repeated in Toronto next Sunday, I was seized and hugged at the airport by George Alevizakis, and Alevizos his brother, the two youngest children of Father John of Alones.[3] The feast and the speeches went very well. I stayed with George, a great dear and v. excited seeing Manoli & me and hearing all about Aleko [Xan Fielding]. We drove to the Niagara Falls in the morning, and gazed in wonder.

[1] George J. Doundoulakis (1921–2007), wartime espionage organiser and physicist.
[2] i.e. the speech at the inauguration of the bronze memorial tablet in Crete (see *Dashing for the Post*, pp. 328–9).
[3] Father John Alevizakis, described by PLF as 'brave and saint-like', one of the most outstanding figures of the resistance, 'who sheltered and befriended many of us for years'. Another of his sons had been executed by the Germans.

I got away for a few days between these week-ends, and stayed at a fairly seedy hotel in W. 44 Street, called the Royalton, but led a double life by having breakfast and final drinks at the Algonquin, being opposite. (As the waiters were Macedonians and Epirotes,[1] I was never allowed to pay for the latter.) Our agent, Lois Wallace, is terribly nice and a little eccentric. We had drinks, then went to see a private view of a not v. good film about the Rosenbergs, written and produced by Mr Doctorow, author of Ragtime[2] – they insisted on sneaking out at the side, to avoid having to lie to him, as he was a friend. I only saw Mrs Sifton – Elisabeth now – for a minute early on, as she had to go to Washington but we had a v. good luncheon Chez Hubert. She's outstandingly nice, I really adored her. We talked lots about the Winds,[3] and she said she felt ashamed of having to publish books which were not half or a quarter as good, owing to the bloody state of the book trade, and she really meant it. I felt she was going to have another serious look at it. Anyway, you'd love her. She's the daughter of a philosopher theologian called Reinhold Niebuhr. I went to the P. Morgan Library – dazzling – with an absolutely charming girlfriend of Anthony Sheil's called [Constance] Anson Jordan, who teaches English & Italian renaissance literature at Columbia University. There was a wonderful Holbein Exhibition. Here I bumped into Milton[4] and had dinner with his new and very nice and pretty Roman wife (called Monica Incisa) next day. I spent ages in the Frick collection – my word! – and went to the Metropolitan Museum again and again; apart from its seemingly limitless wonder, there was an exhibition of Vatican Treasures there, also Henry Moore and a lovely Constable one that brought tears to my eyes. Alas the whole Museum of Modern Art, to my chagrin, was being pulled to bits and rearranged – nothing but a dim exhibition of photographs

[1] From the ancient Hellenic state of Epirus, in the western Balkans.
[2] *Daniel* (1983), directed by Sidney Lumet, adapted by E. L. Doctorow from his novel *The Book of Daniel* (1971).
[3] Fielding planned a book about the wind, eventually published posthumously by a small private press in 1991 as *Aeolus Displayed: A Book of the Winds*.
[4] Milton Gendel (b. 1919), formerly married to Judy Montagu. See p. 348.

in the shrouded ground floor. On the last night I was taken out to dinner by Leo Lerman.[1] Do tell me about him – he adores you, Magouche, as everyone did. We had delicious soft shelled crabs at the <u>Cafe des Artistes</u>, both of which I loved. We drank, gassed away, and laughed a lot. I still feel a bit bewildered by New York, and long to have another look under less strange circumstances. I feel it's full of waiting wonders I scarcely glimpsed.

Manoli & I were seen off by all our Cretan pals, got back safely, he's back in Koustogérako, and here I am, with Joan & Graham – we all squeezed on to the evening plane the same day.

No more now, mes enfants. Petro's off to the village – only thanks for responding so nobly to my S.O.S., and tons of love from us both

Paddy

Do get hold of a book called *Eleni* by Nicolas Gage[2] (Random House). Joan, Niko, Barbara and I are wild about it – so will you be. It's all about Epirus, the round up of children, and the trials and executions by the People's courts, during the Civil War. All true, by the son really called Niko Gatzoyiannis, whose mother was executed near the Albanian border. It's about as exciting as *For Whom the Bell Tolls* and might be as important, when it comes out here, as *Darkness at Noon* was. I had a long talk with the author in Los Angeles (who sounds brilliant and v. nice) by telephone.

Forgot to say I went with a chap called John Chancellor[3] & his son (English) and Meg Fitzherbert (E. Waugh's daughter, who has just written a book about her grandpa, Aubrey Herbert[4]) by subway to see the fireworks for the Centenary of Brooklyn Bridge, and got there just as it finished. Chop Suey round the corner.

---

[1] Leo Lerman (1914–94), writer and editor at Condé Nast. The son of a housepainter in East Harlem, Lerman was at the centre of fashionable New York society for almost fifty years, thanks to his work at magazines such as *Vanity Fair*, *Vogue* and *Mademoiselle*.

[2] Nicholas Gage (b. 1939), Greek-born author and investigative journalist.

[3] John Chancellor (1927–2014), publisher, author and bibliophile – not the NBC television star of the same name.

[4] Margaret Fitzherbert, *The Man Who Was Greenmantle: A Biography of Aubrey Herbert* (1983). Her uncle was PLF's friend Auberon Herbert (see footnote on p. 86).

When Philip Toynbee died in 1981, Paddy wrote the entry for him in the Dictionary of National Biography, *and was one of several old friends who contributed a memoir to the* Observer *(21 June 1981). Another was Jessica Treuhaft (1917–96), known as 'Decca', second youngest of the Mitford sisters, who wrote to Paddy from her home in America, after getting his address 'from my old Hen' (Debo). She asked for his help with a book she was compiling, based on personal memories of Toynbee. Paddy responded with a long letter, which Decca found so amusing that 'you could hear my shrieks all the way to Greece'. Paddy later wrote her a five-page letter of line-by-line comments and corrections (18 March 1983) on her manuscript. The book was published in 1984 as* Faces of Philip: A Memoir of Philip Toynbee. *Decca would acknowledge her special debt to him in her foreword: his handiwork, she wrote, could be detected 'on almost every page, ranging from organisation of subject matter to style, grammar, syntax' – despite the fact that 'we met only once, glancingly, years ago'.*

The letter below was written during the preparation of the book; one problem was inconsistencies between the memories of different contributors.

To Jessica Mitford
3 August 1983

Dear Decca,

I'm dreadfully sorry being such an age writing. I simply don't know how it happened: except that I have been forging ahead like Billy-o on my book, & about time too.

Yes, wasn't it funny, the bit about Julia and PT [Philip Toynbee] in the book,[1] and that you should have clean forgotten.[2] It must have been a great surprise. Did you read Mary Berenson, by her half-sister Barbara Strachey, about their Aunt and I Tatti etc.?[3] Simply

[1] *Julia: A Portrait of Julia Strachey by Herself and Frances Partridge* (1983).
[2] Julia Strachey had an affair with Philip Toynbee in the 1930s.
[3] Barbara Strachey and Jayne Samuels (eds.), *Mary Berenson: A Self-portrait from her Letters and Diaries* (1983). Mary Berenson, née Smith, lived with her second husband, the art historian and connoisseur Bernard Berenson, at I Tatti, a villa outside Florence.

fascinating, because M.B. is so riveting, but Julia writes far better than B.S., who I've never met. A minor mystery is that though Julia mentions Barbara several times, Barbara doesn't mention J. once, not even listed in the index. Bad blood, I bet. I was taken only for a stay at I Tatti by the pal Debo calls Honks [Diana] Cooper. Berenson was a surprising old thing, in appearance half-saint, half-arms-manufacturer: silver bearded & transparent as candle wax.

How mysterious, Isaiah [Berlin] getting it wrong about Philip & Richard [Wolheim]![1] I'm perfectly certain he's wrong. I should say it was a week after the first stormy meeting at the Gargoyle, a fortnight at the very most. They had certainly never met before, nor had I, nor Xan. More recent confirmation: when last in Blighty, I had dinner with Alan Hare,[2] & we were talking about this, & to my astonishment Alan confirmed every detail, as – which I'd clean forgotten – P., X & I had been having dinner with Alan & wife just before going to the Gargoyle, and remembered every detail exactly as I did, and even gave me a pat on the back for seeing that R. was taking it all far more to heart than Philip meant. It was really no more than one of his fearfully tight, routine teases. I'm a great admirer of Isaiah's, but he's not right here (P.S.: Sudden inspiration: Why not write to Alan Hare, and get his version, saying I'd suggested it? Explaining why, and with your reassuring provisos about quoting etc, & Richard's permission? We – Xan, I & other pals shared a house in Cairo during the war. His address: Hon. Alan Hare MC, Flat 12, 53 Rutland Gate, SW7. 581–2184).

---

[1] Richard Wolheim, philosopher, who in the late 1940s was a young don teaching at University College, London. As Paddy remembered, Wolheim (never having met Toynbee before) had been distressed by his teasing during a chance encounter in the Gargoyle Club. PLF (who, with Xan Fielding, was there with Toynbee) had intervened to stop Wolheim becoming too upset. A few days later Toynbee met Wolheim again and apologised; when he learned that Wolheim's girlfriend had just run off with another man, he invited Wolheim to stay with him and his wife Anne on the Isle of Wight, in a typical gesture of spontaneous generosity. Berlin (who, as another academic philosopher, knew Wolheim professionally) denied the truth of this story. Anne Toynbee would marry Wolheim shortly after divorcing Philip in 1950.

[2] See footnote on p. 63.

What a pity about the Bowdlerisation of the Commune part.[1]

In my original long thing about P., I talked about our time in Athens together,[2] & mentioned our spending much of the morning in our neighbouring beds in the New Angleterre Hotel in writing limericks.[3] I've just come across a few of them, all written jointly I think – some pretty laboured & imperfect. (Not for publication, I need hardly add!)

I did enjoy that Mrs. Thatcher's England piece[4] – not so much for the sentiments – I rather fear that in terms of hands and bell I wring when you ring, and vice versa: too late for this old ocelot to do anything about his spots, I fear[5] – but for the splendid jokes – stick & carrot, Beetle and the ham, Debo in the lav etc.

All the best, yrs ever, Paddy

---

[1] In the early 1970s, Toynbee and his second wife, Sally, initiated a self-sufficient farming community in Wales, which soon became a commune. Toynbee, Sally and their youngest daughter moved out, into a nearby cottage.

[2] In the mid-1950s PLF was asked to report on the Ionian Island earthquakes for the *Sunday Times*, and Toynbee had come out to Greece to cover the story for the *Observer*. On their last night together in Athens, 'we ended up with two English girls in their flat; very pretty but perfectly respectable. After a few drinks together Philip made the navvie's gesture of pretending to spit on his hands, then clapped them together, saying, "Now! What about a great deal of SEX? And just in case anyone's feeling shy, I'll kick off and set the ball rolling by rogering Paddy." Their faces were a study.'

[3] One example, remembered by John Julius Norwich, went as follows:

'It's no use, in talking to Toynbee, To pay him back in his own coin, be – Cause if you do this, He goes on taking piss – But how would a kick in the groin be?'

[4] Jessica Mitford's correspondence with Maya Angelou reveals that she was encouraged to write a piece on 'Mrs Thatcher's Britain' for the *Observer*, and PLF's comments suggest that she did so, but for unknown reasons they seem not to have published it.

[5] Jessica was known for left-wing views, in contrast to those of her sisters Diana and Unity.

By the late 1970s Paddy had become disenchanted with his American publishers, Harper & Row. He felt that they were 'bored stiff with my stuff', which he found demoralising, at a time when he was struggling to write the follow-up to A Time of Gifts. *In contrast he had received, soon after the publication of that book, a letter of warm appreciation from Elisabeth Sifton, then senior editor (later editor-in-chief) at Viking Press in New York; and he was very pleased when, several years later, she became his publisher. 'It is a great stimulus to get a move on,' he wrote to her on Easter Sunday, 1982, though he declined her request to see what he had written so far. 'The trouble about letting anyone see work in progress is that I can't bear doing it until it is finished and as presentable as I can possibly make it. I leave most of the rewriting, cutting, grafting, topping and tailing to the end, when the heat's off and all the faults stand out coldly and can be dealt with in a dispassionate and critical way. While work is going on, anything but unmitigated praise sends me into a decline; and as, in its temporary form, it is far from deserving anything of the kind, it remains under wraps. It's an absurd phobia, but I believe not unique. When everything is cleaned up and polished I feel steeled and detached enough for any amount of knocks, and can act on them.'*

The following letter, written some months after an enjoyable meeting with Sifton in New York, exhibits Paddy's propensity to distraction, simultaneously endearing and exasperating.

To Elisabeth Sifton   Kardamyli
undated [late November 1983]   Messenia
                                                    Greece

Dear Elisabeth,

I've been meaning to write to you for ages. I know I'm long overdue with Vol 2. I'm very distressed that it should be so, and I know that you are too. This book is quite different from any other writing I've ever been involved in, and <u>why</u> it takes such an awful long time is chiefly because it's about such a long time ago, and it often takes a long time to bring it to life again, and fill in the gaps; then suddenly it comes in a rush. It seems absolutely incalculable.

But it is getting on, and I'm fairly pleased with it up to date, though there are bits which will need polishing. The other reason for delay is that I do think it's fascinating material, and could turn into a book we will all be pleased about, and I don't want to rush it (please don't swear!), and make a hash of it. But I am working away at it diligently, so please go on being patient. The trouble is, I can't do this book any other way. I long to have it finished and out, and embark on others that will gallop ahead. I bear very much in mind your excellent and most convincing reasons for getting it out soon – i.e., to form part of a broadside – and the consideration really does egg me on, though it may not seem so. One of the things that has been holding me up – Transylvania, all its complications and problems and marvels – is now safely behind me and things should be much easier now.

I've just knocked off for an hour to copy out the enclosed,[1] which needs a word of explanation. I bet you know all about King Robert the Bruce begging Douglas on his death-bed to take his heart on a crusade, in order to fulfil an old vow. Douglas did as he was bidden, and it turned out more or less as told in the enclosed poem; with the difference that it happened in Spain, at a place called Teba, in Andalusia. (I've just been there with the Fieldings, who live nearby at Ronda.) I remembered there was a German poem about it, so, on getting back here, I made a dash for the *Oxford Book of German Verse*, with the enclosed result. It's not great poetry – let alone the translation – but it is full of go, and I love to think of Graf Strachwitz, aged 19 or 20, pacing up and down his grim Silesian *schloss*, mind teeming with Scott, Border ballads, Chevy Chase, Otterburn etc. He was only 25 when he died. It seems he belonged to a Berlin literary *cénacle* [discussion group] called '*Der Tunnel über der Spree*' [The Tunnel over the Spree][2] which seems a very odd place for a tunnel to be, let alone a *cénacle*.

[1] PLF's translation of the 1842 ballad '*Das Herz von Douglas*' ('Douglas of the Bleeding Heart') by Moritz Karl Wilhelm Anton Graf von Strachwitz (1822–47). He wrote out the German in black ink alongside his translation in red – all sixty stanzas.

[2] A German literary society based in Berlin, active in the mid-nineteenth century. The Spree is the river that flows through Berlin.

344

The battle described happened in 1330 (part of the Spanish *Reconquista*), between Alfonso XI, the Avenger of Castile and Leon, and one of the later emirs of Granada. Apart from the mistake about the venue,[1] Bruce died at a place called Cardross, not Scone at all. But I don't think this matters a damn. My German's very rusty. I've probably put my foot in it here and there – end of verse X almost certainly. Never mind.

It's late November here (olive picking in full swing), and I'm counting on the hideous delay in postage between here and America for this to arrive only in late December, and to bring Christmas greetings and love

from Paddy LF

It seems that Paddy also sent his translation of 'Das Herz von Douglas' to Steven Runciman.

To Steven Runciman
5 January 1984

Kardamyli
Messenia
Greece

Dear Steven,

Re: Heart of Douglas

I am sure your *Blue Bonnets* solution is the right one![2] I've always loved the poem, and am particularly fond of the second line, where the ratty bottleneck of syllables almost causes a traffic-block.[3] I should think it highly likely that's where Graf S got the idea from.

---

[1] Von Strachwitz set the battle in Palestine.
[2] Runciman suggested in a letter of 29 November 1983 that 'Angus and Lothian', which PLF had taken to be individuals, should be understood as 'districts, not people', and cited Scott's poem, which refers to 'Eskdale and Liddesdale', in support of this interpretation.
[3] 'Why, my lads, dinna ye march forward in order?' PLF may also be thinking of the German version, *'gürt um dein lichtblau Schwert?'*

Paddy aboard a boat off Hydra, 1959.

Paddy's lover Enrica 'Ricki' Huston. This photograph was taken at her house in Ireland in 1958, after she had met Paddy but before they began an affair.

A cruise aboard Stavros Niarchos's second-best yacht, *Eros II*, in 1955. Sitting in the stern are (left to right) an unidentified man in white; Joan; the foreign correspondent Frank Giles; Paddy; Lady Diana Cooper; Anne Norwich; and (head cut off) Lady Katherine 'Kitty' Giles. A crew member stands in the foreground. The photograph was taken by Diana's son, John Julius Norwich. Note the Jolly Roger.

'I liked Maurice very much, which makes the whole thing even gloomier,' Paddy wrote mournfully, after reading two vicious poems Bowra had written about him, 'The Wounded Gigolo' and 'On the Coast of Terra Fermor'.

Paddy's pal Alexander 'Xan' Fielding, probably in the 1940s.

Paddy and Joan lived in tents during the summer months while their house at Kardamyli in the Mani was under construction. This photograph was taken in 1964.

For several years the building work was a repeated distraction from writing.

Paddy, Joan, Barbara and Niko Ghika and several of the builders on the terrace of the house at Kardamyli, 1967.

The house at Kardamyli under construction, mid-1960s.

Paddy and Joan relaxing on one of the terraces at Kardamyli.

Paddy and 'Debo', Dowager Duchess of Devonshire, close friends and correspondents for more than half a century. This photograph was taken during the celebrations for their book *In Tearing Haste*, published in 2008.

Paddy inscribes a book at Kardamyli, 2008.

He was obviously up to his neck in Sir Walter. But I wonder what makes St James the Good swear by 'Sankt Alban'? According to the amusing note at the end of *The Lay of the Last Minstrel*, the Douglases always swore 'by the right of God' or 'St Bryde' (it doesn't explain why. But I know she was very popular in Scotland – though she never immigrated – as well as England. I'd always looked on St Alban as a Home Counties Roman). Sir W says that the relevant Earl of Angus was very addicted to her. These notes are so riveting – and the poem – I can see I'm going to be sucked in.

I happened to go into the church of St Germain des Prés before setting out for Spain, and admired once more the two splendid Douglas tombs there, in black marble and alabaster: 10th Earl of Angus on the North side, in knee-length armour and a ruff, and, on the S. side, a much younger man, with shoulder-length hair, a Van Dyck moustache (not beard), cavalier knee-length armour and wide lace collar, recumbent on one arm, nursing a claymore: lots of armorial hearts on both. I showed them to Stewart Perowne[1] and Freya years ago, and she said he (the younger one) looked just like a subaltern in a good Scottish regiment. I forgot to note his name, and thought he must be a son of the 10th Earl Angus. I've run him down at last (D.N.B.). He's Ld James Douglas (1617–1645), a grandson, who fell as a general in the French Scottish Brigade, in a skirmish between Douai and Arras. Freya was really right, except for the rank.

I'm very pleased that you liked the poem and that it's all local. Your house looks perfect.[2] It would be lovely to halt there one day, and see the background to all these poems. The nearest I've been is the Cold Comfort Farm where Toby and Emma Tennant live, a once great passage for rievers, Emma says.[3] It looks bleak enough.

All good wishes for 1984,
Yours ever, Paddy

[1] Freya Stark's estranged husband. They had separated when she discovered that he was homosexual.
[2] Runciman lived at Elshieshields, a house dating from the fifteenth century near Lockerbie.
[3] Shaws Farm, home of the Hon. Tobias Tennant and his wife Lady Emma Tennant, one of the Duchess of Devonshire's daughters, is about fifty miles from Elshieshields.

P.S. Stop press! *The Times* of Dec 31st has just arrived with your splendid news, so I've reopened the envelope to enclose our v. warm congratulations.[1] I'm very glad for Sachie, too. His photo makes him look like one of Frederick the Great's generals. I stayed with him a few months ago and found him very cheerful, but a little forgetful about what themes had been touched on. Also very good news about Dimitri Obolensky; but the precedence of prefixes presents a problem.

To Rudi Fischer   Adrianople
30 November 1984   Turkish Eastern Thrace

Dear Rudi,
    About 10 days ago, I sent you and Jock wads of *Woods and Water*[2] typescript, and heard three days ago that Jock's had arrived, the envelope (open, but closed with paper-fasteners) in tatters, but the contents intact. His only contained the last chapter but yours contained 4, 5, 6 and 7, and this makes me anxious about its fate! All's not lost if it has gone astray, as I have another photocopy I can send; but only when I get back to Kardamyli in a month, to finish the final chapter. So, the moment it arrives, <u>could</u> you put me out of my agony by sending a card to K[ardamyli], and another % British Consulate, Istanbul? We will be there in a couple of days.
    You will see, reading the chapters, what a tremendous help you have been, <u>and</u> the literature on Transylvania you sent me. But there are bound to be plenty of faults. I don't want to hurt either Hungarian or Romanian susceptibilities – it's not a polemic book;

---

[1] Both Runciman and Sacheverell Sitwell had been made Companion of Honour. Prince Dimitri Obolensky (1918–2001), Russian-born historian who settled in Britain and became Professor of Russian and Balkan History at the University of Oxford, had been knighted.
[2] The follow-up to *A Time of Gifts*.

but I don't want to suck up, either. For totally different reasons, I'm very fond of both countries. I gave the Transylvanian chapters to Dimitri Obolensky (who has just been to stay) and he said he thought they read distinctly biased on the Hungarian side, and rather pooh-poohed the Romanians. As he is completely neutral himself, this worries me a bit. Constantine & Ioana Soutzo came to stay immediately after. I only gave him Chap 6. to read, 'Carpathian Uplands', which he liked; but, as a Romanian, he was a bit puzzled by my talking about the *Mávos* for *Mures*, and *Temesvár* for *Timisoară*. He accepted my reason viz. 'I'd never, among friends there, heard the river called otherwise.'

When the book comes to Zam and Guraszáda, you will see that there is some funny business viz., 'Angy' doesn't (didn't) really exist, but had to be brought into play for reasons of discretion. By the way, is Angela-Angy a plausible name for a Hungarian girl?[1] She arrived on the page almost without my thinking about it. Also, the journey 'In the Blue' is farther flung than it really was, though otherwise the adventure was roughly as written; but, as I won't be writing about Transylvania again, I was determined to bring more of it in.

Joan and I joined Xan and Magouche in Salonica two days ago, and, after having had a look at the quake-shaken churches, set off east,[2] halting on the site of Philippi, and staying the night in Kavalla, with the sun setting over Thasos. Then on through Xanthi in E. Thrace, plenty of women in *feredjé* [veils pinned in a straight line above the brow and joining under the nose] and *shalvar* [baggy trousers], but, apart from *hodjas* [schoolmasters], no fezes or turbans, as there were thirty years ago. We got to Soufli, then

[1] In *Between the Woods and the Water*, PLF mentions fleetingly meeting a 'very pretty and altogether unusual' young woman named Xenia near the Transylvanian village of Zám; and describes several encounters with 'a pretty and funny girl in a red skirt called Angéla', with whom he has an affair. In fact, these two were the same: a young Serb woman called Xenia Csernovits, unhappily married to a Hungarian husband.
[2] An earthquake in the Thessaloniki area in 1978 was felt throughout northern Greece, Yugoslavia and Bulgaria.

Didymóteicho yesterday afternoon, drove along the poplar-lined Hebros river (Bulg. Maritza), then over the bridge into Turkey and here, arriving at sunset – a great forest of minarets and domes, pigeons and rooks, and have spent the day looking at the mosques of Sinan, and a beautiful one built by Bayazet. It's now October 1st, and in a couple of hours we push off to Constantinople, but not before climbing one of the tallest minarets – if, as of yore, one is still allowed to – and looking upstream into Bulgaria and the field where Valens was defeated by the Goths and the Emperor Baldwin captured by the Bulgars.[1] Barbarossa sacked it on the way through.[2]

All greetings to you and Dagmar!
Yours in haste Paddy

The American photographer Milton Gendel (b. 1919) married Judy Montagu in 1962. He has continued to live in Rome since her premature death at the age of only forty-nine.

To Milton Gendel   Kardamyli
The day after we talked on the blower [mid-1980s]   Messenia
                                                          Greece

My dear Milton,
    I was rather over ambitious and optimistic about participating in the Tiber Island evening. The truth of the matter is I have slowed

---

[1] Valens (328–378), Eastern Roman Emperor from 364 to 378, was defeated by the Goths and killed at Adrianople, a major city of inland Thrace, near the modern border of Greece and Bulgaria. Over the centuries there have been numerous battles on this site; for example, in 324 Constantine the Great defeated his rival Licinius here. Another Battle of Adrianople occurred around in 1205, when the Bulgars defeated an army under Baldwin I (or Baudouin) (1172–c.1205), Count of Flanders and one of the leaders of the Fourth Crusade, who only months before had been crowned Emperor of Constantinople. Baldwin was taken prisoner and some time later put to death.
[2] The city of Adrianople was sacked by the Holy Roman Emperor Frederick Barbarossa during the Third Crusade, late in 1189 or early 1190.

down to such a snail's pace comprising <u>anything</u> that I'll have to, most reluctantly, give up the idea. I've such a stack of waiting work that this would merely become another item at the end of a long list. I wish it were not so. I tried out, as an example of a scheme emerging from yours and Judy's house, my settling in the castle at Passerano, the flag, the rats, the mice, and the final retreat to Ischia – this over dinner last night – and they thought it a <u>fairly</u> amusing tale, but the link with San Bartolomeo too slender. And as for our adventure with Cybele, unpublishable! Stolen antiquities ...[1] But I do want to put these stories into a late autobiographical narrative, so I think we ought to leave it till then, if I am spared. I am terribly sorry to be such a broken reed.

What fun all that was! And Bomarzo[2] and the holy foreskin ...

I bet J.J. [John Julius] will do brilliantly with Rahere.[3] He's a fascinating subject. The Kipling story I ran on about was called 'The Tree of Justice', at the end of a book of stories called *Rewards and Fairies*, sequel to *Puck of Pook's Hill*, all about English history from the Romans down, told by Puck to two children, Dan and Una. They were also read aloud by my mother to my sister and me, and we adored them, and the interspersed poems – 'Cold Iron' – 'A Saint Helena Lullaby' – 'The Road Through the Woods' etc. ...

Rahere, in early life, was a member – 'a minstrel' – even a knight jester, wearing brightly coloured tights, in the wickedly degenerate and sodomitical circle of William II, the Conqueror's successor, called Rufus after his hair or complexion (the King, that is, who was always swearing by the Holy Face of Lucca – Volta Santa?) I think it was after his pilgrimage to Rome, and a vision of St Bartholomew – on the Island – that he took orders

[1] PLF had bought a stone statue of the Roman goddess of fertility from an Italian farmer, and smuggled it back to England. See pp. 145–7.
[2] The Garden of Bomarzo is a mannerist complex of sculptures and small buildings created in the sixteenth century in a wooded valley, in the province of Viterbo, Italy.
[3] Rahere, a young monk and a favourite in the court of Henry I, established St Bartholomew's Hospital in London and the nearby Church of St Bartholomew the Great, to give thanks for his recovery from malaria, contracted on a pilgrimage to Rome.

and built the hospital and marvellous church. I long to know more about him. I wonder if J.J. has written it down. Wm Rufus was shot dead – by mistake or on purpose? – by an arrow loosed off during a hunt in the New Forest in 1100, I think, 34 years after Hastings.

I was best man to Rowly St Oswald in the church [of St Bartholomew], when he married Enid Bagnold's daughter.[1] It didn't last very long … A dash for the post!

Love Paddy (love to all)

The American writer David Mason (b. 1954) and his then-wife, Jonna Heinrich, went to Greece in 1980 and lived for just over a year in Kardamyli, where they became friendly with Paddy and Joan.

To David Mason   Kardamyli
27 April 1985   Messenia
                         Greece

Dear David,

I was – am – delighted and overcome by your generous and splendid review in *Sequoia*,[2] and very ashamed of myself for being such a long time in writing. It arrived very late – what a nice thought to try and get it here for my birthday; but you know Greek posts! – and when it did, I was absolutely in the throes of finishing the last chapter of the sequel to *A Time of Gifts*, and didn't dare break off, knowing full well that you would accept this as a valid excuse. Anyway, I have just put the manuscript in the Oitylos-Athens bus,[3] where it is to be met by the typist, who will get to

[1] In 1953 Rowland Winn, 4th Baron St Oswald (1916–84), married Laurian, daughter of Sir Roderick Jones and Enid Bagnold, author of *National Velvet* (1935). They were divorced in 1955. See p. 66.
[2] Mason had written an essay on PLF's books entitled 'Walking to Byzantium' for the spring 1985 number of the Stanford magazine *Sequoia*.
[3] This was the regular bus route from the Mani up to Athens; before the recent toll roads this was a long trip of around six hours, with two food stops en route.

work at once: now for pruning, revision, scissors and paste, the moment I get it back …

I've just re-read 'Walking to Byzantium' and I am not only – naturally – overjoyed by the contents, but enormously impressed by the style, marvellous mixture of ease and seriousness and euphony: the work of a poet. I'm getting it photostatted to send to my publisher Jock Murray. He'll fling his hat in the air. I do hope Elisabeth Sifton of Viking-Penguin has seen it. I think I'll send it to her too. Bruce Chatwin has just been here, and I think is coming through again, so I'll put it in his purview as well …

Apart from a trip to London and then Ireland this time last year, and a journey to Turkey in the autumn, we have been here all the time, but leave for England for a month next week. Lela and Petro have opened a taverna in the village, and it is doing very well – but we don't see much of them here – one of them for an hour in the morning, so we have become better at doing things for ourselves. It's not been a severe winter, but this last couple of weeks it has rained a lot, so everyone in the village is wreathed in smiles; it is just what the olives needed, so it looks as if we will have a splendid crop.

The sequel to *A Time of Gifts* is just about the same length, so, though it takes us on about 500 miles, Murray has decided to get it out, and publish the rest, when written, as Vol III. This takes us from Esztergom, where A T of G ends, to Budapest, then across the Great Hungarian Plain on a borrowed horse, into the Transylvanian part of Romania (half the summer), then south through the Carpathian mountains and forests to Orsova, the Iron Gates and the Kazan pass: then stop, with the words *to be concluded,* viz., at the Bosporus. The name is to be *Between the Woods and the Water*, the water being the Danube, and the woods the forests mentioned above. Now for Bulgaria, E. Romania, the Black Sea and Turkey … I'll send you a copy when it appears.

Thank you very much again for an indescribable shot in the arm. I feel enormously binged up by it!

Joan sends her love to you both, and so do I.

Yours ever,
Paddy

Paddy responded enthusiastically to a proposal that his poem 'Greek Archipelagoes', originally published in 'Penguin New Writing' back in 1949, should be republished in a new anthology, to be edited by the poet and children's book writer, Kevin Crossley-Holland.

Crossley-Holland was then living in the East Anglian village of Walsham-le-Willows, the site of Walsham Hall, where Paddy had been at school for a year or so in the 1920s. As he had related in A Time of Gifts, *Paddy had been sent to this 'co-educational and very advanced school for difficult children' after being expelled from a more conventional equivalent.*

Paddy thanked Crossley-Holland for a copy of his Penguin Book of Norse Myths *(1980). 'Oddly enough, I first came across Scandinavian myths during my brief sojourn at Walsham Hall, where I remember hearing "The Death of Baldur" read aloud; so I have just re-read it. It is beautifully done, and I very much look forward to the rest.'*

<table>
<tr><td>To Kevin Crossley-Holland</td><td>Kardamyli</td></tr>
<tr><td>19 July 1985</td><td>Messenia</td></tr>
<tr><td></td><td>Greece</td></tr>
</table>

Dear Mr Crossley-Holland,

I am delighted at the idea of 'Greek Archipelagoes' going into *The Oxford Book of Travel Verse.*[1] I had forgotten all about it, and, alas, can't put my hand on it. I would be enormously grateful if you could send me a photocopy of it, so that I can have a last look ...

I am amazed by your knowing about my brief scholastic sojourn in Walsham-le-Willows! I must have been about ten years old[2] at the time. If you come across a book I wrote a few years ago entitled

---

[1] Published in 1989.

[2] He was nine when he arrived, and ten when he left.

A Time of Gifts, it is touched on in the introduction,[1] where I called it, rather transparently, Salsham-le-Sallows,[2] and the headmaster, who was called Major Faithfull,[3] becomes Major Truthful, changes made for the sake of descendants (he had two sons, called Glynn and Bernard.) I am sorry the Hall has been destroyed.[4] I remember it very clearly, also climbing about in the attics, one of which had a chestful of parchment and documents in what I remember as various scripts from about Elizabethan times. I wonder what family lived there.[5] I also remember what seemed a very tall belfry to the church, with four pinnacles.[6]

The gardener's daughter, two years older than me, was called Eileen Fairweather. I was very keen on her, and she became the Maid Marian of a sort of amateur Robin Hood gang.[7] I wonder if the name – or she herself – exists, aged about 72?[8]

With every good wish,

Yours sincerely,
Patrick Leigh Fermor

[1] 'English schools, once they depart from the conventional track, are oases of strangeness and comedy … It was run by a grey-haired, wild-eyed man called Major Truthful, and when I spotted two beards – then very rare – among the mixed and eccentric-looking staff, and the heavy bangles and the amber and the tassels and the homespun, and met my fellow-alumni – about thirty boys and girls from four years old to nearly twenty, all in brown jerkins and sandals … I knew I was going to like it. The nature-worshipping eurhythmics in a barn and the country dances in which the Major led both staff and children, were a shade bewildering at first, because everybody was naked,' *A Time of Gifts*, p. 4.
[2] 'Sallow' is goat-willow, once used locally in building.
[3] Major Theodore Faithfull, inventor of the 'Frigidity Machine', had been commissioned into the Veterinary Corps. His granddaughter is the singer Marianne Faithfull (b. 1946).
[4] The Hall had been demolished, to be replaced by a substantial neo-Georgian house on the same site.
[5] Walsham Hall passed through various hands before coming into the ownership of the Holmes family in the early eighteenth century.
[6] St Mary the Virgin, Walsham-le-Willows.
[7] 'To choose a Maid Marian and a band, to get the girls to weave yards of Lincoln green on the therapeutic looms and then to slice and sew them into rough hoods with crenellated collars, cut bows and string them, carry off raspberry canes for arrows, and to take to the woods, was a matter of days.' *A Time of Gifts*, pp. 4–5.
[8] Crossley-Holland wrote a piece for the parish magazine about 'Maid Marian', and subsequently met Eileen Fairweather, who was amused and delighted by PLF's memories.

To Janetta and Jaime Parladé   Kardamyli
27 August 1985   Messenia
                                                Greece

Darling Janetta and Jaime,

I keep wondering how you all got on in Kashmir, and whether you went to Ladakh, and had a look at all those Tibetan monasteries I've just been reading about, by that gifted chap we met at Cressida's wedding.[1] It does sound extraordinary, and I long to hear about it all, so does Joan, so send news when you can.

I can't tell you what a blessing Lennox Gardens was![2] I got through a tremendous amount of work, and loved camping there with you, even dealing with the baptism of the flat by total immersion. The last two days at Hampstead – up till 3.30 both mornings, slogging away all day, with relays of retyping being rushed up from Albemarle St every few hours. It was a sort of trance, breaking off for dinner with nothing visible except millions of leaves and the spire of the church next door surrounded by starlings and a mass of birdsong hard by – I bet blackbirds, as you suggested, and not thrushes.

A frightful shock awaited me here. Stepping onto the scales, I saw I'd gone up 5 kilos during my English stay, and stepped off again filled with horror; but since then thanks to delicious but suitable grub, clean living and swimming a mile a day, I've managed to shed 8, and am still waning. I get out of the waves svelter and browner with every passing day. The only trouble is, we are meeting Xan and Magouche in Frankfurt on the first of October for a lovely tour of the baroque buildings of S. Germany and perhaps of Austria and I dread to think of all the temptations there, and every [illegible] round guzzling like ogres …

[1] Andrew Harvey (b. 1952), author of *A Journey in Ladakh* (1983); Cressida Connolly (b. 1960), daughter of Cyril Connolly, married Charles Hudson in 1985.
[2] The Parladés had allowed PLF and Joan to stay in their London flat.

It has been bakingly hot here, but, thank God, this is a cool house, and if there ever is a breeze about – and there usually is – we get it. We've had a carpenter in all day – at last – for the past week, a charming old boy, who is repairing all the shutters, which were beginning to crumble away. We've got to have the place looking as nice as we can, as I have written something about it for one of those books Alvilde Lees-Milne edits. This one is called *The Englishman's Room*, an idiotic title, but an excuse for describing the big room here, which I enjoyed. Little Ld Moore, Garrett Drogheda's son,[1] is flying out on the 4th Sept specially to take photos of it, so we're a bit nervous.

Almost three weeks ago, Coote telephoned, and rather shyly announced that she and the Mad Boy had decided to marry.[2] It's the most marvellous news, and I love to think of her in the house, after all her vicissitudes.

I forgot to say that a second shock awaited us here: a prefab, put up a couple of years ago, had blossomed out balefully, with bright lights announcing DISCO; and two nights after we arrived it struck up, making the night hideous with its jittering pandemonium. We thought we would have to go away forever. It went on for a fortnight: listening to the din only 800 yards away, we imagined the place bursting with people, all going mad. Well, do you know, not a single person went, and suddenly, one night, there was silence; then closed shutters. My word, it was an anxious time. It does seem wrong that anyone with the necessary machinery has everyone, for a mile around or more, at their mercy.

[1] Henry Dermot Ponsonby (b. 1937), photographer, known professionally as Derry Moore, Earl of Drogheda since his father's death in 1989.
[2] Coote Lygon had unwisely agreed to marry her old friend, the 'Mad Boy' Robert Heber-Percy, former companion to Lord Berners, from whom he had inherited the estate at Faringdon. ('A Darby and Joan engagement just announced in *The Times* has led to much chuckling on the grouse moors this week,' reported the *Daily Express*.) As might have been predicted, the marriage was not a success, and Coote soon retreated to a nearby bungalow.

John Julius Norwich and his Molly[1] are turning up tomorrow for a few days, then one or two more people during the course of Sept, and David Sylvester and his girl[2] at the end of it, before we buzz off.

Latest news. Two mornings ago, we found a very brightly coloured snake, with gaudy patterns of orange, black and white leopard spots, dead on the bathroom floor, presumably after a tremendous Riki-Tiki-Tavi[3] fight with one of the pussies, although there are no marks on it. We looked it up: it was a totally harmless rat-snake, and I forgot to mention that, halfway along, it had a bulge, obviously caused by a rat. Perhaps it expired of tummy ache, and no cat at all. It looked just like a miniature version of those pictures illustrating sleepy pythons or boa-constrictors digesting buffaloes in the Wonder Book of Nature.

I was terrifically pleased to hand over the book at first. Now, of course, I pine for it back, to go on topping and tailing forever …

Thank you both so much again for making me the first to shelter in that kind haven. I don't know whether – or how? – to send this to Cous-Cous,[4] or to Tramores, so I'll play safe and do the latter, trusting that somebody will send it on. I long to hear about the great move.

Tons of love from us both,
Paddy

---

[1] John Julius Norwich's second wife, the Hon. Mary (Makins) Philipps, née Makins, known as 'Molly'.

[2] David Sylvester (1924–2001), art critic, and the writer Shena Mackay (b. 1944).

[3] The mongoose in the Kipling story who fights cobras.

[4] The Parladés' new house in Andalusia, Alcuzcuz.

Between the Woods and the Water, *the follow-up to* A Time of Gifts, *was published towards the end of 1986.*

To George 'Dadie' Rylands   Kardamyli
8 December 1986

My dear Dadie,
     'and ALL are vain'[1] – I know, I know, or rather I soon discovered, after sending the proofs back and telephoned the rectification from here, but too late! Also ['scorn and hate'] in the next line are in the wrong order. I can't get it into my head that I have a brain which is half scrambler and half-colander and I should look up and check the simplest thing. I wring my hands in the watches of the night ... I wish I could find the Max Beerbohm passage which says, in, no doubt, totally different words: 'Some people say I am bitter. Well, perhaps I am: twenty [illegible] years ago they printed a semi-colon when I had written a colon ...'[2]
     But all this is not the reason for this letter, which is to bring our love, and a thousand wishes for a Happy Christmas and New Year from your devoted

Joan and Pad

---

[1] 'All thoughts to rive the heart are here, and all are vain:/ Horror and scorn and hate and fear and indignation'. These lines, from A. E. Housman's *A Shropshire Lad*, were misquoted in the first printing of *Between the Woods and the Water*. Rylands also pointed out that the 'r' in 'Azay-le-Rideau' should be capitalised, though he failed to note that 'Rideau' is singular, not plural, and therefore should be 'le-Rideau', not 'les-Rideau'.

[2] 'On page 24 of my Works,' Beerbohm told a friend, 'there is a misplaced comma, which has darkened much of my life and has often made me appear more bitter than I really am. It and the death of Lucien de Rubempré are the only things I have never been quite able to dismiss.' Beerbohm was paraphrasing Oscar Wilde, who wrote that the death of Lucien de Rubempré was 'one of the greatest tragedies of my life ... a grief from which I have never been able completely to rid myself'. Lucien de Rubempré is a character in Balzac's sequence of novels, *La Comédie humaine*.

To Philip Sherrard   Kardamyli
14 December 1986   Messenia
                                                         Greece

My dear Philip,

Thank you very much for your letter and many apologies for being such an age answering. I feel very buoyed up by your kind words [about *Between the Woods and the Water*], and am particularly delighted that the bits you liked are my favourites too. It's marvellous being got the point of! All your grammatical points are right, except I think 'scatter' can be either intransitive or transitive. 'The farmer's wife scattered the grain, the White Leghorns scattered over the yard pecking it up, while the Rhode Island Reds, scattered the other side of the wire-netting, gazed enviously ...'

Many thanks, too, for your splendid lecture.[1] Dimitri [Obolensky] told me that it was by far the most popular and cheered to the echo. It's tip-top and I have showed it to many. Do you want it back eventually, or can I hang on to it? If not, I'll get it mimeographed.

I like your idea of the dedication to all the people who were so kind to me, and who are dead now. The end of some of them was shattering, and I carefully kept that out of the book, as it would have cast a blight over the whole thing. But I might write an appendix to the last volume, saying who everyone was who was unnamed, and what happened. It wasn't all tragic, but everyone was uprooted, which they took with wonderful stoicism. István – Elemér v. Klobusiçky (he chose the name himself) – had fled to Budapest, where he toiled away doing translating. We spent several days together in recent years, and corresponded frequently. But the year before last, I found his flat locked, and went through all Budapest till I found him in an old folks' home and he couldn't recognise me (having broken a leg and being in bed) but kept on

---

[1] Given at the centenary celebrations of the British School at Athens, and entitled 'The Greek View of Life'.

saying 'if you are going to Greece give my love to L.F, my dear old friend …' He died a few months after. The home, oddly enough, was very nice, he was obviously loved by the other four chaps in the same room, and the nurses were nice. Angéla is really Xenia of the preceding chapter: I had to blur things a bit. She also retired to Budapest, when Romanian anti-Magyar harassment and dispossession were at their height. She was billeted in a small flat with an odious woman who never stopped shouting and quarrelling, until, as Elemér told me, 'her hot Serbian blood was too much for her. She seized a knife and stabbed her stone dead.' There was a famous trial, but all the neighbours in the building said that she was such a fiend, and so hated by all, that Xenia-Angéla was declared innocent and set free at once! The young boy Hansi Meran, 13 then, I found (after meeting some cousins in London) living at a cottage outside the castle, surrounded by geese and pigs, enormously tall and strong, just widowed from the village girl he had married. We sat up drinking whisky till late. There were one or two pictures I recognised, and a nice print of M. Antoinette. He pointed to a big Biedermeier table, rescued from the *kastély*, and asked me if I remembered it. 'It's where you sat and wrote in a big green book. We peeped at you through the door slit by the hinges, as you hadn't shut it.' He had been arrested by the Russians on the way back from the Eastern Front and sent to Siberia for nine years. A fine chap.

The only thing that worries me about the otherwise marvellous Yeats quotation is 'gazebo'.[1] Otherwise perfect. One dikker says 'etymology doubtful', another said 'a latin future, like *videbo*'?? *Gazo, gazebo, gazui, gazitum*? Well well.

No more now, except all the best and a happy Christmas to you both, and to all,

Paddy

[1] 'We the great gazebo built./ They convicted us of guilt;/ Bid me strike a match and blow', from W. B. Yeats's 'In Memory of Eva Gore-Booth and Con Markievicz' (1927). Sherrard had suggested printing this poem as an epigraph to the final volume of PLF's trilogy. In the event it was not used.

To Rudi Fischer   Kardamyli
10 February 1987   Messenia
                                                          Greece

Dear Rudi,

<u>At last!</u> I've managed to clear the decks, and the last item was writing a review of a book called *A Bonus for Laughter* (a Betjeman quotation) by Alan Pryce-Jones.[1] I undertook it on behalf [of] a v. nice young journalist in *The Times* who gave the book a smashing review.[2] He implored me to write the leading review for <u>another</u> new daily, whose name escapes me, coming out soon, and of which he is to be literary editor.[3] I am going to try and avoid them in future, as they take me days and days.

Rudi, I have been a bad correspondent. But I have a bundle of Rudiana before me, and I will try and deal with what crops up as I go through this. (By the way, I hope I have written <u>something</u> to wish you and Dagmar a Happy 1987? If <u>not</u>, I do so now, with knobs on.)

It's disgraceful, but the top letter is a November one. Alas, I somehow missed the Meridian review.[4] I didn't take Jan Morris's one as bitchy, or meant to be, really, but what she thought – after

[1] *The Bonus of Laughter* is a memoir by Alan Pryce-Jones (1908–2000), writer, critic and editor of *The Times Literary Supplement* 1948–59, who in the early 1930s had been briefly engaged to Joan. The quotation is from Betjeman's poem 'The Last Laugh', published in his last collection *A Nip in the Air* (1974):

'I made hay while the sun shone. /My work sold. /Now, if the harvest is over /And the world cold,/ Give me the bonus of laughter /As I lose hold.'

[2] Allan Massie (b. 1938). His review of *The Bonus of Laughter* was published in *The Times* on 15 January 1987.

[3] Presumably the *Independent*, founded towards the end of 1986. Sebastian Faulks was the first literary editor.

[4] 'I liked the chap on [the BBC] World Service [arts programme] "Meridian" best,' wrote Fischer on 9 November 1986. 'In a few sober words he put his finger on precisely why it is such a wonderful book, so unique among travel books these days. Instead of telling us about missed trains, complaining about being cheated, bedbugs and bureaucracy, it truly conveys how a man of seventy remembers the great times he had when he was nineteen.'

all, she gave me a tremendous preliminary pat on the back![1] I must say on the whole they were marvellous. Apropos of Athos, I'll try and get *Mönchsland Athos*.[2] Ought I to read *The Waters of Marah*?[3] Twenty years ago, writing about Greece, I would probably have taken a Bulga-phobe line, but I won't now – <u>nor would I have at the time</u> – it just shows how affected one is by adopting nationalisms. Yes! I have read the Atiya Aziz Suryal Nicopolis book![4] I took it out of the London Library in early summer. St[even] Runciman obviously used it a lot, but Barbara Tuchman tackled him on several points in *A Distant Mirror*, and, I think, wins.

Back to reviews (next letters): I am surprised there haven't been a lot more hostile ones. I think promotion and 'hype' signing sessions etc., of which Jock (bless him) had arranged a lot, and the concomitant (I <u>won't</u> say consequent!) best selling is bound, by natural reflex, to put some backs up. But the hostile reviews, if one feels they are unfair, <u>are</u> upsetting. Betjeman used to say, after some trouncing in the Press, very sadly, 'The trouble is, Paddy, that I'm afraid unmitigated praise is what one wants ...' I agree about the index. It's frightful, and I'm trying to get something done about it.

I think your part about the 'I' figure in BWW seeming much older and more self-possessed than the same figure a month or two before is a very good one, and I'll watch it in Vol III – anyway, the fact that I'm no longer having a swell time in *schlösser* will simplify things a lot; also, the Athos part is recorded at so much greater length, that it will <u>have</u> to be in tune. I'll take these hurdles when I come to them.

What a nice idea, a boxed 3 vol edition when all is over! I agree about T of G being the best overall title. No inspiration so far about

---

[1] 'Journey in the Balkans to the Land of Dreams', *The Times*, 24 October 1986. 'Mr Fermor is beyond cavil the greatest of living travel writers, and in this work he is exploring the very farthest boundaries of the genre ... Mr Fermor is perhaps more fascinated by the ways of the lost Austro-Hungarian aristocracy than most of us are; and in this as in other pursuits he is led very nearly into self-parody'. Jan Morris subsequently wrote an introduction to the paperback edition.

[2] F. Dölger, et al., *Mönchsland Athos* (Munich, 1943).

[3] Peter Hammond, *The Waters of Marah: The Present State of the Greek Church* (1956).

[4] *The Crusade of Nicopolis* (1934).

a name for [volume] III! I adore Andrew Devonshire's suggested 'Shanks's Europe', but of course it won't do.

Later. About breaking silence re 'Angéla'.[1] I thought we had stopped the interview (which took place, probably against the rules, in White's).[2] I was a bit vexed when I saw it – then delighted with the rest – and regretted having not kept my mouth shut. (N. Shakespeare is an extremely nice chap.) I don't quite know what to do about it. I'd love to do X[enia] a good turn if I could. Should I send her a book? Would she be embarrassed? If you have any idea, do let me know. Everybody loves that part of the book. I feel rather ashamed of the *Dichtung*[3] being such a success, but it's only geographical *Dichtung*, and, I feel poetically right; but hush! When I was staying at Zám, there were some relations of X – I don't think of Gábor's – who lived very close to the gates of the *kastély*, and, after I'd been there a few days disapproved highly of my presence there. The only other person in the house was an old servant of her father's, rather an amusing old boy, who did not disapprove at all. (Gábor was in Pest, I think.) But it was because of their badgering (quite rightly, I suppose, from a formal point of view) that I moved on to Gureszáada and the slightly shorter ranged adventures that ended at Déva. Elemér was not only an ally, but an ex-favourite of X's, so in league with X and me, the way it sometimes washes out. I remember Elemér's wondering – rather more than wondering – whether it was he who had, as it were, initiated X's wild ways. Graf Jenö [Teleki], who was amused by her, thought that these ways began in extreme youth, when she was at school during the Béla Kun period, when, he said, everybody mated as freely as birds.

How interesting that *pisztráng* – and all the Slav words except Russian, including the Greek πέστροφα [trout] comes from a word for mottled – speckled?

No, the Romanian journey doesn't go as far as Băleni, I hadn't met Balasha yet. We met in Athens in May next year. She had been *en poste* there with her Spanish diplomat husband, Paco de

[1] See footnote on p. 347.
[2] An interview with Nicholas Shakespeare, literary editor of the *Daily Telegraph*.
[3] Literally 'Poetry', used here to mean Art, as a justification for Fantasy. See *Dashing for the Post*, pp. 363–4.

Amat y Torres, a dashing scamp who eloped with the wife of his British opposite number's (and great friend's) wife Bill Cavendish Bentinck, who was also a great friend of B's. He's now pretty old, and very nice, and later Ambassador to Poland (while Paco became Ambassador to Delhi, still with Clothilde, Bill's wife. In 1979, Bill succeeded his brother as 9th and last Duke of Portland).[1] I arrived in Athens a year after these events, when Bill and Paco had both been appointed elsewhere. Balasha remained, painting portraits in a charming little house in the Plaka, in a lane under the Acropolis, which is where I moved into, before we did a bunk to a watermill opposite Poros at Lemonodassos, catching a boat for Constantza that autumn, then Galata and Băleni.

The furthest I went on the journey was to a Villa Eftimia in Sinaia, where I stayed with the beautiful daughter of the Foreign Minister mentioned in the Teleki chapter, Filipescu (the one shot through the bladder in a duel in Paris).[2] She was married to an Irish *Reichsgraf* called Ambrose O'Kelly of Gallagh and Tycooly (!). The passionate bridge-playing lady with the long cigarette holder was also there, called Marthe Mitelinen. In Bucharest I stayed with Jo v. Rantzau.[3]

As you see, I'm trying to work through questions methodically! I'm catching up with my bit, and putting the pages into the Fischer file as I go …

12 Feb. Marvellous timing! A letter from you has just arrived, overflowing with kind wishes for the anniversary! Couldn't have been better! Also, I ate not a mouthful yesterday, so your dietary advice doesn't fall on deaf ears! I'll answer that in my next, as this ought to leave now. All greetings to you and Dagmar for 1987,

Yours ever, Paddy

[1] The diplomat and businessman Victor Frederick William 'Bill' Cavendish-Bentinck, 9th Duke of Portland (1897–1990) had married Clothilde Bruce Quigley (d. 1984), an American, in 1924. In 1939 he received a telephone call at his office from his Hungarian maid to tell him that his wife had left him, taking their children with her. He was obliged to resign from the Foreign Office as a result of the publicity surrounding his subsequent divorce.
[2] See *Between the Woods and the Water*, p. 133.
[3] The German diplomat Josias von Rantzau, known as 'Joey'. He encouraged PLF to help himself to drinks, cigarettes and cigars – 'we get them practically free'. A relative of his Romanian mistress, Marcelle Catargi, would marry Balasha's niece, Ina.

P.S. The book is out in America, to my astonishment, and a bundle of reviews has arrived, all nice, except a real stinker in something called *The New Republic*, by an English teacher called Verlyn Klinkenborg.[1] Another lady, rather old, I should think, with whom I've exchanged a letter or two in the past (I spoke in German) after asking [illegible] what she [illegible] to send me, knowing I liked songs, got a niece to photostat a collection called *Der Zupgeisenhausel*. It looks splendid. A nice professor from Sussex has sent me the musical notation and words for 'Érika buza' [by] Bartok, 'so now you will be able to sing it in your bath'.

P.P.S. I got a nice letter from Egon Ronay[2] (whom I don't know) containing one or two Transylvanian cooking recipes. Also, letters from two English women who had stayed at O'Kígyós[3] just after me, one of them playing bike polo a lot, the other I think governess to Sergei W[enckheim]'s younger brother, Christian. S[ergei] was killed in the War, the younger got away to Algiers, and, it seems died of some illness there, poor fellow.

Marie-Lyse Ruhemann, née Cantacuzène, was a distant cousin of Balasha's. When Paddy was at Dumbleton he would often go over to a cottage on the Sudeley Estate that she and her husband Frank rented for their holidays.

To Marie-Lyse Ruhemann   Kardamyli
17 January 1989   Messenia
                                            Greece

Dear Marie-Lyse – if I may make so bold
    How lovely to see those photographs of Dărmăneşti.[4] I'd heard of it so often, and now it has reality. How you must miss it.

[1] Verlyn Klinkenborg (b. 1952), writer on rural topics and newspaper editor.
[2] Egon Miklos Ronay (1915–2010), Hungarian-born food critic, author and publisher of a series of guides to British and Irish restaurants and hotels.
[3] The house of Count Józsi Wenckheim, where PLF learned to play bicycle polo.
[4] A town in eastern Romania.

<u>What</u> a good article in *The Spectator*. He's awfully good and writes very well. <u>Admirable</u> final remarks about Ceausescu.[1] I'm also v. impressed with what Jessica Douglas-Home writes about Romania. She's charming and v. pretty – and v. nice – I'd no idea how intelligent she was.

I think Băleni did have something to do with the Băleann family, and that they were relations. I think Balasha and Pomme's branch was called C-Deleni, like Ghyka-Deleni. Their grandfather's mother was a Ghyka-Deleni from that extraordinary rambling house near Botosani, where old Pr. Gregoire G.D. lived. He was grandfather of Alexander Mourouzi and Alex Ventura, second cousins of B's, who lived at Golosei about fifteen miles from Băleni, a marvellously eccentric household. Mourouzi is at Vitry, in Switzerland, now, Ventura still in Bucharest. I heard from him last month.

About the post-war foregathering. I wrote a long thing about the Danube for an American magazine, told Balasha (living with Pomme & Constantine Donici in a rather charming roomy attic in Pucioasă, near Ploesti, where they had settled after being chucked out of Băleni) where I would be staying – all paid for, that is – at the Athenes Palas, and there nice Ina Catargi (a schoolgirl when I last saw her) came and picked me up and off we went to Pucioasă, with me on the back of her motorbike. I stayed 24 hours there – we didn't dare more – with Balasha, Pomme, Constantine and Ina, talking and laughing nonstop. It was marvellous. Back in Bucharest, I saw Ina and her husband Michel Catargi several times, and also her 1st cousin (distant of Michel's) Bishy, Mic's son, totally unchanged. (Heard from but recently, too. He, Ventura and Ileana Sturdza are my three surviving correspondents in Romania.) Pomme & Ina came to stay here twice, which was lovely – Balasha somehow couldn't face it alas. We corresponded very frequently, and when cancer killed her twelve years ago, I went to see Pomme, and she gave me all <u>my</u> side of the correspondence. I saw Pomme in Paris, about ten years ago, when poor Ina was struck down by the same illness; then Pomme, six years ago, Constantine having died soon after my first visit. The reaper has

---

[1] Noel Malcolm, 'Living with the Collaborators', *Spectator*, 6 January 1989. 'A crude internal policy of Romanian chauvinism was one of Ceasescu's favourite tools.'

been very active. I was impressed, in all this by their absolutely indestructible morale, and the humour and spirit which never left them.

What I meant to tell you was not all this, but that the first thing Balasha did when I arrived on the back of the motorbike was to give me back my old diary, which I had left at Băleni. It has been an unbelievable help with these books.

We are just back from the Massif Central and the Lot. Back to work! All fond wishes for 1989 to you and yours. Do give my [best] wishes to Marina, if you are in touch. It was lovely her turning up here a few years ago with Costi.

Yours sincerely
Paddy LF

Their mother was Anna Vacaresco, dr. of Rudu V., and gr.gr.dr of Furtuna V. Their father, known as 'le Knéaz', also had an estate in Bessarabia and was largely [brought] up in Russia. Not a close relation of the C. Speranskys but friends. We saw Serge C[antacuzène], in Paris, charming. Their son Mihai lives in America.

After he was evacuated from Crete following the German invasion in May 1941, Ralph Stockbridge (1917–2010) volunteered to return almost immediately, operating undercover, constantly on the run, posing as a village schoolmaster; on one occasion he bumped into a German soldier and said 'Gosh! Sorry!' in English, but fortunately the German did not react. When Paddy arrived on the island the two worked together to achieve their objectives – though Paddy was SOE and Stockbridge SIS, two organisations which did not always work happily together. After the war ended Stockbridge remained with SIS; the two men occasionally corresponded, usually on Cretan matters.

To Ralph Stockbridge   Kardamyli
11 February 1989   Messenia
         Greece

Dear Ralph,

Thanks for your letter – also for the first refusal of the typographical colonel's book;[1] but I think I'll stick to Ld B[yron]'s letters, which I expect you've got, in that multi-volume edition.[2] He really is wonderful, wherever you pick him up, not anywhere near the shit that his detractors maintained, extremely clever, packed with common sense, also with warm feelings and humour. I wonder what he would have been like as a portly mid-Victorian worthy with a watch-chain and a top hat, fit subject for one of those Max Beerbohm youth and age caricatures?

I only saw the TV South Bank video[3] last week, and am v. upset about it for certain specific reasons. They recorded <u>8 hours</u> of gassing away. I had specifically asked them to underplay the Kreipe operation, as everyone is sick of it and it always seems to lead to complications. I went into Crete a certain amount, the battle, and

---

[1] Stockbridge had been offered a copy of Colonel Leicester Stanhope's rare book on the war of independence in Greece (1825), which included his reminiscences of Byron. 'He and Byron were chalk and cheese,' Stockbridge commented. Stanhope was known as 'the typographical Colonel' because of his attempts to set up newspapers.

[2] Leslie A. Marchand (ed.), *Byron's Letters and Journals* (twelve volumes, 1973–82).

[3] London Weekend Television's *South Bank Show* had broadcast a television documentary about PLF.

John Pendlebury[1] as the *fons et origo* [spring and source] of what
we were all up to, saying that I was a v. late comer after you, Jack,[2]
Monty[3] and Xan, then mentioned all the rest of us by name. Then,
I was led away to the general, gave a brief account of the operation, and managed to mention every single one of the Cretans
and, of course, Billy [Moss] many times. In the process of cutting,
they got rid of all this, except the Kreipe op. The TV people were
bombarded by bitter complaints ... but I think, and hope, that it is
all straightened out now. I don't know about the readings, some (in
letters) were for, some against. I'd forgotten all about *The Violins*, and
I don't think they had heard of it (except director David Cheshire,[4]
a v. literate Cambridge figure, often a bit tight, but v. nice, sometimes weeping on Joan's shoulders 'They all hate me so!'). I wish J.J.
Cooper [Norwich] had done it instead of Barg,[5] who knew nothing
about the whole thing, whereas J.J. does about everything, and is
a friend since a toddler. He and David did a v. much better and
less pretentious thing on the same theme four years ago. I'd got
George Ps[ychoundakis] over especially to give his books a boost,
but none of this emerged in the final version. No close ups. I don't
think the photography was very good. Jock Murray was excellent, a
Cruikshank illustration to Dickens, but poor Xan looked terrible,
and distorted. Actually, he looks splendid, younger and livelier than
ever, totally white hair merely giving him a Louis XV look. He's
v. fresh in [my] mind, as we (J and I) and he and Magouche spent

[1] John Devitt Stringfellow Pendlebury (1904–41), archaeologist and intelligence officer,
killed during the battle of Crete. PLF said that he 'got to know the island inside out ...
He spent days above the clouds and walked over 1,000 miles in a single archaeological
season. His companions were shepherds and mountain villagers ... He knew all their
dialects'; 'John Pendlebury and the Battle of Crete', *Spectator*, 20 October 2001; PLF in
Cooper (ed.), *Words of Mercury*, pp. 186–91.
[2] John 'Jack' Smith-Hughes (1919–94), who was sent by SOE to work alongside
Stockbridge in German-occupied Crete. Though captured by the Germans during the
invasion, he had managed to escape.
[3] C. M. 'Monty' Woodhouse (1917–2001), DSO, SOE officer in occupied Crete in 1941
and then commander of the Allied military mission to Greece; later an author and
Conservative Party politician.
[4] David Cheshire (1944–92), television director.
[5] Melvyn Bragg (b. 1939), the presenter, lampooned as 'Barg' by the satirical magazine
Private Eye.

Christmas and New Year together, 1st chez a v. nice self-defrocked Benedictine[1] who lives amid masses of books in the Massif Central near Le Puy, involving tremendous trudges through those icy highlands, and 2nd at another old pal's called Julian Pitt-Rivers, who lives in a Puss-in-Boots château in the Lot, continuing on our own to Albi, Montauban, Cahors and Toulouse. I was rather starved of that sort of thing, and flew back from Marseilles rather heavy-hearted ...

All hail to all of you,
Yours, Paddy

Heyward Cutting (1921–2012) was an architect and book collector. Though American, he was educated in England, and during the Second World War enlisted in the British Army with a group of four other American volunteers. All five were wounded in October 1942 at the Battle of El Alamein; two were later killed further up the desert. After a long convalescence in Egypt, Cutting returned to active duty in Italy following the Salerno landings, and was mentioned in dispatches for distinguished service. After the war, he travelled extensively in Africa, Asia Minor and Europe, before returning to America to study architecture, in which he made a distinguished and successful career. In his retirement he and his wife concentrated on their collection of modern British literature and making a garden at their home in Concord, Massachusetts.

To Heyward Cutting   Kardamyli
[posted 27 December 1989]   Messenia
                                              Greece

Dear Heyward,
    I blush with shame for being so late in thanking you for *Fancy Goods* and *Open All Night*.[2] I simply don't know how this delay has occurred. And thank you very much for the book.

---

[1] Jean-Dominique de Hemricourt de Grunne (1913–2007), elegant, sophisticated and worldly Roman Catholic priest at Oxford University in the 1950s, who left the priesthood after his mother's death. De Grunne lived in a house tucked into the hillside below the chateau of Ribes, not far from Le Puy.
[2] Both novels by Paul Morand, translated into English by Ezra Pound and issued in one volume in 1984.

It was very odd: on the same day as yours, another friend sent Paul Morand's *Lettres du Voyageur*, a collection of letters to friends in the last year of his life. Had we mentioned him before in an exchange of letters?[1] Or was it a choice out of the blue? In Romania, where I was living just before the war, in a broken-down, charming estate near the Bessarabian border, I translated a book he had recently written, *Isabeau de Bavière*. It was in the form of dramatic dialogue, rather like le Comte de Gobineau.[2] It was excellent, and a great success. I had tackled it, because Hélène Morand was Romanian, and a friend of the Cantacuzènes with whom I was sojourning. I took it back to England, and corrected it between parades at the Guards' Depot and handed it over to Paul M. over luncheon at the Ritz – he was in Blighty on some mission – and I think it was the first time (Nov. 1939) a private soldier had broken bread there. (A common sight a few months later.) By the time the war was over, and Paul, as an ex-Vichy minister, was in disgrace in Switzerland, oblivion had taken over as far as the book was concerned, until Hélène got hold of me and handed the book back. I gave it to Jock Murray, saying I would correct it again one day. Oblivion returned to her throne and it now occurs to me that I ought to do something about it, when I'm through with my present task. Both Morands are dead, so there's no immediate urgency. (I don't think Jock M. liked the idea when first broached.)

When I set off for the Middle East, a few months after the lunch, I left all my papers and things – two trunks – chez Catherine d'Erlanger,[3] who had moved from Byron's old abode in Piccadilly [no. 139] to Stratton House. (She later left for Los Angeles, stored them at Harrod's depot, and they were sold unclaimed post-war, alas.) I mention all this as Catherine was 'Clarisse' in the first of the *Fancy Goods* stories. She was v. extraordinary, rather like a Renaissance pope, red-haired and rather wicked. She had taken up painting and I was one of her first sitters. She and a man called Bertie

[1] PLF had mentioned Morand to Cutting before.
[2] PLF seems to be referring to one of the novels by Gobineau, probably *Les Pléiades* (1874).
[3] Baroness (Marie Rose Antoinette) Catherine D'Erlanger (née de Robert d'Aqueria) (1874–1959), society hostess; wife of Baron Emile D'Erlanger.

Lansberg had spent ages restoring and cleaning La Malcontenta, the Palladio villa beside the Brenta,[1] which B.L. had bought. It was rather marvellous. It looked v. padlocked and derelict again when I drove past it last year, heading for Venice. I don't know who 'Delphine' is, in the second story, but 'Aurore', in the third, was a Lady Constance Stewart-Richardson who was a big game shot and professional dancer. I never met her, but her niece Gladys [?] S-R lived in Athens for years; we had her house [the house in Kallirhoë Street] for a while, when she died. It was a small cottage near the temple of Olympian Zeus, and there is a lot of her furniture there.

We don't seem to have a French copy of *Ouvert la Nuit*, but have a fine *Tendres Stocks* (*vignettes en couleurs*) de *Chas Labordes*, chez Emile-Paul Frères, on thick hand-made paper, No 260 of 550, *imprimé à Argenteuil le 30 Janvier, 1924*. The vignettes are all thin decorative pen and ink drawings, washed in with pastel tints and shaded with black criss-cross shading, in pure mid-twenties style.

I have changed the bowling[2] in the hopes of reducing the level of almost total illegibility. I think some part of Ezra Pound's translation very clear and good; but very often he lapses into pure translationese e.g. '*Pour moi, Delphine était l'univers. Un univers d'une inspiration plus personnelle, moins soucieux des suffrages que celui dont je faisais partie*'; 'For me D. was a universe. A universe of more personal inspiration, less anxious about ballots than the one that I lived in' (there has been no talk about elections); '... *parapluies sous lesquels des Annamites abritaient de jaunes unions*' '... umbrellas under which Annamites sheltered young unions' and a few lines on '... *dans les prés, en contre-bas, un bétail taché s'avançait en suivant sa langue*' becomes 'in the meadows the spotted cattle moved slowly (in) *contrebass*, after their tongues'. Doesn't mean an awful lot; and a bit further on: '*Londres était devenu une masse incandescente, saccagée de plaisirs, où des autobus, vêtus de réclames, passaient, avec des bruits de tiroir ...*' 'London had become an incandescent mass ravaged with pleasures where advertisement-covered

[1] A river running into the Adriatic, lined with splendid villas.
[2] PLF had changed to a finer nib.

buses passed with the noise of a rifle-range …'. Apart from the difference between a drawer and a rifle-range, I think he might have tried a bit harder! There are lots more. It's fascinating and instructive to compare the two. I think Morand is extremely idiomatic and hard to translate – which makes me anxious about my dormant translation. It may be a tissue of howlers. In spite of everything, I'm a great admirer of some parts of Pound – his Chinese bits in the *Cantos*, for instance, as opposed to the Usura nonsense.[1]

I've asked John Sandoe's[2] to send you a small book called *Remainders*,[3] which I think you might enjoy. Did I ever send you my introduction to a book by Matila Ghyka,[4] a vanished Romanian friend? I ask, because the Nuit Scandinave, in *Open All Night* [*Ouvert La Nuit*], is entirely based on an experience of Matila's, as a young diplomat *en poste* in Stockholm, and recounted to Paul M.

This letter was interrupted by a friend in Budapest[5] (not Bucharest, which it seems is still cut off) telephoning me that Ceausescu has fallen.[6] I can't get over it, it's the best news I've heard for a long time. The whole country, it seems, is torn between mourning for several thousands shot in Timisoara, and delirious rejoicing at freedom regained after so many years of hell.

I apologise for this tangled screed. It's a well-known failing of country-dwellers in winter.

Niko Ghika the painter (different spelling), newly bereaved, arrived this evening for Christmas, looked after by fellow painter

[1] *The Cantos* by Ezra Pound is a long, incomplete poem in 116 sections, each of which is a canto. Canto XLV is a litany against 'Usura' or usury, which Pound later defined as a charge on credit regardless of potential or actual production and the creation of wealth *ex nihilo* by a bank to the benefit of its shareholders.
[2] John Sandoe, bookseller near Sloane Square in London.
[3] A selection from Eric Korn's 'Remainders' column in *The Times Literary Supplement*, published in 1989.
[4] *The World Mine Oyster* (1961).
[5] Rudi Fischer.
[6] A period of violent civil unrest, which started in the city of Timisoara and soon spread throughout the country, culminated in the deposition of the dictator Nicolae Ceausescu and end of communist rule in Romania.

John Craxton. I foresee an evening in front of the television in the village taverna, to see the Romanian news. We refuse to have it in the house, but miss it at times like this.

All wishes – not for Christmas, too late – but for the winter solstice season, and 1990, for you and yours.

Yours ever
Paddy

To Ralph Stockbridge   Kardamyli
25 August 1990   Messenia
                                                       Greece

Dear Ralph,

Yes, in a strange way there was something marvellous about Lili's memorial service, and I think the enormous congregation must have cheered John up, if anything could.[1] He sounds very downcast, poor chap. It was nice seeing Leftheri,[2] and particularly nice seeing Nico[3] who is about to embark on his memoirs, and about time too. We must all help as much as we can. Henry Saridakis has sent me an enormous mass of minute, close-written memoirs I haven't yet read, and I must say the thought of tackling sends my heart into my boots.

Bruce [Chatwin] was an extraordinary bird, and a great loss.[4] He didn't write the book he was always planning, which was a vast thing on Nomads and Nomadism, but he did jolly well with the others. His wife Elizabeth brought his ashes out here, as he had asked, and we buried them under an oak outside a microscopic 11th century church of St Nicholas in the Taygetus foothills, about an hour's climb from here.

---

[1] A memorial service for Lily (Lili) Stanley, née Malandrakis, who had married PLF's radio operator John Stanley in 1945, was held in Athens.
[2] Leftheri Kallithounakis, whom PLF described in an annotation to this letter as 'my own right-hand man'.
[3] Lieutenant Nikolaos Soures, an SOE officer on Crete during the war.
[4] Bruce Chatwin had died on 18 January 1989.

I agree about Wilfred Thesiger.[1] I know him fairly well, from the Travellers and common friends. He is either half naked in Kenya, surrounded by assegai-wielding Masai even nakeder, or pacing along Pall Mall in glittering Lobb shoes, dog skin gloves, a stiff collar with an old Etonian tie, a bamboo-handled umbrella tightly rolled, and a Lock bowler hat, staring down dead straight over a nose like a beak, scowling and glowering eyes, and clenched teeth. He really is very extraordinary. There's a very nice glimpse of him which you must know at the end of the *Short Walk in the Hindu Kush*.[2] Apropos of which, I hotly recommend *The Great Game* by Peter Hopkirk.

We went to Portugal, and then Santiago, with Xan & Magouche a few years ago, and found it absolutely marvellous, as you describe. I would love to see that giant censer in action on St James's day.[3] I'm sure that the other James, St James the Less – San Giacomo di Meno – is the one that comes into the nursery rhyme

I'll tell you a story
About Jackanory …
… another
About Jack and his brother (our one)
etc.

All the best to you both.
Yours ever

[1] Sir Wilfred Thesiger (1910–2003), explorer and travel writer. Stockbridge had been enjoying his autobiography, *The Life of My Choice* (1987).
[2] Eric Newby's *A Short Walk in the Hindu Kush* (1958) describes an encounter with Thesiger on a wild mountain pass.
[3] The censer, three feet high and solid silver, that is swung in a great arc between the north and south transepts of the cathedral of Santiago de Compostela (burial place of St James the Great) on the Feast of St James, 25 July.

Jock Murray tried to help Paddy to make progress with the final volume of his trilogy. He produced multiple copies of a form letter, to free Paddy from the distraction of having to answer correspondence individually. 'It was very kind of you to write and I appreciate the thought,' it read. 'The trouble is that I am having to work to a strict dead-line for the completion of my new book. This makes me a poor correspondent until I have finished it and reached Constantinople – I am not sure when this will be, but I am doing my best! So please forgive this most inadequate mark-time form of thanks.'

To Jock Murray   Kardamyli
5 February 1991   Messenia
                                                  Greece

My dear Jock,

 <u>Please</u> don't take seriously my remark about 'hating the book' on the telephone! Of course I don't. But I wish I were not so slow and scatter-brained, and that distractions were less. One would think one was safe here, but far from it. I sometimes think of St Wandrille with longing – but I couldn't have Joan there! and can't do without. The cold here is fiendish at the moment, in spite of plenty of logs. I went for a brief trudge in the mountains this afternoon, and nearly got blown to bits, and dashed back to tea laced with Famous Grouse, then some work, some delicious lentil soup I heated up (left by Ritsa[1]), then a sip of Coote/Billa and Freda's port,[2] and a chapter of Mr Sponge [*Mr Sponge's Sporting Tour*] huddled over the blazing logs.

All the best, Paddy

P.S. Have you re-read *Huckleberry Finn* lately? Amazing!

---

[1] The cook/housekeeper at Kardamyli.
[2] Coote Lygon, 'Billa' Harrod (see p. 407) and Freda Berkeley, by this time a widow.

Paddy and Joan were longstanding friends of the cookery writer Elizabeth David (1913–92). She was one of several friends to whom he sent his account of swimming the Hellespont in 1984. Early in 1985 he sent her a note to say that he and Joan were 'both deep in' her book, An Omelette and a Glass of Wine. *'It's wonderful,' he wrote: 'You <u>are</u> a glorious writer.' He thought that she should be awarded a DBE,[1] 'just for literature alone – quite apart from the blessing of having reformed our rough island cooking. Your stuff is worth a hundred and one knights,' he continued. 'I think "E for Dame!" demos should begin at once.'*

To Elizabeth David   Kardamyli
10 February 1991

Dearest Elizabeth,

Have I inflicted this stuff[2] on you already?[3] If so, please chuck in fire. It fell out of an old notebook last month. There is a Xerox machine in the village now; it's gone to my head and I can't keep away from it and it makes me a public nuisance. What a lovely letter from you, to which this is not an answer. I've [You've] just been talking to Joan on the telephone so you know the Xan news. It was lovely to find him <u>so</u> much better than we had thought. We were in Paris ten days at the Hotel du Quai [Voltaire]. Lovely it was. I had lots of correction to do – a wonderful translation of *A Time of Gifts* by a v. civilised [illegible] called Guillaume Villeneuve – and whenever I looked out of the window, there was the Seine and some gulls. The whole length of the Louvre being opposite, then the Tuileries, and, the other side of the bridge, that nick in the R. de Rivoli (Place des Pyramides), over which Xan and Magouche's flat is perched. On the other side of the Place stands the Hotel Regina,[4] which is the first roof abroad I ever slept under,

[1] Elizabeth David had been awarded an OBE in 1976, and a CBE in 1986.
[2] The verse 'Voix D'Outretombe' and the accompanying sketches. See *In Tearing Haste*, pp. 268–71.
[3] He had, only a few weeks earlier.
[4] The Hotel Regina stands in the Place des Pyramides on the Rue de Rivoli, with the statue of Joan of Arc in front.

at the age of eight, on the way to and from the nursery slopes of the Bernese Oberland, with my mother and sister. The first thing my mother did, after arriving, was to dash through the traffic, dragging us both to the plinth of Joan of Arc's faded gold equestrian statue. We knew all about her, and it was a thrill. So, the other day, [I] was wandering about this rather old-fashioned but now v. expensive hotel, with long green tiled passages. I strolled along them, a-brim with Proustian vibrations. I remembered that in the loos they used to have bumf with a serial story on it, perforated leaf after leaf, which must have brought them to the brink of ruin – v [illegible]. I wasn't surprised to see that they had changed this at some moment in the last sixty-eight years, at the command of some thrifty *custos rotulorum*,[1] a minor Dark Age setting in.

Lots of love, Paddy

To Jock Murray
22 December 1991

Kardamyli
Messenia
Greece

My dear Jock,

I meant to write much earlier, but these days have been rather hectic. First of all, Niko Ghika and Johnny were expected for Christmas, but couldn't come a) because Nico's doctors didn't want him to get so far away from Athens, and Johnny said his teeth were all falling out, he couldn't possibly tackle turkey – all this mentioned casually when ringing about something quite different, the rotter. Joan and I both felt a bit like Charlie Chaplin in *The Gold Rush* …[2] Fortunately, some very nice Greek friends – at least he's Greek, she's

---

[1] A play on words: a *custos rotulorum* is a keeper of the rolls.
[2] In the silent film *The Gold Rush* (1925), Chaplin plays The Lone Prospector, who invites a dance-hall girl to a New Year's Eve dinner. When she does not arrive before midnight, he walks alone through the streets, desperate. She remembers his invitation and decides to visit him. Finding his home empty, but seeing the meticulously prepared dinner and a present for her, she writes a note for him.

American – and his concubine, Alexis Ladas[1] and Barbara are coming instead.

The other worrying thing has been, of course, poor Xan's illness. He's got the same thing I had a few years ago but far worse, and the outlook is bleak ...[2] Rather worryingly, the *Daily Telegraph* have asked me to do a pre-emptive obituary, which I find oddly hard, and rather harrowing: also, lots of details missing which of course I can't ask Magouche on the blower. I've written to her daughter Antonia Amis,[3] so I hope all will be well. About fifteen years ago, Xan told me he'd been asked to do one of me for *The Times*, and when he'd finished it, read it to me out loud, asking for complaints or suggestions. It was a corker, so I think there were none, only a great deal of bad-taste hilarity.

I'm slogging along quietly at the great task, I wish faster, but I'm doing my best. In the evenings, I've taken to reading through the *Odyssey*, book by book. I was never really up to it at school – left too soon, but could just stumble v. slowly along and am now hopelessly rusty. But someone – Alexi Ladas – sent me a marvellous new translation by Robert Fitzgerald, which manages to retain all the poetry, unlike most,[4] so I read them side by side with Butcher and Lang[5] handy, also a Homeric Dictionary, bought (but unused) years ago. It's so marvellous ploughing slowly through it, one's in a sort of trance ...

No more now, dear Jock except – too late for Christmas in three days' time – a v. Happy New Year from Joan who sends love and me to you and Diana.

Yours ever
Paddy

From a very old notebook (all unconnected)

[1] Alexis Ladas (1920–2000), Greek wartime resistance fighter. He had been arrested by the Italians and condemned to death as a spy, but was saved after his American brother-in-law, Cy Sulzberger, had made representations on his behalf.
[2] Fielding had contracted cancer.
[3] Magouche Fielding's daughter Antonia was married to the novelist Martin Amis.
[4] The American poet Robert Fitzgerald's translation of the *Odyssey* was first published in 1961.
[5] An English translation of the *Odyssey* by Samuel Henry Butcher and Andrew Lang was published in 1906.

When the specialists in Harley St made a ludicrous diagnosis
And my 'galloping diphtheria' turned out merely halitosis
I demanded, (and, in time, received) a sort of an apology
For the wretched man's defective otorhinolaryngology.

The operas of Benjamin Britten
Should never be actually written
Within, or sung loud
But inscribed on a cloud
With the tail of a Siamese kitten.

A young protonotary apostolic
Bathed his privates in beer and carbolic
It was sovereign, he said,
Against colds in the head
And carbuncles of quinzy & colic.

Paddy had been delighted by the French version of A Time of Gifts, *which appeared in 1991. He wrote a letter of appreciation to the translator, Guillaume Villeneuve. Comparing it with the English text, 'I realised what an atrociously hard task you were tackling, and what immense pains you had taken to get exactly the right shade of meaning and tone of voice and what a beautiful and resonant and soigné style you had brought to bear.' He was equally appreciative of Villeneuve's translation of the sequel.*

To Guillaume Villeneuve   Kardamyli
25 January 1992   Messenia
                                              Greece

Dear Guillaume,

I've just posted off – registered and express, which may be a contradiction in terms – the [French] typescript of *Between the Woods and the Water*. It reads beautifully, and you have dealt with the most difficult parts with the utmost skill. Except for the very rare cases where you have been led astray by those terrible traps that the English language sets for everyone, however erudite, who has not been conceived and born in our rough island, all the points that I have commented on with suggestions – they are nothing more – are minor points on which you, as translator, must make the final choice.

I am afraid that the accents in Hungarian names are [a] continuous scourge, but we should observe them as much as possible, as their omission puts Magyars beside themselves, and the same, alas, applies to those maddening diacritics in Romanian, of which the cedilla is the most important. They are all ugly, but there is all the difference in the world between Serban and Sherban and *tuica* and *tsuica*. Out of over-anxiety in this matter, I have made a gross mistake: there is no accent on Hunyadi, and I have officiously and erroneously added one throughout! Please forgive.

The only problem that really worries me is the name of the inhabitants of Transylvania. In Transylvania itself, and in my Romanian years, where nothing but French was spoken, I never heard anyone say 'Transylvanien'; it was always 'Transylvain'. I know that both exist, but the *Grand Larousse* gives priority to the shorter word: Transylvain –e, ou Transylvanien –enne, adj. et n. *Relatif à la Transylvanie ou originaire de cette région.* I can't help feeling that Transylvain is more elegant, the other rather clumsy. Do you think you could bear to change it? It would be a terrible *corvée* [unrewarded labour]. I only started marking it ¾ of the way through.

Thank you so much for Gibbon's memoirs – marvellously done![1] I have always loved them, especially the Oxford bit about the deep potations of the old excusing the brisk interference of the young. He's a marvellous writer, and such a witty one. I am very fond of the passage in *Decline and Fall* (Chapter LXX – Council of Constance) when it talks about the trial of the antipope John XXIII. '... he fled, and was brought back a prisoner: the most scandalous chargers were suppressed; the Vicar

[1] Villeneuve had translated Gibbon's *Memoirs of My Life* for Pierre-Guillaume de Roux at the publisher Critérion.

of Christ was only accused of piracy, murder, rape, sodomy and incest …' The book is beautifully produced and printed, looks and feels just right. Please give M. de Roux my greetings and congratulations. I wonder if you can hear les trompes de Chasse[1] from where you work?

All greetings, and very many thanks again!

Yours ever
Paddy

To Jock Murray   Kardamyli
12 March 1992   Messenia
                                                  Greece

Dear Jock,

You <u>are</u> a brick getting hold of that tape of the interview, which arrived this morning. I was very keen to have it, as I consciously tried to keep the 'er' and 'sort of' level down, and I do believe they have sunk about a millimetre! I'll get at the travel book.

The Violins, Woods and Water and *Peru*[2] are all coming out in Paris in May or thereabouts and I am being urged by all these publishers (all different!) of the importance in every way of going to a great travel writing gathering for two days at St Malo, organised by a man called Michel Le Bris. Anthony Sheil also says it's important to go <u>once</u>. (I oiled out of it last year, with Crete as an excuse.) But I am tempted because I love the idea of my stuff being liked in France. I certainly won't go if it involves anything like making a speech or 'reading a paper', because those take me ages. I've been absolutely swamped by things I couldn't get out of, 'forewords' etc. most of them concerned with Greece and Crete, killing work. I sometimes wonder whether we were right to settle here when

[1] Hunting horns. Villeneuve lived in Fontainebleau, which is surrounded by forest.
[2] Published in English as *Three Letters from the Andes* (1991).

so many ties like this exist. Oh, for Chagford or Saint Wandrille! I've started clearing all this stuff, written a hundred letters I had allowed to mount up, and hoping Vol III will get forward a bit faster. I do feel guilty about this, and rightly. It's now 6.20 a.m., so I am making early starts.

I long for brekker, but Ritsa doesn't come for another hour and a half ...

Magouche was here for a week or so, and we went for terrific walks in the mountains, which, in spite of the markedly cold winter, have burst out in thousands of irises, mauve and scarlet anemones, snow falls of daisies, masses of asphodels, and globes of spurge 2 yards in circumference. Next came Barbara's daughter, Miranda Rothschild, bringing a tiny Korean monk with her, who brushed in calligraphic texts on yards of rice paper, a joy to watch; then Elizabeth Chatwin, who has just gone. None of them were any sort of distraction, thank God, being old Kardamyli hands and knowing the form.

Grindstone calls!

Yours ever
Paddy

Billy Moss, Paddy's deputy in the operation to kidnap General Kreipe, never really settled in the post-war world, and he died in 1965, at the age of only forty-four. Paddy continued to correspond with his widow Sophie, and with their two daughters, Gabriella and Isabelle.

To Sophie Moss   Kardamyli
13 June 1992   Messenia
                                                          Greece

Dearest Sophie,

I'm so sorry being such an age answering, it's all thanks to being on the move, due to the publication of a book (*Between the Woods and the Water*) in France: *Entre Fleuve et Forêt*, and, I must say, beautifully translated. It got quite well received by critics; but all reproached me for being such a slow writer. One simply called his article: 'P.L.F, l'Escargot des Carpates'.[1] So I must get a move on. That was followed by a sort of travel-writer jamboree at Saint Malo, acres of striped marquee built out from the castle, choked with travel-writers from all over the world, a sort of literary Champ du Drap d'Or[2] and great fun.

I'm so sorry you've been going through a 'flagging' period, I know just what you mean! I am too, a bit, depressed by my awful slowness … but I'm determined to get a move on. I'm still plodding across Bulgaria and long for Turkey …

Back to the grindstone! Love from Joan and me too,

Paddy

P.S. Enclosed: something to buy a dozen slates; well, half a dozen … What a <u>curse</u>! At least I've got overhead covering[3] from now on:

'The Snail of the Carpathians'

To Jock Murray   Kardamyli
29 July 1992   Messenia
                                        Greece

My dear Jock,

I've just been talking to Joan on the telephone, as she told me what a <u>wretched</u> time you've been having, assaulted simultaneously on two fronts, as it were![4] I'm so sorry, and do hope you are on the

---

[1] Jean-Baptiste Harang, writing in *Libération* (7 May 1992); PLF wrongly remembered this as having been in *Le Monde*. Harang began his review: 'Patrick Leigh Fermor est un Hercule de la lenteur [slowness].'
[2] Field of the Cloth of Gold.
[3] PLF refers to his snail shell.
[4] Jock had been ill, and had less than a year to live. 'Old age is not for sissies,' he would say to PLF near the end.

mend, now, though obviously feeling pretty rotten. I was beginning to be a bit uneasy, as you are such a sturdy correspondent, prompted half by things that crop up, and half for fun – not erratic like me, & was about to telephone to see how things were. But Joan says, thank heavens it's all over now and just needs taking care and recuperation. Poor Diana![1]

This is not a proper letter, merely a message of fond solicitude to you both. I'll send some more solid stuff later on.

It's very strange being alone here. The house is wholly given over to cats' feuds and intrigues. One who just wandered in as a kitten (Gisella) early last year from nowhere, now has three very active kittens of her own, sired by a very unscrupulous but rather charming tom called Johnny (named after Johnny Craxton rather cheekily, by Ritsa, the Caucasian-Macedonian girl who looks after us now) and the five of them form a sort of mafia, terrorising our two dear old she-cats Papáki and Lilith. The former won't leave Joan's bedroom, the latter lurks in the wilderness outside our domain, only announcing herself every 24 hours or so with a plaintive mew, when I dash out with a plate-full of grub which she devours in haste, looking over her shoulder nervously. They long for Joan, who will put everything right in a jiffy. But it's good for me to see how the other half lives …

I'm glad to say the book is moving forward. One of the exciting bits, later on, is shadowed forth in the last paragraph of that piece about Macedonia I sent on, viz., the Bulgarian reaction to the news of the King of Yugoslavia's murder in Marseilles in autumn, 1935 …[2]

The sun set some time ago, I'm writing outside the studio, and it's getting darker and darker, bats wheel about among the cypresses, the sea is a fading zinc and lilac hue, and I bet this is getting less and less legible, so I'll break off and post this tomorrow morning before breakfast, just after my 7.00 a.m. half-hour swim, about half

---

[1] Jock's wife, and, like him, a friend.
[2] Alexander I, King of Yugoslavia 1921–34, was assassinated by a Bulgarian nationalist in Marseilles during a state visit to France. In *The Broken Road* (pp. 90–3), PLF describes the euphoria in Bulgaria when the news came through.

a kilometre. It's much the best time, and on the return journey, I see the sun coming up behind the Taygetus skyline, and sending the shadows of our cypresses out over the water.

'Περαστικά σου' – may it all pass soon – viz., the tiresomeness of illnesses – as Greeks say at the bedsides of invalid friends.

Much love to Diana and you.

Yours ever
Paddy

Patrick Reade was Paddy's godson.

In November 1942 Patrick Reade's father, Captain Arthur Reade, had been infiltrated alongside Xan Fielding from a submarine on to the coast of German-occupied Crete. During a rest in the mountains he had sponsored Paddy and Xan as candidate members of the Travellers Club. 'We were all three at the time SOE captains dressed up as shepherds, deep in ash and lice, huddling cross-legged over the embers and under the stalactites of a cave,' recalled Paddy many years later. 'Arthur sealed the envelope putting us up. Obviously it would take some time before it could be handed to the next caique or submarine, longer still to reach Pall Mall.'

To Patrick Reade	Kardamyli
19 November 1995	Messenia
	Greece

Dear Patrick,

Last month Joan, Magouche Fielding and I, and about twenty of Xan's old Cretan friends took his ashes up into the White Mountains, dug a hole, buried them under a tree, said a prayer, poured a libation, then had a picnic in the snow with spectacular ravines traversed by sunlight and mist alternately, running away in all directions below … It was very moving, and Xan would have loved it!

We are coming back [to England] some time after the New Year. I have just written to a friend of yours, Alex Martin, shamefully late. He plans to do a BBC interview in celebration of my Methuselah tally of years.¹ Do tell me about him. He wrote a v. nice letter.

We were bathing till late Oct then suddenly all Hell broke loose with thunder, lightning and a deluge of rain, the first since last winter, so the villagers are all wreathed in smiles. Tomorrow morning we set off for Berlin for a week, my first time, so I'm v. excited.

All the best!
Yours Paddy

Joan sends love.

To Peter Levi   Kardamyli
22 February 1996   Messenia
                                                 Greece

Dear Peter,

I'm so glad you enjoy George's *Iliad*.² I think it's <u>very extraor-dinary</u>, a v. surprising literary event. When I think of George's father, [illegible] Nicolas, being able to recite the entire *Erotokritos*³ without a stumble or a halt from end to end – which I heard him doing in our cave above Asi Gonia,⁴ although he couldn't sign his name, it seems akin to Iron Age Greeks reciting the *Odyssey* long after the Mycenaean alphabet had come to bits, with a new alphabet only fumbling its way into being: when the doings of their Bronze Age ancestors only survive in their [illegible] brains and on the tongues of their Iron Age descendants … Dark Age recitals …

---

¹ PLF was eighty in 1995.
² George Psychoundakis had translated the *Iliad* from the original Greek to the Cretan dialect, a remarkable achievement for someone with only basic education.
³ See footnote on p. 311.
⁴ The Psychoundakis family's home village of Asi Gonia was a resistance stronghold during the war.

I envy your Horace studies. I can't think of anything nicer to be doing. I often dip into the Fraenkel book[1] you recommended to me years ago, always finding something new.

We were four weeks in Blighty, which passed in a flash. I went with Joan and Magouche to the Dulwich Picture Gallery, which I thought I had never been to. But suddenly, confronted by Sir J. Reynolds's huge portrait of *Mrs Siddons as the Muse of Tragedy*,[2] I suddenly remembered that I <u>had</u> been there before, aged five or six, trailing round with my mother and sister; then, as by a Proustian cake,[3] all the rest began to cohere, picture after picture surfacing. It <u>was</u> odd.

When we got back here, it had been raining forty days and forty nights; it still is, with no dove leaving the Ark. But we've got lots of wood from the olive pruning, so we sit on either side of the fire, Joan at grips over the chessboard with a ghostly computer competitor and often winning, while I read *Sense and Sensibility*, alternating with the *Satyricon*, a beautifully balanced literary regimen … Joan sends her love, also ours to you and Deirdre, if you see what I mean.

Yours ever, Paddy

[1] Eduard Fraenkel, *Horace* (1957).
[2] There are three versions of the painting *Mrs Siddons as the Tragic Muse*; the one in the Dulwich Picture Gallery is now not thought to be the original, but a copy from Reynolds's studio. The other two are in the National Portrait Gallery, London, and the Huntington Library, California.
[3] PLF refers to Proust's *madeleine*, the taste of which unlocks memories.

On 11 November 1996 Paddy gave the address at the unveiling of the memorial to John Betjeman in Poets' Corner at Westminster Abbey. As well as being a popular poet, Betjeman was celebrated as an advocate for Victorian architecture. In his address, Paddy recalled the occasion sixty-five years earlier, when Betjeman had come to speak at the King's School, Canterbury. 'His discourse was light, spontaneous, urgent and convincing,' he told those present, 'and it began with a eulogy of the spare and uncluttered lines of the Parthenon, and this led on, astonishingly as it may sound today, to a eulogy of the spare and uncluttered lines of the modern architecture of the Le Corbusier and Bauhaus School – the year was 1931 – and then the merits of ferro-concrete and the simplicity of tubular steel furniture were rapturously extolled.'

This letter to Betjeman's daughter, Candida, was written a month after the unveiling of the memorial.

To Candida Lycett Green   Kardamyli
11 December 1996   Messenia
                             Greece

Dearest Candida,

I did love the whole thing in the Abbey and after. I wish I had done better with the address. I am afraid it was rather clumsy and badly put together. I would have liked that procession, out of the chancel, then into the shadowy nave, then into a maze of small Gothic doorways and into a Plantagenet tiring [dressing] room, then back to the south transept, to have gone on forever ... In the Jerusalem Chamber, I couldn't stop thinking about Henry IV, part 2.[1] Then that lovely feast at Christopher Sykes's[2] – I left much too early, it seems, so Rupert[3] told me, over the Colchester natives at Bentley's[4] with Magouche next day: lots of singing and strumming, just what I like.

[1] Scene 4 of Act IV is set in the Jerusalem Chamber, and at the end of Scene 5, the King is carried there to die.
[2] Christopher Simon Sykes (b. 1948), writer and photographer.
[3] Candida Lycett Green's husband.
[4] Bentley's Oyster Bar & Grill, close to Piccadilly Circus.

I've got to stop now, as we are busy packing, as we set off for Blighty tomorrow, chez Janetta as a base, then to Dingley Dell[1] for Christmas with Debo and Andrew and a lot of other old souls, which I look forward to keenly; then the Mill House I expect.

The archivist at my old school looked out John's visit as recorded in the School mag. It was just as I remembered, which gave me a good kick off at any rate (enclosed).

Two days ago, after a day of fitful thunder, there was a sudden crash and a bang and flash louder and brighter and more sinister than anything heard in the war, then everything electric – lights, telephones, street lights etc. – konked out all round. A sudden deluge set in for 24 hours, and Joan and I felt we were in an emptied Ark, with a candle or two flickering, two shaken bipeds and four puzzled cats mewing from room to room. Nothing to show for it, alas! We searched the valley; whatever it was fell about 150 yards off and we hoped for [a] meteorite of unknown mineral nestling in the bracken, but found nothing …

Lots of love
Paddy

Various people were asked to contribute to an album to be presented to Sophie Moss on her eightieth birthday. Paddy's contribution was a piece about 'Tara', the villa on Gezira Island in Cairo which they and several others had shared during the war. As was his wont, he went to enormous trouble with this. 'At one stage every post was bringing me amendments,' remembers Sophie's daughter Gabriella, who was compiling the album. Even when it was done, Paddy continued to fret about it.

To Sophie Moss   Kardamyli
8 April 1997   Messenia
                                                            Greece

(Must type as I'm becoming illegible)
Dearest Sophie,

Renewed Happy Birthday! I do hope that stuff about Tara got to you in time for the great day. How I wish I could have been there!

---

[1] PLF's nickname for Chatsworth, after Mr Wardle's house in *The Pickwick Papers*.

I've just been looking at the pages I sent and I'm overcome with embarrassment, because it's almost entirely fiction! I feel sure I have jammed two totally different occasions together, viz., the First Party – or Ball as I rather pompously call it – and the night of the Burning Sofa.[1] And I don't think it was Burnet[2] at all who played the piano, or Geoffrey Ghali[3] who fixed up the loan of the instrument from the Indian Officers Club. I'm glad I avoided inflicting a monocle on Andrew[4] but I feel pretty sure that it was he who dealt so heroically with that enormous window. At several points I'm afraid Oblivion supervened and Invention slunk out of the shadow and guided my pen. I really ought to be locked up for complete and abysmal unreliability. Also, I made it all sound too smart – but then sometimes a sort of semi-formal eccentricity was interwoven with our particular brand of bohemianism. Another thing: the text is a bit sloppy in places. Of course, nobody quoted Anthony and Cleopatra about the flaming sofa.[5] I changed it to 'might have quoted' on frantic p.c. to poor Gabriella, but too late, I might pull it together one day and go on about some of our friends and add one or two more accurate anecdotes. The whole point of the pages was to cheer you up on your birthday in the hopes of a laugh here and there and to write a bit about Billy and to capture a faint echo of the fun and the oddity of Tara, if I could manage it.

I've got to dash to the post, late as usual, because of typing this out, *tant mal que bien*.[6] Tons of love, dearest Sophie, and also to those outstandingly nice daughters.[7]

from Paddy

[1] PLF had fallen asleep, with a lighted cigarette in his hand. The burning sofa was hurled through a window, to extinguish itself on the lawn outside.
[2] Burnet Pavitt (1908–2002), piano player at Tara, later a wealthy businessman and member of the Royal Opera House board.
[3] Geoffrey Boutros-Ghali, from a prominent Coptic family in Cairo, uncle of Boutros Boutros-Ghali, UN Secretary General 1992–6.
[4] Goaded by others present, who were smashing the glasses from which they had been drinking vodka, Andrew Tarnowski, Sophie Moss's first husband, picked up an occasional table and flung it against an enormous picture window, which shattered 'with a crash and shower of splinters. A moment of awed silence was followed by an outbreak of applause.'
[5] 'The barge [s]he sat in, like a burnish'd throne,/ Burned on the water …', *Antony and Cleopatra*, Act II, Scene 2.
[6] PLF probably means *tant bien que mal* – 'after a fashion'.
[7] Gabriella and Isabelle.

Jock Murray died in 1993. He 'took such trouble about his authors, and in so many ways, and so unobtrusively, that perhaps they – or we, for I am one of them,' Paddy wrote in an obituary published in the Independent *on 23 July 1993, 'were inclined to take it for granted. But not quite: other publishers at home or abroad – not that I know much about them as I have only had one – would remind us now and then of our luck and our spoiled and privileged estate. This was because of Jock's passionate interest in the work of his authors, his great kindness, and his gift for friendship. Nobody, in the Doctor Johnson sense, kept his friendships in a state of better repair.'*

After Jock's death, his son John – John Murray VII – became Paddy's publisher.

To John Murray
10 February 1998

Kardamyli
Messenia
Greece

Dear John,

I'm so sorry not to have been in touch while I was in Blighty. We meant to stay a week or two longer, but suddenly had to get back here for tiresome local problems. Never mind. We'll be back in May. I <u>do</u> feel a bit absurd, not turning up at No 50 with a mass of typescript, but this won't last forever. Hope has revived about Vol III as I briefly said on the postcard with the pussy-cat.

<u>All</u> the Vol III stuff I was making such a nuisance of myself about is here, on very thick paper and weighing a ton, at the bottom of a Japanned tin trunk in the attic, now in the studio. I remember that Jock struggled out with this great weight about twenty years ago, so all is well. I do hope that Jinny[1] didn't have a terrible time hunting for it. I am very much looking forward to getting at it. I will be delayed a bit more by involvement in two other people's books – correction, introductions, etc. Absolute hell, in fact, but it won't last forever: totally unremunerative self-inflicted wounds.

---

[1] John Murray's wife, Virginia, who took on responsibility for the firm's archive.

When we got back here the other day, I found, at the bottom of a pyramid of mail, a rather extraordinary book, long out of print, sent by an old Romanian friend from Bucharest. It is by Paul Morand – all the rage in the twenties and thirties in France, and elsewhere – called *Isabeau de Bavière*, published by Les Editions de France in 1938. It is the life of Isabella of Bavaria, Queen of France, married to K. Charles VI, *le Bien-Aimé*, all told in dialogue, rather like the *Imaginary Conversations* of Landor,[1] and, in France, the Comte de Gobineau, but much less philosophical and far more dashing, covering the grimmest part – for Frogs – of the 100 Years' War, Isabeau(ella) herself rather a fascinating fiend and femme fatale, and her dotty husband, Charles; Jean Sans Peur of Burgundy; Visconti, Orléans, Valois; Henry V, the Regent Bedford – a whole late mediaeval dramatis personae: rebellions, battles, massacres, feasts, adultery in high life, assassination. It's a grim period of French history, rather like that marvellous speech of the Duke of Burgundy in the last act of *Henry V*.

I expect you wonder why I'm going on about all this? All shall be revealed.

I spent a lot of the winter of 1938 and the following spring translating this into English, at the rambling snow-bound house in North Romania where I had settled, and brought the result back with me in Sept 1939, got it typed, and handed it over to Paul Morand (he was a diplomat) when I was a recruit at the Guards' Depot. (I think it was the first time a private was seen lunching at the Ritz.) Morand, who had been at Oxford and was a great Anglophile before the War, didn't behave well in the War – pro-Vichy Ambassador in Romania, etc., and was rather in disgrace after it, which didn't stop him being elected to the Academy a few years later.[2] I didn't know what had happened to my translation, forgot all about it, and only remembered it when his widow – a v. intelligent and handsome Romanian pss[princess], though rather

---

[1] Walter Savage Landor's five volumes of *Imaginary Conversations* (1824–9).
[2] Not as straightforward as PLF makes it sound – see footnote to his 1961 letter to Jock.

wicked, I think – got in touch and handed it over to me over lunch in the Champ de Mars, and I handed it over to Jock for safekeeping and later reference, perhaps, and, after wondering who had the copyright, and deciding that, if we wanted to know, the Académie would be the place to ask, forgot about it all over again; and here memory fades out again. Did I ever retrieve it, <u>or is it still gathering dust at No 50?</u>

I had forgotten what the book was like, and having just re-read it after half-a-century, (in French), I'm rather dazzled and long to have a look at my version. The French seems to me very unusual and fascinating.

You see where I'm heading! Do you think Jinny could steel herself with patience and see if it's lurking somewhere? If it <u>is</u> there, I'd love to have a look at it. I don't know if it's up Murray's street, but <u>if</u> it's there, do cast a first-refusal eye. I can't help feeling it would be a pity if it never appeared in England, in spite of Paul M's war-time delinquency!

Anyway, all hail to you both. Also to Diana.

Yours
Paddy

P.S. I'll be 83 tomorrow. I can't believe it.

To Candida Lycett Green
22 July 1998

The Mill House
Dumbleton
Evesham
Worcestershire

Dearest Candida,

You and Rupert were sports to come to Faringdon,[1] and I thought it was a lovely evening. The only thing that worries me is that I have a faint memory of promising to send you a book – not by me, some

[1] Following Robert Heber-Percy's death, Faringdon House passed to his granddaughter, Sofka Zinovieff.

reference book, I think – and I've clean forgotten what it was. I'm rather apt to do this when I've had a couple. Can you remember what it was, or is it an illusion?

It was marvellous to sit at that huge and well-remembered table again after so many years. The last time I was there was when Mad Boy and Hughie Cruddas[1] held sway. Did you read Mark Amory's book about Gerald?[2] He asked for contribution[s], and I sent one or two, but the best item I could remember I <u>didn't</u> send, because I thought it was such a chestnut, everybody else would have. I heard it from Sachie Sitwell, during that first Christmas of the war, at Weston, on leave from the Guards' Depot. Gerald was staying too. I asked Sachie about Robert, who, it seemed, was leaving the army, and he told me the following. The Mad Boy had joined some suitable regiment and was in charge in the Orderly Room one day when the telephone rang. The voice said:

'General Robinson here. I want to talk to your commanding officer.'

<u>R.</u> (after a pause – no 'Sir') 'He isn't here.'

<u>Gen R.</u> 'That's queer. He was there yesterday.'

<u>R.</u> 'Ah. Yesterday isn't today.'

<u>Gen. R.</u> (exploding after a long pause) 'When your commanding officer comes back, kindly tell him that I told you to tell him that when I asked where his commanding officer was, and he told me you were out, and I said that was queer because you – he – had been there yesterday, you said "Yesterday isn't today" and slammed the instrument down.'

Soon after, Robert's C.O. came in and asked if anyone had telephoned.

Robert said, 'Oh yes. A man who said he was called General Robinson told me to tell you that yesterday isn't today.'

---

[1] Known as 'The Captain', Heber-Percy's companion between the 1950s and 1970s. His arrival at Faringdon prompted Evelyn Waugh's comment to Diana Mosley: 'The Mad Boy has installed a Mad Boy of his own. Has there ever been a property in history that has devolved from catamite to catamite for any length of time?'

[2] Mark Amory, *Lord Berners: The Last Eccentric* (1998).

There was a tremendous row and the Mad Boy was very soon in Civvy Street.

But nobody <u>had</u> sent it to Mark so it never got in, alas!

Tons of love
Paddy

And from Joan

Paddy felt increasingly guilty about his failure to complete his account of his walk across Europe – so much so that he felt obliged to write this letter of excuse to Murray when he came to England.

To John Murray   The Mill House
10 August 1998   Dumbleton
Evesham
Worcestershire

Dear John,

Here we are, back in Blighty. <u>NO SKULKING</u>, only total rustication in the hopes of getting rid of a mass of accumulated impediments. It is bliss to be in this green haven after the oven-like heat of the Peloponnese and the forest fires, both unprecedented in fierceness and extent.

No more just now, except that when I resurface in the capital, I hope to have got rid of cumbersome stuff, and will be able to feast with a lighter heart and conscience. The days have been discouragingly blue so far, but today, promising grey clouds are assembling overhead so all prospects glow.

Love to all
Paddy

and from Joan

To John Murray   Kardamyli
22 April 1999   Messenia
                                                                  Greece

Dear John,

Thank you very much for your letter from the Penelope country,[1] and apologies for delay in answering. We spent two very ad hoc nights with her there once, well worth it, as we spent a whole afternoon rounding up lots of ponies she was looking after, and got in the last stray, with terrific cowboy tactics, just as the sun went down. I also wrote a chunk of, I think, *Roumeli*, in that strange hotel among the Llanthony ruins, donkeys' years ago, haunting the Honddu & Capel-y-Ffin.

It's splendid news about the Murrays' paperback. I've lost Iradj Bagherzade's[2] address, so could you most kindly post the enclosed note? I wish George [Psychoundakis] hadn't behaved so baselessly suspiciously towards No 50, and, I believe, so badgeringly to poor Eleo Gordon,[3] his (via you) benefactress. I'm about to write to her and say that her name, like Abu Ben Ezra's under the pen of the recording angel, will be found to be the first of all.[4]

I love the idea of my stuff returning to roost.[5] We must hang on to Johnny Craxton! His covers are so much part of the books that I almost feel that he wrote them and I drew the pictures. Someone told me recently that she thought they were the best book-jackets she has ever seen.

[1] Following her separation from John Betjeman, his wife Penelope had retreated to a cottage in Cusop, near Hay-on-Wye.

[2] Iradj Bagherzade, founder of the publishing house I. B. Tauris.

[3] Psychoundakis's editor at Penguin Books.

[4] A reference to Leigh Hunt's 'Abou Ben Adhem' (1834), which concludes:

'The angel wrote, and vanished. The next night It came again with a great wakening light, And showed the names whom love of God had blest, And lo! Ben Adhem's name led all the rest.'

[5] PLF had decided to donate his papers to the John Murray archive.

Vol III has had another setback, but a delible one: viz., I somehow promised to write a foreword to a book of reminiscences about the Cantacuzène family, that I can't very well oil out of – there are all sorts of pre-war leverages at work. But it won't be a long job, and then all is clear for full steam ahead. <u>So please take heart.</u>

<u>Next Day.</u> I had hardly written those words when the telephone, on a very bad line, told me Mr (I think) Rudd wanted to talk to me from Magdalen, Oxford. They had just decided one luncheon that they would like to bestow an honorary degree on me: would I accept it? <u>Can a duck swim?</u> He said they would be in touch again soon, to England (where we are due next week). I do hope it wasn't just a slightly tight lunchtime fancy. He sounded awfully nice.

Jacob and Serena Rothschild[1] asked us to go to Nico and Barbara's old Corfu house, Canona (now theirs), for English Easter. Joan now recoils from all *mondanités*,[2] so I went alone, and found Debo which was lovely, and a tremendously nice gardening expert called Mary Keen[3] (whose daughter's just written a book on the Jersey Lily), and Mr Mandelson[4] and his very cheery Brazilian pal,[5] who gives Japanese calligraphy lessons at £100 an hour. Halfway through I was smitten down by a *grippe* virus that ranges the island seeking whom it may devour. It certainly devoured me, in spite of ladlefuls of linctus spooned in by Mr M. So I missed most of the fun, including a visit to the ruins of Butrint[6] on the coast of Albania. I stayed on a day when the

---

[1] Jacob, 4th Baron Rothschild (b. 1936), son of Barbara Rothschild (1911–89), and his wife Serena, née Dunn.

[2] Society gatherings.

[3] Mary Keen (1942–2009), garden designer, worked for the Rothschilds most of her career. Her daughter, Laura Beatty, wrote a biography of Lillie Langtry (1999).

[4] Peter Mandelson (b. 1953), Labour politician and spin doctor. In December 1998 he had resigned as Secretary of State for Trade and Industry after it was revealed that he had bought a home in Notting Hill with the aid of an interest-free loan of £373,000 from Geoffrey Robinson, whose business dealings were subject to an inquiry by Mandelson's department.

[5] Mandelson's partner, Reinaldo Avila da Silva.

[6] An ancient Greek and later Roman city.

others buggered off, which was marvellous in a way; I was able to take Marie Aspioti out to lunch (aged 94). We reminisced about happy Corfu days at Canona, when 40–50 years ago, she used to make us all play 'Up Jenkins' …[1] 'That's right, Peggy. <u>Proper</u> creepy-crawlies, Mr Rylands. Sir Maurice, yours is a disgrace! Now… <u>Smashums</u>! etc.' We slumbered in armchairs in front of the fire, till my plane left.

We are coming back to Blighty hotfoot on this letter, and will be at Janetta's, then the Mill House, and in touch at once.

Love to all
Paddy

P.S. There's an incredible mess going on in Paris – Payot, Flammarion and Phébus all at war about rival translations of *Mani*. I've told them I've only had one publisher in half a century, *et en cette foi je veux vivre et mourir* (François Villon).[2]

To George Jellicoe	Kardamyli
11 October 1999	Messenia
	Greece

Dear George,

I <u>am</u> sorry to be such a slowcoach with the pen – it's a foible that gives rise to continuous complaint in Albemarle Street – but whenever my back is turned a sudden mountain of mail seems to mount up here. Unlike you, who tackle it at once, and polish it off, I become an immediate martyr to Oblomovism,[3] and get stuck for days. Pelion piles up on Ossa,[4] and I behave like Buridan's

---

[1] A game in which contestants try to conceal a coin in their hands, while their opponent orders them to perform various actions which may reveal who has it.

[2] 'In this faith I want to live and die.'

[3] Fatalistic slothfulness, named after the nobleman who rarely leaves his bed in *Oblomov* (1859) by Ivan Goncharov.

[4] When the twins Otus and Ephialtes attempted to storm Olympus, they piled Mount Pelion upon Mount Ossa. The phrase is used to mean 'make something worse'.

Ass,[1] and little gets done. If only it was fascinating reading matter! But it's mostly tedious bosh.

It's jolly seldom I get anything fascinating, like your future son-in-law's[2] admirable disquisition on the Corfu gorgon.[3] It's always intrigued me, and I've longed to know all about it. Well, now I do, so please administer an admiring pat-on-the-back by proxy, and wish them both the best of luck. It's odd to remember that the brightest star in the constellation of Perseus is Algol, to the Arabs, i.e., *El ghoul*, the Monster, viz. the Gorgon's head, which Perseus kept in a bag, and when he wanted to get rid of enemies, he just whisked it out, flashed it round the room, – looking the other way of course – and turned them all to stone. Apotropaic,[4] and how! I enclose a p.c. of one of those occasions. The really odd thing about it is that Perseus seems to be wearing a tam o' shanter, a plaid, and a kilt, as though to <u>illuminate</u> some terrible clan massacre in the Waverley Novels …

No more for the moment, except love to Philippa and everyone there.

Yours ever
Paddy

[1] Buridan's ass is an illustration of a paradox in philosophy in the conception of free will. It refers to a hypothetical situation wherein an ass that is equally hungry and thirsty is placed precisely midway between a stack of hay and a pail of water.
[2] Colin Heber-Percy (great-nephew of Robert Heber-Percy) married Lady Emma Rose Jellicoe in December 1999.
[3] The western pediment of the Temple of Artemis in Corfu depicts the Gorgon Medusa.
[4] Magic that diverts evil onto another course. Among the ancient Greeks the Gorgon was the most widely used image to avert evil.

To Rudi Fischer   Kardamyli
Καθαρή Δευτέρα ['Clean Monday', i.e. the first   Messenia
day of Lent], 2000   Greece

Dear Rudi,

Written in sackcloth and ashes, as usual. It's my letter-writing uniform … <u>Your</u> letter was written on the 4th Sunday in Advent, and here I am, only answering on the eve of Shrove Tuesday … My excuse is that your letter wasn't forwarded, as we overstayed our usual solstice-sojourn in Blighty, for two-fold medical reasons: Joan had to have an operation for a slipped retina, and I for cancer of the tongue, for the second time. It sounds worse than it was. The growth on the side was excised overnight by the laser process three weeks ago. Both patients are thriving; but total anaesthetics do take about six weeks to get over, and I still feel a bit wobbly, but am managing to go for longer & longer walks.

How very nice that people are talking flatteringly of George's *Odyssey*[1] in Cambridge. I'll tell him so.

The pumpkin seeds <u>did</u> arrive just before I left, but I forgot them on my desk, and have just taken one, so the next few hours [will show if it works]. Ritsa, bringing coffee (*metrio*[2]) half an hour ago, noticed them, and asked what they were, and what for. I told her as decently as I could[3] and she laughed and cried 'Α! Διὰ Συχνουρία! Ολος ὁ κόσμος ὑποφέρει ἀπ᾽ αὐτό!' ['Ah! For sychnuria![4] Everyone suffers from that!'] – so we may need some more. I'll start collecting … Our doctor in London said my blood pressure was a bit – not very – higher than it should be, and I must try and drink less coffee,

---

[1] George Psychoundakis's translations of the *Iliad* and the *Odyssey* from Ancient Greek to modern Cretan dialect were published in 2003.

[2] Greek coffee, medium sweetened.

[3] Pumpkin seeds are said to have a number of health benefits, including enhanced male sexual function.

[4] Sychnuria is the medical condition whereby one needs to urinate frequently.

so the tinnitus level may drop too. I'll try and send some of our olive oil, to make up for the lack of inoculation.

I'm sorry to hear that Xenia's nephew is ailing, Περαστικά του! ['May it all pass soon!'] How odd that he was only three when his aunt and I were having such a lovely time in Transylvania! Very many thanks for the P.C. of Gurasada Church. I'd forgotten it was such a splendid example. It looks Saxon? Which, of course, Elemér was. I think you said that Mr Vaida didn't care for Xenia much. Quite apart from everything else, I can't help admiring her fiery spirit in slaying her horrible [illegible] co-lodger.

We had Christmas at Dumbleton, very quiet, and watched the New Millennium fireworks on TV, with Peter Levi and his wife Deirdre, Cyril Connolly's widow. Almost immediately – a few days later – Peter died painlessly in his sleep. We were very fond of him. I'll enclose a sort of Postscript, at the *Independent*'s request, to a much longer obit by Julian Mitchell (v. good) dealing with his marriage, the Soc. of Jesus etc.

I'll also shove in two things that came out round about my 85th birthday, one rather serious, the other more ebullient by Debo Devonshire. I thought there was something odd going on when I went up to stay [at Chatsworth], Debo asking unexpected questions, and scribbling down the answers, so I asked her what was going on, and she admitted Ch. Moore of the *Telegraph*[1] had asked her to do something. I thought it would be a chatty paragraph and nearly fainted when a whole page came out, with a very scruffy wartime snap, in which the Anzora or Brylcreem is much shinier than the Sam Browne[2] ... It was an old-fashioned houseparty there, with the P. of Wales staying, among others, and I sat next to Camilla P.B.[3] twice, whom I'd never met. She is absolutely charming, and very funny. I'd forgotten to put my hearing aid in, so did so, and it let out a bit of a shriek, as these things do. When I said I was sorry, she said, 'Oh, I'm absolutely used to one. A great

[1] Charles Moore, editor of the *Daily Telegraph*, 1995–2003.
[2] A leather belt worn over a uniform, usually supported by a diagonal shoulder strap.
[3] The Prince of Wales and Camilla Parker Bowles married in 2005.

friend of mine has one, and it's always happening. Once she was just about to put it in, but dropped it on the floor, and her dog, seeing something small and pink, promptly swallowed it, and the battery-squeak went on for ages.' 'What happened in the end?' She laughed, and said 'Oh, it was just a question of patience …'

Please give love to Dagmar, and from Joan

Yours ever, Paddy

In a few days' time Janetta is giving a huge party for Frances Partridge's 100th birthday! Also enclosed, an obit of Noel Annan,[1] who will also be much missed.

John Julius Norwich's daughter, Artemis Cooper, was selected as Paddy's authorised biographer. She was an obvious choice, both as an old family friend and as an experienced and successful writer, who had already produced a biography of Elizabeth David and a book about Cairo during the war. Originally it had been suggested that she might write the biography jointly with her husband Antony Beevor, author of a highly regarded work on wartime Crete, but this idea was later dropped.

To Artemis Cooper   Kardamyli
5 November 2000   Messenia
                                           Greece

Dearest Artemis,

Thank you so much for your letter and for telling us by telephone that you had arrived safely. We <u>did</u> enjoy your stay, and you were a saint of goodness, helping with everything so heroically. All this gusto spent for those not only painless but very enjoyable hours of colloquy, if that's the word. Your flair, speed and industry

<hr>

[1] Noel Gilroy Annan, Baron Annan (1916–2000), wartime intelligence officer, author and academic; Provost of King's College, Cambridge 1956–66, Provost of University College London 1966–78, Vice-Chancellor of the University of London 1978–81.

were dazzling! You were determined not to exhaust your patient, but I was ready to go on for hours more.

I've been going through all my letters to Joan for the past half-century. Lots of them seem to have points about them which might be a help to you, though the stacks of bulletins about building the house become a bit prolix and repetitive. The trouble is that many of them are almost illegible, the writing is so so bad and in some cases, faded away. I've been writing over some of the worst ones in pencil or ink in the hopes of legibility. This present writing, though pretty bad, is calligraphy compared to the really bad ones, I think married couples are inclined to drop into a sort of arcane short-hand, especially when scribbled down at high speed.

I wonder what we should do. I can't quite hand the whole [illegible] over to you as they stand, in the corrected form, as I suppose I will need them, or some of them, for Vol III of *A Time of Gifts*. Ought I to choose the likeliest ones, and get them photo-copied? But perhaps you would like to go through the whole lot? I've put lines round any over gossipy or scandalous bits with <u>OMIT</u> written in the margin. There are not many of them.

I'm getting <u>this</u> written in such haste as I want to dart down to the post with it this morning.

It's lovely weather still. Joachim Voigt[1] came two days ago, and we have lovely far-flung swims and walks. My name day (S. Michael & Gabriel[2]) looms in a few days, when the whole village seems to cram into the house, ending up with dancing which culminates by everyone in a chain dance through the French window and round the fountain in a very complicated Oranges and Lemons formation.

Love to you both!
from Paddy and Joan

No time to re-read!

[1] A comparatively new friend, originally a friend of Joan's brother Graham.
[2] PLF was known as 'Mihali' in Greece; his Greek friends addressed him by his second name, Michael, because they found Patrick too difficult to pronounce.

To Sophie Moss   Kardamyli
13 December 2000   Messenia
                                                       Greece

IN TEARING HASTE. WRITTEN IN SACKCLOTH AND ASHES.

Dearest Sophie,

The above should be the title of a published volume of my letters – if published one day in a hundred years' time – as <u>all</u> my letters start with abject apologies for lateness in answering, <u>like this one</u>. It must be an inherited curse – my mother was the same; also, due to fidgeting about the place. Anyway, I <u>am</u> truly sorry and plan to improve.

What's more, this isn't a true letter, only to thank you for yours, and take note of Kyril's[1] whereabouts. I'd love to go and see him with you. Memories of feasts at Marie Riaz's.[2] The other thing is, I've just written to the Folio Soc. to say I'll do a short foreword or P.S. to a Folio copy of *Ill Met*, hoping it might help.[3]

Please thank (or apologies) Gabriella and Pussa [Isabelle] for writing. P. sent a lovely illustrated letter full of your ancestral architecture.

Please forgive lateness again, and lots of love

from
Paddy

I'll be coming back later in the month, so be in touch.

---

[1] Kyril Zinovieff, later FitzLyon (1910–2015), long-lived Russian émigré who joked that his memory stretched from Rasputin to Putin. An acclaimed translator of works from the Russian, he worked for the Foreign Office, and served in military intelligence in the Middle East during the war.

[2] A cousin of the photographer Costa Achillopoulos, married to a rich Egyptian sugar merchant, whom Paddy came to know in Cairo during the war. It was at one of her parties that he had met Joan.

[3] A note on the Folio Society website outlined what happened after they had invited PLF to contribute an introduction to the Society edition: 'He rang up from his home in Greece. It was indeed, he said charmingly, "delicate" and for various reasons he'd always felt the less said the better. We parted genially, my suggesting that we might ask Michael Foot, historian

(cont'd opposite)

Since 1962 Rudi Fischer had been married to Dagmar von Melchner, a second cousin.

To Dagmar Fischer   Kardamyli
Orthodox Easter Monday 2002   Messenia
                                            Greece

ΧΡΙΣΤΟΣ ΑΝΕΣΤΗ! [CHRIST IS RISEN!][1]

Dear Dagmar,

I was talking to Rudi on the telephone the other day – exchanging Easter greetings – and he said you were rather sad because I wrote so seldom! I <u>am</u> sorry, and it's entirely my fault! The trouble was that I had written to the wrong address, in an old address book, and, as you see by the enclosed, they didn't contain anything very exciting, alas, and one of them I am totally unable to read myself, so it is just as well you <u>didn't</u> get it, as it would have been like trying to decipher Coptic or Cuneiform. Thank God, I <u>have</u> your correct address in a more up-to-date address book and I am taking especial care about my handwriting, though it may not look like it.

Easter is just over, here, but we had a very quiet one, as ten days ago Joan fell down in her bathroom and cut her forehead badly on a tap, so we had to take her to hospital for stitches and she is still not walking much, but very much better. Luckily, we had a very nice and efficient old friend, Miranda Rothschild, who has been half doctor, half nurse, and everything looks much better.

of the Special Operations Executive and an old friend of his, to do it instead. This we did. A week later, Paddy telephoned again. He'd been thinking about it, and he felt that there were things he would like to say: the coup had, in his view, been diminished by being reduced to the level of a "tremendous jape" and he hoped to restore the balance by providing something of the context for the enterprise. He did not wish to interfere with Michael's introduction, but would contribute a short Afterword, describing his own experience. It would be 500 to 1,000 words. It eventually emerged at 6,500 words, all of which had to be wrested from him in hand to hand combat, so anxious was he that nothing could be misinterpreted.'

[1] This, with the response at the end of the letter, is a standard form of Easter greeting and response in the Orthodox Church at Easter time.

It wasn't very nice weather, but improved over Easter, which was a lovely sunny day, so I boldly dived into the sea and it wasn't very cold at all, so I think I will start every day. The <u>latest</u> I have swum here is the 25th of November, which is just about when winter storms and huge waves begin.

I do hope all goes well with you in Munich, and that we will see you here this summer. We have to go back to England sometimes, but don't know when it will be. But I hope we strike lucky!

Joan sends her love, and so do I.
Paddy

I end with the formal response to the phrase at the beginning, viz.:-
ΑΛΗΘΩΣ ΑΝΕΣΤΗ! [HE IS RISEN INDEED!]

Joan died suddenly on 4 June 2003, aged ninety-one. This letter was written in reply to a letter of condolence from Paddy's former lover, Lyndall Birch, by this time herself the widow of an Italian count.

To Lyndall Passerini-Hopkinson   The Mill House
9 August 2003   Dumbleton
                                               Evesham
                                      Worcestershire

Dearest Lyndall,

Many, many thanks for your kind words about poor Joan. It was a cheerful morning at Kardamyli, I went in to see her just as she was finishing breakfast with nine kittens scattered about the bed – skewbald, black, white and gold, occasionally bumping into the pieces on the chessboard where she was grappling with a problem, occasionally pushing them off. We made plans for lunch, with Olivia Stewart[1] who was staying, and Elpida, who looks after us.[2] An hour later, when I was working in the studio in the garden, Elpida dashed in in floods saying 'Kyria Ioanna' – Mrs Joan – so I ran across and there was Joan

[1] Olivia Stewart, film producer and script consultant. The daughter of Michael and Damaris Stewart, she was also Joan's god-daughter.
[2] PLF's housekeeper and cook, Elpida Belloyannis. During PLF's final illness she never left his side.

dead on the bed. She had fallen in the bathroom, banged on the edge and death was immediate. The following days were a sort of trance of shock and semi-disbelief. The only strange thing was the day of the service [at Dumbleton] – brilliant mid-summer, sheep baa-ing all over the hills and fields, woods full of birds, sunbeams slanting into the late Plantagenet church through stained glass and seeming to fill in gaps of the liturgy. Wild flowers everywhere. It's hard to see what the end of the half-century together will be. I constantly find myself saying 'I must write – or tell – that to Joan', then suddenly remember that one can't, and nothing seems to have any point. Then I remember all these happy years, and what undeserved luck one had had, and the focus shifts a bit. No more now, dear Lyndall, except thanks for your kind and moving words. Keep in touch!

Love from Paddy

P.S. Back to Greece in about a month.

Wilhelmine ('Billa') Harrod, a friend of Joan's for seventy years, had often been a guest at Kardamyli. Born Wilhelmine Cresswell in 1903, she had been married to the Oxford economist Sir Roy Harrod until his death in 1978. The character of 'sensible Fanny' in Nancy Mitford's Love in a Cold Climate *was modelled on her.*

To Lady Harrod   Kardamyli
15 March 2004   Messenia
                                        Greece

Darling Billa,

How are you? No Mill House over Christmas time, alas, [illegible] I would be gallivanting in the North, because no Joan! It seems incredible, and hard to get used to. Oddly enough, it's over jokes that the absence is brought home most: during the morning, slogging away in the studio, something crops up and I say to myself 'I <u>must</u> remember to tell Joan that at lunch, it <u>will</u> make her laugh.' All sorts of things like that. All the freesias she planted last year are shooting up through the grass, a marvellous display. She <u>would</u> have been pleased. (I don't know if that's how the flower is spelt – it's <u>pronounced</u> almost as if the 's' were a French 'J', isn't it? – but Chamber's dikker says <u>FREESIA</u>, a south-African genus of the iris family, scented greenhouse plants – E. M. <u>Fries</u> 1794–1878; Swedish botanist.[1] The vowel still looks a bit queer.) Anyway, they smell marvellous. I've a tumblerful on my desk. They smell lovely, glass or no glass.

The cats miss her terribly, so do I.

I'm in solitary grandeur here, struggling with letters, and longing to post the <u>last</u> one and get on with the book I've been toiling on for ages, viz. Vol III of that long youthful trudge across Europe; I'm always <u>about</u> to begin when a new driblet arrives …

I notice that my handwriting seems to shrink progressively as the letter goes on, as though there were a terrible shortage of stationery, and illegibility looms. I propose to make a fresh start: here and now!

I very much enjoyed the investiture.[2] I wasn't quite sure when it was to be so Artemis Cooper rang up someone who knows about this sort of thing, and he said he thought the next investiture was in June: 'No, let me see! There's one in February – yes, here we are, Feb the Eleventh.' Well it was my 89th birthday! Can you beat it? It seems the Queen likes to chat briefly to about 1 honoured out of 10. I struck lucky. As she handed the blade to a courtier (who had probably fed her with the tidings anyway), she said, 'I believe it's your birthday.' 'Yes ma'am' 'Well, many happy returns of the day.' I nearly swooned away …

Chatsworth was lovely and YOUR FRIEND[3] was there. I'm now going to the village, hoping there are no letters except one or two handwritten ones; then <u>back</u> to this desk and to work in my new larger writing – it's beginning to shrink already.

I'm coming back for a lot of May, so we might fix something with that nice driver! Anyway, tons of love, dear Billa,

from Paddy

---

[1] Friedrich Freese (1794–1878) was a German physician and botanist.
[2] PLF had been awarded a knighthood in the 2004 New Year's honours list, for services to literature and Anglo-Greek relations.
[3] The Prince of Wales. In a letter to his French translator Guillame Villeneuve (11 November 1991), PLF wrote that the prince and Billa were 'very friendly'; they 'regularly collaborate on the preservation of old churches in Norfolk and go for long walks, pique-niqueing *à deux*, seeking out holy places which need saving'.

In 2004 Paddy received a letter from Henry Hardy, who was preparing a volume of Maurice Bowra's verse for publication. Between 1920 and 1965 Bowra had written a sequence of poems described by Hardy as 'skilful but extremely coarse and scurrilous parodies'. Many of these contained disobliging references to living people. Bowra had not permitted them to be published in his lifetime, merely circulating them around a small circle of friends, provoking the quip from his Oxford colleague and literary executor, John Sparrow, that Bowra's 'prose was unreadable and his verse was unprintable'. But by the dawn of the twenty-first century Bowra had been dead thirty years, and most of those referred to in the poems were no longer alive to be hurt by them. Almost the sole exception was Paddy, the subject of two clever but exceptionally nasty poems written in 1950, 'The Wounded Gigolo' and 'On the Coast of Terror Fermoor'. Though not obliged to do so, Hardy courteously sought Paddy's approval to publish these two poems; and after some vacillation, Paddy chose to exercise his veto. 'Could Maurice's shade ponder all this now, I think I might emerge as more of a saviour than a spoilsport,' he argued. It was clear from the correspondence that he was hurt by Bowra's poems: one sign of this, perhaps, was that his letters on the subject were less coherent than usual, with missing words and incomplete sentences.

Bowra's undisguised admiration for Joan may help to explain his spite towards her lover. Paddy's anagram for Maurice Bowra, 'Eroica Rawbum', suggests a degree of mutual hostility, perhaps suppressed because of their mutual fondness and respect for Joan. But if this hostility ever existed, it was soon forgotten on Paddy's part. 'I like[d] Maurice very much, which makes the whole thing even gloomier,' he wrote to Hardy.

To Henry Hardy
undated [postmarked 3 November 2004]

Kardamyli
Messenia
Greece

Dear Mr Hardy,

This is an afterthought to my letter of two days ago.

You most considerately gave me the chance to say 'yes' or 'no' about two of Maurice's poems,[1] and, rather disappointingly, I want to extend the 'no' to include 'The Coast of Terra Fermor' [sic].[2]

A few years ago Joan (wife) read through the whole collection, and said she had decided to do away with them, as they would seriously hurt the feelings of friends who figure in them; and she told me next day that she had done so, and felt very relieved. I did too, though neither she nor I had read the 'Hero-Gigolo' one. She would have hated it (for the reasons in my letter and the book[3] I asked Sandoe's to send you). She thought that all the people mentioned in the collection would have been cut to the quick, however much they put on non-spoilsport faces.

I think she was right. It's rather like playing limericks or *bouts rimés*, rather tight after dinner, putting friends and foes alike into comic and scurrilous fictitious adventures. The more improper and ridiculous the better, as they are all eventually to be chucked in the fire. But to be carefully preserved and read in cold blood by total strangers a couple of generations later, like Catullus or Martial, when all the characters – and, above all, the tones of voice and the mood – have vanished, is very different.

Many thanks again for your compunction.

Yours sincerely
Patrick Leigh Fermor

I have striven to be more legible. I didn't bring the destruction of the poems into my other letter as I thought it would sound too depressing.

---

[1] The poems themselves, with Hardy's helpful glosses, can be found at: http://berlin. wolf.ox.ac.uk/dugdale/bowra/websiteplf.pdf. In 2012 they were reproduced on the website of the Patrick Leigh Fermor Society, provoking much comment, almost all of it negative.
[2] In a letter preceding this one, PLF had written that he thought 'the Hero-Gigolo poem', about his relations with Balasha Cantacuzène, 'a bit cracked', and did not want it to be printed.
[3] Artemis Cooper (ed.), *Words of Mercury*, which reprints PLF's favourable review of Bowra's *Primitive Song*, originally published in *The Spectator*, 6 July 1962.

To Milton Gendel   Kardamyli
21 April 2005   Messenia
                                     Greece

My dear Milton,

I've just been talking to Magouche on the telephone and, naturally, <u>you</u> cropped up, and then reciprocal praise of your wonderful book of Roman photographs – and in the middle of this, it suddenly shot through me like a <u>lance</u> that I don't think I wrote and thanked you for them. Do forgive me for being such a swine! I absolutely loved them, and I was <u>most honoured</u> to figure among all those marvellous people, reading Pius II's letters to our friends on Lake Bolsena (?). It's at the Mill House, and all visitors have gone slowly through it, and joined me in hosannas.

Olivia Stewart came here for a few days and then went back to Rome. I'm fighting an unequal fight against all the things I <u>ought</u> to have done years ago. When I've polished all these off, I plan to get down to finishing the last vol. of that *Time of Gifts* trilogy, describing my youthful trudge across Europe. I have got all Bulgaria, half Romania, a chunk of Turkey to polish off; then I pine to finish not a long sojourn in Mt Athos in midwinter 1933–34. I've got all the notes.

Wish me luck, dear Milton, and again, forgive my bad manners!

Please give my love to any survivors. I don't know what's happened to them all – Natalie, Sandrino etc. I thought Domietta[1] looked spiffing.

Yours ever,

Paddy

---

[1] Princess Laudomia Hercolani (née del Drogo), known to friends as 'Domietta', style icon and set designer, who worked with Luchino Visconti on the film *The Leopard* (1963). In reply, Gendel wrote that Domietta was 'not displeased that you found her spiffing'.

To Henry Hardy
May 2005

Kardamyli
Messenia
Greece

Dear Mr Hardy,

I write in sackcloth and ashes.

All sorts of impediments have been cropping up, including the arrival of bulldozers and lorries, preparing to put up a large building hard by, visits to Athens, lawyers etc. Also a visit, unannounced but unrefusable. One nice (properly announced!) visitation was from Mr [James] Morwood, the Dean of Wadham,[1] which was very agreeable. He was collecting information for a colleague who is doing a biography of Maurice,[2] so I did what I could, touching lightly on the nerves. He was mainly in search of impressions of Adrian Bishop[3] whom I met once or twice in Cairo before he set off on his fatal mission, and of Dr Zaehner,[4] whom I only met once, and spent a hilarious evening with Prue Pelham (who soon after married a great friend of Maurice's – Guy Branch – also of mine and Balasha Cantacuzène – alas killed as a fighter pilot in the battle of Britain.)[5] The chief memory of this wildish evening is Zaehner reciting a highly pornographic alphabet which I had never heard, before or since. He was also in search of details about Sir Walter Smart, 'Oriental Minister' at the Embassy in Cairo, a great friend of Joan's and mine. We spent two winters working in their house in Normandy [Gadencourt].

I was half way through a letter to you when he arrived, in which I had imparted the fact that about 2½ years ago, Joan, just having

[1] Bowra was Warden of Wadham College, Oxford, 1938–70.
[2] Leslie Mitchell of University College, Oxford. His *Maurice Bowra: A Life* was published in 2009.
[3] Adrian Bishop, a longstanding friend of Bowra's and perhaps his lover. In 1942, while on an intelligence mission in the Middle East, he fell to his death from the third floor of one of Tehran's smartest hotels.
[4] Robert Charles Zaehner (1913–74), academic and intelligence officer, Spalding Professor of Eastern Religion and Ethics at Oxford University, 1952–74.
[5] Flying Officer Guy Branch was killed in action on 11 August 1940 while flying a Hurricane over the English Channel.

dug out and re-read the poems, said she was going to destroy them, as they would give too much pain to the 'figuranti', and, next day, she told me the deed was done. I hadn't mentioned this to you,[1] as it seemed to make the whole theme darker than it need be. (She hadn't seen the Gigolo Hero one. At least, I never saw it until sent by you.) Joan's opinion was that the destruction could not be compared to the Byron conflagration in Albemarle Street,[2] as Maurice had already given sets to other people, including Pam Berry, so there was no question of their not surviving, but Joan didn't want to be the carrier.

If it is not too late, I would be *much happier* if Terra Fermor [*sic*] vanished. I feel very guilty. I stick to my idea that Maurice was temporarily cracked in those two poems. They introduce me as a swine, and [Joan], it seems to me, as an idiotic but beautiful idiot for putting up with such a swine, so all three come out as [incomplete sentence] …

I'm afraid I think Eroica Rawbum ought to go. Maurice was unpredictably sensitive on some points. When Gide went to visit Magdalen *à la recherche* after undergraduate days of Oscar Wilde, rather hoping for Maurice's company, M. kept out of the way and Gide merely wandered through the rooms in silence, passing the flat of his hands over the panelling – or whatever it was – in a [*illegible*] gesture, and went away.

He obviously had mixed feelings about me. When I gave a nice review of M's *Primitive Song* in a learned publication [h]e wrote a v. cheery thank you letter saying 'If you want someone to pour a kettle all over Steven Runciman (who had sacked me from the British Council in Athens for idleness), I'm your man!'. When Joan and I married he gave us the magnificent 20-volume Bonchurch Swinburne,[3] which takes up nearly two yards [of] shelf room. I've just come across the enclosed letter.[4]

---

[1] In fact he had – see letter postmarked 3 November 2004.

[2] In 1824 John Murray burned the manuscript of Byron's memoirs in an Albemarle Street grate.

[3] Sir Edmund Gosse and Thomas James Wise (eds), *The Complete Works of Algernon Charles Swinburne*, Bonchurch Edition (1925–7).

[4] A letter from John Sparrow to PLF, 5 October 1971, about which books of Bowra's he would like to have.

As this is an indiscreet and I hope private letter, here is a charming slice of life told by Guy Branch to Prue, Joan and me. Guy was in Maurice's rooms when Isaiah Berlin came in, looking worried. Maurice asked what the matter was, Isaiah embarked on a long tale of European travel and its discomforts, in deep, hardly audible flow of rhetoric which described creepy feelings on the torso, at great length, at the end of which Maurice said briskly, 'Up with your shirt, Shia! Let's have a look!' The shirt went up, and after a minute's fumbling in the undergrowth, Maurice joyfully cried 'Why, it's a dear little C R A B!'

I've got to motor to Athens this afternoon to lay a wreath there, with Geo. Jellicoe – he for SBS, I for SOE – celebrating the anniversary of the war's end, and so all this has been written in rather a rush.

With all kind regards
Yours sincerely
Patrick Leigh Fermor

To Janetta Parladé   British Embassy
17 October 2006   Athens

Darling Janetta,

I'm sitting in the garden here on a rather cloudy morning. It may rain soon, but it's under a sort of a shelter, beside a fountain in which carp and goldfish swim to and fro, and I would be writing far more legibly if an enormous Labrador dog would take his head off my lap for five minutes. I think he's got me mixed up with an old friend. He's been accompanying the Ambassador on a ten-kilometre run – training for an enormous marathon run in a week's time, so he's probably rather tired.

I came up for a beautiful service to a chap called David[1] who blew up a lot of aeroplanes and sank enemy ships without number

[1] Colonel David Sutherland (1920–2006) served with the SBS and SAS during the war. He was on the British military mission to Greece in 1946.

during the war, and go back to Kardamyli tomorrow. I wish you and Jaime were going to be there!

Do you remember when the sudden sad news about Ralph's death put a stop to a planned trip to Delphi? It seems about five years ago, but is probably fifteen.[1]

I wish you both lived five miles away, at the outside, instead of the other southernmost tip of Europe …

tons of love
Paddy

The project to publish a volume of Paddy's correspondence with Debo Devonshire helped to relieve his loneliness and depression at being unable to finish the third volume of his trilogy. The two old friends had exchanged lively letters for almost half a century. The book, edited by Charlotte Mosley, was published by John Murray in 2008 under the title In Tearing Haste: Letters between Deborah Devonshire and Patrick Leigh Fermor.

To Deborah Devonshire   Kardamyli
29 March 2007   Messenia
(Oh, if only I'd learnt to do this[2] three-quarters of a   Greece
century ago!)

Darling Debo,

Don't be downcast at the <u>thinth</u>[3] of this, it's just that I can't bear to look at the Somerset Maugham letter anymore.[4] I pretty well finished all yours, and they are tip-top. I'm not sending any yet, as

---

[1] Actually forty-six. Ralph Partridge died in 1960.
[2] Date his letters fully. PLF was having difficulty in establishing the dates of his letters to her.
[3] Thin-ness.
[4] A letter to Debo written on 26 August 1956, describing his disastrous visit to the Villa Mauresque. See *In Tearing Haste*, pp. 19–22.

I hope they will be a help with all the non-existent dates on mine. Just think what a difference <u>one second's</u> more penmanship would have made today. I keep looking hopefully for your absent letters, but have drawn blank so far. The thing is, I've always <u>treasured</u> your ones, and would be v. surprised if any had been allowed to stray from the fold. It's terribly worrying.

Christina[1] has just been on the telephone, in tremendous form as always. She's having my Rita of the Mill House[2] up for a night with one of her children, and is planning to take them to the pictures and Madame Tussaud's. She really is a marvel.

I've got to dash off with this.

Tons of love
Paddy

I was toiling away in the studio yesterday when, at one o'clock, Elpida came and said three people had turned up, and were waiting on the terrace. They were a v. nice elderly & scholarly American, head of the American College of Athens (he made me a U.S. DLitt a few years ago) and his just as nice and amusing Greek wife.[3] The third was a cheerful chauffeur. I had asked them to lunch, last week, when they said they had some scholarly local duty. I'd utterly forgotten. There was only a single [illegible] in the fridge, so I took them to the only taverna open in the village in winter, and all was well. Talk about Dr Oblivion![4] It all ended with lots of chat and laughter, and even song …

---

[1] The Dowager Duchess's GP, Dr Christina Carritt.

[2] The cook/housekeeper at the Mill House.

[3] Dr John Bailey, president of the American College of Greece for many years, married to Irene Korre-Bailey.

[4] A joke name PLF used for himself to indicate his failing powers.

To Deborah Devonshire
27 July 2007

MANY APOLOGIES FOR DEPRESSING STATIONERY
AND UNTIDY WRITING, BOTH SAID TO BE DUE TO
A PASSING OPTICAL AFFLICTION CALLED TUNNEL
VISION

Darling Debo,

What about the banner headline above? Olivia Stewart has just been here for a few helpful days and ran off these banners by the hundred, so it'll be in time to stop me from being a bore from the word GO. She's a brick and a great standby, and, somehow, vaguely akin to Charlotte [Mosley]. <u>One's jolly lucky to have such friends</u>. What with Christina and her magic motor, driving one all over the Metropolis, i.e., first dropping me at the 1st specialist, then vanishing for a quarter of an hour to park, then trudge back to the specialist, and when he has finished specialising with me, trudging another quarter of an hour to retrieve the chemist, and drive onto the next one, the other side of our capital ... and a king's ransom has to be slid into a slot <u>each time</u>. At least I've found a part solution to this: halting at White's Club and getting a roll of glittering coins off the barman, to be forced on one's charioteer, against protest.

Charlotte's sojourn was far too short, but jam all through, great fun and lots of ground covered. Nothing could have been more congenial, the veg went down like ambrosia, helped down by lots of nectar (consult Lemprière's Classical Dictionary – have you got one? I loved it).

I hope this side [of the paper] won't show through? (Turn over.) It looks all right. I love talking about her grandfather Napier.[1] Why was I scribbling about him <u>before</u> all this in some fairly recent letter? I worshipped her[2] in Athens when I had just turned twenty,

[1] Napier Sturt (see footnote on p. 283).
[2] Balasha Cantacuzène.

and for long after. We eloped to a water-mill in the heart of a steep lemon-forest. Crichel was the last roof I slept under before sailing from Glasgow to Alexandria, as part of a solitary mission to the Greeks fighting the invading – and openly retreating – Italians.

I've had to break off our book for three days, but start again tomorrow, enjoying it like anything. I've tempered one or two bits of ardour in case the reader would conclude I was a bit of a rotter, if you see what I mean; but crushes are hard to look different! Anyway, I'm sure it will all work out gloriously.

I'm writing this in the studio, clad in Indian sandals, and shorts. Outside, meanwhile, the sun beats down to the rage of man and beast.[1] The back of my hand is scattered with such purplish maps. I'm going to get them looked at. If your new eye-chap isn't perfect, do try mine (via Christina), as I've taken to him like anything … Write soon.

Tons of love,
Paddy

It must be uphill work without Henry.[2] Thank heavens for Helen.[3] Please tell me truthfully: could you read this letter or was it impossible work? – Beyond the Pleasure Principle.[4]

---

[1] 'In a jungle town/ Where the sun beats down/ To the rage of man and beast/ The English garb/ Of the English sahib/ Merely gets a bit more creased.' From 'Mad Dogs and Englishmen' by Noël Coward.

[2] Henry Coleman, the Devonshires' butler for half a century, had retired.

[3] Helen Marchant, the Dowager Duchess's secretary.

[4] The 'pleasure principle' is a psychoanalytic term, meaning the guiding force behind the id; but PLF is using it here playfully, to suggest that reading his letter might have been hard work.

Paddy generously encouraged many younger writers, as William Blacker (b. 1962) would acknowledge in an address he gave at Paddy's memorial service in 2011.

To William Blacker
16 May 2009

Kardamyli
Messenia
Greece

Dear William,

I promise that I will get at the book[1] as soon as I can, but there's a sort of a literary traffic-block at the moment, so do forgive if I am on the slow side.

Meanwhile, here's a conundrum! After reading your letter, I made a dash for Debo Devonshire's last book[2] which only arrived a few days ago, and I <u>thought</u> I had read it all: the only chapter I had only skipped through, out of barbarous ignorance, was the one about flowers (publisher John Murray, like me). But then I found the chapter, where Debo describes the author as being a dashing military man, called 'C. E. Lucas Phillips'.[3] I've obviously got into a frightful tangle somewhere! Perhaps it is another book and I've got the whole thing [wrong]. Where did I read about your father being one of the earliest people to fly over Mt Everest and deeply involved in Central Asia during WWI?[4] It's obviously a different book!

I'm terribly worried about a trouble to the eyes called 'Tunnelvision', which very much limits one's efficient seeing, and sends one

---

[1] William Blacker's account of the eight years he had spent living in rural Romania, *Along the Enchanted Way: A Romanian Story*, was about to be published by John Murray.
[2] *Home to Roost, and Other Peckings* (2009), which contains a chapter about the book *Flora Domestica*, written by William Blacker's mother, Mary Rose Blacker.
[3] Brigadier C. E. Lucas Phillips (1897–1984) MC, Croix de Guerre, author of *Cockleshell Heroes* (1956), *The Greatest Raid of All* (1958), etc., as well as *The Small Garden* (1952), a book that Debo admired; she wrote an introduction for a reissued edition in 2006.
[4] Major Stewart Blacker (William Blacker's grandfather), planned, navigated and photographed the first flight over Mount Everest in 1933, piloted by the future Duke of Hamilton. In 1919–20 he raised a private army of Turkoman levies and White Russians to counter Bolshevik infiltration of Persia, for which he was awarded the OBE.

off the line when writing. It slows one up terribly. I wish I'd learnt to type. I'd always rather despised it, but not now.

The best of luck in your new habitat! It's rather impressive to live so near what Macaulay calls 'the great Volsinian Mere'.[1] Joan and I once spent a week visiting all the place names that come into *Horatius* or *Lake Regillus*.

> The harvests of Arretium
> This year, old men shall reap
> This year, young boys in Umbro
> Shall plunge the struggling sheep
> And, in the vats of Luna,
> This year, the must shall foam,
> Round the white feet of laughing girls
> Whose sires have marched to Rome.[2]

Yours ever, Paddy

---

[1] 'Best of all pools the fowler loves/ The great Volsinian mere ...' Macaulay, *Lays of Ancient Rome*, 'Horatius', VI.

[2] Macaulay, *Lays of Ancient Rome*, 'Horatius', VIII.

Jeremy Lewis (1942–2017), publisher, author and editor, had been in touch with Paddy about his biography of Cyril Connolly (1997), and had visited him in Kardamyli. As assistant editor of The Oldie *magazine, he asked Paddy to write a review.*

To Jeremy Lewis   Mill House
very early August 2009   Dumbleton

Dear Jeremy,

Many thanks for your letter, and *The Oldie*. My trouble is that my handwriting has deteriorated to such a degree that I found it hard to read the letters on the page. At this moment I am making a terrific effort to be legible – which I've never done since I was ten years old, and so far it is emerging fairly legibly, but the effort is very exacting, and I feel in danger of going off the lines at any moment. I've just been having a terrific struggle to write a review for the *Sunday Telegraph* of a marvellous book called *Along the Enchanted Way* ('A Romanian Story') by William Blacker. But the first results were so awful that I had to dictate it to Olivia Stewart. Results very little better, so re-dictated, with some changes, to another old friend, Artemis Cooper. The result was better, but still hopeless, so yesterday – 3rd time – I re-wrote as dictated to Cressida Connolly (another pal, a few miles away), and the result seems <u>just</u> bearable (by the skin of its teeth) so I'm going to send it to Mr Michael Todger,[1] at the *Telegraph*, beautifully amended (again!) and retyped by Cressida. <u>More or less presentable</u>. The result of all this is that I have got to learn to type, though 94, or find some other solution. But, alas, it looks as if I'll be out of action for quite a bit, back in the Peloponnese at the end of the month.

The name of the affliction that causes all the trouble is Tunnel-Vision, but privately known to me as Simplonitis, after that tunnel through which, to learn to ski, one was taken every winter.

With all kind regards
Paddy LF

Please forgive all this fuss.

---

[1] Michael Prodger, then literary editor of the *Sunday Telegraph*.

For some years Paddy had been in intermittent correspondence with Paul Pollak, archivist at the King's School, Canterbury. In 2006, for example, he thanked Pollak for sending him some 'fascinating' cuttings about the family of Nellie Lemar, the girl who had inadvertently caused him to be expelled from the school so many years before. 'I wonder if any photographs of Miss Lemar exist?' he asked. 'I didn't realise that there were so many sisters, all wonderful looking. I was told that the Duke of Gloucester – Pr[ince] Henry then – used to take her out to lunch in his dashing sports car, to Folkestone or Dover – en tout bien, tout honneur [intentions entirely honourable], I'm sure – when he was stationed at Canterbury in a cavalry regiment.'

To Paul Pollak   (as from) Kardamyli
undated [postmarked 23 February 2010]   Messenia
                                                 Greece

Dear Paul,

Before I write another word, I would like to apologise for my appalling writing, which, as you will see, refuses to stick to the rails. It was already deteriorating when I came [to England] from Greece for Christmas and the New Year. But, a couple of days before Christmas, I somehow managed to sleepwalk in the dark, outside my bedroom, and fell head over heels down a fifteen-foot staircase, arriving with a thump in the hall. Nothing was broken, thank heavens, but I was black and blue with bruises. It didn't spoil Christmas and New Year, and is now getting better. But it was a serious fall, and will take a month or two to recover. I was very lucky to get off so lightly. This was followed by the worst weather I have ever seen in England. I was supposed to be spending a cheerful Derbyshire Christmas at Chatsworth, but everything was cancelled – or postponed till later on – and I had a few friends here, who arrived before the really paralysing weather began.

Thank you very much for the fascinating Canterbury literature. Nellie Lemar, the wonderful looking cause of my scholastic downfall, must be in Australia, if surviving. What a long time ago it all seems! She really was the most beautiful looking being imaginable.... I wish I had a photograph or memento of this totally innocent romance.

I'm still toiling away on the third volume of my youthful trudge to the Balkans. I had abandoned it rather, but have started again, and find it is not so hopeless as I had imagined. Anyway, I am going back to the Mani in a couple of weeks, so wish me luck.

Please give my greetings to Marc,[1] and warm greetings to you. I'll write a bit later, when I hope my script will be a bit less tiring.

Yours ever, Paddy

[1] Marc Dath, housemaster of the Grange (PLF's old house). He and PLF had been in correspondence before and after PLF's opening of the new Grange in 2007.

In the spring of 2011 Paddy was diagnosed with cancer of the throat. An operation was performed to remove the tumour. By then ninety-six years old, he chose to refuse further treatment. He was able to return to Kardamyli from hospital in Athens, and talked excitedly about resuming work on the third volume of his trilogy, completing the story of his great walk begun in A Time of Gifts. *But only a few weeks later another operation proved necessary. On 9 June 2011, Paddy left Greece for the last time, hoping to see his friends in England before the end. He arrived at Dumbleton that night, and died the next morning.*

Dramatis Personae

John Betjeman (1906–84), popular poet, writer, broadcaster and advocate for Victorian architecture, knighted in 1969. He married Penelope Chetwode in 1933, but the two became estranged after her conversion to Catholicism in 1949. As a schoolboy at the King's School, Canterbury, in the 1930s, PLF had heard Betjeman lecture long before they met. His daughter, Candida Lycett Green, was also a friend of PLF's.

Lyndall Birch (b. 1931), later Lyndall Passerini-Hopkinson, daughter of the journalist Tom Hopkinson and the novelist Antonia White. She had married Lionel Birch, Hopkinson's successor as editor of *Picture Post* (a man only five years younger than her father), but the marriage failed after only a few months. When she first met PLF, in 1958, she was working as a proofreader for the United Nations Food and Agriculture Organisation in Rome.

(Cecil) Maurice Bowra (1898–1971), classical scholar and Warden of Wadham College, Oxford, knighted in 1951, renowned as a wit, often vicious. He was devoted to Joan but not so friendly towards PLF.

Marie-Blanche ('Balasha') Cantacuzène (1899–1976), a princess from one of the great dynasties of Eastern Europe. Her family owned a house in Bucharest and an estate in Romanian Moldavia, near the Bessarabian border. In 1924 she had married a Spanish diplomat, who abandoned her while serving as ambassador in Athens, where PLF met and fell in love with her in 1935.

(Charles) Bruce Chatwin (1940–89), travel writer, novelist and journalist. He had known PLF and Joan slightly since 1970, but he and PLF came to know each other well when he visited Kardamyli in the winter of 1984/5 and stayed for seven months. After his premature death at the age of only forty-eight, his ashes were buried at a chapel nearby, at his own request.

Cyril Vernon Connolly (1903–74), writer, critic and editor, briefly Joan's lover. PLF referred to him satirically as 'The Humanist'.

Alfred Duff Cooper (1890–1954), 1st Viscount Norwich, politician, diplomat, author, and British Ambassador to France, 1944–7.

Artemis Cooper (b. 1953), writer, daughter of John Julius Norwich and granddaughter of Duff and Diana Cooper, married to the military historian Antony Beevor (whose books include *Crete: The Battle and the Resistance*, 1991). Her biography of PLF, *Patrick Leigh Fermor: An Adventure*, was published in 2012.

Diana Cooper (1892–1986), née Lady Diana Manners, famous beauty and London socialite, the youngest daughter, in theory, of the Duke of Rutland (in fact daughter of the Hon. Henry 'Harry' Cust). In 1919 she married the Conservative politician and writer Alfred Duff Cooper, who was appointed British Ambassador to France in 1944. Towards the end of his life he was made Viscount Norwich; she preferred to remain known as Lady Diana Cooper, claiming that Viscountess 'Norwich' sounded too much like 'porridge'. She and PLF became friends in the early 1950s: in the words of PLF's biographer, 'Paddy and Diana each discovered that the other was the sort of person they liked best.'

Deborah ('Debo') Vivien Cavendish, Duchess of Devonshire (1920–2014), née Mitford, the youngest of the six Mitford sisters, who married Andrew Robert Buxton Cavendish, later 11th Duke of Devonshire (1920–2004), in 1941. PLF had first seen her at a ball in 1940, though she had scarcely noticed him. In the post-war years they became close friends, and he was a frequent visitor to the Devonshire seats, Chatsworth in Derbyshire and Lismore Castle in Ireland. The correspondence between the Duchess and PLF over a period of more than half a century was published as *In Tearing Haste*, edited by Charlotte Mosley, in 2008.

Lawrence Durrell (1912–90), poet, novelist and man of letters. Though British, he lived most of his life abroad, in Corfu, Crete, Egypt and France. He came to know PLF while serving as a press attaché to the British embassies in Cairo and Alexandria.

Pamela Egremont see **Pamela Wyndham-Quin**

(Henry) Robin Romilly Fedden (1908–77), writer, diplomat and mountaineer. In the 1930s he served as a diplomat in Athens and taught English literature at Cairo University, and co-edited the literary journal *Personal Landscape* with Lawrence Durrell and Bernard Spencer. Henry Miller thought him effete. After the war, he worked for the National Trust.

Agnes 'Magouche' (also known as Magouch) Fielding (1921–2013), née Magruder, then Gorky, Phillips and finally Fielding, was the daughter of an American admiral and widow of the Armenian-American artist, Arshile Gorky.

Alexander ('Xan') Wallace Fielding (1918–91), writer, translator, journalist and traveller; met PLF while serving behind enemy lines in Crete during the war, and they became close friends. Before his marriage to Magouche Phillips, he was married to Daphne (1904–97), née Vivian, ex-wife of the 6th Marquess of Bath.

Rudi Fischer (1927?–2016), editor and scholar, a naturalised Australian of Saxon Transylvanian origin who was living in Budapest and working as an editor for the *New Hungarian Quarterly* when he first made contact with PLF in 1978 to draw his attention to errors in *A Time of Gifts*. 'My debt to Rudolf Fischer is beyond reckoning,' PLF would write in *Between the Woods and the Water*. 'His omniscient range of knowledge and an enthusiasm tempered with astringency have been a constant delight and stimulus during all the writing of this book; his vigilance has saved it from many errors, and I feel that the remaining ones may be precisely those when his advice was not followed.'

Ann Gerald Mary ('Annie') Fleming (1913–81), née Charteris, granddaughter of the 9th Earl of Wemyss. Her third husband was Ian Fleming, later the author of the James Bond novels. They lived at Goldeneye, a house in Jamaica, and Sevenhampton, in Wiltshire. A renowned society hostess, she had friends in politics and in the literary world, and became one of PLF's closest friends and most regular correspondents.

Nikos ('Niko') Hadjikyriakos-Ghika (1906–94), artist and sculptor generally considered among the best modern Greek artists, from a wealthy Athens family. He and PLF became friends after the war, and in the early 1950s Ghika allowed PLF to stay for long periods at his house on Hydra. After this house was destroyed by fire, Ghika built a house on Corfu. He married first Antigone ('Tiggie'), and then, in 1961, Barbara Warner.

Enrica ('Ricki') Huston (1929–69), née Soma, socialite, model and ballerina, born in New York of Italian-American parents. She became the fourth and much younger wife of the film director, screenwriter and actor John Huston (1906–87). She died in a car accident at the age of only thirty-nine.

Barbara Hutchinson see **Barbara Warner**

George Katsimbalis (1890–1978), poet and raconteur, a dominant figure in Greek literary life, immortalised in Henry Miller's *The Colossus of Maroussi* (1941).

Patrick Kinross (John Patrick Douglas Balfour) (1904–76), 3rd Baron Kinross, historian and writer, specialising in Islamic history. He came to know PLF while serving as First Secretary at the British embassy in Cairo during the Second World War.

Elemér von Klobusiçky (1899–1986) was PLF's host on his family estate in Transylvania in the summer of 1934. In *Between the Woods and the Water*, PLF concealed his identity under the pseudonym 'István'. 'I admired him very much,' wrote PLF, 'he was tremendous fun, and we became great friends.' They had several adventures together, including a frolic with peasant girls who discovered the two young men swimming naked in a river. PLF especially liked the fact that 'István' had run away to join a hussar regiment during the First World War.

Lady Dorothy ('Coote') Lygon (1912–2001), fourth and youngest daughter of the 7th Earl Beauchamp, the doomed family on whom Evelyn Waugh is said to have modelled the Flytes (Lord Marchmain) in his novel *Brideshead Revisited*. She was a spinster until her unexpected and short-lived marriage to Robert Heber-Percy in 1985, two years before his death.

Sir Aymer Maxwell of Monreith (1911–87), baronet, elder brother of the writer Gavin Maxwell. He had inherited estates in south-west Scotland, but preferred sailing round the Greek islands to more conventional country pursuits. While PLF was waiting for the house at Kardamyli to be built, Sir Aymer let him use his own house in Euboea.

Jessica Mitford (1917–96), known as 'Decca', writer and civil rights activist, the second youngest of the six Mitford sisters. Her left-wing sympathies were in sharp contrast to those of her sister Diana, second wife of the Fascist leader Sir Oswald Mosley. She lived in California, where she met and married the American lawyer and civil rights activist Robert Treuhaft.

Nancy Mitford (1904–73), novelist, biographer and journalist, eldest of the six Mitford sisters. After the war she lived in France. She had married Peter Rodd in 1933, but the marriage did not survive, and she formed a long-term liaison with the Free French officer, and later ambassador in Rome, Gaston Palewski.

Judith Venetia ('Judy') Montagu (1923–72), daughter of the politician Hon. Edwin Montagu and Venetia Stanley, the young woman with whom Asquith had become obsessed during the First World War. Judy was a close friend of Princess Margaret, but had given up her London life and moved to Rome after falling for the American photographer and art historian Milton Gendel (b. 1919), whom she eventually married in 1962. She and PLF had a brief love affair in the 1950s. He was staying in her Rome flat on the Isola Tiberina when he began his affair with Lyndall Birch.

W. Stanley 'Billy' Moss (1921–65), soldier, writer and traveller, PLF's second-in-command in the operation to capture General Kreipe. He wrote an account of this operation, *Ill Met by Moonlight* (1950), which was made into a film (1957) by Powell and Pressburger. In Cairo during the war he met the Polish Countess Zofia ('Sophie') Tarnowska (1917–2009), whom he subsequently married.

John Arnaud Robin Grey ('Jock') Murray (1909–93), publisher, the sixth John Murray in the illustrious family firm, and a patient friend to and supporter of PLF.

John Julius Norwich (1929–2018), diplomat, writer and broadcaster, otherwise known as John Julius Cooper, 2nd Viscount Norwich, son of Duff and Lady Diana Cooper. Among his best-known works is a three-volume history of Byzantium; he credits PLF with having opened his eyes to this great civilisation, in the two weeks they were on board the *Eros II* together.

Mark Ogilvie-Grant (1905–69) was posted to Greece with the Special Operations Executive in the Second World War, but was taken prisoner in the Mani soon after landing. After the war he settled in Athens, where he worked for BP.

Janetta Parladé (1922–2018), née Woolley, a close friend of Joan's, and of Frances and Ralph Partridge, much admired for her beauty and intelligence. Her lovers included Lucian Freud and the Duke of Devonshire. She was married to Humphrey Slater, Robert Kee and Derek Jackson, who left her for her half-sister, Angela Culme-Seymour. Eventually she would marry a Spanish aristocrat, the interior designer Jaime Parladé.

Frances Catherine Partridge (1900–2004), née Marshall, was married to Ralph Partridge (1894–1960), and lived at Ham Spray, where, before marrying Frances, Ralph had lived in a ménage à trois with Lytton Strachey and Dora Carrington. Ralph and Frances were close friends of Joan's and Janetta Parladé's.

George Psychoundakis (1920–2006), Cretan resistance fighter, shepherd and author. PLF translated his war memoir into English and then helped to arrange its publication with John Murray under the title *The Cretan Runner* (1955). Later he translated the *Iliad* and the *Odyssey* into the Cretan dialect.

Peter Courtney Quennell (1905–93), writer and man of letters, knighted in 1993. He was editor of the *Cornhill Magazine*, and co-editor of *History Today*.

Joan Rayner, later Joan Leigh Fermor (1912–2003), née Eyres Monsell, photographer and muse, the second of three daughters of Bolton Meredith Eyres Monsell, MP, who became Conservative chief whip and then First Lord of the Admiralty, and was ennobled in 1935 as 1st Viscount Monsell. In 1939 she married the journalist and typographer John Rayner, but the marriage did not succeed, and they were living apart by the time she met PLF in Cairo towards the end of the war. She and Paddy formed a lifelong partnership, despite his affairs with other women. She was devoted to her brother Graham, who succeeded his father as 2nd Viscount on his father's death in 1969. Joan's mother, Caroline Eyres, had inherited Dumbleton Hall in Worcestershire, a mid-Victorian pile, said to have been considered as a refuge for the House of Lords during the war. This was sold after her death, and thereafter Joan and Graham shared the Mill House on the Dumbleton estate.

George Humphrey Wolferstan ('Dadie') Rylands (1902–99), literary scholar and influential theatre director. Elected Fellow of King's College, Cambridge, in 1927, he lived there for the rest of his life. Virginia Woolf, for whom he worked at the Hogarth Press, outlined some of his qualities in her diary: 'His silver grey suits, pink shirts, with his powdered pink and white face, his nerves, his manners, his love of praise.'

Edward ('Eddy') Sackville-West (1901–65), 5th Baron Sackville, novelist and music critic. He converted to Roman Catholicism in 1949.

Georgios Seferiades ('George Seferis') (1900–71), poet, career diplomat, and a major figure in Greek letters, awarded the Nobel Prize for Literature in 1963. His close relations with PLF were strained by the tensions over Cyprus in the 1950s. Seferis served as Ambassador to the United Kingdom from 1957 to 1962. He took a stand against the dictatorship of 'the Colonels' who took power in 1967, and by the time of his death he had become a popular hero in Greece for his resistance to the regime.

Philip Owen Arnould Sherrard (1922–95), author, translator, poet and philosopher, whose work includes important translations of modern Greek poets, and books on modern Greek literature and culture. He lived on the island of Euboea, near Sir Aymer Maxwell.

Sir Sacheverell ('Sachie') Reresby Sitwell, 6th Baronet (1897–1988), art critic and writer on architecture, one of the famous three Sitwell siblings. In 1925 he married Georgia Doble (d. 1980). PLF was taken up by them in the late 1930s. They lived at Weston Hall, a Jacobean house in Northamptonshire.

Amy, Lady Smart, painter, Lebanese wife of Sir Walter Smart. PLF had come to know them both in Cairo during the war. In the 1950s PLF was often a guest at Gadencourt, their house in Normandy.

Walter Smart ('Smartie') (1883–1962), diplomat, knighted in 1942.

Freya Stark (1893–1993), explorer and travel writer, had met PLF in Egypt during the war. She was awarded a CBE in 1953 and made a dame in 1972.

Michael Stewart (1911–94), diplomat, British Ambassador to Greece 1967–71, knighted in 1966. He and his wife (Katharine) Damaris (b. 1923; née du Boulay) became close friends of the Leigh Fermors, as did their daughter Olivia. PLF's last years were eased considerably by Olivia, who shouldered all the administrative tasks in Paddy's life that had been done by Joan in her lifetime.

Philip Toynbee (1916–81), writer and journalist, son of the historian Arnold Toynbee, an old friend of PLF's and an exuberant drinker.

Iris Tree (1897–1968), poet, actress and muse, daughter of actor-manager Sir Herbert Beerbohm Tree. As a young woman she had been sought-after as an artists' model, being painted by Augustus John, Duncan Grant, Vanessa Bell and Roger Fry; sculpted by Jacob Epstein; and photographed by Man Ray. She was first married to the New York artist Curtis Moffat; their son Ivan, a successful screenwriter, was also a friend of PLF's. Her second marriage was to the actor and ex-officer of the Austrian cavalry, Count Friedrich von Lebedur-Wicheln. After their divorce they both appeared in the 1956 film, *Moby Dick*. She also appeared in a cameo in Federico Fellini's *La Dolce Vita*.

Guillaume Villeneuve (b. 1960), French translator, whose work includes translations of *A Time of Gifts*, *Between the Woods and the Water* and *The Broken Road*, under the collective title *Dans la Nuit et le Vent*, as well as of *A Time to Keep Silence* and *Abducting a General*. His translations include works by several of PLF's friends, including James Lees-Milne, Steven Runciman and Osbert Lancaster.

Barbara Warner (1911–89), née Hutchinson, had been married to Victor Rothschild, 3rd Baron Rothschild, and Rex Warner before marrying Niko Ghika in 1961.

Rex Warner (1905–86), classicist, writer, poet and translator. As director of the British Institute in Athens, Warner had been PLF's boss for a brief period after the war.

Janetta Woolley see **Janetta Parladé**

Pamela Wyndham-Quin, later Egremont (1925–2013), society beauty, wife of John Wyndham, 1st Baron Egremont (1920–72), and a long-standing friend of PLF's.

Acknowledgements

I wish to thank Paddy's literary executors – Artemis Cooper, Olivia Stewart and Colin Thubron – for their continued faith in me as editor of Paddy's letters. Each of them has helped me in various ways. I am especially grateful to Artemis Cooper for her assistance throughout.

I am grateful to Artemis too for reading the text of this book and providing me with her comments and corrections – as did her father, John Julius Norwich, who died as this book was going to press. Several other readers performed this invaluable service for me: Penelope Dening; Sir Michael Llewellyn-Smith, former British Ambassador to Greece 1996–9, and Visiting Professor to the Centre for Hellenic Studies, King's College London; Charlotte Mosley, editor of *In Tearing Haste*, Paddy's correspondence with the Duchess of Devonshire, and *Love from Nancy: The Letters of Nancy Mitford*; and Henry Woudhysen, Rector of Lincoln College, Oxford. Each of these readers has helped to make the book better than it would have been otherwise. I must state, however, that any remaining mistakes are my sole responsibility.

In compiling a volume of this kind an editor incurs many debts. My hunt for Paddy's letters has ranged across two continents, and taken me to locations I should otherwise never have seen – a castle perched on a cliff in Umbria, an apartment overlooking the Tiber in Rome, a romantic Wiltshire garden, the terrace of one of England's grandest houses; and many other interesting locations. I remember in particular a day in a Budapest flat with the late Rudi Fischer and his wife Dagmar, who fortified me throughout with strudel and Transylvanian schnapps (*tuica*). I also recall lunch at a taverna in Athens where the two of us consumed three carafes of retsina. I am grateful to all those who made me welcome, listed below. I am especially grateful to Myrto Kaouki and Irini Geroulanou of the Benaki Library for allowing me to stay at Paddy's house at Kardamyli, and to Elpida Belloyannis for making my stay so comfortable.

I want to thank the following individuals for supplying me with letters, helping me to find them or commenting on them: Brigid Allen, Alan Bennett, William Blacker, Hugh and Gabriella Bullock, Matthew and Cressida Connolly, Kevin Crossley-Holland, Max Egremont, the late Rudi Fischer, Milton Gendel, Henry Hardy, Denise Harvey, Philippa Jellicoe, the late Jeremy Lewis, Imogen and Rupert Lycett Green, David Mason, Alan Ogden, Janetta Parladé, Dan Popescu, Patrick Reade, Ann Shukman, Elisabeth Sifton, Matthew Spender and Guillaume Villeneuve.

I also wish to thank Charlotte Mosley again, and John Murray publishers, for permission to include two letters to Debo Devonshire from *In Tearing Haste: Letters between Deborah Devonshire and Patrick Leigh Fermor*; Mark Amory, for permission to quote from his edition of *The Letters of Ann Fleming*; and Anna Lontou, stepdaughter of George Seferis, and Fotios Ar. Dimitrakopoulos and Vasiliki D. Lambropoulou, editors of a volume of correspondence between Paddy, Joan and Nico Ghika published in 2007 by the Cyprus Research Centre, for permission to publish a letter from that volume.

I am grateful to the staff of the National Library of Scotland, where Paddy's archive is kept, and Helen Symington in particular; also Kirsty McHugh, the recently appointed curator of the John Murray archive, and her predecessor, David McClay. I also want to acknowledge the help of the following archivists and archives for supplying me with copies of Paddy's letters and giving me permission to publish them: Heather Dean, John Frederick and the Special Collections and University Archives of the McPherson Library of the University of Victoria, for access to the papers of John Betjeman;

Melissa Kunz of the Department of the Special Collections and University Archives, McFarlin Library, the University of Tulsa, for permission to publish a letter to Cyril Connolly; Wes Davis for alerting me to the existence of Paddy's letter to Annette Crean and the Imperial War Museum for permission to publish it; Hannah Weinberg of the Schlesinger Library, Harvard, for access to the papers of Elizabeth David; Jenny Watts of the Norfolk Record Office, for access to the papers of Wilhelmine ('Billa') Harrod; Dr Natalia Vogelkoff-Brogan and Dr Eleftheria Daleziou of the American School of Classical Studies at Athens, for access to the papers of Richard Hubbard Howland; Gayle Richardson of the Huntington Library in California for access to the Patrick Kinross papers; Catherine Taylor of the Waddesdon Archive, for access to the papers of Candida Lycett Green; Helen Marchant, James Towe and the Mitford Archive at Chatsworth for access to the papers of the late Dowager Duchess of Devonshire, and her sister Nancy Mitford; Peter Henderson, archivist of the King's School, Canterbury, for access to letters in the school archives; Peter Monteith and the Provost and Fellows of King's College, Cambridge, for access to the papers of 'Dadie' Rylands; Nicola O'Toole and Oliver House of the Bodleian Libraries, University of Oxford, for access to the papers of Stephen Spender and (Charles) Bruce Chatwin; and Elizabeth L. Garver of the Harry Ransom Center, the University of Texas at Austin, for access to the papers of Freya Stark.

I should like to extend particular thanks to Ioanna Moraiti of the Benaki Museum in Athens for help with the photographs.

I want to extend renewed thanks to John and Virginia Murray for their hospitality at the John Murray building in Albemarle Street during the days when I was there. It seemed appropriate to be reading Paddy's letters to John's father in the very room where Paddy himself had often laboured on his own manuscripts. If I needed inspiration, his portrait by Derek Hill hung on the stairs outside.

Once again I am indebted to Peter Mackridge, Emeritus Professor of Modern Greek at Oxford, who translated all Paddy's Greek and provided me with transcriptions.

I also want to thank Ceri Evans for her stalwart help with the transcription. Much of what she typed might as well have been written in Romanian in that it was so far from her own experience, but she did an excellent job all the same.

I should like to thank my editor, Michael Fishwick, for his faith in the book, and for his skilled editorial guidance; my copy-editor, Kate Johnson, for protecting me from several blunders; Sarah Ruddick of Bloomsbury, for her professionalism in seeing the book from typescript to print; and Douglas Matthews, for compiling the index. I also wish to thank my agent, Andrew Wylie, and Tracy Bohan of the Wylie Agency, for their steadfast support.

Illustration Credits

Index

NOTES: Page numbers in **bold** indicate the first page of a letter to a correspondent. Titles and rank are generally the highest mentioned in the letters and notes. Patrick Leigh Fermor's works appear directly under title; works by others under author's name.

Acheson, Dean 158
Achillopoulos, Costa 109, 222–3
Acton, Sir Harold **271**, 14, 116, 280;
    Nancy Mitford: A Memoir 271
Adrianople 348nn1–2
Agioi Theodori (village) 177
Ainsworth, William Harrison 87
Albin Michel (French publisher) 93–4,
    110
Alcover, Paul Zanesco 20
Aldwick, near Bognor Regis 84
Alevizakis, George and Alevizos 336
Alevizakis, Father John 336
Alexander, Field Marshal Harold, 1st
    Earl 62
Alexander I, King of Yugoslavia 384
Alington, Napier Sturt, 3rd Baron 283
Amat y Torres, Francisco de ('Paco')
    362–3
Amiot-Dumont (French publisher) 94
Amis, Antonia 378
Amis, Kingsley 307n4

Amory, Mark: *Lord Berners: The Last
    Eccentric* 394
Angelou, Maya 341n4
Annan, Noel, Baron 402
Anne, Princess 264
Annesley, Mrs (of Annes Grove, Cork)
    279
Anson, Lady Clodagh 278
Anstruther, Sir Ralph (Hugo) 205–7,
    210, 215
Antrim, Randal McDonnell, 8th Earl
    of 63
Apocalypse Now (film) 319
Arcos, Duquesa de 283
Ariadne (mythical figure) 30
Arnold, Matthew: 'The Scholar Gipsy'
    80
Arundel, Thomas 317
Ascham, Roger 59
Ashley-Cooper, Lady Lettice Mildred
    107
Ashton, Frederick 64, 87, 110

Aslan, Grégoire 138
Aspioto, Marie 296, 398
Asquith, Raymond 13
Astor, Judy 289n1
Astor, Michael 189, 217, 294, 301
Astor, Polly 289
Athens: PLF works for British Council in 5; Nancy Mitford disparages 108n1; Joan buys house in 153n1
Auden, Wystan Hugh 104, 315–16, 332
Austen, Jane: *Sense and Sensibility* 387
Avanzo, Renzo 143
Avila da Silva, Reinaldo 397n5
Ayer, A.J. ('Freddie') 101, 171n1

Bagherzade, Iradj 396
Bailey, John and Irene 416
Baillie, Lady Maud 164
Bainbridge, Peggy 50
Bairnsfather, Bruce 107
Baldwin I, Count of Flanders 348
Baldwin, Ken 206n1
Bali 233
Baltazzi, Nicky 49
Balthus (Balthasar Klossowski de Rola) 116, 157, 159–60, 244–5
Balthus, Setsuko (*née* Ideta) 244
Barber, Eric Arthur 68n1
Barcelona 236, 320
Bardrochat House, Galloway 290, 292
Baring, Mona Montgomerie 222
Bath 188
Bath, Henry Thynne, Marquess of 62, 151, 169, 188
Bath, Virginia, Marchioness of 151, 169, 188
Baudelaire, Charles: 'L'Albatross' (poem): parodied 307
Beckford, William 98
Beerbohm, Max 357
Beevor, Antony 402
Beistegui, Don Carlos de 81

Békássy, Eva 331
Békássy, Ferenc 323
Bell, Gertrude 97
Bell, Quentin 322n1, 323
Belloc Lowndes, Maria 49
Belloyannis, Elpida 406, 416
Bendern, Patricia de (*née* Lady Patricia Douglas) 42
Bennett, Alan and Jonathan Miller **170**
Berenson, Mary (*née* Smith) 338–9
Berkeley, Freda 375
Berkeley, Lennox 264
Berlin 386
Berlin, Sir Isaiah 340, 414
Bernard (unidentified) 35–6
Berners, Gerald Tyrwhitt-Wilson, 14th Baron 107n6
Bernier, Georges 116
Betjeman, Sir John **307**; at Easton Court, Chagford 10, 129; invites PLF for weekend 33; PLF parodies 94; portrait sculpture by Angela Conner 265; Alan Pryce-Jones quotes 360; on reviews 361; memorial unveiled at Westminster Abbey 388; visits PLF's school 389
Betjeman, Penelope, Lady 33, 396
Between the Woods and the Water (PLF): on PLF's walk across Europe 4; copy sent to Rudi Fischer 346; title 351; published 357, 358; reception 360–1; US publication 364; French translation 379, 381, 383
Bibesco, Priscilla Helen Alexandra 66
Birch, Lyndall (*later* Passerini-Hopkinson) **142**, **150**, **406**; PLF's relations with 142, 156; PLF dedicates 'Two Marble Feet' poem to 152n1
Birr Castle, Ireland 82
Bishop, Adrian 412
Blacker, Major Stewart 419n4

Blacker, William **419**; *Along the Enchanted Way* 421

Blackwood, Lady Caroline 327

Bloomfield, Paul: *Uncommon People* 119

Bloomsbury Group 322

Bogarde, Dirk 11, 124, 126

Bognor Regis, Sussex 84

Bogomilism 311

Boigne, Adèle d'Osmond, Comtesse de 273

Boldini, Giovanni 223

Bologna 158

Bolton Abbey, north Yorkshire 294

Borghese, Prince 'Tinty' 142

Boulanger, Jane 92

Boustead, Colonel Sir Hugh 291–2

Boutos (PLF's neighbour) 323

Boutros-Ghali, Geoffrey 390

Bowen, Elizabeth 278

Bowra, Maurice: scurrilous poems 12, 409, 412–13; PLF meets in Palombara 73; PLF anagramises name 89; visits PLF in Greece 93, 107; and death of Richard Dawkins 105; visits Gadencourt 120; and PLF's book on Greece 190; death 257; Mitchell's biography of 412; PLF's anecdotes on 413–14

Bradley, Mrs (agent) 110

Bragg, Melvyn 368

Branch, Bridget ('Biddy') **19, 24**

Branch, Guy Rawstron 4, 412, 414

Branch, Lady Prudence (*née* Pelham) 21, 24, 281, 412

Brenan, Gerald 254, 283, 288

British Acropolis Appeal Committee 324n3

British Council 5, 28

Broglie, Marie de 242

Broken Road, The (PLF; third volume of trilogy; posthumous) 4, 375, 378, 381–2, 384n2, 395, 397, 408, 411, 423

Brooke, Rupert 322n1

Brooks-Richards, Sir Francis and Hazel, Lady 296

Browning, Robert 105

Bruce, Bernard 98

Bruce, Robert VIII 343

Bryant, Arthur: *The Age of Elegance* 149

Budapest 198

Buffet, Bernard 33n4

Byblos 98

Byron, George Gordon 6th Baron 12, 270, 367

Cadiz 52

Caetani, Cora 110

Callimachi, Anne-Marie 21

Cameron, James 80n1

Cameron, Roderick ('Rory') 113

Cameroon (French Equatorial Africa) 135–9

Campbell, Lady Mary Sybil (*née* St Clair Erskine) 44

Campbell, Robin Francis 44, 283

Campiña, Enrique Granados 301n4

Cantacuzène, Princess Balasha (Marie-Blanche) **200, 238, 263, 270, 280, 294**; persecuted and isolated in communist Romania 8, 34, 198–9; PLF's love affair with 8, 19, 34, 222, 417; PLF first meets 19; sends love to Biddy Branch 25; PLF revisits (1965) 108–9, 196, 204; death 300, 365; family background 365; returns PLF's old diary 366

Cantacuzène, Hélène ('Pomme') 21, 25, 196, 201, 204, 222, 300, 365

Cantacuzène, Mihai 366

Cantacuzène, Serge 366

Cantimir, Dmitri 204

Capri 151

Carr, Raymond 327

Carrington, Dora 254

Carritt, Dr Christian 416–18
Castiglione, Baldassare, Count 322
Castle of the Immortals, The (film) 255
Catargi, Ina ('Ins'; *née* Donici) 20, 25,
    201, 222–3, 242, 365
Catargi, Michel 223, 365
Catroux, General Georges and
    Marguerite 113
Cavafy, C.P. 175; 'The Canon' (poem)
    139
Cavendish, Lady Elizabeth ('Feeble')
    307
Cavendish, Peregrine ('Stoker'),
    Marquess of Hartington (*later* 12th
    Duke of Devonshire) 189, 199
Cavendish-Bentinck, Clothilde Bruce
    (*née* Quigley) 363
Ceausescu, Nicolae 365, 372
Celebi, Kadi 249
Chagford *see* Easton Court
Chancellor, John 338
Channon, Sir Henry ('Chips') 125
Chantilly 111–13, 117
Chaplin, Charlie 377
Charles, Prince of Wales 401, 408
Charles VI, King of France 154n3
Charteris, Martin 327
Chatsworth House, Derbyshire
    ('Dingley Dell') 263, 265, 389, 401,
    408
Chatwin, Bruce 308, 351; death 373; *In
    Patagonia* 308
Chatwin, Elizabeth 373, 382
Chaudhuri, Nirad C. 234
Cheshire, David 368
Chester Row, Pimlico: Joan buys
    house in 162
Chitto, Pierino 60–1
Cholmondeley, Lady Caroline 293
Chrissoveloni, Nicky 20, 155
Churchill, Pamela (*later* Harriman)
    114–15

Cicogna, Countess Anna-Maria 301
Clifford, Dr 299
Cobb, Carolyn Postlethwaite 131–2
Cockburn, Claud 114
Cocullo, Abruzzi, Italy 76
Colefax, Sibyl 322
Coleman, Henry 418
Colonna family 245
Conner, Angela 265
Connolly, Cressida 421
Connolly, Cyril ('the Humanist' or
    'the H') 40; infatuation with Joan
    32–3, 40; and PLF's contribution
    to *Horizon* 43; visits PLF in Greece
    93, 246–7; wife's infidelity 107; in
    Tangiers 114; PLF meets in London
    188; declines to write book on
    Greece 190; illness and death 279;
    Jeremy Lewis's biography of 421; *The
    Unquiet Grave* 299n4
Connolly, Deirdre *see* Levi, Deirdre
Cook, Peter 170
Cooper, Artemis 402; as PLF's
    biographer 12, 402; at Bognor
    as child 85; takes dictation from
    PLF 421; *Patrick Leigh Fermor: An
    Adventure* 30
Cooper, Lady Diana 57, 61, 65, 69,
    74, 81, 84, 94, 120, 133, 226, 229,
    258, 259, 261, 304, 333; PLF's
    correspondence with 1, 3, 9, 13;
    PLF stays at Bognor home 7, 84;
    PLF meets 57; PLF loses letters of
    condolence on death of husband
    88n; in Chantilly 111–12, 276; at
    Paris ball 114, 116–17; depression
    150; moves from Chantilly 157, 161;
    burgled 216; takes half of Fieldings'
    house 224; performs in *The Miracle*
    231n2; and PLF's dog Troilus 251;
    home in London 264; PLF visits in
    London 299; disparages Bloomsbury

321–2; falls and breaks ribs 333; takes PLF to I Tatti 340; *The Rainbow Comes and Goes* 134n2

Cooper, Douglas 225

Cooper, Duff *see* Norwich, 1st Viscount

Corberó, Xavier 235n2

Corfu 326, 331, 397

Cornhill (magazine) 54, 93–4

Craxton, John: writes obituary of Joan 28; travels with PLF 63, 207; in Crete 185; on Kardamyli house 234; designs for PLF's books 301, 396; friendship with Niko Ghika 373, 377; pet cat named for 384

Crean, Annette **26**

Cretan Association of New York 335–6

Crete: PLF's wartime activities in 5, 26; Joan visits 185; PLF visits with Xan Fielding 295; PLF visits with Joan 333

Crossley-Holland, Kevin **352**

Crowley, Aleister: and 'Thelema' 318n3

Cruddas, Hugh 394

Csernovits, Xenia 347n1, 362

Culme-Seymour, Captain George 281

Curtis, Dunstan and 'Tony' 185

Curwen, Eldred 50–1

Cutting, Heyward **369**, 5

Cyprus 96, 109, 113, 296n2

Daintrey, Adrian 264

Dakin, Douglas (ed.): *British and American Philhellenes during the Greek War of Independence* 119

Danquah, Paul 197

Dashing for the Post (PLF's published letters vol.1) 2–3

Dath, Marc 423

David, Elizabeth **376**, 188n1

Davis, Bill and Anne 50–1

Dawkins, Richard MacGillivray 67, 105

Delfino, Marina ('Mimosa') Parodi 151

Dennis, Nigel: *Cards of Identity* 101, 103

Devonshire, Andrew Cavendish, 11th Duke of: marriage to Debo 121; at Lismore Castle 164, 277; as government minister 189; at Chatsworth 263, 389; sculpted by Angela Conner 265; recovers from drink problem after infatuation with Janetta Parladé 266; suggests title for PLF book 362

Devonshire, Deborah, Duchess of ('Debo') **121, 147, 415, 417**; PLF's correspondence published 1, 3, 415; PLF writes to by hand 14; friendship and correspondence with PLF 121, 151; and PLF's stay at Lazio 142; at Lismore Castle 164–5, 189, 277; at Chatsworth 265, 389; and Andrew's drinking 266; and sister Nancy 277; at Ann Fleming's funeral 327; at Rothschild's Corfu house 397; *Home to Roost* 419

Dirk Hatterick (boat) 250

Djem (Cem), Ottoman Sultan 204

Doctorow, E.L. 337

Dominic of Sora, St 75

Donici, Constantine 20, 23, 25, 196, 201–2, 365

Douglas, Lord James 345

Douglas-Home, Jessica 365

Doundoulakis, George 336

Dropmore Press 53–4

Du Cane, Peter 79

Dulwich Picture Gallery 387

Dunn, Ann 42

Durrell, Lawrence 209, 224

Durrell, Margaret 224

Easton Court Hotel, Chagford, Devon 10, 129–30

Eaton, Peter 323

Eden, Sir Anthony 11, 19, 69, 96n2

Eden, Clarissa, Lady (*née* Spencer-
Churchill) 69–70

Edwardes, Miss (of Tivoli) 69, 71–2

Edwards, David 79n3

Egerton, Thomas 151

Egremont, John Edward Reginald
Wyndham, 1st Baron 271

Egremont, Pamela, Lady **289**, 270,
292–3

Eliot, Valerie 307

Elizabeth II, Queen: coronation (1953)
74, 79

Elizabeth the Queen Mother 87

Encounter (magazine) 101

Erlanger, Baroness Catherine d' 370

Eros II (yacht) 95, 101

Escobar, Luis (Luis Escobar
Kirkpatrick, 7th Marqués de las
Marismas del Guadalquavir) 284

Esztergom 316

Euston, Hugh Denis Charles FitzRoy,
Earl and Fortune, Countess of (*née*
Smith) 66

Fairweather, Eileen 353

Faithfull, Major Theodore
(headmaster) 353

Fargue, Léon 241

Faure, Hubert 157

Fedden, Robin 49, 128, 185, 188, 256n1,
302, 304

Fellows, Sir Charles 247

Fenton, Vanessa (PLF's sister) 263

Fermor, (Muriel) Aileen (*née* Ambler;
PLF's mother): in Brighton 263

Fermor, Joan Leigh (*earlier* Rayner)
**28, 32, 41, 43, 49, 72, 109, 123,
135, 138, 174, 176, 180, 181,
185, 205, 221**; PLF's relations
and correspondence with 7; at

Kardamyli 10; PLF meets 28;
Connolly attracted to 32, 40; PLF's
jealousy of other admirers 32; travels
to Rome with Hamish St Clair-
Erskine 40–1; travels in Greece with
PLF 54; stays at Gadencourt with
PLF 56; complimented by stranger
in Paris 61; on conflict over Cyprus
109; at Passerano with PLF 149;
inheritance from mother 176; in
Crete 185, 333; in Singapore 229;
in Athens 237; flu 239, 241–2; stays
with brother in Gloucestershire 264,
294; writes to Balasha 280–1; meets
PLF in India 306; pet cats 384;
operation for slipped retina 400;
death 406–7; Bowra's admiration
for 409

Fermor, Sir Patrick Leigh
('Paddy'): letter-writing 1–2,
14–15; fall in old age 4, 422; throat
cancer and death 4, 425; walk to
Constantinople 4; translating 5;
war service 5; works for British
Council in Athens 5, 28; settles in
Kardamyli 7, 10, 176; romances and
affairs 8–9; horseriding and hunting
10, 22–3, 130, 132, 174, 287; interest
in aristocracy 11; manner 11–12; as
subject of poems by Maurice Bowra
12, 409, 413; swims Hellespont 12;
memorises and quotes poetry 13–14;
daily routine in Greece 14; hand-
writes letters 14; wins Heinemann
prize 54; writes on snake-catchers
in Abruzzi 76–7; provokes brawl
at Kildare Hunt 82–3; slowness in
completing book 102–3; attends
Paris ball 114–17; at filming of *Ill
Met by Moonlight* 123–5; catastrophic
visit to Somerset Maugham's villa
126–9, 415; financial concerns

131–2, 144–5, 154; writes script for film *The Roots of Heaven* 135; hospitalised from riding accident and haemorrhoids 141; affair with Lyndall Birch 142; acquires marble objects found in Italy 145–6; affair with Ricki Huston 156; depressions 174–5; travels in East 229–33; acquires dog from Maxwell 250–1; keeps turkeys 261–2; portrait sculpture by Angela Conner 265; considers publishing European walk book as two volumes 267–9; treated for cancer of the tongue 270, 294, 400; visits Crete with Xan Fielding 295; walking in Himalayas 302–4; car blown up by Cretan communists 313; on etymology of surname 315; Guards training 330; translates von Strachwitz's 'Das Herz von Douglas' 343–4; TV documentary on (*South Bank Show*) 367–8; and writing of third voume of trilogy (*The Broken Road*) 375, 378, 381–2, 384, 395, 397, 408, 411, 423; eightieth birthday 386; gives address at Westminster Abbey memorial for John Betjeman 388; contributes to 80th birthday album for Sophie Moss 389–90; donates papers to Murray archives 396n5; contributes to Folio Society edition of *Ill Met by Moonlight* 404; knighthood 408; suffers tunnel vision 417, 419, 421

Festugière, André-Jean: *Personal Religion Among the Greeks* 119

Feversham, Charles William Slingsby ('Sim') Duncombe, 3rd Earl of 99

Fielding, Agnes ('Magouche'; *earlier* Phillips): on PLF's Englishness 11; in Portugal 187–8, 374; PLF meets in London 188, 388; in Morocco 189; Xan leaves Daphne for 283, 287; in Athens 294; calls on PLF 298–9, 310; introduces Bruce Chatwin to PLF 308; Lev Lerman admires 338; PLF meets in Salonica 347; in Frankfurt 354; spends Christmas with PLF 368; travels to Santiago with PLF 374; apartment in Paris 376; and Xan's illness 378; visits PLF in Kardamyli 382; takes Xan's ashes to Crete for burial 385; visits Dulwich Picture Gallery with PLF 387; praises Milton Gendel's book of photographs 411

Fielding, Daphne (*earlier* Marchioness of Bath) 62, 123–4, 223–4, 257, 287

Fielding, Xan (Alexander) **298, 335**; friendship with PLF 12; PLF subscribes to *Horizon* for 40; affair with Daphne Bath 62; and filming of *Ill Met by Moonlight* 123; and PLF's script for film of *The Roots of Heaven* 135; cooking 207; PLF stays with in Uzès 223–4; birth 224; troubled by brother-in-law's machinations 224, 229; in Kardamyli 257, 382; on Debo Devonshire's secret reading 277; stays at Parladés 283; breaks with Daphne and marries Magouche 287; in Greece 294; visits Crete with PLF 295; in Italy with PLF 297; Christmas on Corfu with PLF 310; in Salonica 347; PF meets in Frankfurt 354; in wartime Crete 368, 385; cancer 378; ashes buried in Crete 385; *Aeolus Displayed: A Book of the Winds* 337; *The Money Spinner: Monte Carlo and Its Fabled Casino* 298

Fischer, Dagmar (*née* von Melchner) **405**

Fischer, Rudolph (Rudi) **311, 315, 328, 346, 360, 400**, 189n1

Fisher, Thomas Hart and Ruth (*née* Page) 64n3
Fitzgerald, Robert 378
Fitzherbert, Margaret (Meg) 338
Flecker, James Elroy 97
Fleming, Ann (*née* Charteris; *later* Rothermere) **126**, **129**, **197**; PLF's friendship with 9, 63, 150; PLF meets in Tivoli 69–70; at Paris ball 112, 114, 116–17; at Villa Mauresque 127; proposed for Turkey trip 206; moves out of London to Wiltshire 260; PLF stays with in London 264; PLF stays with in Wiltshire 270; death from cancer 327, 332
Fleming, Ian 53
Flynn, Errol 11, 138
Folio Society 404
Fonteyn, Margot 64, 87
Foot, M.R.D. 404n3
Forbes, Alastair 113–14, 150
Fraenkel, Eduard: *Horace* 387
Fragonard, Jean-Honoré: painting 240n2
Francesca (unidentified) 34–5
Franchetti, Baron Giorgio 143
Franco, General Francisco 52n1
Frederick Barbarossa, Holy Roman Emperor 348
Frederick II (the Great), King of Prussia 243
French Equatorial Africa *see* Cameroon 135
Frere, Alexander Stewart 127
Freud, Lucian 327n3
Frisch, Max: *The Fireraisers* (*Biedermann und die Brandstifter*) 217n1

Gadencourt, Normandy 55–6, 60, 63, 109, 120
Gage, Henry Rainald Gage, 6th Viscount 112–13

Gage, Nicolas: *Eleni* 338
Gál, István 318
Garbo, Greta 242n2
Gargoyle Club, London 44, 340
Garnett, David ('Bunny') 288
Gary, Romain: *Les Racines du Ciel* (*The Roots of Heaven*) 135
Gathorne-Hardy, Edward: friendship with PLF 90, 94, 98, 100, 238, 253, 255, 274, 296; death 307
Gaudí, Antoni 346
Gaulle, Charles de 154n2
Gendel, Judith Venetia (*earlier* Montagu) **130**, 112, 114–15, 142, 157, 160, 163, 337n4
Gendel, Milton **348**, **411**, 337, 348
Georgakis, Ioannis ('Yanni') 239–40
Ghika, Barbara (*earlier* Warner): PLF stays at Pembrokeshire cottage 7; returns to Charlotte Street 68; in Athens 296; PLF visits in Corfu 326
Ghika, Niko: PLF stays at Hydra mansion 7, 90–1; in Athens 237, 296; home in London 264; and Nancy Mitford 271–2; PLF proposes returning painted table to Athens house 324; PLF visits in Corfu 326; visits PLF in Kardamyli 372; ill health 377
Ghyka, Princess Eileen (*née* O'Connor) 95n1, 110–12
Ghyka, Ivan 20
Ghyka, Julie 319
Ghyka, Prince Matila: translates *Violins of Saint-Jacques* 92; and PLF's leaving Greece 95; PLF meets in Paris 110, 112; *Documentary Chronology of Romanian History* 323; *The World Mine Oyster* 95n1, 154, 372
Giacometti, Alberto 241

Gibbon, Edward: *Memoir of My Life* 380

Gibson-Watt, David and Diana (*née* Hambro) 207

Gide, André 413; *Les Caves du Vatican* 103n2, 297

Giles, Frank 115, 118

Giles, Lady Katherine ('Kitty') 115

Giray, Azamat 315

Glenville, Peter 117

Gloucester, Prince Henry, Duke of 422

Goetz, Walter 115

Gold Rush, The (film) 377

Goncharov, Ivan: *Oblomov* 38

Gordon, Eleo 396

Gordon, Jane Maxwell, Duchess of 293

Goring, Marius 124

Gourgaud du Taillis, Lucienne (*née* Haas) 35

Grande Trappe, La (monastery), Normandy 33, 38–9

Gréco, Juliette 11, 138–9

Greece: PLF's attachment to 12–13; politics in 13; PLF and Joan travel in 54; conflict with Britain over Cyprus 96n3, 101, 109

'Greek Archipelagoes' (PLF; poem) 39, 352

Greene, Graham 308

Greuze, Jean-Baptiste: painting 240n2

Grey, Lady Jane 59

Groddeck, Dr George 33

Grosskurth, Phyllis: *John Addington Symonds* 215

Grunne, Jean-Dominique de Hemricourt de 369n1

Guatemala 34

Guggenheim, Marguerite ('Peggy') 116

Guinness, Gloria (*née* Alatorre) 79

Guinness, Thomas Loel 78

Gunther, Jane 335–6

Guys, Constantin 223

Haldeman, Lady Myra Idinia (*née* Sackville; 'Dina') 281

Hambleden, William Herbert ('Harry') Smith, 4th Viscount and Maria Carmela, Viscountess 151

Harang, Jean-Baptiste 383n1

Hardy, Henry **409, 412**

Hare, Alan 340

Hare, Alan Victor 63, 176

Hare, Jill 176

Harper & Row (US publishers) 342

Harper, Allanah 222

Harrod, Sir Roy 407

Harrod, Wilhelmine, Lady ('Billa') **407**, 375

Harvey, Andrew 354n1

Hayward, John Davy **89**

Heber-Percy, Colin 399n1

Heber-Percy, Lady Emma Rose (*née* Jellicoe) 399n2

Heber-Percy, Robert Vernon ('The Mad Boy') 107n6, 355, 393n1, 394

Heinemann (publishing house) 154

Helen of Troy 325

Hepburn, Audrey 131

Herbert, Auberon Mark Yvo 86, 141

Herbert, Aubrey 338

Herbert, David 98

Hercolani, Princess Laudomia (*née* del Drogo; 'Domietta') 411

Herzog, Baron Mór Lipót 328

Hesketh-Prichard, Alfred ('Alfgar') Cecil 309

Hesketh-Prichard, Major Hesketh Vernon 309

Heywood Hill (London bookshop) 103

Hildyard, Myles 302

Hill, Derek 91n2

Himalayas: PLF accompanies Fedden to 302–5

Hinks, Roger 108, 203, 273–4

Hoare, Lucy, Lady (*née* Cavendish-
    Bentinck; 'Joan') 25n1
Hoare, Sir Reginald 25n1
Hockney, David 331
Hodja, Nasreddin 249
Hole in the Wall restaurant, Bath 188
Holiday (US magazine) 196, 203
Hopkirk, Peter: *The Great Game* 374
Hore-Ruthven, Beatrice Mary Leslie
    281
Horizon (magazine) 40, 43
Hornibrook, F. A.: *The Culture of the
    Abdomen* 226
Housman, A. E.: *A Shropshire Lad*
    357n1
Howard, Brian 280
Howard, Cécile (*née* Geoffroy-
    Dechaume) 31n
Howard, Edmund Bernard Carlo
    ('Mondi') 31
Howard of Penrith, Francis Philip
    Howard, 2nd Baron 31
Howard, Trevor 11, 138
Howland, Richard **55**, 86
Hubbard, Thomas Edward 19n1
Hudson, Cressida (*née* Connolly) 354
Hungary 197–8, 317–18, 328–31
Hunt, Leigh: 'Abou Ben Adhem'
    (poem) 396
Huston, Allegra 192, 193n1
Huston, Anjelica 157
Huston, Enrica ('Ricki') **156, 162, 163,
    165, 166, 168, 171, 173, 182, 192**;
    relations with PLF 8, 156; political
    indifference 13; rescues PLF from
    Kildare Hunt brawl 83n2; birth of
    daughter Allegra 192
Huston, John 8, 11, 135, 156
Huston, Walter ('Tony') 157
Huxley, Aldous 220
Huysmans, Joris-Karl 30
Hydra (island) 7, 90–1, 109, 331

Ignotus, Paul 332; *Hungary* 316
Ill Met by Moonlight (film) 11, 123–4, 132
'In honour of Mr John Betjeman'
    (PLF; parody) 94
In Tearing Haste (PLF–Debo
    Devonshire letters) 9, 415
Incisa, Monica 337
India 233–4, 303–6
Ionian Islands: earthquakes 341n2
Isabau of Bavaria, Queen of France
    154n, 370, 392
Ischia 150
Ismay, General Hastings Lionel
    ('Pug'), 1st Baron and Laura
    Kathleen, Lady 113

Jackson, Derek Ainslie 44, 163, 224
Jackson, Janetta *see* Parladé, Janetta
Jackson, Pamela (*née*
    Mitford; 'Woman') 277
Jebb, Sir Gladwyn and Cynthia, Lady
    113
Jellicoe, George, 2nd Earl **398**
Jellicoe, George, 2nd Earl and
    Philippa, Countess 225
Jerusalem 314
John XXIII, Pope 380
Johns, Miss (typist) 130
Jordan, Constance Anson 337

Kalamata 193
Kalianessi, Athina ('Nana') 269
Kallithounakis, Leftheri 373
Kardamyli: PLF purchases land and
    settles in 7, 10, 176, 181, 193, 195;
    construction of house 205–6, 208–
    15, 217, 234; rainstorms 238, 259–60,
    386–7; plantings 253–4
Károlyi de Nagykároly, Count Mihály
    317, 332
Károlyi, Countess Katinka (*née*
    Andrássy; Catherine) 332

Kathimerini (Greek newspaper) 103
Kathmandu 231–2
Katsimbalis, George ('The Walrus'): friendship with PLF 12; and Papadopolos 104; in Athens 237, 296; writes on Seferis's mortal illness 257; PLF enquires about Byron's Cephalonian letters 270
Keay, John 303
Kee, Cynthia 189
Kee, Robert 82n4, 83, 189
Keen, Mary 397
Kell, Henri 116
Kelly, Ambrose of Gallagh and Tycooly 363
Kent, Prince Edward, Duke of 87
Kent, Princess Marina, Duchess of 86
Keyes, Geoffrey, VC 283
Keykúbad, Alaédin, Seljuk sultan 249
Kildare Hunt, Ireland 82
King's School, Canterbury 79–80, 389
Kinross, Patrick Balfour, 3rd Baron **216**; stays at Easton Court, Chagford 10, 129; visits PLF in Greece 93, 100, 107; PLF and Joan stay with in London 216, 237, 262–3; holds friends' possessions in London house 259; loses weight 299
Kipling, Rudyard: *Kim* 306n1; 'The Tree of Justice' (story) 349
Klinkenborg, Verlyn 364
Klobusiçky, Elemér von 358, 362, 401
Knollys, Eardley 187n1
Kornaros, Vikentios: *Erotokritos* 311
Kosztka, Tivadar Csontváry 328
Kreipe, General Heinrich 5, 26, 123, 126, 137, 208, 367–8
Kun, Béla 317

Ladas, Alexis 378
Lahore 306
Lambaréné, Gabon 80n1

Lambert, Isobel 59
Lambert, J.W. 72
Lambton, Belinda ('Bindy'), Lady (*née* Blew-Jones) 114–15
Lancaster, Osbert 99
Landor, Walter Savage: *Imaginary Conversations* 392
Lane Fox, Louisa 261n1
Lane Fox, Martha, Baroness 261n1
Lang, Andrew: *The Olive Fairy Book* 188
Langford, Sam 280
Lansberg, Bertie 370–1
Laracy, Darina 244n1
Larbaud, Valery 140
La Rochefoucauld, François de 33
Laver, James (ed.): *Memorable Balls* 81
Lawrence, T. E. ('Lawrence of Arabia') 314
Lawson, J. C.: *Modern Greek Folklore and Ancient Greek Religion* 119
Laycock, Robin 283
Le Bris, Michel 381
Le Corbusier (Charles-Édouard Jeanneret) 106, 272
Ledebur, Friedrich von 140
Lederman, Dr 299
Lees-Milne, Alvilde 187, 355
Lees-Milne, James 66, 187
Lehmann, John **39**
Lemar, Nellie 4, 422
Leopold I, Holy Roman Emperor 318
Lerman, Leo 338
Levi, Deirdre (*earlier* Connolly) 188, 246n1, 401
Levi, Peter **386**, 246, 401
Lewis, Jeremy **421**
Lisanevich, Boris 231–3
Lisbon 43
Lismore Castle, Ireland 161–5, 277–8
London Library 361
London Magazine 313

Long Crichel House, Dorset 187n1
Longford, Elizabeth: *The Years of the Sword* 242n1
Loti, Pierre 98
Lubbock, Lys 41
Lubbock, Percy: *Roman Pictures* 73
Lucas Phillips, Brigadier C.E. 419
Lucca 64
Lukas, Paul 138
Lutyens, Emily: *Candles in the Sun* 119
Lyall, Archie 76–7
Lycett Green, Candida (*née* Betjeman) **388, 393**
Lycett Green, Rupert 388, 393
Lygon, Lady Dorothy ('Coote') 100, 107, 120, 176, 355, 375

Macaulay, Rose 220; *They Went to Portugal* 45
McCarthy, Mary 332
McDonnell, Randal 72
McEwen, David Fraser 184
McEwen, Rory and Romana (*née* von Hofmannsthal) 293
McGrath, Charles 2
Mackay, Shena 356n2
Mackenzie, Hamish 102
Macmillan, Harold 11, 96, 100, 189n3, 265, 324–5
MacNeice, Louis 250, 301–2
Mafra, Francisco de Mello Breyner, 5th Count of 49
Magouche *see* Fielding, Agnes ('Magouche')
Malcolm, Noel: 'Living with Collaborators' (article) 365n1
Mandelson, Peter 11, 397
Mani (PLF) 6, 130, 132, 142, 267–9, 398
Marchant, Helen 418
Marie (servant) 117, 120
Marnham, Sir Ralph 141

Marques, Luiz and Susan (*née* Lowndes) 49n4
Marsas, Aleko 242
Martin, Alex 385
Mason, David **350**; 'Walking to Byzantium' 350n2, 351
Mason, Jonna 350
Massie, Allan 360n2
Massigli, Odette 63
Massourides, Tony 177, 181
Mathieson, Peggy 28
Maugham, W. Somerset ('Willie'): PLF's disastrous visit to 126–8, 415
Maxwell, Sir Aymer **250, 291, 323**, 205–6, 225, 250, 274–5, 279, 291, 323
Maxwell, Elsa 108
Melas, Nico 49
Melville, Herman 97
Meran, Hansi 359
Mersey, Katherine ('Kitty') Petty-Fitzmaurice, Viscountess 165, 277
Metcalfe, Lady Alexandra ('Baba') 99
Millard, Anne 44
Miller, Jonathan *see* Bennett, Alan and Jonathan Miller 819
Miller, Karl 293
Milward, Charles 309
'Mioritza' (Romanian folk-poem) 201
Mitchell, Julian 401
Mitchell, Leslie: *Maurice Bowra* 412n2
Mitelinen, Marthe 363
Mitford, Jessica *see* Treuhaft, Jessica
Mitford, Nancy (*sometime* Rodd) **106, 141**; visits PLF 100; PLF meets in Paris 110, 242–3; at Lismore Castle 164; death 271; PLF reminisces on for Harold Acton 271–9; 'The English Aristocracy' 107n4; *Love in a Cold Climate* 407; *The Pursuit of Love* 281; *Voltaire in Love* 273n2; 'Wicked Thoughts in Greece' 108n1

Moffat, Ivan 71, 77, 150

Moncreiffe, Sir Iain of that Ilk 312, 330

Monde, Le (French newspaper) 7

Monreith House, Galloway 291

Monsell, Graham Eyres, 2nd Viscount: visits PLF in Greece 25, 334; invites PLF to Mill House 188; illness 201; unable to accompany PLF to Turkey 205–6; home at Dumbleton Hall ('Tumbledown'), Gloucestershire 208, 264, 294, 487; in Singapore and India 229, 231, 233

Montagu of Beaulieu, Edward Douglas-Scott-Montagu 3rd Baron 87n4

Montagu, Judy *see* Gendel, Judith Venetia

Monte San Savino, Italy 175

Montgomery, Field Marshal Bernard Law, 1st Viscount 299n3

Montreux 70

Moore, Charles 401

Moore, Derry (Henry Herbert Ponsonby Moore; 12th Earl of Drogheda) 355

Moore, Doris Langley: *The Late Lord Byron* 166

Moore, Dudley 170

Moorehead, Alan 99, 102

Moorehead, Lucy 99

Morand, Hélène 155, 370

Morand, Paul: *Fancy Goods* 369, 371–2; *Isabeau de Bavière* 153–5, 370, 392; *Lettres du Voyageur* 370; *Open All Night* 369, 372

More O'Ferrall, Roderic 83, 166, 278

Morrell, Lady Ottoline 322

Morris, Jan 360–1

Mortimer, Raymond 187n1, 278, 280

Morwood, James 412

Mosley, Charlotte 3, 415, 417

Mosley, Sir Oswald 11

Moss, Gabriella 382, 389–90, 404

Moss, Isabella 382, 390, 404

Moss, Sophie **382, 389, 404**

Moss, W. Stanley ('Billy') 26, 124, 368; death 382; *Ill Met by Moonlight* 123, 404

Mourouzi, Alexander **34**, 8, 34, 365

Murphy, Dervla 313

Murray, Diana 384

Murray, John ('Jock') **53, 92, 130, 144, 153, 194, 217, 256, 267, 301, 302, 313, 375, 377, 381, 383**; and PLF's concern over writing 6; and PLF's stay in Passerano 9; and PLF's appeal for help to free Greek publisher 13; correspondence with PLF 14; PLF meets 53; publishes Freya Stark 91; PLF dines with in Greece 99; payments to PLF 131, 144, 153; and PLF's move to Ischia 150, 191; PLF urges to publish translation of Morand's *Isabeau de Bavière* 153, 370; proposes publishing PLF's European walk book in two volumes 267; badgers PLF 298; travels in India 314; PLF sends David Mason article to 351; in TV programme on PLF 368; supports PLF over final volume of trilogy 375; illness and death 383, 391

Murray, John VII (Jock's son) **202, 391, 395, 396**

Murray, Virginia 391, 393

Nerval, Gérard de 115

Nevile, Henry 25

New York 335–7

Newby, Eric: *A Short Walk in the Hindu Kush* 374

Niarchos, Stavros 101n2

Nicholson, Jenny (*née* Graves) 81–2

Nicholson-Price, Lynda 283

Nicolson, Harold 39
Niebuhr, Reinhold 337
Noailles, Vicomte Charles de 184, 221,
    244
Noailles, Marie-Laure de, Countess
    114–15, 161, 184n1
Noailles, Natalie de 244
Norton, Clifford and Noel Evelyn
    ('Peter') 91, 244
Norwich, Alfred Duff Cooper,
    1st Viscount: PLF stays with at
    Chantilly 57–8; viscountcy 62;
    illness 74; death 82n1; sends verse
    telegram to Xan and Daphne
    Fielding 258
Norwich, John Julius Cooper, 2nd
    Viscount: on PLF's letter writing 22;
    home in London 264; and verse on
    Philip Toynbee 341n3; and Rahere
    349–50; visits PLF in Kardamyli 356
Norwich, Mary ('Molly'), Viscountess
    (née Makins; then Philipps) 356
Nostell Priory, West Yorkshire 66

Obolensky, Prince (Sir) Dmitri 346–7,
    358
Ogilvie-Grant, Mark 176, 238, 271–2,
    275
Ogilvy, David 158n2
Olga, Princess of Yugoslavia (earlier of
    Greece) 87
Olivier, Brynhild 322n1
Olson, Stanley 320
'On the Quays of Kalamata' (PLF;
    poem) 193
'On Two Marble Feet and a Marble
    Tree Dug Up Last Autumn by a
    Ploughman in Latium' (PLF; poem)
    146, 152
Onassis, Aristotle 239–40
Onassis Foundation 239n1, 324
Onassis, Jacqueline (earlier Kennedy)
    11, 239–40

Oporto 44–5
Oranmore and Browne, Oonagh, Lady
    (née Guinness) 82n4
Origo, Antonio 175
Orr-Lewis, Sir Duncan (?or Douglas)
    50–1
Oxford Book of Travel Verse, The (ed.
    Crossley-Holland) 352
Oxley, David 124

Palewski, Colonel Gaston 110
Pani (Polish coachman) 22
Papadopolos, Kosta 103
'Paradox in the Himalayas' (PLF;
    article) 313n3
Paraskevas ('Junior' and 'Hero';
    Kardamyli workmen) 205, 211–13
Paris 7, 29, 39, 56, 94, 110–11, 114,
    161–2, 240–2, 376
Parker Bowles, Camilla 11, 401
Parladé, Jaime, Marques de Apezteguía
    235n1, 236–7, 266, 282–4, 286–7, 334
Parladé, Janetta (earlier Jackson) 234,
    414; sees PLF in Abruzzi 150; PLF
    considers for trip to Turkey 206; in
    London 216; meets PLF in Spain
    281, 286, 288; marriage to Jaime
    282–3; parentage 282; travels in
    Jordan with PLF 314; visits PLF 334;
    celebrates Frances Partridge's 100th
    birthday 402
Parladé, Janetta and Jaime 318, 354
Parsons, Lady Bridget 82n3
Partridge, Frances 283, 320, 402
Partridge, Ralph 254, 415
Pasolini dell'Onda, Niccolò 143
Passerano, Castello di, Lazio 9, 142–4,
    147–9, 245
Passerini-Hopkinson, Lyndall see
    Birch, Lyndall
Paterakis, Manoli 26, 124, 185, 335–6,
    338
Patinir, Joachim 220

Patmore, Derek 21
Patrizi, Francesca 143
Pavitt, Burnet 390
Peake, Sir Charles and Catherine, Lady 99, 102
Peake, Mervyn 54
Pendlebury, John 368
Penguin New Writing series 39
Perowne, Stewart 91
Perrone, Natalie 157, 184
Perry-Smith, George 188n1
Petronius, Gaius: *Satyricon* 387
Phalireás, Socrates 177
Phillips, Mark 264n2
Piccolomini d'Aragona, Count Alberto 41
Pisa 64
Pitt-Rivers, Julian Alfred Lane Fox 47, 51–2, 87, 286, 369; *People of the Sierra* 286
Pitt-Rivers, Michael 87
Poirault, Roger 222
Pol-Roger, Odette 111
Pollak, Paul **422**
Pope, Alexander: PLF parodies 227–9; *Essay on Man* 226
Portland, William Cavendish-Bentinck, 9th Duke of 363
Portugal 44–9, 319, 374
Pound, Ezra 371–2
Powell, Dilys 100
Powell, Michael 123
Prat, Lily 319
Pressburger, Emerich 123
Primet, Madame 125
Primo de Rivera, Margot 286
Prodger, Michael 421
Pryce-Jones, Alan: *A Bonus of Laughter* 360
Psychoundakis, George 124, 311, 368, 396; translates *Iliad* into Cretan dialect 386, 400; *The Cretan Runner* (transl. PLF) 72–3, 92–3, 100, 103

Pushkin, Alexander: *The Captain's Daughter* 258; *The Queen of Spades* 259

Quennell, Peter 44, 70, 75, 112–13, 184, 188, 218, 221, 229

Rabelais, François: *Gargantua* 318n2
Radziwill, Lee 239
Rahere (monk) 349
Ralli, Joan ('Lilia') 110, 111
Rantzau, Josias von ('Joey') 363
Rawsthorne, Isabel 33
Rayner, Joan *see* Fermor, Joan Leigh
Reade, Captain Arthur 385
Reade, Patrick **385**
Réalités (French magazine) 94
Riaz, Marie 404
Ritsa (PLF's carer) 384, 400
Robilant, Conte Alvise di 184
Robilant, Contessa Elizabeth di (Betty; *née* Stokes) 184
Robinson, Geoffrey 397n4
Rodd, Gustaf ('Taffy') 77
Rodd, Nancy *see* Mitford, Nancy
Rodd, Peter 330
Rodd, Rosie (*later* Baldwin) 77, 144, 206
Rodocanachi, Constantine Pandia ('Tanty') 89
Rolli, Paola 143
Romania 5, 196–7
Rome 40–1, 70–1, 157, 176, 182, 243–5
Ronay, Egon 364
Rootes, Ruby, Lady (*née* Duff) 58
Roots of Heaven, The (film) 135
Ross, Alan 272, 307, 313
Rosse, Lawrence Michael Harvey Parsons, 6th Earl of and Anne, Countess of (*née* Messel) 82
Rothermere, Ann (*née* Charteris) 44
Rothschild, Cécile, Baronesse de 242
Rothschild, Da'ad 310

Rothschild, Jacob, 4th Baron and Serena, Lady (*née* Dunn) 397
Rothschild, Miranda 310, 405
Rothschild, Philippe, Baron de 242
Roufos, Arietta (*née* Scanavi) 208
Roufos, Rodos Kanakaris- 208
Roumeli: Travels in Northern Greece (PLF) 6, 202, 267, 396
Roux, Pierre-Guillaume de 380n1, 382
Royal Society of Literature: awards Heinemann prize to PLF 54
Ruhemann, Marie-Lyse **364**
Rumi, Jalaluddin 249
Runciman, Sir Steven **203**, **344**, 334–6, 361; *The Fall of Constantinople* 200, 203
Russell, Aliki (*née* Diplarakou) 73
Russell, John Wriothesley 73
Rylands, George ('Dadie') **357**, 6, 280

S., Reggie 36
Sackville-West, Edward 164–5, 187n1, 189, 278–9
Sagrada Familia church, Barcelona 236, 320
St Albans, Osborne de Vere Beauclerk, 12th Duke of 278
St Clair-Erskine, Hamish 40
Saint-Jean de Solesmes monastery, Sarthe, near Le Mans 32–3
St Martin's Press (New York) 313
St Oswald, Rowland Winn, 4th Baron and Laurien, Lady (*née* Jones) 66–7, 350
Saint-Wandrille monastery, Normandy 9, 28, 30–1, 38, 41, 133
Sandoe, John (bookseller) 372, 410
Sangallo, Giuliano da 185
Sansovino, Andrea 175
Sant' Antonio monastery, near Tivoli 31n2
Sargent, Sir Malcolm 86

Saridakis, Henry 373
Sartre, Jean-Paul 37
Scarisbrick, Tony 73
Schwob de Lur, Annabel (Mme Bernard Buffet) 33
Scott, Sir Walter 345
Searle, Alan 128
Seferis, George **102**; on PLF's rewriting and revisions 6; friendship with PLF 12, 94; PLF reads extracts from books to 98; urges PLF to finish writing book 102; awarded Nobel Prize 190; illness and death 257
Seferis, Máro 102, 257
Serpieri, Didi (*née* Vlastou) 207
Seville 50–1
Shakespeare, Nicholas 362
Shawe-Taylor, Desmond 187n1
Sheil, Anthony 381
Sherrard, Philip **321**, **358**, 274n1, 321, 324
Shirley, Revd Canon Frederick **79**
Sifton, Elisabeth **342**, 335, 337, 342, 351
Silone, Ignazio (Secondino Tranquilli) 244
Singapore 229–30
Sitwell, Georgia 62
Sitwell, Sir Osbert 102, 346; *Left Hand Right Hand* 26
Sitwell, Sacheverell 62, 294, 394
Skelton, Barbara ('Baby') 93n3, 107n3, 114
Smart, Amy, Lady 43, 63
Smart, Sir Walter 7, 43, 55–6, 412
Smith-Hughes, John ('Jack') 368
Snowdon, Antony Armstrong-Jones 1st Earl of 82n3
Society of Dilettanti 247
Soures, Nikolaos 373
Soutzo, Constantine Ioana 347
Sparrow, John 170, 409
Spears, May, Lady (Mary Borden) 97

Spender, Maro 297
Spender, Matthew 297
Spender, Natasha 334, 335
Spender, Stephen **145**, **190**, **326**, 101, 331
Spratt, Thomas Abel Brimage 247
Staercke, André de 113
Stanhope, Colonel Leicester: *Greece in 1823 and 1824* 367
Stanley, Lily (Lili; *née* Malandrakis) 373
Stark, Freya **91**, 219, 314, 345
Stendhal (Marie-Henri Beyle): *La Chartreuse de Parme* 243
Stewart, Damaris, Lady **219**, **247**, 247, 252
Stewart, Damaris and Michael **252**
Stewart, Sir Michael 219, 239, 247–9
Stewart, Olivia 406, 411, 417, 421
Stewart-Richardson, Lady Constance 371
Stewart-Richardson, Gladys 371
Stirling, William (Bill) 278
Stockbridge, Ralph **367**, **373**
Strachey, Barbara 338
Strachey, Julia 151, 338–9
Strachey, Lytton 254, 322
Strachey, Rosemary 283
Strachwitz, Moritz Karl Wilhelm Anton, Graf von: 'Das Herz von Douglas' 343n1
Sturdza, Ileana 365
Sturt, Napier 417
Sunday Times 72, 80
Surtees, R. S.: *Mr Sponge's Sporting Tour* 290, 374
Suryal, Atiya Aziz: *The Crusade of Nicolopolis* 361
Sutherland, Colonel David 414
Sydney, Sir Philip 318
Sykes, Christopher: antipathy to Peter Quennell 75
Sykes, Christopher Simon 388

Sylvester, David 356

Tarnowski, Andrew 290
Teleki, Count Jenö 362
Teleki de Szék, Count Pál and Countess Johanna 317
Tennant, David 44
Tennant, Toby and Lady Emma 345
Tennant, Virginia (*née* Parsons) 62
Tharaud, Jean and Jérôme 317
Thesiger, Wilfred 374
'They Have Straightened the Tower of Pisa' (PLF; poem) 191
Three Letters from the Andes (PLF; Peru) 256n1, 381
Thubron, Colin 2
Time of Gifts, A (PLF): writing and publication 4, 7, 257, 307, 311, 425; title 250, 301; French translation 376, 379
Time to Keep Silence, A (PLF) 9, 65, 74, 122n1, 194
Tison, Frédérique (Balthus's niece) 157n3, 160
Tito, Marshal Josip Broz 69
Torlonia, Villa: ball 81
Toynbee, Philip 44, 101, 187, 332, 339
Toynbee, Sally 187, 341n1
Traveller's Tree, The (PLF) 6, 9, 28, 54, 267
Tree, Lady Anne Evelyn Beatrice 62
Tree, Iris 71n, 142
Treuhaft, Jessica (*née* Mitford; 'Decca') **339**; and PLF's political indifference 13; stays on Hydra with PLF and Joan 106; *Faces of Philip: A Memoir of Philip Toynbee* 339; 'Mrs Thatcher's Britain' (article) 341n4
Trevor-Roper, Patrick 187n1
Troilus (pet dog) 250–2, 255
Tuchman, Barbara: *A Distant Mirror* 361

Turville-Petre, Francis Adrian Joseph 275

Twain, Mark: *Huckleberry Finn* 375

Tyrakis, George 26

Tzannetakis, Tzannis 13

U and Non-U 107, 272

Vacaresco, Anna 366

Valens, Eastern Roman Emperor 348

Veil, Simone 324

Veloudios, Thanos 104

Venice 300

Ventura, Alex 365

Verney, John: *Going to the Wars* 101

Verschoyle (publishing house) 81

Vesey, Colonel Thomas 330

Viking Press (New York) 342

Villeneuve, Guillaume **379**, 376, 408n3

Villon, François 398

Vilmorin, Louise de 65; *Madame De* 65

Violins of Saint-Jacques, The (PLF; novel) 6, 65, 314n1; French translation 92, 110, 381

Vivian, Anthony Crespigny Claude Vivian, 5th Baron 223n4

Vlad the Impaler 312–13n1

Voigt, Joachim 403

Voltaire, François Marie Arouet 243

Wade, Miss (Lady Diana Cooper's maid) 85, 88

Wales 185–7

Wallace, Lois 337

Walpole, Horace 98

Walsham Hall, Suffolk (school) 352–3

Warner, Rex 190

Warre, Rev. Edmond 45

Waugh, Evelyn: at Easton Court, Chagford 10, 129; antipathy to Peter Quennell 75; marriage to Laura

86n1; caricatures Brian Howard 280; *Put Out More Flags* 330

Wedgwood, Dame Cicely Veronica 261

Weidenfeld, George 107n3

Weiller, Paul-Louis 110, 115

Wenckenheim, Christian and Sergei 364

Wescott, Glenway 335

Whaley, Duncan 197

Wheeler, Mavis 223n4

Wheeler, Monroe 335

Whigham, Ian: visits Kardamyli 176–7, 179, 205, 252, 334; at Mill House 188; on poaching eggs 207; and construction of Kardamyli house 210, 215; in Singapore and India 229–31, 233

Whitehead, John 45

Wilde, Oscar 357n2

Wildeblood, Peter 87n4

Winn, Rowland *see* St Oswald, 4th Baron

Wodehouse, P.G.: *Uneasy Money* 208

Wolfenden Report (1957) 87n4

Wolheim, Anne (*earlier* Toynbee) 340n1

Wolheim, Richard 340

Woodhouse, C.M. ('Monty') 368

Wooley, Revd Geoffrey Harold, VC 280–1 & n4

Woolf, Virginia 322

Wyndham, Harry Hugh Patrick 291

Yeats, W.B. 359

Yeoman's Row, London 110

Zaehner, Robert Charles 412

Zanuck, Darryl 135, 138–9

Zinovieff, Kyril (*later* FitzLyon) 404

Zinovieff, Sofka 393n1

Zurbarán, Francisco de 2

A Note on the Editor

Adam Sisman is an award-winning writer, author of *Boswell's Presumptuous Task*, shortlisted for the Whitbread Prize and winner of the US National Book Critics Circle Award for Biography, and biographer of John Le Carré, A. J. P. Taylor and Hugh Trevor-Roper. He selected and edited *Dashing for the Post*, an earlier volume of the letters of Patrick Leigh Fermor, and (with Richard Davenport-Hines) *One Hundred Letters from Hugh Trevor-Roper*. He is an Honorary Fellow of the University of St Andrews and a Fellow of the Royal Society of Literature. He lives in Bristol.

A Note on the Type

The text of this book is set Adobe Garamond. It is one of several versions of Garamond based on the designs of Claude Garamond. It is thought that Garamond based his font on Bembo, cut in 1495 by Francesco Griffo in collaboration with the Italian printer Aldus Manutius. Garamond types were first used in books printed in Paris around 1532. Many of the present-day versions of this type are based on the Typi Academiae of Jean Jannon cut in Sedan in 1615.

Claude Garamond was born in Paris in 1480. He learned how to cut type from his father and by the age of fifteen he was able to fashion steel punches the size of a pica with great precision. At the age of sixty he was commissioned by King Francis I to design a Greek alphabet, and for this he was given the honourable title of royal type founder. He died in 1561.